TRUFFAUT ON CINEMA

TRUFFAUT
ON CINEMA

Compiled by
ANNE GILLAIN

Translated by
ALISTAIR FOX

INDIANA UNIVERSITY PRESS
Bloomington and Indianapolis

This book is a publication of

Indiana University Press
Office of Scholarly Publishing
Herman B Wells Library 350
1320 East 10th Street
Bloomington, Indiana 47405 USA

iupress.indiana.edu

Originally published as *Le Cinéma selon François Truffaut, Textes réunis par Anne Gillain* © Editions Flammarion, Paris, 1988
English translation © 2017 Alistair Fox

All rights reserved

No part of this book may be reproduced or utilized in any form or by any means, electronic or mechanical, including photocopying and recording, or by any information storage and retrieval system, without permission in writing from the publisher. The Association of American University Presses' Resolution on Permissions constitutes the only exception to this prohibition.

⊚ The paper used in this publication meets the minimum requirements of the American National Standard for Information Sciences—Permanence of Paper for Printed Library Materials, ANSI Z39.48-1992.

Manufactured in the United States of America

Cataloging information is available from the Library of Congress.

ISBN 978-0-253-02575-3 (cloth)
ISBN 978-0-253-02639-2 (paperback)
ISBN 978-0-253-02656-9 (ebook)

1 2 3 4 5   22 21 20 19 18 17

In memory of Helen G. Scott

CONTENTS

ix
Preface to the English Edition (2017)

xxv
Preface (1988)

xxix
Acknowledgments

xxxi
A Note on the Translation

1
1. Childhood

21
2. The New Wave

51
3. The Auteur Theory

58
4. 1954: *Une visite*; 1957: *Les Mistons*; 1958: *Histoire d'eau*

64
5. 1959: *The 400 Blows*

82
6. 1960: *Shoot the Piano Player*

95
7. 1962: *Jules and Jim*

112
8. 1962: *Antoine and Colette*

115
9. 1964: *The Soft Skin*

129
10. 1966: *Fahrenheit 451*

140
11. 1967: *The Bride Wore Black*

150
12. 1968: *Stolen Kisses*

160
13. May 1968

166
14. 1959–1968: Overview 1

189
15. 1969: *Mississippi Mermaid*

197 **16.** 1970: *The Wild Child*	286 **25.** 1978: *The Green Room*
207 **17.** 1970: *Bed and Board*	293 **26.** 1979: *Love on the Run*
218 **18.** 1971: *Two English Girls*	300 **27.** 1980: *The Last Metro*
227 **19.** 1972: *A Gorgeous Girl Like Me*	309 **28.** 1981: *The Woman Next Door*
233 **20.** 1973: *Day for Night*	319 **29.** 1983: *Confidentially Yours*
242 **21.** 1969–1974: Overview 2	328 **30.** 1975–1984: Overview 3
253 **22.** 1975: *The Story of Adele H.*	343 List of Films Discussed by Truffaut
262 **23.** 1976: *Small Change*	351 Sources
272 **24.** 1977: *The Man Who Loved Women*	357 Index

PREFACE TO THE ENGLISH EDITION (2017)

Anne Gillain

While reading Alistair Fox's precise and elegant translation of a volume I edited some thirty years ago, I was transported back to the time when I undertook this project and lived for almost a year with Truffaut's words resonating in my ear. I remember those days all the more vividly because it was in 1984, the year he died. I had actually mentioned to him in the fall of 1983 that I planned to collect his interviews. My letters had remained unanswered.

Our correspondence had started in 1979 after I met him in Paris to discuss my intention of writing a critical book on his films. I lived in the Boston area and, over the years, his letters kept me informed of the progress of his work. For instance, *The Last Metro*:

19 Dec. 79
On the 28th [of November], I started on *Le Dernier Métro* with Catherine Deneuve, Gérard Depardieu, Andrea Ferréol, and Jean Poiret, over the course of 14 weeks in Paris.

29 August 1980
After two or three screenings held for Gaumont and the financiers of the film, I am somewhat more confident. This time, I am hoping to get the same kind of enthusiastic reception that greeted *Baisers volés* and *La Nuit américaine*. We will be finished on the 17th of September. I will send you the press kits through the next mail and the other things for which you are waiting.

1st October 1980
It is not enough just to make films—it is still necessary to assist with their promotion beyond Paris, which is why I am in Brussels, but I am not complaining, everything is going well, the reception accorded the film here, as elsewhere, is exceeding all my hopes.

8 October 80, NY
From New York, where I am staying until Monday. Then Los Angeles for 3 days, San Francisco 4 days, and returning to Paris on the 22nd. As you will have guessed, it's a matter of showing *Le Dernier Métro* at Festivals in the hope of finding a good US distributor.

In the last years of his life, Truffaut seemed possessed by a sense of creative urgency and was making his films at a breathless pace. After the triumphal reception of *The Last Metro*, the film of his that equaled the success of *The 400 Blows* in financial terms, Truffaut, instead of enjoying a pause, immediately embarked on a new venture: *The Woman Next Door* was completed by October 1981. No sooner was this film out than he was already feverishly anticipating the making of the next one:

Sunday, 21 February 82
Next week will be important because of the ceremony for the Césars (our Oscars). We have been nominated for *La Femme d'à côté*, Fanny Ardant and Véronique Silver (Madame Jouve). In particular, Orson Welles will be there to preside over the evening; the day after tomorrow, Mitterand is going to make him an Officier de la Légion d'Honneur (Welles has been wanting this a lot for a long time). I'm a bit behind in my work—I can't wait for the 10th of March, the date on which I will begin writing my new screenplay, a comic crime film that will begin shooting in October–November.

Just over a year later, he was already preparing what promised to be a magnum opus:

9 March 83
I am leaving for 2 weeks for Belgium with Jean Gruault to write the first draft of our great film project.

Sadly, this film in which Proust would have made a cameo appearance, never came to completion.[1] The script would eventually be published as a novel by Jean Gruault in 1996 under the title *Belle Époque*.[2] I met Truffaut in Paris in August 1983 and received his last letter in the spring of 1984, when I was already working on the book of interviews:

January 84
Three days after our evening, I had a hemorrhage in the brain (this was on the 12th of August), and on the 12th of September I had an operation. For a brain aneurism. My convalescence will take a whole year. Even a month ago, I wouldn't have been able to write to you without trembling, but I'm now beginning to climb back up the slope. I'm leaving for the Midi to take some rest, and I will be coming back at the beginning of February....

In the midst of all these injections, these tablets, these drops I have to take, and hours spent sleeping, I think of you and I have found a Céline that you might have missed;[3] please accept it with my affection, and in anticipation of our next meeting.

Truffaut liked to share books with his correspondents, and the project for this volume of interviews was born from a publication he had sent to me back in 1983 to help my research. It was a bibliography edited by an American scholar, Eugene P. Walz, *François Truffaut: A Guide to References and Resources*.[4] Among the numerous works listed, it included all the interviews given in the Francophone and Anglophone press. I began reading these texts and soon realized they were priceless. At the time, there was little web access to reviews, and it seemed important to make these documents available to the audience of the films. I started collecting them systematically, first in American academic libraries for the Anglophone press, and then in Paris during the summer of 1984. I actually hoped that Truffaut himself would edit the volume as a convalescence project. I spent many days that summer in the library of the old Cinémathèque, which was still at Trocadéro, collecting and photocopying interviews in film reviews. It was a long task, since I was not allowed to take more than three items out per day. Then I started going to the offices of famous newspapers and magazines that did not specialize in cinema: *L'Express*, *Le Monde*, *Le Figaro*. During this research, something alerted me. I was told several times that Truffaut's dossier was not available for consultation because it was in use. I knew it was unlikely that several scholars would be using his files at the same time. This is how I first came to the chilling realization of how desperately ill he was: the journalists were writing his obituaries.

Now, thirty years later, after completing my critical book in 1990 and recently editing a volume of articles on his films, I find these interviews even more riveting than before. The passion for cinema they display, their sincerity and lucidity about his craft, are striking. True, the main purpose of these texts was the promotion of the films, but this does not preclude a thorough assessment on Truffaut's part of his own work. In this respect, the remarks he made later, long after a given film had been released, prove all the more revealing. Truffaut can be harsh on himself in the condemnation of some movies—*The Bride Wore Black*, for instance: "Let's forget about it"—or when he lists everything wrong about *Bed and Board*. He also displays regret over the failure of certain films at the box office: *The Mississippi Mermaid* and *Two English Girls*. The sheer number of the interviews suggests that Truffaut devoted a lot of time to this exercise. Did he enjoy it? He once wrote to me, "Although I increasingly enjoy the period during which we are filming, the time that precedes the release of the film becomes more and more oppressive each year." Interviews seem, however, to have played a role in his creative process, as he explained when *Bed and Board* came out in 1970. Reacting to Truffaut's statement "I want to know without being known," the journalist retorted, "In that case, interviews must be a torture for you." Here is Truffaut's answer:

> No, not at all. Everything takes place in a small group, and, in addition, for the filmmaker, it replaces psychoanalysis, as it were: everything one says in films and interviews amounts to a substantial inward clearing. Fellini says that interviews help him a lot in his work. I think that this is true.[5]

In this respect, the interviews can be read as an artistic autobiography, functioning as a twin volume to the official biography by De Baecque and Toubiana.[6] To this important book, packed with invaluable information, especially about the childhood period, it adds the authentic voice of an artist entirely devoted to his craft. One thing we soon learn, without much surprise, is that for Truffaut life came second to cinema. This is one of the leitmotivs of the interviews:

> I don't live outside cinema.
>
> I want to make normal films—that is my life.
>
> I am rather inclined to turn away from real life, I take refuge in cinema.
>
> I like life in moderation.
>
> I nevertheless feel I am living a more normal life when I am involved in a shoot.
>
> Cinema is my country, my family. My religion is cinema.[7]

These statements are not an affectation on his part. They must be be taken quite literally and offer a key to his creative work. One recalls his last film, *Vivement dimanche!*, in which the guilty party, trapped at night in a phone booth, declares in a vibrant monologue before his suicide, "I don't belong to the society of men." In *The Green Room*, a very personal film in which Truffaut himself plays the main role, his character declares, "I have become a spectator of life."

Truffaut seems to have experienced a sense of marginality and, in this respect, it might be useful to evoke the complex aura that emanated from his person. His presence in a room was powerful in spite of his smallish frame and, in particular, the intense, almost piercing look in his eyes compelled attention. He literally seemed to see through people; there was even a slightly haunted quality about him as if he were living simultaneously in two worlds, ours and another one, secret and mysterious. When you were talking to him, suddenly, and without warning, he would appear to be elsewhere and, for an instant, oblivious of your presence. It was odd and slightly intimidating. Then he would come back, smile, and go back with gusto into the conversation. Shortly after his death, in 1985, I wrote a few pages to recall the impression I formed during my first encounter with him, and to capture the galvanizing impact of his presence.

> After our interview, which lasted for an hour, I am left with a sense of contrasts. From the outset there was a contrast between his frail bodily person, lively and mobile, and the imposing dimensions of an office that was covered by books, in all directions—books on shelves that reached up to the raised ceiling, books carefully piled up on his vast desk. The extreme kindness and solicitude Truffaut displayed also contrasted with a distant air that showed right away that he was miles away from daily concerns. Later, when I knew him better, this contrast took a different form, for me. I felt as if I was in the presence of two different men whose personalities alternated in response to the particular day, or even the moment. The first was very young, mischievous, spontaneous, loving to laugh like crazy, enjoy himself, poke fun at people affectionately, note their little foibles and their inconsistencies, a man who could sometimes appear naïve on account of the strength and sincerity of his imagination . . .
>
> The second was a mature, lucid man, who would cast a sharp-eyed glance on people and things ("I immediately spotted that," he would often say), displaying a dazzling intelligence in all his judgments. There was not the slightest trace of eccentricity, even of a genial sort, in his remarks. He was measured, rational, and would always go straight to the heart of the matter . . .
>
> I have often thought that the coexistence of these two different people could not have been easy for him to live with and that his films represent the dialogue between them, the place in which these two contradictory tendencies confronted one another and found their harmony.

The first man was looking for contacts, exchanges, conversations; the second was distant, he was elsewhere. Both of them were generous—generous and shy.

His shyness did not come from any lack of self-confidence. He was aware of his capacities. It was rather a technical problem that remained as a hangover from his youth. For a long time, he had the feeling that he was like an object in the eyes of others, as if he did not exist for them. The effect on him, I believe, was both one of pleasure and pain: the pleasure of observing and understanding everything without anyone knowing it, and the pain of being ignored. As an adult, famous and admired, he found himself in the position of a subject. Wherever he went, people looked at him, they looked for his reactions, they were even intimidated by him. He found this gap problematical. He never became truly used to it. He knew how to handle situations, perform his role and fulfill his responsibilities—he was not lacking in authority—but there was always this gap between the spectator, the observer and the man in the public eye. Every time that he had to change course, on the occasion of a meeting, or in an unforeseen situation, the gears clashed a bit. The clash was his shyness. On the telephone, he would say "hello," and then there would be a silence that would have to be filled. I had learned the need to be talkative, even chatty, because that was the only way to put him at his ease. He did not like the telephone—he said he hated how intrusive its ringing was in his apartment—and, even when I was in Paris, he preferred to write short notes to me. I had the impression that, apart from the making of his films, during which he adored collaborating with others, to work in a team, he felt best when he was alone. Of course, he also hated this solitude, while defending it fiercely. I remember his Antoine-Doinel-like expression when he told me about how his secretaries lied on his behalf: "Elles mentent tout le temps." He liked to point out that the word "secretary" comes from the word "secret."

In the course of the grand commemoration organized by the Cinémathèque of Paris in 2014, in celebration of the thirtieth anniversary of Truffaut's death, a series of lectures and panels took place. A young film director, Axelle Ropert, gave a most interesting talk about Truffaut as an actor, and I would like to evoke a few of the points she made.[8] Starting from the premise that, although her students loved his films, they all hated him as an actor, especially in *The Green Room*—a film she found poignant and beautiful— she was trying to understand their reactions. In her lecture, she made some arresting comments about Truffaut's physical appearance. Using one of his interviews on television as an example, she analyzes the odd quality of Truffaut's body in terms of the way he moves—or rather does not move—and speaks. She describes the general impression as "dissociated" and enumerates the elements that create it: the rapid voice, the blank tone, the fixed body like that of a wax figure, the mask on his face with rapid eye movements. She emphasizes, in particular, the extraordinary quality of the look in his eyes: a blank stare that seems absent, in another reality, and the way he casts anxious sideways glances at certain moments, as if he wanted to escape. She notes that in his films, especially in *The Green Room*, these features are even more accentuated than in real life.

Truffaut the actor, she comments, is hard to love and actually rejects empathy and compassion with his whole body. She summarizes the message he sends as *"Noli me tangere"* [do not touch me] and adds there is not one ounce of narcissism in the attitude of Truffaut, who seems actually unaware of himself. She finds his whole appearance heart-wrenching and concludes that the look in his eyes gives the impression of someone who has seen something terrifying that one cannot get over or forget. In *The Green Room*, this tragic vision is, of course, World War I with its cohort of dead and maimed bodies, but Ropert wonders what it was, outside the fiction of this film, that Truffaut could not forget. For somebody who has met Truffaut, this analysis carries a tone of authenticity and, listening to her, the reality of his presence came back forcefully to my memory. One can only guess as to where this look came from. I would venture two hypotheses. They combine childhood and art.

First, because of his films and what they tell us, I would say it was the look of someone who emerges in an unknown place, feels like a complete stranger, and realizes that there is absolutely no one in sight who can help. It is the look of a somnambulist and probably comes from Truffaut's rough landing in reality during his formative years. Growing up, there is a good chance he often felt trapped in a foreign and scary place with nowhere to hide. This primal sense of terror—and I really don't think the word is too strong—and of homelessness never left him. Then there was cinema.

To understand the role of cinema in Truffaut's life, it has to be situated in this lunar landscape. Early on, he experienced cinema as the only safe place where the wax figure could come to life and experience a firework of rapturous emotions. This accounts for the visceral power it held over him and for the intensely close relationship Truffaut fostered with films. Watching them, he experienced not simply identification with the main character, but an emotional connection and deep empathy with the director. In his interviews, he explains for instance why, as an adolescent, he specially loved films with a first person voice over. "The director was confiding with me, while I was sitting there in the dark."[9] He goes as far as saying that he got annoyed when the hero had a screen confidant and lost interest in his problems. He simply refused to share him with a fictional character and demanded an exclusive intimacy. This is why, in his own films with a voice-over—for instance, *The Story of Adele H.* or *The Man Who Loved Women*—he keeps the main character friendless.

Truffaut's elusive demeanor evokes some striking statements made by another artist whose creations bear profound similarities with his own. In his superb 2014 Nobel Prize speech, Patrick Modiano declared that a fiction writer must remain "at the margins of life in order to describe it, because if you are immersed in it—in the action—the image you have of it is mixed up." He compares the writer to a "somnambulist" whose "altered state is the opposite of narcissism":

> His imagination, far from distorting reality, must get to the bottom of it, revealing this reality to itself, using the power of infrared and ultraviolet rays to detect what is hidden behind appearances. I could almost believe that the novelist, at his best, is a kind of clairvoyant or even visionary. He is also a seismograph, standing by to pick up barely perceptible movements.[10]

I believe that Truffaut is, like Modiano, an artist who fluently read what is "hidden behind appearances" and made this subterranean world accessible in his films. With this in mind, let's go back to the interviews and see how they validate this premise. At first sight, it is not the case. The concept of the artist as a "visionary" and "clairvoyant" actually clashes with Truffaut's clear, measured, and precise statements regarding his craft. What sort of cinema, audience, and subject matter does he advocate? In 1974, Truffaut declared, "I will always adhere to a form of cinema that brought me to cinema."[11] This kind of cinema is popular and designed to entertain. Truffaut stuck to these views through his entire career. In 1983, a year before his death, he was still defining his work as "Saturday evening films designed to give pleasure."[12] What sort of an audience did he wish to reach? "The audience that goes to the movies not for the director but for the actors."[13] What about subject matter? As early as 1966, Truffaut knew exactly what kind of material he wanted to deal with in his films: "I am not gripped by big ideas. Godard, yes, he's the kind of man interested in big problems of our time, but as for me, I can only make a film out of ideas that are personal to me."[14] Ideas simply did not interest him, and he was certainly not about to make films on political, moral, or philosophical issues. This does not mean that his work is devoid of them, but they are incidental, not the core of his fictions. As far as his subject matter was concerned, there were two requirements: they had to originate in the past and—most importantly—to be validated by experience:

> I'm chasing that, to recapture a lost secret, rather than heading toward future innovations.
>
> I am a nostalgic person, completely turned toward the past. I work with material drawn from my own past experience, or that of others.
>
> Basically, I only work with memories from twenty-five or thirty years ago.[15]

Truffaut even asserts that a director only has three to six films to make and that thereafter "one is experimenting with new combinations."[16] In his last interviews, taking Lubitsch as a model, he mentions his ambition to "*faire un film à partir de rien*," or a film where the story is just a pretext.[17] In short, Truffaut wants to make personal films that will touch a wide popular audience without any explicit intellectual content. There is a flavor of provocation in these statements. Truffaut's creative years spanned the domination of intellectuals in France—Foucault, Deleuze, Barthes, Derrida, Bourdieu—and the rebel in him enjoyed describing his craft as lowbrow fictions. Things, of course, are more complicated, even if these statements do not lack in sincerity. In a 1982 interview about *The Woman Next Door*, Truffaut mentions a scene in the film where popular songs are eulogized because their silly words display real emotions. He then adds a personal reminiscence evoking his time in the army, when he was twenty, and how impressed he had been by the fascination that the photo magazine *Nous Deux*—the lowest kind of fiction—held for the young recruits:

> All those young soldiers, what did they throw themselves on? On *Nous Deux*. It was fantastic—I was very impressed by that . . . . So it was from that time that I concluded one should not be contemptuous of things just because they are popular and mass-produced.[18]

There is no doubt that this raw and primal hunger for fiction is exactly what Truffaut wanted to unleash and feed with his films. What is at stake? Control over the viewer's mind. Truffaut describes his work as a "contest between him and the spectators," or a "game" in which the use of "calculation and ruse" is involved.[19] In other words, his concern is not the "What" (subject matter) nor the "Why" (commitment to a thesis) but the "How." The motto "Pleasure has to overcome analysis" is a constant leitmotiv in his interviews: "I am seeking to work on them physically."[20] Hitchcock is, of course, the obvious example of this mental hold that freezes the spectator in his seat. An image recurs twice in Truffaut's last interviews: he wants the spectator to watch his films gaping "with an open mouth":

> I would like people to watch *The Green Room* with their mouth agape, that they go from one astonishment to another.
>
> I try to take people on board . . . I would like people to watch a film with their mouth wide open.[21]

In Truffaut's work there are indeed moments when emotion, instead of skulking in the background, literally bursts onto the screen and lets the hypnotic power of cinema take over. They usually consist of silent scenes that condense formal elements and distill in a few shots the essence of the film. At a first viewing, these scenes often appear like riddles. Something is going on that we don't really understand, but what proves impossible to articulate firmly grips our system. They are scenes one watches with an open mouth and represent Truffaut's stylistic signature. A few examples: in *The Last Metro*, a German officer convulsively grabs Catherine Deneuve's hand in a deserted office; in *The Woman Next Door*, a telegraph operator circulates aimlessly in the middle of a garden party; in *Shoot the Piano Player*, Charlie comes across an unknown cellist in a corridor; in *The Wild Child*, Victor rocks silently in the top of a tree; in *The Story of Adele H.*, Adele, sitting in a tree in the night, smiles enigmatically as she watches her lover inside a house going upstairs with a woman for a sexual encounter. In these moments, what Truffaut calls the "magic of cinema" is totally operative.

What is going on? To answer proves a formidable challenge. Let's start by mentioning that we are at the heart of what Modiano described as an altered state of consciousness where we are transported "behind appearances." Nobody knew better than Truffaut that the minute you enter a movie theater, your perceptual system undergoes a radical modification. Cinema is emotion; cinema is hypnosis. The mental processes involved are both fascinating and wildly elusive. They involve nonconscious and nonverbal mental mechanisms that Raymond Bellour brilliantly analyzes in his magnum opus, *Le Corps du cinéma*.[22] It is sufficient to note here that fiction films activate a perceptual mode linked to the prelinguistic infant's first reception of reality. Radically different from perceptions ruled by language, these fundamental perceptions are kinetic and rely on volumes, forces, energies, beyond and below the linguistic. They are particularly active in the enjoyment of dance and music, but, as Bellour stresses, they are even more operational in cinema.

Truffaut never theorizes about such objectives in the interviews. When asked about formal components of mise en scène, he mentions "instinct" rather than theory. This explains why film directors are more sensitive to his craft than critics. While scholars are sometimes at a loss to define his contribution to cinema, brilliant young directors such as Xavier Dolan or Arnaud Desplechin freely express their debt toward him. Asked to choose between Godard and Truffaut, Dolan answers:

> Truffaut. Why? Because the former enjoys himself alone; the latter enjoys himself with us . . . Godard could never have made a film like *La Femme d'à côté*. Never. Never. Because he [Truffaut] is too moving, too human, also too aware of the need to accord importance to characters and stories, rather than merely to processes, to himself, to a vision, to freedom, to a revolution, to a play on words. You don't find this humanity in Godard's films—that is intentional . . . it is *his* cinema . . . As far as I am concerned—someone who is seeking to extract the very essence of things, however small it might be—I can't nourish myself on a film by Godard.[23]

Arnaud Desplechin, in a long interview that is entirely a tribute to Truffaut, declares for his part:

> When I began to learn from Truffaut again, and I learned from him more than from any other directors, I learned one can be quietly violent, discreetly provocative . . . His art is allusive, complicated, full of implications that create double, triple, and quadruple meanings, because he took the question of cinema so seriously. Still each film presents itself as naked and going straight to emotion, yes, more toward emotion than toward plot.[24]

Significantly, there is one text in which Truffaut does address perceptual issues relating to cinema. In his preface to *Hitchcock/Truffaut*, while not theorizing, he imagines the filming of a scene and details how Hitchcock would use formal elements to create a suspenseful subtext:

> To simultaneously film the first (obvious) situation and the second (secret) one, with the aim of achieving a dramatic effect through purely visual means. Hitchcock, the filmmaker who is the most accessible to all audiences on account of the simplicity and clarity of his work, is also the one who excels in filming the most subtle relationships between human beings.[25]

All these terms—*"situation secrète"* or *"rapports subtils"* as Truffaut calls them,[26] or "quadruple meaning" as Desplechin states—recall Modiano's description of the artist as someone who "penetrates to the depths of reality" with the "power of infrared and ultraviolet light" in order to capture "the most subtle of movements." I would describe Modiano's and Truffaut's creations as works of "pure fiction." The inner workings of human emotions are their exclusive territory and sole concern. Their major goal is to use formal elements to access a perception of reality that radically differs from the "mixed-up image of life" which is our daily bread. Fiction creates an altered state of consciousness where the spectator experiences the circuitry of the mind at work. The fact that these perceptions shirk the categories of language makes them hard to describe, but metaphors are an effective tool to account for their power.

The British philosopher Bertrand Russell proposed one of the most telling. When asked why he liked Joseph Conrad's novels so much, Russell answered that they provoked an intense emotion in him because he felt that the author distinguished between two levels: "One, that of science and common sense, and another, terrifying, subterranean and periodic, that in some sense held more truth than the everyday view."[27] What is this underground level Russell calls terrifying but truer than daily reality? It represents the locus where memories, sensations, sexuality, and the violence of passions operate, a locus where all circuits are active and connected while barriers between the different perceptive modes are lifted, as happens in the hypnotic state. Incidentally, using the opposition mind/body to "name" these barriers completely distorts the problem and precludes any grasp of its complexity. Pure fiction is invaluable because it helps us appreciate the systemic nature of the mind. In Truffaut and Modiano's works the hero's quest (chasing love for Truffaut, or a name for Modiano) imposes a hidden order on these buried drives and brings them to light with exhilarating clarity. We are suddenly face to face with them and love what we see, instead of submitting to them in fear and chaos. Truffaut and Modiano are frontier men. They both explore territories where blocks of experience suddenly touch to create a slightly hallucinatory perception, which resembles the condition of a man about to fall asleep. Like in a daydream, perceptual barriers dissolve. This state is the alpha of modern fiction, documented by Proust at the beginning of *Remembrance of Things Past* when the narrator, going to bed early, suddenly connects with this hallucinatory reality that precedes sleep.

In aesthetic terms, the whole question is, of course, to understand how fiction links the two levels described by Russell. In his films, Jean Cocteau used the elegant metaphor of the mirror: all it took was to enter a mirror to gain access to the underworld. For Truffaut as for Modiano, a constant play on time—flashbacks, temporal ellipsis, remembrances, condensation or superimpositions of scattered instants—and the web they both weave between past and present is an effective tool. For Modiano, the connection is also born from a myriad of elusive sensations displayed on each and every page of the novels. It will be the light noise of leaves in a tree, the pale light of a winter sun, or the strong fragrance of privet in a public garden. Devoid of any discernable narrative function, these notations call attention to body-intense, nonconscious activities that occur while time flies, erasing human bonds. What is impressive is the range of the perceptual ride the novels allow from the most physical—almost flesh-connected—reality to the abstract arbitrary sign: a family name. The result is hypnotic for the user. The work of the novelist is the reappropriation of the word by the flesh.

Earlier on I mentioned that Truffaut's concern is neither with the "what" or "why" of fiction but only the "how." "How" obviously refers to style. All the formal choices made by the artist—colors, shapes, motions within the frame, montage, or punctuation between scenes and so forth—affect our perceptions. Truffaut's style is so rich in hidden details that every time I work on a film I discover a new set of formal connections that I had not detected before. In this preface I will only mention one element: his use of objects and the way they become full-fledged participants in the stories. Hitchcock was, of course, a master at the game and could use a glass (*Suspicion*) or a bottle (*Notorious*), keys (*Dial M for Murder*) or a lighter (*Strangers on a Train*), to signal the violence of the underworld. In his films, objects attract human passions like magnets. Truffaut followed in his footsteps. In fact, Jean Gruault confided, in an interview, that originally each scene in *The Story of Adele H.* was supposed to be built around an object and refer to scenes in Chaplin's films, another magical juggler of daily objects. In Truffaut's films, there are a few regular players: milk, water, fire, scissors, photographs, stairways, windows, doors, lingerie, hoses, broken dishes, or the number 813. Over time, these objects will decrease in number while gaining in power.

Truffaut's interviews display his artistic maturation over the years. Contrary to the stale cliché, the early films are not his only achievement and the later ones academic. As with all artists, Truffaut's work evolved, and three key words can characterize this evolution: economy, condensation, and rapidity. His latter films tend toward a more abstract codification of reality. While filming *The Story of Adele H.*, he likens himself to an electrician: "This is a very rigorous kind of approach, very exhilarating, one that I had already enjoyed adopting in *The Wild Child*; like an electrician, I strip the wires bare, I reduce the number of elements."[28]

Along with the scarcity of visual components, Truffaut also displays an increased attention to color schemes in his work with director of photography Nestor Almendros. One striking trend in his last films is his avoidance of natural light. In *The Green Room*, *The Last Metro*, or *Confidentially Yours*, a large part of the action takes place at night: "night carries the fiction," notes Truffaut. It stimulates the spectator's attention and bars the return of a confused image of life with the colors and noises that television delivers profusely. Reality is condensed and distilled into a set of parsimonious signs.

To illustrate the essence of Truffaut's style, I like to use a scene from his penultimate and probably most perfect film, *The Woman Next Door*. We know the plot: Mathilde and Bernard, who used to be tormented lovers, discover they have become neighbors in a small town. Both are now happily married. Passion will return and kill. In this scene, Mathilde, sitting at night near an open fireplace, is convulsively going through a box of photographs. Armed with scissors, she cuts off the face of her lover from each photo and throws it into the flames. The last shot is a close-up of the fire engulfing the charred face of Bernard. This scene belongs with the silent scenes I mentioned earlier. It also illustrates the sparse use of familiar visual signs: fire, scissors, photos, hand. Let us now focus on one detail that I will call the "Truffaut touch." Mathilde wears a nightgown. This is expected: she is home at night. However, on top of her nightgown, she does not wear a dressing gown but an opened raincoat.

This raincoat will appear in two other significant scenes. In the first, at the beginning, Mathilde and Bernard have a chance encounter in a supermarket and decide to be friends. All it will take is for Bernard to touch her cheek and she will faint. The last time Mathilde will wear her raincoat is in the tragic scene in which, at night, she will shoot Bernard in the head after they have had sex, and then kill herself. As a result of visual associations, the raincoat, an everyday object, signals sexual violence. The scene would be strong without it; its presence reinforces the architecture of the film and imparts elegant coherence to the narrative. The "Truffaut touch" is just that: an uncanny, but pivotal, detail that without warning compels our mind to stand at attention. While it might remain invisible to one's focused vision, it potently affects the viewer's perceptions. This sort of detail imparts not only textual cohesion but also intertextual continuity from film to film. At the end of *The Soft Skin*, the hero's wife was also wearing a raincoat when she left home to shoot down husband.

As this scene attests, Truffaut is expert at capturing the ravages of physical passion in a few elegant signs. This is indeed his distinctive trademark. Along with the collusion between past and present, sexuality is a major element of the subterranean world. For society, unchartered sexuality is not simply scandalous; it carries with it a terrifying power of destruction. This potential remains intact in Truffaut's work. Although the films cover a wide range of sexual situations—masturbation, intercourse, homosexuality, sexual addiction—there is not a single pornographic image in his films. Sexuality is coded in a series of indirect representations such as words ("*Attends/j'attends*") or metaphors (Doinel repeating women's names in front of a mirror). When sex acts are represented, it is done at such vertiginous speed that the spectator does not have a chance to reflect on what he is witnessing (the two little girls in *Two English Girls*)—or else the camera lingers on a magnified detail that divests it of all reality, making it become so crude as to appear grotesque (Muriel's virginal blood on the bed sheet in *Two English Girls*). Exactly as in Modiano's novels, what is remarkable is the perceptual ride the spectator experiences from the most sophisticated language to the physical body of passion: "*Ce papier est ta peau, cette encre est mon sang. J'appuie fort pour qu'il entre*" ("This paper is your flesh, this ink is my blood. I am pressing hard so that it sinks in"). Carole Le Berre rightly insists on the literal nature of this sentence.[29] Bridging the gap between flesh and paper, translating physical impulses into a highly coded symbolic system that is easily readable, is the magic of his cinema.

Truffaut's work endures because of its impeccable logic born from an organic connection between life and fiction. In his work, fictions are paid for, and dearly, by experience. He literally fed his films with his flesh and blood. This is what endows them with incomparable authenticity and humanity. In a minimal, powerful, and elegant language, Truffaut goes beyond the appearances to the heart of human passions. He explains with poignant accuracy how men live, love, and suffer. The same can be said of Fellini, Bergman, or Hitchcock. Truffaut's field of investigation may be more circumscribed than theirs, his body of films more limited, his existential anchoring in life more fragile, but, as for them, the human truth his films capture is eternal and their language universal.

Notes

1. It was, however, turned into a TV miniseries, starring André Dusollier, Kristin Scott Thomas, Isabelle Carré, Claude Jade, and Jeanne Moreau (among others), broadcast in France in 1995.
2. Jean Gruault and François Truffaut, *Belle Époque* (Paris: Gallimard, 1996).
3. Truffaut is referring to a work by the writer and doctor Louis-Ferdinand Destouches, known as Céline.
4. Eugene P. Walz, *François Truffaut: A Guide to References and Resources* (Boston: G. K. Hall, 1982).
5. Anne Gillain, ed., *Le Cinéma selon François Truffaut* (Paris: Flammarion, 1988), 273.

6. Antoine de Baecque and Serge Toubiana, *Truffaut: A Biography*, trans. Catherine Temerson (Berkeley: University of California Press, 1999. Originally published in French as *François Truffaut* (Paris: Éditions Gallimard, 1996).
7. Gillain, *Le Cinéma*, 265, 267, 273, 405, 413, 442.
8. *"Truffaut acteur,"* conférence d'Axelle Ropert, jeudi 6 novembre 2014, https://www.canal-u.tv/video/cinematheque_francaise/truffaut_acteur_conference_d_axelle_ropert.16734.
9. Gillain, *Le Cinéma*, 438.
10. Patrick Modiano, "Nobel Lecture," December 7, 2014, http://www.nobelprize.org/nobel_prizes/literature/laureates/2014/modiano-lecture_en.html.
11. Gillain, *Le Cinéma*, 313.
12. Ibid., 421.
13. Ibid., 321.
14. Ibid., 177.
15. Ibid., 197, 141, 197, 349.
16. Ibid., 332.
17. Ibid., 376.
18. Ibid., 412.
19. Ibid., 220, 423, 220.
20. Ibid., 423, 336.
21. Ibid., 376, 425.
22. Raymond Bellour, *Le Corps du cinéma: hypnoses, émotions, animalités* (Paris: P.O.L., 2009).
23. "Xavier Dolan: 'Mégalo, moi? Depuis toujours!'" *Télérama Officiel*, October 9, 2014; see https://www.youtube.com/watch?v=9F2A2mcNt_4.
24. Dudley Andrew and Anne Gillain (eds), *A Companion to François Truffaut* (Malden, MA: Wiley Blackwell, 2013), 110, 120.
25. François Truffaut, avec la collaboration de Helen G. Scott, *Hitchcock/Truffaut* (Paris: Éditions Ramsay, 1983), 13. [Translation by Alistair Fox.]
26. Anne Gillain, *François Truffaut: Le Secret perdu* (Paris: L'Harmattan, 2014), Postface, 313.
27. Ray Monk, *Bertrand Russell: The Spirit of Solitude* (London: Jonathan Cape, 1996), 317.
28. Gillain, *Le Cinéma*, 332.
29. "Truffaut: la littérature au feu de cinéma. Dialogue entre Carole Le Berre et Serge Toubiana," November 6, 2014, https://www.canal-u.tv/video/cinematheque_francaise/truffaut_la_litterature_au_feu_du_cinema_dialogue_entre_carole_le_berre_et_serge_toubiana.16739.

PREFACE (1988)
Anne Gillain

Between 1959 and 1984, some three hundred interviews with François Truffaut were published, both in French and English. This book brings together the entire set of these interviews, which have previously been dispersed across a multitude of journals and magazines in France, Canada, England, and the United States.

In *Tirez sur le pianist* (*Shoot the Piano Player*), Charlie, when he was still using his first name Édouard, is seen being admonished by his impresario for having "blown" his press conference. Arming himself with an arsenal of books on how to overcome shyness, he prepares for a second encounter with the journalists, and this time presents himself confidently without any trouble. The presence of this vignette regarding success in this domain, in a film that is largely autobiographical, reflects the importance Truffaut attached to his relations with the press. Anxious to promote his films, and concerned above all to have his intentions understood, he would submit himself on the release of each film, with good will and a seriousness that everyone acknowledged, to the ritual of interviews. This is a genre that he himself had cultivated with brio during his career as a critic—as his *Hitchcock* attests—and his experience allowed him to exploit the potential effectiveness of this frequently debased format to the maximum. An interview, for him, provided a forum. It not only allowed him to convey information, but also to intrigue, surprise, and attract the audience to his works. One needs only glance through these texts to see how carefully he prepared his statements, worked on the choice of terms, and honed the cutting edge of his formulations. Truffaut, filled with a passion for explaining and persuading, took pleasure in using words. That is a rare gift in a filmmaker. He was able to bring to this routine the freshness of new critical insights, trenchant summations, and a depth of insight that is often very striking. Above all, he conveyed the vivacity and warmth of his personality. With him, a journalist would find himself facing not only an interlocutor, but also an active collaborator who was full of initiative. Truffaut knew how to steer the conversation by himself, and how to invest responses with an originality of tone and an intelligence that confers on these texts their exceptional quality. Taken as a whole, these interviews will be of interest to readers for three main reasons.

First, they constitute a corpus of precious information concerning the genesis of each film. In them, Truffaut gives an account of the sources of his inspiration, the choice of his themes, and the construction of his screenplays. We learn, for example, about the role played by the Jaccoud affair in the conception of *La Peau douce* (*The Soft Skin*), or by the Brontë sisters in that of *Les Deux Anglaises et le continent* (*Two English Girls*). The technical aspects of the making of each film are tackled, but Truffaut also speaks in the interviews about his relations with collaborators, actors, and of the atmosphere during the shooting. He provides numerous examples of his indirect style, and of the choices that were available to him for the realization of a scene. Anecdotes alternate with critical insights and make the whole as lively as it is informative.

Second, these interviews represent an impressive body of theoretical reflections on the nature of cinema itself. From 1959 onward, Truffaut was concerned with defining the efforts of the New Wave filmmakers, and with measuring them against those of their predecessors. The list of directors whose works he mentions include Rossellini, Renoir, Vigo, Hitchcock, Ray, Lubitsch, McCarey, Welles, Fellini, Bergman, Cocteau, Godard, Resnais, Chabrol, and Pialat, to mention only the most well known of them. Indeed, these texts make reference to the whole history of cinema. In them, Truffaut analyzes the impact of different media, television in particular, on the work of mise-en-scène; he compares literature and cinema; and he defines the dynamic of the relationship between a fiction film and its viewer. The importance and weight of these statements confirm that this man, who described himself as the least intellectual of the French directors, and declared that he had no interest in ideas, exploited them better than those who deliberately cultivated them.

Finally, the interviews provide a mine of biographical information. This is their most unexpected aspect. Truffaut evokes impressions and memories of childhood, reveals his reactions to political events and social phenomena, offers us intimate insights into his favorite reading, his emotional development, and his itinerary as an artist. In this regard, the American interviews are unquestionably the most revealing. That might be owing to the fact that he felt a lesser degree of reserve when in a foreign country, to a desire to assert himself personally in a culture where he was less well known, or simply to a different style of journalism. Even though I was already acquainted with Truffaut himself, as well as his films and the critical writings that had been devoted to him, I was frequently surprised by the amount of additional information I gleaned from reading these interviews.

In order to create this collection of interviews, I first had to gather them from all their disparate sources. Even though many of the relevant magazines had enjoyed merely an ephemeral existence, I was able to find a large number of them in French and American libraries. Moreover, Madame Madeleine Morgenstern assisted me considerably in my work, by giving me free access to François Truffaut's own archive, as well as to the archives of the Films du Carrosse. I would like here to express my gratitude to her.

I thought that the best principle for organizing these texts might be to respect the chronological order in which they were published. By itself, however, this classification was insufficient for anyone who might want to have easy access to all the information pertaining to a given film. After *Les 400 Coups* (*The 400 Blows*), most of the interviews, in fact, make reference to several of Truffaut's works. I therefore decided to isolate the material in each interview relating to a particular film. For each of them, I then created a montage of extracts that bring together the most significant of Truffaut's comments at the time when the film appeared, and added at the end of the chapter any comments that Truffaut subsequently made on the same film, indicating the date of each commentary. This book, then, includes a chapter on each of the twenty-one films Truffaut made, as well as on his four short films. I have also included three preliminary chapters on his childhood, the New Wave, and the *"politique des auteurs,"* a theoretical concept that Truffaut elaborated during the 1950s, when he was writing for the *Cahiers du cinéma*. In addition, I have divided the book into three main periods: 1959–1968, 1969–1974, and 1975–1984, inserting at the end of each of these parts a chapter in which one or two important interviews are presented in their entirety, titled Overview 1, 2, and 3. These three chapters focus on artistic, critical, and theoretical issues that allow one to follow Truffaut's development at different moments in his career.

Truffaut on Cinema presents a cinematic biography that is direct, lively, sincere, often funny, sometimes moving, and always intelligent. The idea for this book came to me when Truffaut was already ill. I had intended to suggest to him—in order to provide something with which he could distract himself—that he should organize these texts himself. I think that this project would have interested him. I am sure that spectators who watch his films will find it fascinating.

ACKNOWLEDGMENTS

Anne Gillain would like to thank the *Cahiers du cinéma* 88 and *Sight and Sound* for permission to reprint a number of interviews. The extracts concerned are included in chapters 10, 14, and 30 of the present book. Detailed references are listed under Sources at the end of the book.

Alistair Fox would like to acknowledge his debt to Frédéric Dichtel for his scrupulous care in reading through a draft of the translation, offering invaluable advice on a number of Truffaut's more challenging locutions, and intercepting several errors that might otherwise have gone undetected.

A NOTE ON THE TRANSLATION

The spoken language François Truffaut used in his exchanges with interviewers was extremely lively, usually relaxed, often colloquial, and always very impassioned. For that reason, I have tried to keep as close to Truffaut's own words and speech rhythms as is consistent with idiomatic English.

In referring to films, Truffaut almost invariably used the title of a film's French release, which can cause difficulties for an Anglophone reader, given that the French title can often be very different from the title of its American release. For that reason, my practice in the translation has been to give the English title (as recorded in the Internet Movie Database, or IMDb) in the text, but to identify each film both by its English title and the French title used by Truffaut in a footnote. In cases where the original title of a film was in a language other than French or English, the original foreign language title is also given. A summary list of the films mentioned or discussed by Truffaut is given at the end of this volume.

To assist Anglophone readers who may not be familiar with the French personalities and cultural and historical contexts to which Truffaut frequently alludes, I have included explanatory annotations where it seemed these might be helpful. In addition, I have compiled an index of names, titles, and subjects to assist the reader in navigating through the wealth of material that Truffaut provides in these interviews.

Alistair Fox

TRUFFAUT ON CINEMA

CHAPTER 1
CHILDHOOD

> A man is formed between seven and sixteen years old; after that, for his whole life, he will live out whatever he has acquired between these two ages.
>
> Interview with Luce Sand, Jeune cinéma, *May 31, 1968*

Did you really have an unhappy childhood?

No. It was just like that of Antoine in *The 400 Blows*. The film was not at all exaggerated. In fact, I have a feeling I left out things that might have struck people as unrealistic. What I do regret is not having shown how closely associated my story was with the years immediately following the War. But, it was my first film—I wasn't yet capable of making a period film. I still have a film to make that will go back to that time, one about a boy under the Occupation. It wouldn't deal with the Resistance, only the more mundane aspects of life at that time . . . I have to say that the fact of having grown up during the Occupation gave me a terrible view of adults.

When were you born? What did your parents do?

My father was a young designer-architect who was especially keen on mountain climbing, along with my mother, who was a secretary at the weekly magazine *L'Illustration*, rue Saint-Georges, where my grandfather Jean de Monferrand worked—also a mountain climber and an official in the French

Alpine Club. They were regarded as real eccentrics in the quarter, because they would leave in shorts with a backpack every Saturday morning, arriving back on Sunday night. There are people like that whom it is impossible to label . . .

I was born in Paris, very near Place Pigalle, on the sixth of February, 1932, being immediately handed over to a nurse, then raised until I was eight years old by my grandmother. When my grandmother died, my parents took me back. They were not mean—only highly strung and preoccupied. My mother was embittered. Undoubtedly, she would have loved to have a more dazzling life. I was not sporty; very quickly it was cinema that attracted me. Not to love camping was considered a dubious business in the household.

Do you remember your first experience of cinema?

I don't have a very good memory of the first film I saw, probably in 1938 or 1939, because of the incompetence of the "permanent" employee in the theater. My aunt took me to the cinema, and we went into the film while a marriage scene was being shown on the screen. Two hours later, the same scene was played again, and my aunt said, "This is the scene that was playing when we arrived," and we left.

This makes me think of a story, the one about the little girl who saw *Joan of Arc* at the cinema, and, when describing the story later, said, "It's about a lady who is put in the fire and then becomes a shepherdess."[1]

My first clear memory of a film was of *Four Flights to Love* by Abel Gance, with Micheline Presle and Fernand Gravey, in 1939 or 1940.[2] It is a film that made everyone in the theater cry, because of parallels between the periods. It was a film about the war of 1914–1918, and the theaters were full of soldiers on leave, men who were going to leave for the war, or were returning from it, so things were really crazy, I think, throughout the whole of France. I heard my mother weeping by my side; my father had just been mobilized. As for myself, I didn't cry, probably because I didn't understand what was going on very well, but I was bowled over; my only fear was that the film would end.

I have often rewatched *Four Flights to Love* since, and each time I do weep, because it is a really irresistible, brilliant melodrama.

Although they weren't cinephiles, my parents were keen on entertainments, and discussed important plays and films between themselves. That guided and directed my taste. They took me to see certain films, but I very quickly adopted the habit of secretly going to see ones to which they didn't take me. When my parents went out together at night, I myself would also leave, ten minutes after them, to go to the cinema, generally at the closest theater. I didn't enjoy these evenings as much as I might have, because my anxiety about getting caught, and of getting home after them, was too great. The second half of the film was spoiled, to the extent that fear would make me leave before the movie had finished, because I had to be in bed when my parents came back. I still retain a great degree of anxiety from this period, and films are associated with anxiety for me, with the idea of secrecy. And so I found it more convenient to go to the cinema in the afternoon, skipping class.

What school did you go to?

Up until 1941 I was at the Lycée Rollin. I failed the examination to enter into the sixth grade. And so my parents decided to put me back into primary school.

At primary school, there was no one else who had come from a high school. I was somewhat of a misfit. At high school, no one played hooky. Here, it was an everyday occurrence. I began by behaving well like everyone else, and then I played up. The more I was punished, the more unruly I was. So I was expelled quite often. I went from school to school. I was taught in the local school in rue Choron, then at rue de la Victoire, then at rue Hippolyte-Lebas, then at the École commerciale in avenue Trudaine—you can see the kind of pupil I was! I played hooky in the company of my friend Robert Lachenay. When one of us was made to go back to a particular school, the other would arrange to follow shortly after, so that we were always attending the same one. I don't know how it happened, but I ended up being placed in classes that were less and less advanced. On one occasion, I found myself in a class I had already taken three years earlier in another school. I attended for some days at the end of the month for compositions. I remember that at one time, we were away so much, Robert Lachenay and I, that we trumped up fake school reports written with India ink on paper folders, which we made our parents sign.

What money did you use to go to the cinema?

When my "pocket money" for the week ran out, I used the money meant for the school canteen, but I also have to admit that I frequented many theaters where it was possible to enter without paying.

How did you do that?

I had a different method for each cinema. At the Delta it required two of us to go: one of us would pay and then let the other in (that was always done through the toilets). At the Images, we had a different strategy, because the lavatories were in the hall, in the basement; we had to go down the stairs and, when we did, we would always find an old ticket in the toilets, on the floor. Then, all we had to do was sling our jackets over our shoulder to make it look as if we had come out of the theater, have this old ticket to show, and then choose a moment in the intermission, and that worked. Even at the Gaumont-Palace, it was possible to get in, but at the peak time, on Sunday afternoon, at the moment when members of the audience were coming out, because of the immense doors, and the four thousand people who were exiting. It involved pretending to be someone who had forgotten something, and moving back through this flood of people. That was also possible.

At that time there were two cinemas facing each other across the boulevard des Italiens: the New York and the Cinéac-Italiens. Both started up at ten o'clock in the morning. Their patrons consisted almost entirely of school kids and high school students. And we could not all come with our satchels because that would have looked funny. Every morning there would be a group of fifty or sixty children there. They would be waiting, and the first cinema that opened would get all the clientele, because everyone was anxious to get out of sight, because we felt very guilty.

What films do you still remember?

The films that I really admired, obviously, were French films, given that I started to go to the cinema during the War. Films like *Le Corbeau: The Raven*, and *Les Visiteurs du Soir*.[3] Very soon, I had seen them several times. At the beginning, that was an accident, as I had seen them secretly without my parents' knowing; then my parents would say, "Come, let's go to the cinema," and I would be taken to see a film again without being able to say that I had already seen it! But that gave me a taste for seeing a film several times.

The best film of the Occupation—and the one that was most talked about—was *Le Corbeau*. *Les Visiteurs du Soir* provoked arguments at school: there were all those who were critical of the castle, and all those who defended the white castle. But yes, that was all we talked about, even the teacher. He would say, "The castle had to be new at one moment or another, and so it is intelligent to have built a white castle." There was a strong vein of fantasy in French cinema. At that time I loved any film coming out that was a little bit crazy. In those days I placed quality things on the same level as things that were definitely less good, like *La Fiancée des ténèbres*. I adored that. It was very strange—with Jany Holt . . . Also *The Phantom Baron* . . . I remember one film I saw . . . I was just a kid, it was at Montauban, it was called *Pontcarral*, do you remember it?[4] At any rate, I was a subversive spectator. Supporting the director, against the audience. Always. Even in the case of films that were being ridiculed, films that people were sniggering at. I was all for the ridiculous, for audacity, cheek... Lyricism, always, always lyricism.

And what did this revolt come from? From your reading? From your temperament?

I think it came from watching films in secret, from the fact that we were playing hooky so often and doing so many stupid things during the war—I identified with every occasion on which someone on the screen was shown to be bored, every time someone found themselves in an irregular situation. Reading *Madame Bovary* was a shock for me because it offered a parallel to my truancy. So many lovers and so many money troubles! That struck a chord with me; I detested everything that was normal.

What did cinema mean to you at that time?

With the passing of time, it has become obvious to me that cinema has been much more than merely a refuge. I'll admit now that the neurotic aspect of my love for cinema is unmistakable. In earlier times, I didn't understand that, I didn't have any awareness of the fact; today, I know it for sure. At the same time, it is difficult to talk about something that is so intimate and personal! It is no exaggeration to say that cinema saved my life. That's why I can't speak about it intellectually. From time to time I would use the expression "drug" before the word became fashionable... The reason I threw myself so avidly into the cinema is probably because I was dissatisfied with my own life during the years of my early childhood—specifically, the years of the Occupation, since in 1942 I was ten years old. Thus 1942 is an important date for me: it is the moment when I began to go and see a lot of films. From the age of ten to nineteen I was obsessed with films. I'm unable to be objective about that.

What kind of cinema formed you?

I often say that the "Minnelli-ites" (fans of Minnelli)[5] and the fans of American cinema are people who are not seeking to see themselves reflected in a film in any way. They are looking for total escape, including a change of visual scenery, which is to say, that they would prefer not to see their own town, their own streets, or their own world. Their need for escape is extreme. As far as I was concerned, perhaps because there were no American films during the Occupation, I was first formed by a handful of French films. I say "a handful" because, between 1942 and 1944, there were no more than forty or fifty, of which the most memorable was definitely *Le Corbeau*. Perhaps this was also because I preferred to encounter a world that was not too far removed from my own in real life . . . I preferred, for example, modern films to period films, and psychological films and crime thrillers to other kinds of films . . . That's all that I can say on that subject; anything else would be more appropriate as part of a study of cinema during the Occupation.

In what respects did you see Le Corbeau *as reflecting the times?*

It's a film I went to see about twenty times. Five or six times during the War, and then repeatedly when, having been censored at the Liberation, it was once again licensed to be shown. It is a film whose dialogue I have learned by heart, which is not surprising, and happens with all films that one sees enough times to know them intimately. From *Le Corbeau* I probably learned 150 words of vocabulary that I didn't know before; it contained a very adult kind of dialogue compared with the other cinema of the time, but also in relation to my own vocabulary. Even today, I still know by heart the text of anonymous letters in *Le Corbeau* . . . I had not yet rebelled at that stage, but was on the verge of doing so, and these films presented a picture of society that spoke to me. The whole world was rotten, and there were things relating to love that seemed to me—it would be wrong to say "new," given that I had not had much experience—at any rate, "original." Even today, I find that the interactions between Pierre Fresnay and Ginette Leclerc are very powerful. They are still compelling, and have not become clichés.

Later, while continuing to love French cinema, I discovered American cinema. To be frank, to a certain extent it was my encounter with [Jacques] Rivette that diverted my attention away from French cinema.[6] I remember that Rivette thought it was absurd to have seen *Children of Paradise* fourteen times,[7] and to know *Le Corbeau* off by heart. For him, none of that held any interest, because he only responded to the mise-en-scène. And probably under the influence of Rivette and the people at the *Cahiers*,[8] I, for a time, forgot all the things that are coming back to me now.

You were saying just now that you felt yourself to be completely a post-War child. Didn't you ever wonder what had happened in France, in Paris, during the War?

Yes, indeed, because I had an uncle who was deported, and I had been struck by the passivity of the people around me. When I was told that France was waiting to be liberated, I truly had the impression that that was not true. I saw such a lot of indifference around me. People would go out at night, to the theater, to the cinema, because the experience of entertainments was very important during the War. I lived at the intersection of rue Henri-Monnier and rue Frochot, at Pigalle. There were musicians in the street with whom I played when I came back from school. There was also blood, gunshots, the settling of scores, as well as many passionate affairs. There were German women in black stockings . . .

German women?

Yes, "grey mice." As for me, I looked at that especially from the sexual angle. There was this whole sexual aspect to the Occupation that no one ever talks about, but which seems to me one of the most significant things about it. For example, people would make love in the street, there were no lights in the whole of Pigalle, one had to have a flashlight to go into the Metro, there were couples in the porches. During air raid warnings we would go to the Metro at Abbesses, Jules-Joffrin, Pigalle, it would be full wherever we went . . .

Did you ever sleep in the Metro?

Yes, one day, Lachenay and I had "missed" so much that we didn't dare go back to school. We said to each other, "The bigger the excuses, the more likely they are to work." I went back and said to the teacher, "My father has been arrested by the Germans." That was in 1943, and my uncle had been arrested eight days earlier. There is always an element of truth underlying the lies of children, but my father came to get me. That caused a big drama, so that I didn't dare go home.

I was eleven. Lachenay told me that one could sleep in the deepest Metro stations that had been turned into air raid shelters. I went there. It was black as pitch. We were given a blanket, but they woke us up at five o'clock so that the Metro could begin operating. At that time you could get a liter of wine for 125 grams of copper, and so we would steal doorknobs and things like that, and then sell the wine. My father caught me, and he sent me to schools where he told them everything I had done. I was a "black sheep." Everything that I did was viewed askance; and so I didn't go back there. I went to the municipal library and devoured Balzac.

Another time, the headmaster of the school summoned my mother and said to her, "We can no longer keep your son here, because he is away sick too often." I got wind of that and didn't dare go home that evening. So I went to sleep in the Metro. The next day, eager to put myself straight with society, I went back to school. My mother, extremely anxious, came to get me, took me back home, and made me take a bath; this episode is replicated quite closely in *The 400 Blows*.

Then there were the holidays, during the summer of the Liberation. I was in a holiday camp. The director was selling off the camp's food, and we didn't have anything decent to eat. We were covered with boils and lice. We wrote to complain, and the director said, "I will sue you for defamation." We were very perplexed; we didn't know what "defamation" meant. We thought that it had something to do with food, because of the word's similarity to *affamer* [to starve]. In the end, our heads were shaved, and I was saved. It was the first time that I had been shorn. I also went back home.

What are your memories of the Liberation?

I was twelve in 1944. That's the year in which I uttered an enormous lie—I have never been able to figure out why. I was in Brittany, and I wrote to a friend to say that I was going to return to Paris to follow the trial of Pétain.[9] What was going on in my head at that moment? I don't know, but I was genuinely fascinated by the Pétain trial and also by the hypocrisy of the Liberation newspapers, which tried to create an impression of unanimity among the French people. Similarly, it seemed strange to me when I would hear my parents talking about Sacha Guitry, and about Claudel's most recent play, while the War was raging.[10]

After the Liberation we went on several occasions to the Gare du Nord, and the Gare de l'Est, to see deportees returning. Most people think of deportees as emaciated people, but in fact, because they had spent the intervening time in hospitals, they were all bloated, enormous. That was even more tragic, making an even bigger impression. We waited for my uncle on several evenings like that . . .

I think that this period left me with a purely defensive attitude. I remember that I would tremble when I went into shops—they would always send boys in to beg—to the point where, even now, I am astonished when a shopkeeper is pleasant. I still enter a shop with humility, truly. I'm programed to view life as very hard; I believe that one must adopt a very simple, basic stance—one has to say, "Yes, yes," and only do what others want you to do. It's because of that that there can't be any violence in my films. Already, in *The 400 Blows*, Antoine is a child who does not revolt . . .

But the Liberation was also the time when American films arrived on the scene. What is the first one you saw?

I don't know, it was a comedy, I was very surprised, it was something that came from another planet. I had never seen anything like it . . . Imagine the shock for young people: in the same quarter of 1946, when the only great actors we knew were Raimu and Pierre Fresnay, we discovered Humphrey Bogart, Cary Grant, Spencer Tracy, James Stewart. Yes, really, the great shock, the decisive shock, was the one we got from seeing American films at the Liberation.

It was really after two or three months of American cinema that, for the first time when coming out from a film, I noticed the name of the director. I set about making a record, identifying each film in terms of its director, and then to have ideas, saying to myself, "It's a film by so-and-so, I'll go to it." It was actually in 1946 that this started, also thanks to a fairly important magazine, *L'Écran francais*. It was very biased, but even so, it was a specialized magazine. It published an article by Jean-Paul Sartre on *Citizen Kane* before its release. This helped to ensure that *Citizen Kane* became an event. I think that must have been on July 6, 1946.

How many times did you see it?

Eighteen, twenty times, I can't remember. I know it very, very well. Suddenly, at the age of thirteen, I registered that a film could be written like a book. Indeed, a lot of men of my generation felt that they could become directors as a result of *Citizen Kane*. Kubrick, Resnais, Frankenheimer, Lumet. This was not a filmmaker's film, but a cinephile's film. Several months later I saw *The Magnificent Ambersons*, which, in many ways, I preferred. I found it more sincere, more moving.[11]

At what age did you leave school?

I was fourteen, and I wanted to work. I applied for a job with an exporter of seeds. It didn't take long before he regretted having hired me. I didn't turn up very regularly. As soon as I got my pay, I would go to the cinema. After four months he fired me. It was Christmas, I had received a bonus and, with my redundancy payment, this gave me a small nest egg. I had been living at Lachenay's place, and we decided to establish a film club at the Cluny-Palace on Sunday mornings. We bought a print of *Metropolis* in 16mm,[12] and we baptized our club very simply *Le Cercle cinémane*. But the quality of the screenings was horrible, and people did not come back. They went instead to André

Bazin's film club at the Broadway, which also took place on Sunday mornings. Then, naively, I went to see Bazin, to ask him to change the day. This was how we came to know each other.

We talked a bit about cinema, but eight days afterwards, my father, who had discovered the advertisement for the *Cercle cinémane* in *L'Écran francais*, stuck my head on a pike and delivered me to the police. The real ones. Not the officers that deal with the under-eighteens. I spent two nights in the police station, just as in my film. Then they shut me away at Villejuif.

At that time, in 1948, half of Villejuif served as an insane asylum, and the other half as a reform school. Delinquents who tried to escape were brought back by those who guarded the mad people. At Villejuif there was a bunch of other boys who had committed a variety of infractions; there were young apprentices who had stolen lead from factories, others who had stolen bikes, and especially the wheels of cars, and a large number of young street kids; during those years, juvenile delinquency was at its height. I was rescued by André Bazin. I wrote to him, and he worked hard to get me out. He went to see the psychologist and arranged for me to be released. My parents waived their rights over me without too much resistance. At Villejuif, moreover, I had not been sad; I was curious about everything. As I recall, none of us were really very wicked. When our guardians were nasty to us we would invent very romantic excuses for them: "It's because his daughter got pregnant, or because his wife screwed around."

I was angry when *The 400 Blows* came out because certain newspapers claimed that it was exaggerated. It's just that there is a big difference between the laws that protect children and the reality of what actually happens. One statute says that no child can be put in an ordinary police wagon, and that they must be conveyed in a special vehicle. In reality, if it's after hours when a kid is taken to the police station, no one is going to call up a car specially for the purpose, and so the child is put in the police van regardless, with the prostitutes and all the other people who have been rounded up . . . These are the things that stick with you, that leave a mark, the funny memories.

In the end, Bazin got me out of there, and found a job for me at *Travail et Culture*, in which he directed the cinema section.[13] My work consisted of setting up document files and organizing screenings in factories. Each program was limited to short films (Charlie Chaplin, Laurel and Hardy), because we were not allowed more than three-quarters of an hour, which was how long the lunchtime canteen services were open. I made other friends who were interested in this formula: Alain Resnais, Chris Marker, Alexandre Astruc. Each evening, at the Cinémathèque, I would meet Jacques Rivette, Jean-Luc

Godard, Jean Gruault, Alexandre Astruc. As a result of finding ourselves there, we would fall into conversation, and became friends.

Did you think that you would become a director?

When I was on a high, yes. In more rational moments, I only aspired to become a film critic. I began to have particular likings and aversions. At first, I began by rejecting French cinema as a whole. I could no longer admire Pierre Fresnay after I had discovered, over the course of three months, James Stewart, Gary Cooper, Spencer Tracy, Cary Grant, Humphrey Bogart, Peter Lorre, Mickey Rooney, John Garfield . . . I discovered *Zero for Conduct*, *L'Atalante*, and *The Rules of the Game* at the Cinémathèque, along with all of Griffith, all of Murnau, Stroheim.[14] It was fantastic!

By the time I was sixteen I had compiled an enormous body of material relating to films: photos, biographies of directors . . . I would write up several records each day, I had archives. To augment my collection I would conduct raids at night, with friends; we would decide that "in this cinema we can swipe twenty-four photos of *La Grande Illusion*,"[15] and we would go there with rocks and bricks, to smash the windows. When I had to leave for military service, I put all my dossiers—which required a real house-moving exercise—on a cart. And I crossed the whole of Paris to offer them to Langlois, for his Cinémathèque.[16] I said to him, "In exchange, I only ask that you let me have free admission to your Cinémathèque, for as long as I live."

In 1949 Bazin fell ill and had to leave for a sanatorium. Because of that I left *Travail et Culture*, and I ended up being an acetylene welder in a small factory near Paris. I earned sixty francs an hour. Welding had the advantage of fostering reflection. With my dark glasses and my bottle of gas in front of me, I passed the time by trying to recall the last film I had seen. In the morning when I arrived I would say to myself, "I am going to try and relive *City Lights* or *Monsieur Verdoux*," and I would do so, scene by scene, in order to spin that out as long as possible.[17] In that way I would get to the end of the morning. Was the welding any good? Ah! I have to confess that it wasn't too bad. I only hope my efforts didn't cause too many blowups later! On Saturdays and Sundays I found something I enjoyed. I would go to the Faubourg club, and when there were presentations on cinema I would create mayhem. People would laugh at how indignant I became.

For a time I worked for the newspaper *Elle*. I was seventeen, and my inexperience showed. For example, they asked me to conduct an investigation, to draw up a table, of how one says "I love you" in all the languages of the world.

I scrounged information from all the embassies, and the whole of the *Cité Universitaire*. They published the results, and afterwards there were I don't know how many letters of complaint, because in entries covering forty countries there were at least fifteen mistakes!

How did you rediscover cinema? You had a fairly difficult time during that period . . .

It happened exactly as I recounted it in *L'Amour à vingt ans* (*Love at Twenty*). I fell in love with a girl I saw a lot, whom I met at film clubs. I was so smitten that I went to live opposite her and, believing that I was closer, I grew more distant from her. I saw her as much as I wanted, but for her I had become a kind of freeloading relative. I became very friendly with her parents . . . In the end it turned out so badly that I joined the army. At the time, the war in Indochina was taking place, and I enlisted for three years.

But, isn't it the case that you were not cut out to respect order and hierarchy?

Yes, but one has moments like that. I had wanted to believe that I could do so. In my first weeks in the army I had a little crisis that was rather strange. I started to believe in God. I wrote raving letters to people in Paris. Naturally, I should have sought the advice of Bazin, who was still in the sanatorium. He would have talked me out of joining, or he would have made me think it through; but it's the kind of thing one does without saying anything to anyone else. Of course, it was not long before I regretted it. After several months, before leaving for Indochina, I was given permission to spend fifteen days in Paris, with the money from my enlistment bonus. In Paris I spent most of it with the girl on whose account I had left and, with her, I blew all my money. I told myself that I was mad, and that I didn't want to go back—so I deserted. There was a moment of panic, because I didn't want to stay in a hotel. I thought I was going to be caught, and so I started to live here and there. I didn't have any civilian clothes, and it was a bad moment at that time: everyone was going away on holiday, it was August, and the month was starting badly. I met Chris Marker in the street who was astonished to find me half hobo, half soldier. He took me to a bar, and I told him all my woes. Bazin was in Paris, but I didn't dare see him. Chris Marker called Resnais, who called Bazin, and then Bazin persuaded me to turn myself in to the military authorities. Then he undertook to arrange for me to be discharged officially. I spent a time in prison at the Dupleix barracks. It was very tough then, there were all these deserters from Korea. That was the time when certain volunteers in the French battalion in Korea were shown holding up a bank in Tokyo! The regime was terrible, especially in the heat of August. There were eighteen of us in a cell meant to hold four, and we had to piss into a tin without being able to leave the cell, a real hell. And Bazin arrived to get me moved from there to a military hospital. After eight days they said, "Given that you surrendered yourself voluntarily, we trust you—we're sending you to Germany." I didn't leave for Germany; I absconded. And then, for some reason or another, I wanted to procure a certificate of health. I had the address of a trainee doctor I could see, and, as I was going to visit this guy, I found myself arrested. This time it was extremely rough: I was taken to Germany in handcuffs in an ordinary train. This was right at the beginning of the *Cahiers du cinéma*. I read the *Cahiers* in the train. All the people who got on to the train stared at this specimen of a handcuffed soldier. I arrived at the barracks I had left two months earlier, and as soon as I got there, my hair was shaved off and I was put in prison! Then there was a psychiatric hospital, with real insane people— those whose military service had made them crazy. Ominous stuff.

My friend Robert Lachenay crossed the whole of Germany to come and see me in the mental hospital. He was not allowed to come in. That was the inspiration for one of the final scenes in *The 400 Blows*, when René goes to see his friend at the reform school for juvenile delinquents, and they can only see each other from a distance through a glass door. That went on for four months, until, finally, I was reclassified as having an "unstable personality"— thanks, again, to the efforts of André Bazin.

With hindsight, how would you explain this difficult period?

I don't know. Probably I should acknowledge the influence of Jean Genet who, without knowing it, played an important role in my life. He was the author of perhaps the most powerful book on disobedience and freedom, *The Thief's Journal*.[18] One day in 1948, fittingly, I stole this book, three months after having taken my decision to join the army.[19] It's not unlikely that it influenced my decision to leave the army by deserting . . . And it probably played a large part in developing in me a taste for "diaries," for "chronicles." As a soldier, I kept a diary each day, and I remember well, at the time of my desertion and then my arrest, that, for several days, there was only one thing I was able to keep with me: a book put out by the NRF[20] in a sufficiently small format to be able to be concealed. It was *Isabelle*, by Gide. And so, I continued to make notes in the margins of *Isabelle*,[21] day after day, in pencil—secretly, of course . . . until André Bazin came to my rescue.

And what did you do when you got back to Paris?

André Bazin arranged for me to work in the cinematic wing of the Ministry of Agriculture. At the beginning, I lived at Bry-sur-Marne with him and his wife; they had a little boy of three. I led a family life there, which I had missed for several years. André Bazin was editing the *Cahiers du cinéma*, which at that time had only published around twenty issues, and contained articles by my old friends from the Cinémathèque—Jean-Luc Godard, Jacques Rivette, Éric Rohmer, and from time to time Alexandre Astruc, who began to make films: *The Crimson Curtain*, and then *Bad Liaisons*.[22]

My time in the army had left me disenchanted with cinema. From the time I was twelve, I would make a record of all the films I saw, in a notebook, arranged in alphabetical order, adding a cross on those that I had seen several times. I had seen films like *The Rules of the Game*, *The Cheat*,[23] and *Le Corbeau* more than ten times. In the army, I calculated that I had seen nearly two thousand films in six or seven years, and that I had therefore lost about four thousand hours of reading time. I was disgusted with myself, and I thought that I couldn't even think of myself as self-taught, given that an autodidact becomes enlightened all by himself, whereas I had learned nothing.

Where does your passion for literature and books come from?

It was in the family. My maternal grandmother, who raised me when I was a small child, greatly loved books. During that time I spent many hours in the rue Lafitte, in a bookstore, where she would buy and rent books. I was six or seven—it was before the War. Several years ago, one day in a fit of nostalgia, I went back to rue Lafitte, but the bookstore wasn't there anymore, having been replaced by buildings. My grandmother wrote a novel about bigotry that she never dared publish because of worries about what the family might think. She was a literary person; she was the one who started me reading books, and who taught me to read. I was too sick to go to nursery school. After that, I lived with my mother, who couldn't stand noise, and who would force me to sit motionless, without speaking, for hours and hours. And so, I read—it was the only thing I could do without getting on her nerves. I read an enormous amount during the Occupation. Given that I was quite often alone, I developed a taste for adult books, the ones that my mother was reading; I would swipe them during her absences. Then, when I was thirteen or fourteen, for fifty centimes a piece, I bought 450 small, grayish volumes: *Les Classiques Fayard*. And I set out to read them, in alphabetical order, beginning with A (Aristophanes), and finishing at V (Voltaire), without skipping over a single title, a single volume, a single page.

I was very impressed by Alphonse Daudet (*Jack, Les Contes du lundi, Le Nabab*). But the great revelation for me was Balzac, and the fact that the boy in *The 400 Blows* erects an altar to him is no accident. What I liked best was *La Peau de chagrin*, on account of the crazy things it depicts. These days I prefer *Le Lys dans la vallée*, *Les Illusions perdues*, and *Eugénie Grandet*. By the time I got out of the army, I no longer had any desire to go to the cinema. The idea was that I was going to read!

What made you "come back" to cinema?

By finding myself in a cinematic atmosphere at Bazin's place. I started to go to the cinema again because he was writing on cinema and would talk about films. One day I said to him, " I think that I might be able to write something on cinema." He encouraged me to try it, and he published my first articles in the *Cahiers du cinéma*. Then I wrote as well for *Arts, La Parisienne*, and *Le Temps de Paris*. Once again, I became completely absorbed by cinema. I left the Bazins' place to rent a room in Paris.

These days, how would you sum up the main stages in your cinematic development?

The first stage—which I would almost describe as a form of therapy—was the cinephilic stage of 1942 to 1950: cinema helped me to survive, and I saw the same films over and over again. Here's a small anecdote about that . . . One day I ran away from my parents, and I didn't exactly know what I was going to do. Basically, I just wandered off! I then went to the place of a friend I thought might help me, by putting me up; nothing doing, he wasn't there. Since I needed to indicate a meeting place to him, I chose a film I liked that was being screened that week, *The Story of a Cheat*. And I told him that I would be at the Champollion for the whole day . . . I had gone to his house at midday, at two o'clock I was at the Champollion, and I was ready to stay there until seven or eight o'clock that night! I intended to remain there until he met up with me—it was a place where I felt safe. People can say all they like about Guitry, but on that day, he was a friend with whom I had found a refuge! After this phase of cinephilia, the crisis of 1949–1950 occurred.

Subsequently, I rejoined my friends Rivette, Godard, et cetera. But that was another stage—of the articles in the *Cahiers du cinéma* and *Arts*. It was obviously a more intellectual stage, given that it involved thinking about films and commenting on them. As for writing! It wasn't a question of being intoxicated by images, but of really analyzing the screenplay. That was an extremely important stage in my development. I began to try and work out why certain films were not entirely compelling, why the first half was good, why the second half seemed to go off in all directions, and so on ... For the first time, instead of saying "It's good! It's bad!," I began to imagine how it could have been made good, or why it was bad. That was what I was doing in the *Cahiers*, but even more so in the weekly *Arts*, in which there was an actual requirement to give a summary of the story ... Having to sum up a story gives one an insight into how it is constructed. This was a very positive period, for me.

Your—short—time in the Ministry of Agriculture, was it simply to earn a living?

That was the main reason, but even so, this institution had an important film library. The first thing I learned there was how to project films, because they had a 16mm projector. And given that I didn't have an enormous amount of work—it amounted to little more than sticking labels on boxes—I could watch, and rewatch, all the films I liked. There weren't many of them: Prévert's short film on Aubervilliers, a little poetic film by Kirsanoff, *Brumes d'automne* ... [24] Several films like that, which, when all is said and done, did not have much to do with agriculture ... Others included *L'Opération du sabot de cheval* [how to use horse shoes to protect the hoof of a horse], and films of that sort. Let's say that the Ministry would have been an important stage if the man who was there had agreed to take me on as an assistant regarding agricultural films; however, he didn't want me to work with him.

Did you make a lot of enemies at that time?

Yes ... quite a few ... but friends also. These days, I realize that I had the reputation of being a destructive type—someone even called me "the grave digger of French cinema" but that is because one always remembers criticisms better than eulogies. When I liked a film, I would defend it vigorously; indeed, I felt compelled to write four or five articles on *Journey to Italy, A Man Escaped, Lola Montès*.[25] The year that ... *And God Created Woman* came out, which I really loved, the press attacked Brigitte Bardot so savagely that she sent me a letter to thank me for being the only one to have defended her![26]

When did you start to want to make films?

I think that I began to want to be an *auteur* from the time I met Rossellini in 1951. We had been defending him fiercely in the *Cahiers*, and I had helped him tackle a Parisian distributor who had completely pirated his film *Journey* to Italy. At that time, Rossellini invited me to work with him as an assistant, as a friend. He was in the habit of improvising, and because people began to mistrust him on account of that, he asked me to write up storyboards for him; thus I prepared a scene-by-scene outline for a version of *Carmen* that was completely faithful to Mérimée, but which was never filmed.

I was Rossellini's assistant for two years, during which, in spite of the fact that he didn't do any filming, I learned an enormous amount from him. To a large extent, he turned me off American cinema, which he hated, giving me instead a liking for simplicity, clarity, and logic. We are still great friends today, and my admiration for him has never decreased.

It was during this time that we really began to get going in the *Cahiers du cinéma*. Having been strongly impressed by a news item of the day, I wrote the screenplay for a feature film, *Breathless*, which I offered to Philippe Lemaire, an actor who was very popular at the time, but in vain.[27] Later, I tried once again to shoot the film with Gérard Blain, who loved the subject matter, then Édouard Molinaro didn't succeed in making it as his first film, so in the end I gave the screenplay to Godard, who had no difficulty in getting it done, two months after the release of *The 400 Blows*.

What were your relations with your parents like when The 400 Blows *appeared?*

After the release of *The 400 Blows*, my parents divorced. They felt threatened by the film. I don't think they even went to see it. Their friends told them not to go. There was a close physical resemblance between my father and the man who played him in the film. It was the same with the apartment in which we filmed. It was located in the same quarter in which I had grown up.

My parents resented the film, feeling that it perpetrated a great injustice, especially given that it won the main prize at Cannes. Obviously, I became the focus of a lot of attention. It is only now that I realize how difficult their situation was. Certainly, I was the object of a lot of bitterness at the time. It would be true to say that the film engages with everything that had not been acknowledged or talked about in our lives.

You never imagined yourself being anything other than a director? A writer, for example?

A writer, just a little bit, perhaps when I was eleven. During 1942–1943, when I read Zola, maybe at that time, but after that, from the time I saw American films—that is, from 1946 onwards—I knew I was going to be a filmmaker. For a long time I loved cinema insanely, to the extent, for example, of refusing to go to see theater, simply because it was theater. Now, I enjoy going to the theater to see actors in advance of making a film . . . There were a few years when I really was very fanatical.

These days, how many times a week do you go to the cinema?

Three times, four times—much less frequently than in the past.

In the past, how often did you go?

There were occasions when I would see twelve films a week. I have diaries, from around 1949, that are absolutely packed full of film titles.

You don't have the feeling, because of having passed half your life in dark halls, that you have missed out, that you have bypassed anything?

If cinema were to come to an end, I would be left high and dry. There is nothing I would be able to do, nothing I would know about: I would be like a disabled person. It is a consuming, total specialization for me. But I don't have the feeling that I am linked to cinema by accident. I have often felt rather uncomfortable in the context of real life. As a journalist, because I didn't complete secondary school, I found that I wasn't qualified to write on a lot of things, or else that I wrote badly. But with cinema, in contrast, I have a feeling that what I do is not so bad. People either like or don't like my films, but they don't dispute the fact that I am a filmmaker. To put it another way, there has been no faking on my part: I am not self-deceived as far as my own vocation is concerned. Around about 1958, 1959, 1960, I was often tormented by the fear of being an "imposter"—time, and the response of audiences have made this feeling recede (which isn't to say that I don't have other concerns . . .). Now, when I think a film is finished, ready to be shown, I don't allow myself to go back to it—I move on to the next film. There is always a new film waiting to be made.

Notes

1. Truffaut is referring to *La Passion de Jeanne d'Arc* (*The Passion of Joan of Arc*, Carl Theodor Dreyer, 1928).

2. *Paradis perdu* (*Four Flights to Love*, Abel Gance, 1940).

3. *Le Corbeau* (*Le Corbeau: The Raven*, Henri-Georges Clouzot, 1943); *Les Visiteurs du soir* (*Les Visiteurs du Soir*, Marcel Carné, 1942).

4. *La Fiancée des ténèbres* (Serge de Poligny, 1945); *Le Baron fantôme* (*The Phantom Baron*, Serge de Poligny, 1943); *Pontcarral, colonel d'empire* (Jean Delannoy, 1942).

5. Vincente Minnelli (1903–1986), an American filmmaker renowned for making musicals, such as *Meet Me in St. Louis* (1944), *Ziegfeld Follies* (1945), and *An American in Paris* (1951).

6. Jacques Rivette (1928–2009), along with Truffaut, Jean-Luc Godard, Éric Rohmer, Claude Chabrol, and others, was a key member of the New Wave—young filmmakers who began making films in the 1950s—and is known for films like *Paris Belongs to Us* (1961) and *The Nun* (1967). He continued making films until 2009.

7. *Les Enfants du paradis* (*Children of Paradise*, Marcel Carné, 1945).

8. Truffaut is referring to *Cahiers du cinéma*, a French film magazine founded by Truffaut's mentor, André Bazin, together with Jacques Doniol-Valcroze and Joseph-Marie Lo Duca, in 1951. It became an important vehicle for articulating and disseminating the ideas and aesthetic principles of the New Wave.

9. Marshal Philippe Pétain was prime minister of the reactionary and collaborationist Vichy government of France between 1940 and 1944. After the Liberation he was tried for treason (July–August 1945).

10. Sacha Guitry (1885–1957) was a French actor, playwright, and filmmaker who was accused of collaborating with the Germans following the capitulation of France during World War II. Paul Claudel (1868–1955), a French poet and dramatist with right-wing views, was also accused of being a collaborationist.

11. *Citizen Kane* (Orson Welles, 1941); *The Magnificent Ambersons* (*La Splendeur des Amberson*, Orson Welles, 1942).

12. *Metropolis* (Fritz Lang, 1927).

13. *Travail et Culture* was an association devoted to political and cultural activism, aiming to promote the right to equal access to culture, especially for the working classes; see Antoine de Baecque and Serge Toubiana, *Truffaut: A Biography* (Berkeley: University of California Press, 1999), 38–39.

14. *Zéro de conduit* (*Zero for Conduct*, Jean Vigo, 1933); *L'Atalante* (Jean Vigo, 1934); *La Règle du jeu* (*The Rules of the Game*, Jean Renoir, 1939).

15. *La Grande illusion* (*La Grande Illusion*, Jean Renoir, 1937).

16. Henri Langlois (1914–1977), an ardent and influential cinephile, cofounded the Cinémathèque Française in 1936, serving as its director. An attempt to remove him by André Malraux, the French Minister of Cultural Affairs, in 1968 provoked protests in which Truffaut was involved, leading to his reinstatement.

17. *City Lights* (*Les Lumières de la ville*, Charles Chaplin, 1931); *Monsieur Verdoux* (Charles Chaplin, 1947).

18. Jean Genet, *Journal d'un voleur* (*The Thief's Journal*, published in 1949).

19. Truffaut has misremembered the date, given that Genet's *Journal d'un voleur* was published in 1949, and that Truffaut enlisted in October 1950.

20. *Nouvelle Revue Française*.

21. André Gide's *Isabelle* (1911), published together with his *La Symphonie pastorale* (1919), is a story about a young man who falls in love with the portrait of the absent daughter of a couple in whose home he is staying.

22. *Le Rideau cramoisi* (*The Crimson Curtain*, Alexandre Astruc, 1953); *Les Mauvaises Rencontres* (*Bad Liaisons*, Alexandre Astruc, 1955).

23. *Le Roman d'un tricheur* (*The Story of a Cheat*, Sacha Guitry, 1936).

24. *Brumes d'automne* (Dimitri Kirsanoff, 1929), which shows how the autumn atmosphere and human feelings correspond to each other.

25. *Viaggio in Italia* (*Voyage en Italie*, *Voyage to Italy*, Roberto Rossellini, 1954); *Un condamné à mort s'est échappé* (*A Man Escaped*, Robert Bresson, 1956); and *Lola Montès* (Max Ophüls, 1955).

26. *Et Dieu créa . . . la femme* (*. . . And God Created Woman*, Roger Vadim, 1956).

27. Truffaut is referring to a script subsequently filmed by Jean-Luc Godard: *À bout de souffle* (*Breathless*, 1960).

CHAPTER 2
THE NEW WAVE

> Each member remained true to himself, but, by so doing, grew distant from the others. Have you seen Rossellini's film on Saint Francis of Assisi? It deals with this very same phenomenon. It illustrates what happened to the New Wave. At the end of the film, the monks are together, and they start to spin round and round very quickly until they fall over. When they rouse themselves, they get up and leave in the direction in which they fell.
>
> Interview with Chris Petit and Verina Glaessner, Time Out, *no. 197,* November 30–December 6, 1973

Does the term "New Wave" reflect the reality?

I think that the reality of the New Wave was something that was anticipated rather than there from the beginning. The term was originally invented by journalists and then turned into something real. Nevertheless, even had this journalistic epithet not been created at the time of the Cannes Festival, I believe that the term, or some other like it, would have been created sooner or later once people started to become aware of the number of "first films" that were being made.

The concept of the New Wave originated as a result of an official survey conducted in France by some statistical service or another on French youth in general. Initially, the "New Wave" referred to future doctors, future engineers, and future lawyers. This survey was published in *L'Express*, which gave it a lot of publicity, and for several weeks *L'Express* appeared with a subtitle on the first page: "*L'Express*, the Newspaper of the New Wave."

Then, as a result of the coincidences that turned festivals into an opportunity for reviewing young filmmakers—not only in France, but also in other countries—journalists writing on film began to use this expression to denote a certain group of new filmmakers, not all of whom were necessarily motivated by a shared critical concern, given that Alain Resnais and Marcel Camus were included among them. This is how the slogan came to be formulated—a slogan which, in my opinion, did not correspond to any actual reality in terms of, for example, an association of young French filmmakers who regularly met together, had shared goals, and a common aesthetic (as some people overseas have believed). In actuality, there was none, with any notion of an association being merely a fiction, an entirely superficial appearance.

Nevertheless, isn't it true that this New Wave shared certain preoccupations?

There is only one thing that I see the young filmmakers as sharing in common: as a rule, they played pinball machines, in contrast to the older directors who prefer cards and whiskey! This is no anomaly, because, all joking aside, I have observed that, above all, there are essential differences between us. Certainly we know each other, we love the same films, we exchange ideas as friends, but when the results of our creative efforts are appraised on the screen, one sees that Chabrol's films have nothing to do with those of Louis Malle, which have nothing to do with mine. The films of the young filmmakers have an extraordinary resemblance to the people who make them, because the latter make them in a state of complete freedom. And that's the only thing that unites them: freedom. The older French directors had long since lost the habit of choosing their subject—I mean, an idea for a film that they carried around with them, feeling it in their guts and their head. In the process of becoming stars, French directors had become very sought-after. What they undertook was therefore determined by the nature of the proposals that were brought to them.

Let us try to define the young cinema in relation to the old.

As a rough generalization, I think it true to say that each of us is trying to bring a certain kind of veracity to cinema, instead of conducting ourselves in accordance with an "acquired truth." The verity of *Chemin des écoliers*[1] is entirely external, constantly drawing upon a cinematographic "truthfulness" to which we have become accustomed. For years now, French cinema has not been truthful—take settings, for example. One thing that all our films have in common is that they are extremely realistic, and each one in a way that is completely different. And the degree to which they are successful depends upon the extent of this realism. In each of our films, what matters is the personal vision of life it projects. For us, the important thing is to depict things we know about. Each one of us is trying to oppose the verity of our own personal experience against the stereotyped representation of reality that had come to dominate French cinema. You won't find in any of our films a breathless girl shutting a door—a cliché of all dramatic and psychological cinema. When we don't know how to do something, we insert an ellipsis; we film things that we believe are interesting, and moments of action that we think we can master.

If our films are jerky, don't flow smoothly, don't seek to invite the spectator to have a good time, it is because they are trying to bring together things that are powerful, important, that urgently need to be said. It seems to me that the young filmmakers are more preoccupied with what happens on the screen than with technique. They attach great importance to the characters, and to the subjects of their films. They have a great respect for the audience and the rather naïve idea that what interests them will inevitably interest spectators. They maintain that if the story pleases them, it will please others, and that their sincerity ensures that spectators will receive a good deal. But there are no aesthetic party lines. There are only similarities due to chance.

> *The New Wave only comprises individuals. But didn't André Bazin, in the* Cahiers du cinéma, *play a very large role as a theorist of cinema, and isn't he your mentor to some extent?*

Six or seven years ago, there were two generations of critics on the scene; there were also two generations of filmmakers. Then a third generation of critics came along, and then everyone was amazed that such young people were making films, just as six or seven years earlier, they were astonished that people were writing at such a young age! And yes, in this respect too, the *Cahiers du cinéma* was very important—no one was concerned about the age of the people who were supplying the articles, but only with the substance of these pieces, and the readership that each one of these articles attracted allowed the journal to shift from a monthly to a weekly. This is how the young critics came to express their ideas in many important newspapers. There was a first stage involving aesthetic evaluation of films, and a second stage in which we wondered why the films were like they were, why films were not better—it was a stage of "practical reflection" on the way in which they were made. There was a heightening of awareness on the part of five or six friends of the *Cahiers du cinéma*, who are now making films; above all, it involved an attempt at simplification. We went back to truths that were not new, but had been forgotten. At the beginning, in the silent era, all you needed to make a movie was to have film and a camera; then, bit by bit, cinema became industrialized to the point of becoming inaccessible to the amateur. This was a crucial turning point—the moment at which amateurs stopped making films, the last French amateur having been Jean Vigo, whose work marked the watershed between silent and talking movies. After three or four years of cinema with sound, a film represented an investment that only cinema industrialists could afford, so much so that the mise-en-scène was constrained on all sides, controlled, forbidden to the amateur.

This simplifying work of the *Cahiers* was salutary, and it seems to me that if one were to write a history of the New Wave, the first film to mention would be *Le Coup du berger*, by Jacques Rivette, which is exemplary both in terms of how it was made and also its style of production and its aims.[2] It was a film produced by Claude Chabrol, shot in Chabrol's apartment, by Rivette, in two weeks, with money being spent only on the film stock, and with a borrowed camera, several actor friends—Brialy, Doniol-Valcroze—and, above all, the desire to tell a story. I came next after Rivette by shooting *Les Mistons* in the following year, in which I also tried to tell a story with dialogue and actors. We wanted to show that we were storytellers—that is what mattered. With these two or three films, a start was made. Young people who were able to raise capital from their families—I believe that that was the case with Louis Malle, Chabrol, and me—made the first films of the New Wave, but the success of these first films allowed those who followed, and were unable to assemble enough capital, to raise finance with small "opportunistic" producers (in the good sense of the word). I think that eventually, after two years, all those (at the *Cahiers du cinéma*, for example) who had wanted to make a film had made one. And to finish with the *Cahiers du cinéma*, I have to say that André Bazin died several months before undertaking a documentary on Romanesque churches, a short film which was very dear to him, and which would have been his first film.

What is the significance of the young filmmakers' movement in the context of cinema history?

To sum it up, one could say that cinema has passed through three stages: the silent era, in which a film involved a physical performance, the time of

Griffith and John Ford. To make a film in that period was like engaging in a wrestling match. The director carried a considerable weight of film and equipment on his own shoulders. He had to orchestrate the movements of thousands of extras. The Deglane[3] of this period, that is, the master wrestler, was Griffith, and the Executioner of Béthune[4] was Cecil B. De Mille.

With the advent of the talkies, cinema was intellectualized. It became a subproduct of the novel, and especially of theater. It was given up to the semi-intellectual. This period was illustrated in the worst case by the duo of Feyder and Spaak,[5] and in the best by Prévert and Carné.[6]

We now come to the third stage: that of the intellectuals, a time in which bodily performance no longer enters the picture, in which all technical problems are taken in hand by a large team and perfectly resolved. The methods employed are just as perfectly executed as in the fifteenth film of this or that great director—whereas formerly, that would have been impossible. Cinema today is given over to intellectuals, that is, to people who in other circumstances would have been able to write novels and plays and who, undoubtedly, a decade ago, would have preferred to write novels and plays out of a fear of technology. We are now in the age of auteur-cinema. An intellectual cinema, of course, runs the risk of quickly becoming dry and abstract, but it also has more chance of becoming intelligent, powerful, and sincere, compared with the cinema of preceding periods.

Should one speak, then, not of revolution, but of evolution?

Exactly. For the young filmmakers, it's a question of rediscovering the healthiness of silent cinema, an amazing health that is the only thing that can prevent our cinema from becoming tense, gnarled, boring, and dry. It is necessary to recover the freshness of the first period of cinema and disown the second period completely, given that from our perspective today it seems like a transitional stage.

Who, in your view, are the most detestable dialogue writers and screenwriters of this second period—those who have most contributed to the undermining of the health of cinema, and whose influence remains the most dangerous?

Excluding the three names that dominated cinema before the War, by which I mean Renoir, Gance, and Jean Vigo, the screen was merely a by-product of theater and the novel. In my view, Charles Spaak seems the most compromised figure from this time. I should also mention Jeanson,[7] who vulgarized boulevard theater. When Jeanson declared that he was fighting against the cult of the director in affirming that the real author of a film is the dialogue writer, he was right, because all the films that he wrote were made by men who were effaced by him, who had nothing to say, and he, indeed, was the real author of those films. But if I were in his shoes, I wouldn't boast about it!

Even though it is impossible to identify a single formula for the young cinema, one can attempt to evaluate the intellectuals who drove it.

Above all, it involves people who were not afraid. They do not experience any fear in the face of the technology that had previously scared off others. They are not at all fearful of haggling with producers. They make it a point of honor to assert themselves forcefully in business dealings. They have completely abandoned the old idea that money is against art, and industry against cinematic art. They want to reconcile art and money instead of making them antagonists. The danger, of course, is that success will oblige them to work in accordance with established norms. They risk being approached very quickly by producers who say, "You made your film with 30 million; we are going to give you 120 for your next one. You see how much easier everything is going to be." Yes, the danger arises with the second or third film.

What is your own position on this subject?

There are only particular cases. Clearly, one can make three cheap films, but still want to make an expensive one. It can also be useful to use certain stars. The problem is to safeguard freedom to the utmost extent.

Has the fact of having made your films on a shoestring brought something new to your works?

Yes, indeed. Whereas a seasoned director used to take fifteen shots, we will use only one or two. That motivates the actors who know that we are not going to do it again, and so they take the plunge. Consequently, our images do not have the glacial perfection usually found in French films, and audiences have been moved by the spontaneous impression created by our films.

But that is an unpredictable effect that arises from a lack of polishing, if I understand correctly.

Absolutely. And there has been a lot of that in cinema already. It confers a veracity on the films that, while not profound, being an external one, nevertheless has its own importance. For example, in normal films, when one shoots a scene with characters who are talking inside a car, it is done in a studio by projecting images filmed beforehand by the cameraman, through a process called "transparency," that scroll past behind the windows. We clearly see that the actor is not driving, and that he is reciting his text without paying any attention to the steering wheel. All the spectators who drive a car wonder why the car doesn't crash into a tree. Now, because we cannot permit ourselves to use transparency in a studio for this kind of scene, we have fixed a camera on the front of the car, for the first time in years. As a result, we have achieved a greater sense of realism, the reality of the streets, the reality of the acting and the actor, and this kind of scene has touched the viewers. But this practice, forced upon us by circumstances, must not be allowed to become a method. At any rate, one gets to profound truth through surface truthfulness, and sophisticated cinema had lost even the superficial appearance of truthfulness. The actors' clothes, for example, were never rumpled, the characters never in a disheveled state.

> *Most of the young filmmakers who have come to notice, have, it seems, one thing in common. They are all students of, or at least regular attenders at, cinémathèques. They have not learned their craft behind the camera, but by watching films.*

In former times, people used to go to the cinema casually. These days, in fact, it is because of watching films and loving them that we want to make films. We no longer go to the cinema casually, but because of a desire to make cinema. As far as I am concerned, I was twelve when I decided to be a director, as a result of watching films.

Obviously, in such circumstances one runs the risk of not seeking to reinvent cinema in the way one should, but rather of copying it. It's at that point that temperament can intervene.

> *Have the young directors fully digested their cinémathèque culture? Are they not in the position of certain teachers of literature, former "khâgneux,"[8] who approach a novel a little too influenced by their study of the history of literature? Don't they run the risk of imitating too much, rather than inventing?*

In my opinion, this film culture is not a handicap. It even marks a step forward in comparison with preceding generations, when one became a filmmaker by passing through a craft industry. Assistants used to imitate the methods of their bosses, and not the classics. That's what led to the style one can call the "French cinema" style—artificially elegant, fearfully monotonous, and very inferior to the flexibility of American cinema. We have adopted the casualness of the latter with respect to technique and fluidity of camera movements. Naturally, as far as our creative sources are concerned, our legacy is French.

Can one say that the young filmmakers aim to bring something new to their conception of dialogue?

Negatively, yes, insofar as we disapprove of dialogue written in the style of Audiard or Jeanson, who only present witty characters seeking in every sentence to sum up their experience in happy and brilliant aphorisms—the dairywoman who talks like an engineer, in a definitively authoritative way, voicing an opinion on the fate of the world, and of life. Our desire is to portray things realistically. We try to de-theatricalize the dialogue.

In *The 400 Blows*, my dialogue writer, Marcel Moussy,[9] had a decisive input in this respect. I called him after having seen his TV broadcasts, *Si c'était vous*. He excelled in creating dialogue for familial conflicts, and his experience as a teacher inspired him to write exchanges between teacher and students that struck everyone with their accuracy. We make films in which almost nothing happens. No blood, no fistfights, no dramas, no violence, but a succession of small daily incidents that form the substance of a film. The danger, of course, would be to create a new fashion, or to merely look at oneself.

One problem is soon going to present itself to you: that of stars. How are you going to resolve it?

Personally, I would systematically refuse to make films with five particular stars: Fernandel, Michèle Morgan, Jean Gabin, Gérard Philipe, and Pierre Fresnay. These are artists who are too dangerous, who make decisions concerning the screenplay, altering it if they don't like it. They don't hesitate to dictate how it is going to be distributed, or to veto certain partners. They influence the mise-en-scène, demand close-ups. They don't hesitate to sacrifice a film's interests to what they call their "standing" and bear the responsibility, in my opinion, for many flops. I am happy to have made this statement, because henceforth I will have less chance of succumbing to temptation! But, cinema does not depend, fortunately, on these five A-listers. It is even the case, as we've seen recently, that stars sometimes have commercial failures. But there are some intelligent actors, and I will mention, for example, Jeanne

Moreau, who is renowned for her flexibility and her kindness—she does not even want to participate in the projection of the rushes, so as not to form hasty impressions about her acting. It would be ridiculous not to accept the collaboration of artists of this type.

Where has the New Wave found its audience?

The films that are going to come out either at the end of the year, or at the beginning of next year, are going to appeal, obviously, to a variety of audiences, but it is important to understand one thing, that these films have been made in exactly the same way as that of *Hiroshima*[10] and other films that have enjoyed a success this year: that is, *by expecting the worst*. These are films that have been shot so economically, generally with budgets of between thirty and forty million [francs], that it only takes a small-scale distribution to recover their costs. And when they are as successful as *Black Orpheus*, or *The Lovers*, or *The 400 Blows*, or *Les Cousins*, it is all to the good—but none of that was predicted in advance.[11] For our films, a release at the Caumartin art cinema would be sufficient—in other words, to be successful at specialized cinemas. Venomous articles are inevitably going to appear mounting new attacks that are stronger than ever on films by young directors, films that will achieve no distribution beyond the left bank, where they will enjoy a success comparable to that of the films of Ingmar Bergman or *Ivan the Terrible*[12] at la Pagode, and to *Il Grido*[13] at the Caumartin art cinema. This would amount to a real success, and would be sufficient. But, it will be in the interests of the people in the profession to say, "Look at these French films that don't even get a release on the Champs-Élysées," whereas this is not a valid criterion, given that there are films that come out on the Champs-Élysées which do not run for even a week, and whose box office returns are so disastrous that producers do not want to make them public.

I think, therefore, that the outlook is positive, and that the year 1960 will be even more amazing on account of the multiplicity of interesting films, their quality, and their quantity, that it will be more conclusive than the year 1959. For me, the New Wave is a phenomenon of 1960. Earlier, I wrote an article in *Arts* on the crisis affecting the ambition of French cinema, in which I said that, whereas in literature 80 percent of novelists aspire to win the Prix Goncourt, in cinema there are only three filmmakers each year who can hope to win the Prix Delluc. All that is changing with the young cinema. Whether successful or not, all the films that we make are ambitious in their nature. And this is very important. One can argue for hours over whether a film is good or bad, but if it has an ambitious quality, one very quickly becomes aware of the fact. This ambitious character could perhaps be made the basis of financial assistance to cinema. A reward for quality should be designed to encourage intentions, that is to say, ambition. We need to hope that, not long from now, the jury for the Delluc prize will be considering thirty filmmakers instead of three or four—that there will be an embarrassment of choices. When that happens, French cinema will be saved.

1961

All the newspapers are saying that the New Wave is now finished; what do you think about this?

I recognize that there is a malaise, a bad moment to get past, and solutions to be found. I attribute this malaise to a particular irony: the essential effort of the "new cinema" was about emancipating itself from the cinema industry. Films had become impersonal because of the various constraints placed on them—foreign actors, too many screenplays, the views of distributors, excessively large technical teams, excessively high financial estimates. We thought that it was necessary to simplify everything in order to work more freely, and to make *low-budget* films on *simple* subjects. This is what gave rise to the mass of "New Wave" films that had only one thing in common: a shared refusal. A refusal to have walk-on parts, a refusal to have theatrical plots, a refusal to use sumptuous decors, a refusal to include explanatory scenes. These are often films with only three or four characters, with very little action . . . Unfortunately, the linear appearance of these films has been construed as the reworking of a particular literary genre that irritates many critics and the present-day highbrow audience, a genre one could nickname "*saganisme*":[14] low-slung cars, bottles of scotch, fleeting love affairs, et cetera. The desired lightness of these films is regarded—sometimes wrongly, sometimes rightly—as frivolity.

This is where confusion has arisen: from the fact that the qualities of this new cinema—gracefulness, lightness, modesty, elegance, swiftness—move in the same direction as its faults—frivolousness, recklessness, naïveté.

The result? All of these films, the good ones as well as the bad ones, annoy some person or another. Every critic has his list of good and bad "new" films, but the list is never the same! What is paradoxical is the fact that this laudable effort to achieve lightness is bearing fruit three years too late—that is, precisely at the moment when filmmakers are contriving to hem spectators in by offering them the most *solemn* movies ever made. In earlier times, super-productions—often, but not always, biblical—would appear once a year. These days, there is one every month. *Ben Hur, Spartacus, King of Kings* are the opposite to television films, and our cheeky little films, shot in a devil-may-care manner, don't stand a chance against them.[15]

In conclusion, films that have a "New Wave" character generally have the following disadvantages:

- they resemble a TV broadcast, and therefore don't justify being seen outside the house;
- in their rejection of a convoluted plot that is then resolved, they give the impression of a short film that has been drawn out in length;
- they only address a part of the general audience, and are unable to be understood in the same way by a spectator entering the theater casually, and by a viewer who would have read all the articles and interviews relating to the particular film concerned;
- they do not conceal the modesty of the means by which they were made, achieved by paying more attention to things that don't cost much;
- they appear to want to deliver an entertainment, while not respecting any of the laws of an entertainment.

But, is all of that your own opinion, or the opinions you have found expressed by detractors of the New Wave?

It's a little of both. Aesthetic considerations matter more to me. I think, for example, that there are two kinds of cinema: the "Lumière branch" and the "Delluc branch." Lumière invented cinema to film the nature of actions, as in *Tables Turned on the Gardener*.[16] Delluc, who was a novelist and a critic, believed that one could use this new invention to film ideas, and actions that have a meaning other than what is apparent, through the possibility of incorporating the other arts. The result? The history of cinema comprises the "Lumière branch": Griffith, Chaplin, Stroheim, Flaherty, Gance, Vigo, Renoir, Rossellini (and closer to us, Godard); and, on the other side, the "Delluc branch": Epstein, L'Herbier, Feyder, Grémillon, Huston, Bardem, Astruc, Antonioni (and closer to us, Alain Resnais). For the former group, cinema is a *spectacle*, for the latter, it is a *language*.

Critics have always understood the Delluc branch better, which is natural, given that Louis Delluc is their boss.

Agreed, but isn't it true that this spectacle-cinema, in the sense in which you characterize it, is often very affected and contrived?

I want to emphasize that the first group shot their films with a spontaneous *innocence*, in recreating such things as the arrivals of trains in stations, a baby's meal, and sprayers sprayed,[17] and that the latter group—in a more contrived and intellectual manner—filmed moral conflicts between characters who most often are talking behind each other's backs. I'm simplifying, but it's a bit like that. Check it out, and you'll see for yourself.

The view you are expressing is rarely found in accounts of the history of cinema, but do you think that it is just as valid since the arrival of the new filmmakers as it was before?

In actual fact, it is becoming less and less true, given that people like Agnès Varda, Doniol, and Chabrol are practicing a kind of double game involving both Lumière and Delluc. What is correct, I think, given that the literary aspect of New Wave films is so heavily criticized, is to identify two fairly clear tendencies that I can detect:

(a) *The Sagan tendency*: involving a greater frankness concerning love relationships and matters of sex; self-portraits given by intellectuals and artists; cultivated characters, who are well-to-do, with a seeming air of coldness, et cetera. Several titles: *Les Cousins, L'Eau à la bouche, La Récréation, Les Mauvais Coups, Shadows of Adultery, Time Out for Love, La Morte-Saison des amours, The Girl with the Golden Eyes, Tonight or Never* . . .[18]

(b) *The Queneau tendency*: involving a search for the truthfulness of an ordinary vocabulary; unexpected, comical relationships between characters, who are generally lower-class or eccentric; a taste for the mixing of genres and shifts of tone; the search for a bittersweet tenderness, et cetera. Some titles: *Zazie dans le métro* and *A Couple* (and for a very good reason!), but also *The Good Time Girls, Shoot the Piano Player, Lola, Une femme est une femme, Adieu Philippine* (unreleased).[19]

What do you make of Resnais?

His impact surely escapes classification, but all the same, let us entertain the possibility of a third tendency that we might call, without too much racking of the brains, "the *Éditions de Minuit* cinema,"[20] in which one would include films that correspond to the "new novel" and those that aspire to be sociological "documents" or "testimonials": *La Pointe courte, Hiroshima mon amour, Lettre de Sibérie, Seven Days . . . Seven Nights, The Human Pyramid, The Long Absence, Last Year in Marienbad*, and two films that have not yet been released: *Chronique d'un été*, and *Le Temps du ghetto*.[21]

But, I repeat, such classifications are arbitrary. They allow us, perhaps, to see more clearly why the detractors of the new cinema are so irritated, but it's not merely a game. To speak candidly, there are some good films and some not-so-good films within each category, in each genre, in each tendency.

People always claim that a film has to please, but no one has ever said that a painting must please.

If a painting doesn't please you, you look at the next one; cinema is an entertainment—you are immobilized, trapped in your seat, at the mercy of the filmmaker.

Does that mean that for you it's like a circus?

You don't know how right you are! My films are circus entertainments, and I want them to be like that. I never show two elephants in a row. After the elephant comes the juggler, after the juggler, the bear. I even manage to have an entr'acte at about the sixth reel, because people get tired, their nerves fray. In the seventh reel, I pick them up again and try to finish with what I can do best.

Are you joking, or not?

I swear to you, I'm not. I genuinely think in terms of the circus when I am working. I would like people to whistle and boo at bad sequences and applaud those they like. Given that people have to be pent up in the dark to watch my films, I never fail near the end of the film to lead them into nature, by the seaside, or in the snow, in order to be forgiven.

It is just like at the Cirque d'hiver[22] when I was a boy, where shows often ended with water pouring on the circus ring; it was a matter, in short, of giving the last word to nature. I have made up rules for myself, which may be naïve, but I stick to them, and try to improve on them from film to film.

It's a *cinema of compromise*, if you like, in the sense that I'm always thinking about the audience, but that doesn't mean that it is a *cinema of concession*, because I never include a comic effect that doesn't make me laugh beforehand, or a sad effect that doesn't move me. That said, I have never really liked any of my films—there is always some important element that hasn't come off as well as I had hoped. It is very difficult to succeed in pulling off a good circus entertainment!

It was just three years ago that you abandoned criticism in order to make films. Have any of your ideas on cinema been modified since?

At the time, I was very aware of an enormous gap between cinema as I conceived of it and cinema as practiced by filmmakers. Today, I consider that every film is abstract and even experimental, whether it pretends to tell a story like *Psycho*,[23] or no longer even pretends, like *Marienbad*.

The question that most interests me currently is the following: does one have to continue to pretend to tell a story that is strictly controlled, supposed to have the same meaning and the same interest for the filmmaker and the spectator, or rather, to the contrary, should one admit that one is putting out there the rough version of a dream-movie, in the hope that it will advance us in exercising an art that is fearsomely difficult to practice on account of the multiplicity of elements that need to be controlled?

I think that all the filmmakers who have emerged from the Cahiers du cinéma *have this in common—panic at the thought of anything that could resemble the taking of a stand vis-à-vis the problems of our age. Do you share this phobia?*

Let me reply only for myself, not for my friends from the *Cahiers*—you would need to ask them each individually. Actually, in my films, I never address the "problems of our times," and if I were to tackle them, I wouldn't be capable of adopting a position. It's a question of temperament. For example, in a film, I am much more interested in the characters than in the events, and so I cannot make films about ideas. To take one example, I greatly admired Brecht's play about Hitler, but even if I were to have Brecht's genius, I would never have been able to create an Arturo Ui who was so antipathetic.[24] But I have read that Hitler, like Napoleon, liked to take short naps in the middle of work, and would bring along an old mattress that was flattened in the middle; it's a moving detail, like all details that relate to childhood for an adult. If I were to make a film about Hitler, it would be bound to be awful, because I would pay too much attention to details of this sort. It's this kind of thing that captures the paradoxical aspects of life. You know that the Israeli secret agents were only able to identify Eichmann when they saw him returning to his house with a bouquet of flowers.[25] By searching in their files, they found that it was his wedding anniversary. Gotcha! I find that phenomenal.

To make a war film, one is obliged to focus on men in the plural, rather than a man in the singular, something I could never imagine doing in my work. On the other hand, I don't believe that an artist today needs to treat the problems of his time any more than in any past centuries. One is always between two wars—I belong to a generation that is very pessimistic in that regard. The notion of "bad conscience" is all very good, I think, but imagine the career of Matisse if he had suffered from "bad conscience." He was too young to join the war of 1870, too old for that of 1914–1918, and a patriarch in 1940. He died at the end of the war in Indochina, and at the beginning of the war in Algeria. It is unbelievable! I maintain that the five wars in which he didn't take part constitute trivial events in the context of a life that was entirely devoted to painting flowers, and women with sections of window frames. He was good to other painters, he brought good to men generally, and what he did was good for him. You will say to me: why Matisse and not Picasso? I cite whatever suits me!

But I don't want to evade your question. The best perennial subject is love, and it is wrong to reproach the young cinema for being too preoccupied with it. We are criticized for not dealing with Algeria, which is currently the hottest topic. When a critic condemns a film for frivolity on the grounds that "in our times there are more urgent things to say," my view is that if these things are "urgent to say," then they are also "urgent to write," and that such a critic would be better occupied in doing precisely that. To report on a frivolous film constitutes an even more frivolous act than making a frivolous film, is it not so? In fact, in cases of this kind, the critic is attacking the filmmaker for not being a journalist—because "urgent" matters are the purview of journalism.

The important books on Algeria are not novels, but eyewitness accounts, files, and documents. A novel inspired by the "Audin affair" would deprive the real event of its impact, just as films based on the Dreyfus affair were disappointing.[26] When I was in Canada, I saw a filmed broadcast on the problems in Algeria made at the time of the Generals' putsch.[27] It was absolutely extraordinary: it had images that we had never seen in France, showing crowded villages, internment camps, and all kinds of interviews. It was very objective, very disturbing, and that gave the feeling of a situation that will be much more difficult to resolve honestly than anyone has admitted in any of our newspapers, regardless of their political leanings.

Personally, I have opted for fiction; it does not exclude ideas about life, the world, and society. I only notice details that relate to such issues, or, in the other direction, I become enraged when I read in a newspaper that the

Association of the Blind has decided to stop accepting the eyes of criminals condemned to death! I'm not certain I've answered your question very well.

> *Your heroes are almost always outsiders living on the margins of society. Is that a conscious choice on your part? Do you think, like Chabrol, that it's impossible to depict a worker on the screen?*

It is true that we are all more or less right-wing or left-wing anarchists, and that our characters resemble us: they can't be placed easily. Nevertheless, a French filmmaker has scruples of a sort that you will never find in American cinema. Many French filmmakers—Becker is the clearest example[28]—only like to deal with what they themselves know at first hand.

I used to work in a factory, as a welder, and I remember enough about that to be able to depict workers fairly accurately, but what's the point of filming people who, for eight hours each day, work at something they don't like? To glorify their work would be hypocritical, just as encouraging them to resign themselves to it would be . . . At that time in my life, I used to "escape" from my work by mentally reconstructing the three or four films that I had seen on the previous Sunday. And believe me, nothing in the world would have made me go and see a film about workers. In France, there are five or six directors who are communists, and about fifteen who are genuine leftists. It's those ones—Le Chanois, Lara, Menegoz, Paviot, Enbiani, Daquin—who should be asked to film workers and the problems of workers.[29]

What prompts me to make a film is generally a vague idea, or a feeling, or a need to do something different from my preceding film. One day I might film a worker, but only if I am led to it naturally—it is not something that I would decide arbitrarily to do in advance. Obviously, I am aware that there are more idle and wealthy characters on French screens than ordinary workers . . .

Apart from children—there are always some in my films—I am particularly interested in thieves, beggars, prostitutes, all of which are asocial characters whom I would not like to see excluded from society. Even if society would prefer to do so . . .

1962

> *Where is the New Wave today?*

That depends on the day. Not everything is going smoothly at the present time, but we should remember that, when everything *was* going well, it surpassed anything we were anticipating. At the end of 1959 we were caught up in a dream, everything was happening in conditions that had been unimaginable two years earlier.

I remember, for example, an article by Marguerite Duras in *France-Observateur*, in which she describes her work on *Hiroshima* with Resnais. Resnais said to her, "We must start with an assumption that it will be a miracle if we manage to get a theatrical release." The international success of *Hiroshima*, compared with the modesty of this point of departure (which also reflected, to some degree, a principle of modesty) is particularly meaningful.

I believe that it was like this for us all. When I shot *The 400 Blows*, I was alarmed to see that my estimate—around twenty-eight million—had blown out to thirty-five. I was panic-stricken, I had the feeling that I had embarked on something that would be difficult to make profitable; but, once it was finished, with the Cannes Festival and foreign sales, the film more than recovered its costs. In America, for example, it was bought for a hundred thousand dollars: fifty million [francs].

So we were swept along in a state of euphoria. In 1959 the situation was unusually propitious. It is only natural that it should have encouraged dreams, even ones that were a little bit crazy. This was also true of certain producers who, believing that the secret to everything was youth, novelty, et cetera, threw themselves in turn into looking for new talent.

There is one thing that it's probably good to recall: the first flops began with compromises. For example, a producer, presented with someone who had not yet made anything, would tell himself that all that was needed was to give the aspiring filmmaker a good cameraman. Now, it's a very bad mistake to give a beginner a cameraman who is used to making classical films: the product is a mongrel, shapeless. It would be impossible for such a cameraman to help a young director in the way, for example, that Decaë or Coutard could have done,[30] or a cameraman used to semiprofessional conditions (as in the case of Melville's films). Moreover, he would no longer be able to make a classical film, shot according to the usual norms.

The same error occurs in different forms. For example, the intrusion of traditional scriptwriters or stars into films that were not made to be like that, not to mention other similar kinds of faulty combinations. In Hanoun's case,[31] this was because of the intervention of the whole studio machine, among other things—something he had not foreseen, and for which the film was not suitable, given the mixture of improvisation and prepared staging that characterizes it.

As for the rest of us, we, too, have inevitably succumbed to some wrong-headed ideas about how we should approach cinema.

At the time when we were beginning to make films, it was Rivette who was the most active. During this period, Astruc was the only one who could truly consider himself a filmmaker. The rest of us were thinking about cinema without being excessively adventurous in formulating our ideas. Rivette was the most clearly decisive one, and he provided an example, by making films in 16mm. Rohmer, too, thought of himself as a filmmaker, but he was looking for this to develop more in the future.

Rivette was the first to propose concrete solutions. He made us get together, proposed plans, suggested the idea of establishing an association of filmmakers, a group for directors, and other comparable ideas.

By studying estimates—which had been quite well documented—we had worked out that one could comfortably make films for twenty-five million francs. That's right! Our thinking went something like this: we would say to so-and-so, "With a hundred million, you make a film without knowing whether it will be profitable or not; we, with a hundred million, can make four of them, and its very unlikely that one of them won't be a success."

Resnais was interested (at the time, he wanted to make *Les Mauvais Coups*).[32] We all went to see people like Dorfmann and Bérard,[33] with a screenplay that he had drafted with Rivette, as well as with Chabrol, Bitsch, and me,[34] which was called *Les Quatre Jeudis*. We presented this screenplay, but it didn't enthrall anyone, and no producer followed it up.

Our mistake was to believe that producers were interested in making cheap films. We were ignoring the time-honored law of French cinema that the producer is not the one who *has* the money, but the one who is *looking* for it, and that his only assured earnings come from his percentage of the budget for the film. The higher the estimate for the film, the higher this percentage would be. That explains why they would make films for two hundred or three hundred million that could have cost half as much, and why so many producers—when it comes to the crunch—basically don't care about how the film does at the box office.

This was the reason this project did not go forward, which was why it was necessary for the film's author also to be its producer—so that the different interests invested in the film resided in the same person, and were not working against one another.

Is it true to say there was a failure to change distribution practices that had been designed for a form of cinema that is now outdated?

That's absolutely right. But, temperamentally, I am against any kind of discrimination. Accordingly, I would not like to see a chain of theaters established that specializes in the screening of New Wave films, in parallel to a larger or more comfortable chain, et cetera. I believe that a film should not limit its aims. In my view, that seems incompatible with the vocation of cinema. We are in the domain of entertainment—all films should have the same circulation. In this respect, we should accord them the same value at the point of departure: in those circumstances, all kinds of miracles are possible.

The exploitation of *Marienbad*, which consisted of distributing small handouts at the entrance to the theater urging people to go and see something special, telling them that they would not need to look for any precise meaning, but only an atmosphere, an enchantment—this was a very loyal thing to do. At the same time, it seems wrong, to me, because it runs counter to the very concept of an entertainment, which is that it doesn't matter who can go in, or where it is (unfortunately, often, it also doesn't matter when or how), and that one should expect to see an entertainment, with, simply, the possibility of a surprise arising from the subject of the spectacle.

As far as I am concerned, I am more in favor of the photos one sees at the entrance to the theater. It is often said these days that people, even in the provinces, know beforehand what kind of film they are going to see, but I continue to believe that most choose a film by looking at the pictures at the entrance to the cinema, as I used to do when I was a boy.

Isn't it true that those who think there should be two circuits of distribution nevertheless put their finger on a reality that one needs to consider, irrespective of the solutions they propose for the problem, some of which are too theoretical?

Obviously, the person handling the exploitation has to know what he is doing. There are certain errors one shouldn't commit. If, in a cinema that is used to showing westerns, one suddenly switches to *Lola*, it is obvious that there is going to be some fallout: the film, the audience, and the theater owner will all suffer. Of course, the ideal situation would be for everyone who goes to see westerns to go and see *Lola* as well, and vice versa, but nothing is going to be achieved by attempting to go down that route.

Similarly, a distributor needs to understand certain things. Unfortunately, too often he doesn't know them. If a distributor is almost certain that a film is going to be torn to shreds by the critics, it is perhaps preferable in this case to release it in the provinces first. If not, then it is better to try it in Paris—all the more so, if one has reason to believe that the reviews are going to be favorable.

For example, the last two films of Constantine, Givray, and Jean-Louis Richard have had an infinitely more favorable press than their earlier ones.[35]

Now, by the time these reviews appeared in Paris, the films had almost finished their run in the provinces, which is stupid. If the films had been released in Paris first, in the provinces they would have attracted spectators whose interest had been aroused by the press, in addition to Constantine's regular fans. Certainly, there are people who are now saying to themselves, "We have missed the opportunity to see these films, we didn't know that *A Swelled Head* and *Good Luck Charlie* could interest us." It's the same story with *The Honors of War*.[36]

This is a good example of incompetence on the part of the distributor, who didn't take into account the nature of the product he had in his hands, someone who let himself get caught up in the machinery of a routine that consists of giving things over to regional peddlers. Because the latter have occasionally secured rentals over a long period (it is easier, actually, to obtain them in the provinces that in Paris), the distributor believes he is on the right track.

And what about films that are considered, rightly or wrongly, incapable of being released commercially?

These films have all ended up being released eventually, one after another. The experience of 1959 was an intoxicant that led to certain excesses. In fact, I don't think that a film should try to be innovative on all levels at once. It might be that it's necessary to have some element in a new-style film that links it to classical cinema: a simple subject with impact, the presence of a star, or something else. One senses that many films have been made in a state of naïveté. You cannot depend on flukes forever. Among films that have been flops, there are, for a start, those that are quite successful artistically, but which floated above the head of the audience; there are those that are merely interesting; and there are those that are just outright failures.

There is no issue concerning those that are failures: they are panned in the *Cahiers*, and elsewhere, which is to be expected.

The problem arises with those films that are interesting, but without being entirely successful. These films have one thing in common: the screenplay doesn't have the same meaning for the audience as it does for the director. Currently, these faults are probably caused by an excess of self-confidence on the part of the director, or else from the fact that he has chosen a kind of subject for which sincerity alone is not enough. There are subjects that allow one to speak from the heart—what one has to say is so simple that everybody will understand it, no matter what. In this case, there is no issue to be resolved.

There are other kinds of subject, however, that do pose problems worth pondering—for example, problems of construction. One moves from one character to another character, and from one group to another group of characters; the film shifts from one place to another. At this stage, professional considerations must come into play. When you are in a particular location, it must be able to be recognized. The director is sometimes persuaded that people will recognize an apartment or characters when they reappear after half an hour, whereas the audience will probably not recognize anything at all—such things are very important. We can say that there are two kinds of film, if you like. The first sort comprises films that are quintessentially personal, reflecting the state of mind of the artist at the time when he shot the film—for example, *Breathless* (which, above all, in my view, is a kind of cry from the heart). The second type consists of films that are shot "cold," fabricated objects that one has to construct in the best way possible; for instance, all films with a crime-thriller format need to be well constructed. There are several ways of doing this. In this regard, I have a feeling that Paviot's *Portrait-Robot*, Doniol's *Dénonciation*, and Chabrol's *The Third Lover* would have benefited from having been carefully discussed before the films were shot, perhaps in collaboration with someone like Kast, who is fairly rigorous and logical, or a screenwriter like Moussy.[37] There is no doubt that, even though all three of these films are interesting, what the audience takes from them is not exactly what the filmmaker intended—there is "a bone in the cheese."

When all is said and done, I don't think that too much injustice has been done. I have to confess that I'm more likely to notice justice than injustice. I believe that, in a great number of cases, the according of success, or lack of it, was deserved: a hierarchy of values has been respected. Thus, I find it appropriate that *Seven Days . . . Seven Nights* was far less successful that *Hiroshima*, given its pretensions to be a remake of the latter for everyone, whereas, in actual fact, it turned Renais's film into a remake for no one.

As far as I am concerned, I have still had only one misunderstanding with the audience: *Shoot the Piano Player*, and I believe that the blame for that lies entirely with me—quite apart from the fact that there was not a very good match between the distribution of the film and the kind of film it was.

1967

Given that it has now been three months since the last interview between you and the Cahiers, *and that a lot of things have happened in French cinema in the meantime, we want to ask you what you think about the evolution of the New Wave?*

The other evening I heard a vague polemic on television between Claude Mauriac and Melville.[38] And the only thing they agreed on was in saying, "Naturally, the New Wave has been very disappointing." Then they moved on to another topic, as if what they had said was self-evident. That shocked me. If one considers the New Wave in terms of what it was in the beginning—an ambition to make a first film with fairly personal content before one is thirty-five—then it has displayed an impressive richness, has kept all its promises, and has inspired similar movements in almost every other country in the world, which was beyond anything we had hoped for.

The New Wave was born in 1959, and since the end of 1960 it has been scoffed at; as far as public opinion was concerned, it was regarded as something prestigious for a year only. The turning point at which eulogy shifted to denigration was marked by a film by La Patellière and Michel Audiard, *Rue de Paris*, that was promoted as an "anti-New-Wave" film: "Jean Gabin settles his account with the New Wave."[39] That is when demagoguery started up—in other words, when the very same journalists who had launched the movement decided it was time to feed people the clichés they wanted to read, and nothing else. Prior to *Rue de Paris*, when we were interviewed—Jean-Luc [Godard], Resnais, Malle, myself, along with others—we would say, "The New Wave doesn't exist, it doesn't mean anything," but afterwards things had to change, and since then I have proclaimed my membership of this movement. Today, in 1967, one should be proud of having been, and still being, part of the New Wave, like having been a Jew during the Occupation.

The New Wave is constantly being insulted, always in a cowardly manner, because those who attack do not take the trouble to define it, or to mention specific titles and names. Despite this, without succumbing to a mania for lists, one should note that in the past three years we have seen the successful arrival of Alain Jessua, Claude Berri, José Giovanni, René Allio, Luc Moullet, and several others. These are not one-off filmmakers, they will continue working; they belong, of course, to the New Wave, to French cinema; their films will be included in festivals, and will be shown overseas . . .

I imagine that people who shout that "the New Wave has failed," without specifying any reasons for their judgment, are thinking of "intellectual" films that have not been successful with the audience. In their minds, they refuse to accord the "label" to films they have enjoyed, or which have proved successful. This selective discrimination is arbitrary, however, given that the New Wave comprises *That Man from Rio* as well as *L'Immortelle*; *The Two of Us* as well as *La Musica*; *Les Cœurs verts* as well as *A Man and a Woman*; and *A Matter of Resistance* as well as *Brigitte et Brigitte*,[40] which is why it is foolish to make any kind of generalization—and, as they say, that in itself is a generalization! The New Wave did not have an aesthetic program, it was simply an attempt to rediscover a certain kind of freedom that had been lost around 1924, when films became too costly, shortly before the advent of the talkies. In 1960, for us, creating cinema was to imitate D. W. Griffith in the days when he was making his films under the California sunshine, before even the birth of Hollywood. At that time filmmakers were all very youthful. It is staggering to realize that Hitchcock, King Vidor, Walsh, Ford, and Capra all made their first film before the age of twenty-five. It was a craft for boys, rather than cineastes, and that is how it should be. So the young filmmakers needed to come along, like Guy Gilles and Lelouch, and others even younger, camera in hand, leaning out perched on the side of helicopters, prepared to get eaten by mosquitoes in the Amazon, et cetera.

You have just given a very broad, indulgent definition of the New Wave... It encompasses many men: Lelouch, Rappeneau...

I don't see how one can define them by any criterion other than that of age. If Lelouch, who shoots with a handheld camera, without cuts, is not part of the New Wave, then it doesn't exist...

Yes, but the notion of "New Wave" also implies a moral point of view on cinema. There is also the problem of the nature of success, of the audience: what do you think about the commercial future of NW films?

In that regard, things have been more difficult, because distribution is the hardest system to change. Nevertheless, I believe that the art house cinemas have lacked a bit of courage in their programming. The films exist, they only have to project them, from *Adieu Philippine* to *The Glass Cage*, to *Le Signe du lion*, *The Enclosure*, *Le Coup de grâce*, *Le Joli Mai*, *La Longue Marche*, *Muriel*, *Lola*, *The Soldiers*, the list would be a long one...[41]

1968

How would you now situate yourself in relation to your friends in the New Wave? Do you feel that you have all followed an almost parallel path, each one in accordance with his own personality, and that you have all remained true to what you were in the beginning, to the original conception of cinema that you had?

I think so, but doesn't that come from the fact that we know each other too well? I think that Rohmer's films resemble him enormously, just as Godard's films resemble him. Rivette is a little more unpredictable—he is the most ardent cinephile of us all, the one who most struggles against himself, meaning that it is fairly difficult to predict what he is going to make. But, yes, I believe in being true to oneself.

To oneself, but what about to the group that you constitute?

Oh! We were not always a group—we are split up. These days we are coming together again because of what has been happening over the Cinémathèque.[42] But I find it difficult to give you an answer. I happen to have made new friends through cinema: Claude Berri since *The Two of Us*, Kast, whom I didn't understand earlier; I have come to like them better through their films. In this business, it is certainly difficult to be friends with people for whom one does not feel a degree of admiration. Even so, an element of judgmental criticism enters into our relations with one another, however attenuated, however softened. That's inevitable.

Do you continue to discuss your work together?

Yes, certainly much more than anyone else has ever done in France before. That's because of the *Cahiers du cinéma*, and because of the training we had as a group. We met at the Avenue de Messine, at the Cinémathèque, we came together in the film clubs; there were famous sessions at Montparnasse in which we would argue every Tuesday night! All that led to us talking about cinema as a group. Later, at a more intimate level, it seemed entirely normal for us to read our screenplays to two or three close friends, and to take heed of their advice.

1974

Today one can gauge the importance of a movement like the New Wave, but, in your case, we don't know a lot about how you came to be aware of your own role . . .

In the beginning I didn't have very well developed ideas; they arose out of the influence of friends like Rivette and Rohmer. As for me, I would instinctively like, or dislike, this or that film. At a certain moment it was Rivette, perhaps, who alerted me to the clichés in French cinema, and it was from 1950 onward that we began to revolt a bit against that . . . Our hostility may have been excessive, but all the same, in my opinion, between 1950 and 1955 no films appeared that were as important as *Le Corbeau* or *Children of Paradise* had been. We were interested in Bresson, Tati . . . After 1950 Cocteau wasn't making anything . . . It was as if there was a void. From 1950 to 1955 French cinema was a facsimile, an artificial extension of what had been strong between 1940 and 1950. Darkness and cruelty, which had been quite sincere in the beginning, had become a routine. There was almost a snobbery surrounding the unhappy ending. Naturally, because of that, we defended American cinema, which was then being viciously attacked by the critics, to a much greater degree than it is today, owing to the fact that now they are intimidated! Basically, we succumbed to the temptation that besets all critics: to oppose things instead of talking about them objectively. The refrain went like this: one can't like French cinema if one likes American cinema, one cannot like Mizoguchi if one likes Kurosawa, one can't like this if one doesn't like that!

With almost fifteen years hindsight, how would you judge your actions today (I am speaking here of the phenomenon of the New Wave)?

I don't like such questions because I think that we are not the right people to ask. They are more appropriately addressed to external observers. I do not like giving the kind of answers critics deliver—I never think of doing that. The process of working turns one into an individualist. I don't mean to say that one ceases to be curious about the work of others, but everything becomes enormously individualized. I have an opinion on Bergman, but not on Swedish cinema! What were we trying to achieve? Probably a greater fidelity to life. However, I don't know if we were all aiming to achieve the same thing! That becomes apparent afterwards, in the works we have created. We didn't know at all, any one of us, what kind of film we were going to make. Obviously, one can sense certain preferences. If you read Godard's collection of articles today, troubling things emerge. We can see, in 1950, his interest in films that were, in the end, to anticipate *La Chinoise* and *Pierrot le Fou*. Then one says to oneself, "Ah yes, there is a continuity there!" I think that it would be the same if one were to read the articles by Rivette and Rohmer. Very striking, Rohmer! And, probably, if one rereads mine too. But an evaluation of whether goals have been attained, or not, that is not for us to do! There are now going to be many studies of the New Wave . . . With this contradiction, that whereas discussions of the New Wave in France are almost always pejorative, in America they remain eulogistic. Recently I was reading reviews of the New York Festival in which someone wrote that the festival had been saved by French films, whereas the American films had been pitiful: the very opposite of the refrain at Cannes the year before. In both cases, it's untrue; the truth probably lies somewhere between the two . . .

I would like to hear you talk about your first experience as a producer with Paris Belongs to Us.[43]

In reality, when we produced it, the film had already been made, because *Paris Belongs to Us* was shot with nothing: several loans, some people who lent a bit of money, and an apartment, and film stock that came from another movie . . . The fact remains that, at the end, there was an enormous mass of film, at which point it was necessary to spend money to reimburse people, tackle the editing . . . All of that happened after the release of *The 400 Blows*, and thus at a fairly propitious time for me, since I was a producer on this film at 50 percent. Chabrol, for his part, had just had a good success with *Le Beau Serge*, and especially *Les Cousins*.[44] Between the two of us we made it possible for Rivette to finish his film, pay back his debts, rent an editing suite, and get down to work. Work that, it seems to me, took a very long time, since *Paris Belongs to Us* was still not quite finished when I completed *Shoot the Piano Player*. Simultaneously, I contributed to the production of the film *Testament of Orpheus*—partially by subscription, because cinema circles had turned away . . .[45]

During this period, one thing was very apparent: the close collaboration that existed between you all, from Rivette to Godard, through Chabrol . . . Today, it seems that there might not be the same frame of mind . . .

As for that, I don't know. It's a frame of mind that belongs to youth, to beginners; you would have to see if it exists in other teams of young people. With people who have succeeded in doing what they want to do, it is more difficult. I often think of this phrase, "With art it's everyone for himself, just as it is in a shipwreck!" That's normal: when Rohmer is making *Claire's Knee*, he doesn't need me.[46] One needs to make a distinction between different things: there can be an artistic collaboration—it's rare—and material aid when one believes in something, when one wants to assist a project. At that time, it was called coproduction. I have sometimes done this, as have Rohmer and Chabrol. At the same time, I have preserved my own habits: I have often had occasion to resort to Rivette—for example, concerning *The Bride Wore Black*—to ask his advice, both before and after the shoot. And then I stopped, as far as making films was concerned, because we had ideas that were too opposed about what was happening at that time. He is in favor of uncut versions, whereas I still believe in arranging and making adjustments to the film! He thinks—and it's a very beautiful, very honest idea—that one should allow the audience to witness one's mistakes, to show everything, including what hasn't been successful. I, in contrast, have a more sneaky idea: to disguise weaknesses, to plug the gaps. I believe that every stage of the process is an opportunity to intercept mistakes, improve the film . . . In contrast, I don't think I have ever finished the editing of a film without having worked with Jean Aurel, which often amazes people.[47] But it's true: Aurel has been a big help with all my films from *Jules and Jim* to my recent ones. He is a man who has a phenomenal critical mind. To return to your question, I also think that differences become more marked with the passing of time, because when one is setting out, one has the impression that everyone is the same, and it is not until later that one is struck by the differences. That is why the articles on the New Wave cannot be taken too seriously, insofar as they try to draw things together into themes. Finally, I am more impressed by the differences that are becoming more accentuated, probably because we are also working with an awareness of what each of us is doing, and in reaction to it. That's only human!

Notes

1. *Le Chemin des écoliers* (Michel Boisrond, 1959).
2. *Le Coup du berger* (Jacques Rivette, 1956).
3. Henri Deglane (1902–1975), a French wrestler who won a gold medal in Greco-Roman wrestling at the 1924 Olympic Games, held in Paris.
4. Jacques Ducrez (1932–2009), a professional French wrestler who went under the name of "le Bourreau de Béthune."
5. Truffaut is referring to Jacques Feyder (1885–1948), a Belgian filmmaker who worked mainly in France, and Charles Spaak (1903–1975), a Belgian screenwriter who worked as secretary for Feyder and wrote the script for the latter's adaptation of the play *Les Nouveaux Messieurs* (Francis de Croisset).
6. Jacques Prévert (1900–1977), a French poet and screenwriter; Marcel Carné (1906–1996), a French filmmaker known for *Port of Shadows* (1938), *Le Jour se lève* (1939), *The Devil's Envoys* (1942), and *Children of Paradise* (1945).
7. Henri Jeanson (1900–1970), a journalist and screenwriter, whose pre-War screenplays included those for *La Dame de chez Maxim's* (Korda, 1933), *Marchand d'amour* (Gréville, 1935), and *Naples au baiser de feu* (Genina, 1937).
8. A slang term for students preparing for the competitive entrance examination for entry into the École Normale Supérieure, one of the élite *grandes écoles*.
9. Marcel Moussy (1924–1995), a French screenwriter and television director born in Algiers.
10. *Hiroshima mon amour* (*Hiroshima Mon Amour*, Alain Resnais, 1959).
11. Truffaut is referring to *Orfeu Negro* (*Black Orpheus*, Marcel Camus, 1959); *Les Amants* (*The Lovers*, Louis Malle, 1958); and *Les Cousins* (Claude Chabrol, 1959).
12. *Ivan Grozniy* (*Ivan the Terrible*, Sergei Eisenstein, released in two parts: Part 1 in 1944, and Part 2 in 1958).
13. *Il grido* (*Le Cri*, Michelangelo Antonioni, 1957).

14. A term Truffaut is coining from the name of Françoise Sagan (a.k.a. Françoise Quoirez), a French writer best known for her novel *Bonjour Tristesse* (1954), which became a cult work on account of its depiction of a disillusioned teenager.
15. *Ben Hur* (William Wyler, 1959); *Spartacus* (Stanley Kubrick, 1960); and *King of Kings* (*Le Roi des rois*, Nicholas Ray, 1961).
16. *L'Arroseur arrosé* (*Tables Turned on the Gardener*, Louis Lumière, 1895).
17. Truffaut is alluding to three of the earliest films to be made, *L'Arrivée d'un train à La Ciotat* (*The Arrival of a Train*, Louis Lumière, 1896), *Repas de bébé* (*Baby's Dinner*, Louis Lumière, 1895), and *L'Arroseur arrosé* [literally, "the sprayer sprayed"] (*Tables Turned on the Gardener*, Louis Lumière, 1895).
18. *Les Cousins* (Claude Chabrol, 1959); *L'Eau à la bouche* (Jacques Doniol-Valcroze, 1960); *La Récréation* (Fabien Colin and François Moreuil, 1961); *Les Mauvais Coups* (François Leterrier, 1961); *La Proie pour l'ombre* (*Shadows of Adultery*, Alexandre Astruc, 1961); *Les Grandes Personnes* (*Time Out for Love*, Jean Valère, 1961); *La Morte-Saison des amours* (Pierre Kast, 1961); *La Fille aux yeux d'or* (*The Girl with the Golden Eyes*, Jean-Gabriel Albicocco, 1961); *Ce soir ou jamais* (*Tonight or Never*, Michel Deville, 1961).
19. *Zazie dans le métro* (Louis Malle, 1960); *Un couple* (*A Couple*, Jean-Pierre Mocky, 1960); also *Les Bonnes Femmes* (*The Good Time Girls*, Claude Chabrol, 1960); *Tirez sur le pianiste* (*Shoot the Piano Player*, François Truffaut, 1960); *Lola* (Jacques Demy, 1961); *Une femme est une femme* (Jean-Luc Godard, 1961); *Adieu Philippine* (Jacques Rozier, 1962).
20. Les Éditions de Minuit, founded in 1941 in Paris during the German Occupation, functioned as an underground publisher until the Liberation in August 1944. After the War, it published experimental novels by authors associated with the "Nouveau roman," such as Samuel Beckett, Alain Robbe-Grillet, and Marguerite Duras.
21. *La Pointe courte* (Agnès Varda, 1956); *Hiroshima mon amour* (Alain Resnais, 1959); *Lettre de Sibérie* (Chris Marker, 1957); *Moderato cantabile* (*Seven Days . . . Seven Nights*, Peter Brook, 1960); *La Pyramide humaine* (*The Human Pyramid*, Jean Rouch, 1961); *Une aussi longue absence* (*The Long Absence*, Henri Colpi, 1960); *L'Année dernière à Marienbad* (*Last Year in Marienbad*, Alain Resnais, 1961); not yet been released: *Chronique d'un été* (*Chronicle of a Summer*, Edgar Morin and Jean Rouch, 1961), and *Le Temps du ghetto* (Frédéric Rossif, 1961).
22. The Cirque d'hiver ("Winter Circus"), situated at the juncture of the rue des Filles Calvaires and rue Amelot in Paris, was opened by Emperor Napoleon III in 1861, and renamed Cirque d'hiver in 1870. It hosts circuses, musical concerts, and other entertainments.
23. *Psycho* (Alfred Hitchcock, 1960).
24. Bertolt Brecht, *Der aufhaltsame Aufstieg des Arturo Ui* (*The Resistible Rise of Arturo Ui*, 1941).
25. Truffaut is referring to Otto Adolf Eichmann, a Nazi who organized the mass deportation of Jews to ghettos and extermination camps during World War II, who was captured in Argentina by Mossad agents, tried and found guilty of war crimes, and hanged in 1962.
26. Maurice Audin was a young French mathematics assistant at the University of Algiers who was arrested by French soldiers during the Battle of Algiers, and died under torture in June 1957.

The "Audin affair" was the subject of indignant discussion in a number of newspapers. The "Dreyfus affair" concerned the unjust conviction for treason of Captain Alfred Dreyfus and subsequent cover-up of the true culprit, which provoked an intense political and juridical scandal.
27. A failed coup d'état, organized in Algeria in 1961 by retired French army generals, aimed at overthrowing President Charles de Gaulle.
28. Jacques Becker (1906–1960), best known for films like *Casque d'or* (1952), *Touchez pas au grisbi* (1954), and *Le Trou* (*The Hole*, 1960).

29. Truffaut is referring to Jean-Paul Étienne Dreyfus, better known as Jean-Paul Le Chanois (1932–1976); Claude Autant-Lara (1901–2000); Robert Menegoz (active in filmmaking between 1951 and 1979); Paul Paviot (1926–); and Louis Daquin (1908–1980). Neither the IMDb nor Allociné have any record of a director named Enbiani.

30. Henri Decaë (1915–1987), who worked closely as a cinematographer with Jean-Pierre Melville, Louis Malle, and Claude Chabrol, as well as Truffaut on *The 400 Blows*; Raoul Coutard (1924–), notable for his work as a cinematographer with Jean-Luc Godard.

31. Marcel Hanoun (1929–2012), known chiefly for *Une simple histoire* (*A Simple Story*, 1959).

32. A film based on a novel by Roger Vailland, which was eventually made as *Les Mauvais Coups* (1961) by François Leterrier.

33. Robert Dorfmann (1912–1999), the producer of *Last Year in Marienbad* (1961); Henri Bérard, producer of *Rififi* (Jules Dassin, 1955), and *Celui qui doit mourir* (*He Who Must Die*, Jules Dassin, 1957).

34. Truffaut is referring to Charles L. Bitsch (1931–), an assistant director and director, known for *Chance at Love* (1964) and *Le Dernier Homme* (1969).

35. Jean Constantine (1923–1997), a soundtrack composer who worked with Truffaut on *The 400 Blows*; Claude de Givray (1933–), a director and writer who supplied the screenplay and dialogue for Truffaut's *Stolen Kisses* (1968) and *Bed and Board* (1970); Jean-Louis Richard (1927–2012), a French actor, writer, and director who appeared in Truffaut's *Jules and Jim* (1961) and *The Last Metro* (1980), and wrote the screenplays for *The Soft Skin* (1964), *Fahrenheit 451* (1966), *The Bride Wore Black* (1968), and *Day for Night* (1973).

36. *Une grosse tête* (*A Swelled Head*, Claude de Givray, 1962); *Bonne chance Charlie* (*Good Luck Charlie*, Jean-Louis Richard, 1962); *Les Honneurs de la guerre* (*The Honors of War*, Jean Dewever, 1961).

37. Truffaut is referring to *Portrait-robot* (*Portrait-Robot*, Paul Paviot, 1962); *La Dénonciation* (Jacques Doniol-Valcroze, 1962); and *L'Œil du Malin* (*The Third Lover*, Claude Chabrol, 1962). Pierre Kast (1920–1984) was a writer and director, as was Marcel Moussy (1924–1995), who contributed to the scripts for *The 400 Blows* and *Shoot the Piano Player*.

38. Claude Mauriac (1914–1996), son of the novelist François Mauriac, was a French writer and journalist who wrote cinema criticism for *Le Figaro*.

39. *Rue des Prairies* (*Rue de Paris*, Denys de La Patellière 1959), for which Michel Audiard (1920–1985) wrote the script.

40. *L'Homme de Rio* (*That Man from Rio*, Philippe de Broca, 1964); *L'Immortelle* (Alain Robbe-Grillet, 1963); *Le Vieil Homme et l'enfant* (*The Two of Us*, Claude Berri, 1967); *La Musica* (Marguerite Duras, Paul Seban, 1967); *Les Coeurs verts* (Édouard Luntz, 1966); *Un homme et une femme* (*A Man and a Woman*, Claude Lelouch, 1966); *La Vie de château* (*A Matter of Resistance*, Jean-Paul Rappeneau, 1966); and *Brigitte et Brigitte* (Luc Moullet, 1966).

41. *Adieu Philippine* (Jacques Rozier, 1962); *La Cage de verre* (*The Glass Cage*, Philippe Arthuys, Jean-Lous Levi-Alvarès, 1965); *Le Signe du lion* (Éric Rohmer, 1962); *L'Enclos* (*The Enclosure*, Armand Gatti, 1961); *Le Coup de grâce* (Jean Cayrol, Claude Durand, 1965); *Le Joli Mai* (Chris Marker, 1963); *La Longue Marche* (Alexandre Astruc, 1966); *Muriel ou Le temps d'un retour* (*Muriel, or The Time of Return*, Alain Resnais, 1963); *Lola* (Jacques Demy, 1961); *Les Carabiniers* (*The Soldiers*, Jean-Luc Godard, 1963).

42. In February 1968, the French Minister of Culture, André Malraux, attempted to fire Henri Langlois, the founding director of the Cinémathèque française, provoking indignant protests in which Truffaut and other directors actively participated.

43. *Paris nous appartient* (*Paris Belongs to Us*, Jacques Rivette, 1961).

44. *Le beau Serge* (*Le Beau Serge*, Claude Chabrol, 1958).

45. *Le Testament d'Orphée* (*Testament of Orpheus*, Jean Cocteau, 1960).
46. *Le Genou de Claire* (*Claire's Knee*, 1970).
47. Jean Aurel (1925–1996) was a writer and director who collaborated with Truffaut, most notably, on the screenplays of *L'Amour en fuite* (*Love on the Run*, 1979), *La Femme d'à côté* (*The Woman Next Door*, 1981), and *Vivement dimanche!* (*Confidentially Yours*, 1983).

CHAPTER 3
THE AUTEUR THEORY

> The entire oeuvre of a filmmaker is contained in the first reel of his first film.
>
> Interview with R. M. Franchi and Lewis Marshall, New York Film Bulletin 3, no. 3, Summer 1962

Let's talk about the famous "author theory" ("la politique des auteurs"). You were the one who launched the theory during the 1950s. It has had a very big impact.

These days, I tend to repudiate the idea of an "all-encompassing author" that I propounded when I was a critic. Nevertheless, even if he does not write one line of the screenplay, it is the director who counts, it is he whom the film resembles like fingerprints; his film can mirror him for better or for worse, but it is he, and he alone, that it resembles.

However, the notion of a "complete author" has wreaked havoc during the past few years, giving rise to the fact that many people, out of pride or vanity, have aspired to work alone, whereas they really needed to have been assisted. Indeed, everyone needs to be helped, unless they are going to end up like Lisbona: "Produced, written, conceived, and made by Joseph Lisbona."[1] He might very well have added "and seen by Lisbona," given that he was almost the only person to see *Le Panier à crabes*.

It all began with your 1954 article in the Cahiers du cinéma: *"Une certaine tendance au cinéma français."*

This was not so much an article on the author theory as a very ferocious article attacking the state of French cinema at that time. Because it was very violent, they only published the first part of the piece. Among the parts that were cut were a number of insults leveled at René Clair, Clément Delannoy... I was very angry at the time, and found it difficult to attain any moderation or restraint. I was excessive. But, be that as it may, it was this article that opened the doors of other journals to me, such as *Arts*, for which I worked for three years.

Perhaps you could try to define the ideas you developed in the politique des auteurs.

At that time, there existed what we call the "French quality tradition." All the big shows and festivals would present a film that was invariably described as a product of this "tradition." These films were generally a collective effort, being made by large teams. They were often directed by filmmakers committed to the so-called "French quality tradition." Such films would employ a very famous person for the decor, a great name for the music, and each year they were hugely successful, commercially and critically—all this to the detriment of auteur films, films made by more cultivated people who preferred to work on a film that was not inspired by a famous novel, and who worked in a more personal, more individual way. During this period, there were four or five French filmmakers who were making films in a more personal manner: Jacques Tati, Robert Bresson, Max Ophüls, Jacques Becker, and Jean Renoir... and the *politique des auteurs* was a declaration of support for the kind of cinema these filmmakers were creating. Above all, however, it revolved around the idea that the man who has the ideas and the man who makes the film should be one and the same. That being said, I am also convinced that a film resembles the man who makes it even if he has not chosen the subject, has not selected the actors, has not created the mise-en-scène entirely by himself, and has left the editing to his assistants. Even this kind of film profoundly reflects—in its rhythm, its cadence, for example—the man who made it, because the overall effect of all these elements will result in idiosyncrasies that inevitably appear in the film, owing to the fact that in cinema there are basically two commands: "Action!" and "Cut!" A film is constructed out of what occurs between these two directives during a minute-and-a-half of shooting each day.

To put it another way, the director is responsible for determining how the representation is going to be staged for one and a half minutes per day, and, when I am watching a film, I like to try and guess what the filmmaker has done to fill this minute-and-a-half, and very quickly one comes to feel what has gone on. Now that I make films and the issue of a film's quality does not interest me any more, this is what I look for: to try and see if the man who made it was violent, calm, happy, or angry. I watch it scene by scene, and in this way, I try to go back to the source, to its origins in the character, the personality of the director. I can almost sense, for example, whether in this scene or that the filmmaker was happy with his actors, or was annoyed by what they were doing. I now look at films almost like one examines a temperature chart at the foot of a hospital bed.

So this is no longer a critical attitude.

Not anymore. Now I'm not concerned about that.

It's the director that you focus on.

That's right. I've just remembered one aspect of the author theory that I had forgotten, and which I would now like to bring up. The *politique des auteurs* was a critical concept, essentially polemical—meaning that, for certain critics, there are good films and bad films—and the idea I had was that there are not good or bad films, there are simply good or bad directors. It could occur that a bad director might give the impression of being a good one because he has been lucky enough to have a good screenplay, talented actors . . . nevertheless, this "good" film would not have much value in the eyes of a critic because he would see that it was merely a fluke, resulting from a convergence of circumstances. On the other hand, one could encounter a situation in which a good filmmaker makes a "bad" film, owing to the convergence of adverse circumstances, and yet this film would hold more interest for the critic than a "good" film by a bad director. Moreover, given that the notion of success or failure is not important in itself, what's interesting in the career of a good filmmaker is the way in which it reflects his own thought from the early stages of his career to its maturity. Each of his films will mark a particular stage in his thinking, and it doesn't matter whether such a film was "successful" or not. I illustrated this idea with an example for which Jean Delannoy has never forgiven me. I said that Jean Delannoy's best film would never be worth the worst film by Jean Renoir. And this is really what the *politique des auteurs* is saying.

According to what you have just said, the essential basis of the author theory is the personality of the director as it is reflected in his work.

Exactly.

You have mentioned Tati, Bresson, Max Ophüls, Becker, and Renoir...

I would like to add Cocteau to this list. You can see that I don't want to repudiate the *politique des auteurs* today, but all the same, it was a product of its time. It was a necessary intervention at the time, because of the situation that prevailed in France. I practiced it. I still believe in it today, but with regard to a much more limited range of directors. The absence of great auteurs ten years ago even led us to invent some, and I have to admit that quite a few of them were of this order. Now I would say that there are about ten directors whose work I would always go to see, whose films I watch systematically, and whom I consider fabulous. But as far as the others are concerned, to speak truthfully—unlike the critics in *Le Figaro* and the *New York Times*—I think that there are good Bergman films, good Aldrich films, and Aldrich films that are bad, sometimes very uneven, and that, when all is said and done, there are very few standout figures.

Do you think that the author theory could be a valuable critical tool for those who are working?

For critics? Yes, because when filmmakers are good filmmakers, have potential, and are capable of making progress, when you like them in the way we appreciated them at the *Cahiers du cinéma*, and you have the patience to go and rewatch their films and examine them several times in a row, you get to the point where you see their films in a more precise, more acute way, and you understand why they made such and such a film, and why this particular film marks a stage in the development of this particular man.

Can you give us an example of this idea that the personality of a man is expressed in his films? How would you apply the author theory to the works of Jean Renoir?

French critics used to routinely disparage Jean Renoir every two or three years. By that, I mean that he was an excellent filmmaker at the time, and recognized as such, but precisely because of the law determining that some films should be successful and some not, critics could not accept the idea that all of Renoir's films were praiseworthy. As a result, an almost mechanical formulation eventuated. When Renoir had had two successes, it was almost certain that his next film would be attacked. This was a critical rule of such exactitude that I called it the "law of alternation." It also applied in the other direction: after two flops, the critic, thinking it would be helpful, would describe the third as a great event, even if the film was as bad as the two preceding ones. Because of a complex critics have, they feel a need to give the impression that they are being helpful, efficacious. Renoir's career is typical in this regard, given that he always tried out everything, and because he was always out in front. In 1936 he made *Toni*, which was ten years ahead of Italian neorealism. The following year he made *La Bête humaine*, which, in contrast, was a brilliant film, finished and polished like a Hollywood product, in the best sense of the word. After having explored everything and having been the first in each domain, he made *The Rules of the Game* in 1938. Everyone gave it the thumbs-down. *The Rules of the Game* was the first psychological film in which the notion of good and bad characters had been entirely eliminated. After that, he left for America, and the French only got to see his American films at the Liberation in 1945. The refrain then changed into "Renoir, the most French of filmmakers, has been lost to Hollywood and his films are no longer worthwhile," whereas, in my view, this change of atmosphere greatly helped him to move on, to evolve. In 1942 or 1943, he made a film called *The Diary of a Chambermaid*.[2]

Yes, with Paulette Goddard.

Yes, this film represents an enormous step forward, in my opinion, even in comparison with *The Rules of the Game*, because although it reprises *The Rules of the Game*, psychology was no longer interesting him. It is the same film, but completely poetic instead of being psychological. Its characters were stylized to an extreme degree. There was one who danced in a garden and ate a rose. This effort was completely misunderstood. It's accurate to say that critics, in general, are disconcerted by any kind of new work, and most of the time, they don't know what to say. They look for arguments, evidence in the most insignificant factors. Taking a filmmaker who was an emigrant, they treated him like an immigrant: "He attempts to adapt our national author, who is so subtle, but, because of his Germanic ponderousness, it was hopeless before he even began."[3] That's what they said about Max Ophüls in France. If Renoir makes a Hollywood film in which all the action takes place in France, it is obvious that the streets are not going to be French or Parisian, and that the extras will be Hollywood extras. But critics have no idea about looking for a deeper truth. As soon as critics were informed that the film had been made in Hollywood, they simply asserted that one could not detect anything

French about this film. In the case of many films, it is very easy to foresee what the critics' reactions will be.

Do you think that the work of an auteur gets better over time, and that his most recent film is always the best? Is this consistent with the politique?

No, not exactly. It evolves. What is true is that his last film ought to be the most engrossing. For example, first films are impetuous, somewhat experimental, often containing virtuoso passages, since they involve a kind of love play with the camera . . .

In some ways, a love affair with a camera.

Exactly, and just as in a normal couple the relationship stabilizes itself, the camera becomes more restrained, and what is in front of the camera becomes more important. Generally, a young filmmaker does not achieve success very easily, given that his work invariably contains a lot of provocation. Furthermore, because the audience for films is mostly middle-aged, most filmmakers, in fact, become successful when they are thirty-five, forty years old, given that this is the time when their age corresponds with the average age of their audience, as well as their preoccupations. And then, once the filmmaker has more or less established some communication with his audience, he normally detaches himself once more. That is, he continues to move on by becoming more abstract, and from that moment he is lost, finally lost, as far as the industry is concerned. That is when, however, his films become most fascinating to study. A man like Hitchcock, who has enjoyed commercial success, and regards the need to attain it as a supplementary discipline, succeeds in remaining at the top of the box office. But other filmmakers, who are artists only, end their career completely misunderstood by the audience, and very often by critics as well, which is the case with Buñuel at the present time, Max Ophüls at the end of his life, and Chaplin.

And also Orson Welles?

Yes, Welles too.

You were saying earlier that you no longer maintain a critical perspective on cinema. What is your relationship with films these days?

I am no longer a theorist; I am interested in films with less passion, more detachment, a lot of curiosity, and also more tolerance. I can now enjoy a film if it contains ten minutes that are good, which once would have been impossible for me. I set much less store by the *politique des auteurs*, applying it less frequently. The idea that a good director can mess up a film comes much more often into my mind. But I still have a huge curiosity about cinema. From time to time when a film excites me, I become passionately enthusiastic, but I no longer want to reform French cinema, or European cinema, or world cinema. As far as what I wrote in the *Cahiers* is concerned, I think that everything I advocated and everything I hoped for has been achieved.

Notes

1. Joseph Lisbona (1932–) is a director and producer known for *Le Panier à crabes* (1960), and *La Corde au cou* (1965).
2. The IMDb lists *The Diary of a Chambermaid* as having been released in 1946 in the USA, and in 1948 in France.
3. *The Diary of a Chambermaid* was based on *Le Journal d'une femme de chambre*, a novel by Octave Mirbeau published in 1900.

CHAPTER 4
1954: *UNE VISITE;* 1957: *LES MISTONS;* 1958: *HISTOIRE D'EAU*

> When I was making *Les Mistons*, I would say: "This is the first film made by Martians." It seemed monstrous to me, and, once I knew it was projectable, I was very happy.
>
> Interview, *Télé-Ciné, no. 94, March 1961*

Let's talk about your first short film, which was called Une visite, *and which you shot in 16mm . . .*

What exposure to filmmaking had I had before that? I had seen Rivette shoot one or two films in 16mm . . . I think that was all . . . Rivette, moreover, was the director of photography for this film, which was shot in Doniol-Valcroze's apartment. I have nothing much to say about it. The idea was to make a film in 16mm that would not be at all like an avant-garde film—that is, one in which there would be no dead people, no pools of blood, no poetic effects—and which would be light gray. It was a film in black and white, but I wanted it to be light gray like Cukor's comedies. That was what most intrigued me at that time, probably because, as I've told you, I was becoming more and more interested in how screenplays were put together. I was very impressed by films like *Adam's Rib* and *It Should Happen to You*,[1] and I wanted to make a film in half-tones, not extremely funny, but slightly strange, and one that artistically resembled American films. That was absurd, since I was shooting without sound, but I proceeded as if people were talking, without asking myself what would happen. The film was thus incapable of being distributed, or even screened. But it had been made! With Jean-José Richer as an actor, François Cognani, a boy who was my assistant—has died since—and a girl who has become a continuity girl for television . . . It was not very good. I am often asked for copies—I'm very happy that none exist any longer!

Not even a single copy?

One copy had to stay around at Doniol-Valcroze's place because his daughter, who was three or four years old, had acted in it . . . I can no longer remember whether I gave him the copy, and he no longer knows where the film is. It is a film that has been lost.

You never watched it again?

Resnais wanted to see it subsequently. I told him that I couldn't show it to him—that it was merely a string of sequences joined end-to-end. He asked me whether I would like him to work on tightening it, and he made a new cut that wasn't bad. I seem to remember that I was pleasantly surprised when I watched it again . . . But I don't know any longer! Frankly, there's nothing to say about this short film. For me, my first film was *Les Mistons*! *Une visite* didn't count! What did I learn from it? To be wary of unnecessary shots, which is to say that I had never realized until then that to show someone going from a telephone booth to an apartment requires so many shots of the entry to the building, of stairs, of the guy who is knocking on a door, whom one shoots again from the other side . . . A little bit about the nature of cinema, as everyone does when he realizes that these simple actions that one has in one's head require a certain number of shots, and that you then have to try to synthesize them, and create ellipses. It's the same as with writing: someone finds himself in front of a blank page and suddenly wonders whether he is going to write in the present or past tense, in the first or the third person, using short phrases or long phrases!

Rivette was very important during your apprenticeship in cinema . . .

Because he was a terrorist! He would assert things so forcefully that there was no question of not sharing his opinion. He has changed a lot; now he is genuinely interested in everything, in all forms of cinema. Today it is difficult to get him to speak ill of a film. But at that time he practiced a terrorism that was more fanatical than that of Rohmer, who nevertheless was the "boss," if one has to speak of a leader. Rohmer exercised a great deal of authority, but he was no cinephile. Rohmer did not need to see a film twice, as he had a fantastic memory. He watched few films, only saw them once, knew them very well, and basically was not interested in any of the others. He instinctively knew what would interest him. Of all of us, Rohmer was the one who saw the smallest number of bad films during his life, simply because he didn't go to watch them! Rivette, on the other hand, saw everything, was interested in all of them; it was he who promoted a number of names to come: Nicholas Ray, Richard Brooks, Preminger . . .

Then, four years after Une visite, *you made* Les Mistons. *Four years is a long time; why this interruption in your work as a filmmaker?*

You think it was four years? *Une visite* dates from 1954 and *Les Mistons* from 1958 . . . Perhaps *Les Mistons* was in 1957 . . . I think the delay was owing to the good time I was having in *Arts, spectacles*, which happened after 1954.[2] I was working for the magazine *Arts*, but the articles were not signed; it was the style of the magazine at that time. There were four or five of us writing: Paul Guimard, Antoine Blondin . . . I even think Boris Vian may have been writing anonymous articles . . . There was a strange practice there, which was to give a report on all films. If twelve films came out in a given week, there were twelve unsigned reviews, all of which expressed a personal opinion, often an impertinent one. And then there was a change of direction at *Arts*: Jacques Laurent arrived with his friend Jean Aurel. And I, without knowing why—it's an attitude I find myself often adopting—said to myself, "There's no longer anything for me to do in this magazine!" And I didn't so much as set a foot back in there, thinking that they were going to fire me . . . because there was no reason to keep me! Aurel had to call me very solicitously while I was shooting my short film, to tell me that it would need both of us to deal with all the reviews. From then on, the articles were signed, and the cinema page of the magazine started to attract attention. It was an arrangement that worked well, and so we began to talk. The result was that Aurel and I were crushed under the weight of work: we would make a selection, we invented a system of little stars, a selection of films with slogans . . . Many things that took off from this time! The thought of making films was rather pushed to one side. But then it came back after Rivette had made *Le Coup du berger*! Let's put it this way: we were uncertain. The one who was most sure that he wanted to make films was

Rivette. Also Resnais, who was making short films, and Astruc, obviously . . . but, in our group, we were not at all sure that we would become filmmakers, at least not in my case. From time to time Rivette would draw us together and say, "Come on, it's all about making films! Let's write some screenplays!"

After that, Les Mistons *was your first idea?*

My first thought was to make five stories about children. Because I had a good memory of working with Doniol-Valcroze's daughter in my little film in 16mm—I enjoyed doing that greatly. I even had a feeling I was getting more out of children than from people my own age, or older. Apart from *Les Mistons*—which was based on a novella by Maurice Pons—I had other scripts, original stories. The fact I started with *Les Mistons* was simply because it was very economical to do: it didn't require much money, it didn't entail interior scenes . . . all I needed was a small stock of film. Especially as I had been put in contact with an operator in Montpellier who had all the material . . . Let's say that I had no financial problems! On top of that, I had met Gérard Blain who was very keen to work, and Bernadette Lafont, his wife, who were living near Nîmes . . .

One usually thinks of Les Mistons *as a film that is very close to you . . .*

It is fairly close to the novella by Maurice Pons, but I never thought of it as being close to me. What drew me to it? Probably the fact that in *Arts* there had been an item on a collection that was called *Virginales*[3] . . . I had read all of the stories—around fifteen, as I recall—and I liked this particular one a lot because I could visualize it well. I think it may even have been the phrase about "Bernadette playing tennis" that sparked it off . . . And then there was the cinematic potential inherent in the situation: five children spying on a young couple . . . That said, I didn't feel very comfortable as I was working on it, I was full of doubts: I wasn't happy with the vignette. I was happy enough when I was shooting inessential scenes, but when I had to deal with the story itself, it slid through my fingers. I thought it was weak. That the children should persecute the pair of lovers was fair enough, but that the young man should then go off on a mountain climbing course because of that (or maybe not because of that) and end up being killed . . . In the end, I didn't think that worked—I was not happy with it. As a result, the narrative side of the film is very uneven. The film is merely a collection of minor incidental events. Also, during that period—it's no longer true of what he writes now—Maurice Pons was in a precious phase, as a result of the influence of Radiguet and Cocteau. This was a kind of verbal music with which I was familiar, and which I liked; inevitably, I must have liked his phrasing, cast in the form of commentary. I was bound to want to attempt writing dialogue, at the same time as I was fearful of doing so. I wrote some lines for the lovers that I have since discarded. In the version you see now, there are no love scenes—an omission I find awful. I asked myself, "Am I capable of writing dialogue for films?" It was something that tormented me. I don't know whether or not I had already seen *Sommarlek*,[4] but Bergman's film was an important event for me. It was the film that made me think that everyone could write dialogue for films, at least that I, at any rate, could write it. The idea, I thought, was to be natural: to write down what one says, and what one hears in real life. What I find curious is the fact that a Swedish film subtitled in French should have put this in my mind; I could just as readily have derived it from the films of Renoir, given that I knew the musical cadences of their dialogue by heart. But in the end it was *Sommarlek* that triggered this desire in me. I thought, "When it comes down to it, I can write the love scenes!" Similarly, *Monika*[5] would turn out to be important for *The 400 Blows*, of which it was, to some extent, a feminine version. It encouraged me, giving me some ideas. I am not one of those people who invents everything, who starts from scratch; if someone shows me a contraption, I ask how it works! I am not much of an experimenter, I have a need to rely on what already exists, and, from that point on, to do with it whatever I like.

Was it to undertake Les Mistons *that you established your production company,* Les Films du Carrosse?

Yes.

Out of a desire to enjoy greater freedom, or because the very structure of French cinema necessitated it?

I no longer remember. I think the idea was to enjoy freedom, exactly the same idea as today. Also, at that time, short films received a quality bonus based on the completed film, and this bonus went to the producer ... Given that there were two or three of us associated with this film, it made sense to proceed in that way!

After Rivette, Godard and Une histoire d'eau[6] ...

People often want to know how that came about. In reality, it was very simple. I had a very strong liking for floods—as for fire—because each year in the news, at the same point in the year, they would show people in a rowboat abandoning their house . . . I like this image a lot. And one day, I saw floods in the region of Montereau, where I had been staying in a summer camp, just when the Germans were leaving and the Americans were arriving. And I said to Braunberger, the producer who most strongly believed in me, and was always suggesting things to me, "If you give me some film, I will go with Jean-Claude Brialy and a girl, and we will try and improvise something about floods!" He gave me the film. And with Michel Latouche, a cinematographer who had also shot with Godard, we worked for two days. But, in truth, we lacked a structure for the film. There was too much improvisation in it; we really needed to devise a small story. Given that I was simply filming shots, I was not very happy about my work—especially as I was reluctant to annoy people who had actually been flooded, by taking a boat for the purpose of shooting the film! There were all kinds of things that made me sorry to be there, causing me to feel unhappy about this venture. So I apologized to Brialy and said to Baunberger, "I'm abandoning this material—I will reimburse you for it," and I know not what! And then Godard asked to see the rushes. At the time he was very interested in editing; he even did some editing on films about exploration for Connaissance du Monde . . .[7] Just like Resnais had done three years earlier, he said to me, "I am interested in editing and finishing it!" He did the editing and the commentary, and showed it to me; he may have changed a thing or two—I'm not even sure about that. And considering that it was a film by both of us, we cosigned it. It was released with *Lola*, and that was loudly booed![8]

Notes

1. *Adam's Rib* (*Madame porte la culotte*, George Cukor, 1949); *It Should Happen to You* (*Une femme qui s'affiche*, George Cukor, 1954).

2. *Arts, spectacles* was a French periodical that appeared from 1953 to 1959.

3. *Virginales* is a collection of stories written by Maurice Pons dealing with the awakening of the senses in adolescents as they are in the process of turning into adults. It was published in 1955 by Julliard.

4. *Sommarlek* (*Summer Interlude*, Ingmar Bergman, 1951).

5. *Sommaren med Monika* (*Summer with Monika*, Ingmar Bergman, 1953).

6. *Une histoire d'eau* (*A Story of Water*, Jean-Luc Godard and François Truffaut, 1961).

7. Connaissance du Monde is a French organization founded in 1945 dedicated to presenting "filmed lectures" about discoveries and adventures in different parts of the world.

8. *Lola* (Jacques Demy, 1961).

CHAPTER 5

1959: *THE 400 BLOWS*

> Cocteau intimates the frightening gap between the world of adolescents and that of adults in this passage from *The Holy Terrors*: "In the absence of the death penalty in schools, Dargelos was expelled."[1]
>
> Interview, Arts, June 3, 1959

What gave you the idea for The 400 Blows?

At first, it involved a project for a short twenty-minute film called *La Fugue d'Antoine*. As I said, my intention was to make a series of sketches focusing on childhood. When *Les Mistons* was finished, at first I couldn't raise enough money to shoot my other short films, and on top of that I realized that they were going to be too different from my other projects, all of which were more or less autobiographical, or else drawn from news reports—I didn't want to get them mixed up with *Les Mistons*. Originally, *La Fugue d'Antoine* was to be a story about a boy who, having lied at school to explain his absence one day, after he had played hooky, didn't dare go home, and so spent a night in Paris outdoors. This idea gradually became transformed into a kind of chronicle about the experience of the boy during the year when he was thirteen (which was the most interesting time, for me). It entirely left out, however, an aspect that had been very important to me: how it was in Paris during the Occupation, black market ploys, et cetera. I didn't feel I could undertake a cinematic recreation of this period—not only because of financial reasons, but also for artistic ones, given that it is easy to descend into the ridiculous when evoking the style of this period.

Why did you choose an adolescent adventure as the first subject for a film?

The subject had been on my mind for a long time. Adolescence is a state recognized by educators and sociologists, but denied by the family, the parents. To speak in the language used by specialists, I would say that emotional withdrawal, the awakening of puberty, a desire for independence, and a feeling of inferiority are characteristic signs of this stage in one's development. A single upset can trigger a rebellion, and this crisis is accurately described as "juvenile originality." The world is unjust, therefore one needs to fend for oneself, and one starts to act out: "one becomes a bit wild."[2]

Just now, you were talking about autobiography.

I also had an eventful schooling; but not everything in The 400 Blows is autobiographical. On the other hand, everything is true: whether these adventures were experienced personally by me, or by others, the important thing is that they were actually experienced.

The idea for this film came to me owing to a television broadcast—*Si c'était vous*—in which the filmmakers, Bluwal and Marcel Moussy, aimed to interest the spectator in conflicts between parents and children.[3] Naturally, I recruited Moussy as my dialogue writer.

Had I been left to my own devices, I would have been tempted to stereotype the parents as caricatures in order to create a vicious satire—but this would have lacked objectivity. Moussy helped me to make these people more human, more normal. He had never worked for cinema, and was quite tempted to do so; we understood each other very well. I saw at once that it was impossible to write dialogue for children. We decided we would describe the situation to them, and then leave it to them to come up with the words. On the other hand, all the dialogues for the parents, the teacher, et cetera, were written out by Moussy, and have been kept just as they were—I think their speeches are very good. Formerly, Moussy had been a schoolteacher himself, and he was clearly drawing on that experience when writing the school scenes. In addition, Moussy greatly helped to give the screenplay a structure. I had pages and pages of notes, but all of that was so close to me that I couldn't manage to give it any structure. Moussy is amazing in that respect. There is no one who can equal his ability to grab hold of a small part of the screenplay, enhance it, and make it bounce. He succeeded in giving the film a dramatic framework without in any way modeling it on a theatrical play.

How did you direct your actors?

To shoot a film with children is very enticing beforehand, entails a lot of panic while it is happening (because it is a fearsomely challenging business that is always slipping through one's fingers), and is immensely satisfying afterwards. Even when I have a feeling that everything is going adrift, there is always something that is salvageable, and no matter what happens, it is always the child who comes across best on the screen.

I also think that I get more pleasure from directing a child than an adult because I am just starting out as a director, whereas adults have already had experience at acting. I tend to be intimidated by their "seniority," and when they don't want to do what I tell them, I sometimes give up the struggle, or else allow myself to be pulled along when they do their thing, and I am never sure I'm right. A child's sincerity is something I think I can feel absolutely. For example, through the whole length of the film, I had to wrestle with Jean-Pierre Léaud. He was terrific, but he was scared that he was going to come across as unlikeable, which meant that he continually wanted to smile. For three whole months I prevented him from smiling . . . and I'm sure I was right.

That said, I was amazingly lucky to come across that kid. He *was* the character. Better still, he improved the film. I had been seeing Antoine as more fragile, more timid, less aggressive, whereas Jean-Pierre gave him his robustness, his truculence, his courage. He was an invaluable collaborator. He was able to find the right gestures spontaneously, he adjusted the script, always for the better, and he used the words that he wanted to use.

How did you recruit your young actors?

I was able to find all these children thanks to France Roche who put an advertisement in *France-Soir*, with results that exceeded our expectations, given that we received more than two hundred letters. I systematically ruled out all those who came from the countryside, because I didn't want to make any kid have to relocate specially to Paris, and we summoned the hundred who remained for screen tests in 16mm. Straight away, Jean-Pierre grabbed one's attention and stood out from the rest. Furthermore, he had already acted a small role in *King on Horseback*,[4] two years earlier, and had done a bit of dubbing.

The scene in which Jean-Pierre Léaud is questioned by the psychologist is rightly celebrated. How did you make it?

Originally, this scene was conceived in a classical manner with the standardized tests, ink spots, et cetera, that one uses in such situations. Only we had been very careful not to make use of the tests used in *The Little Rebels*.[5] I felt that it needed to be done differently, but I didn't know how. On top of this, it was impossible to find the right actress to play the role of the psychologist. I wanted an unknown face, and I had precise ideas about this character. In describing the woman I was looking for to others—someone who was both carnal and intellectual—I realized that I had unconsciously drawn a portrait of Annette Wademant.[6] Unfortunately, she was not in Paris, and so we decided to film the shots with the boy, leaving the reverse-shots to be filmed later. We had no written script, nothing that had been rehearsed before the shooting. I had only had a brief discussion with Jean-Pierre, and had vaguely indicated to him what the general direction of my questions would be. I left him completely free to reply to them in his own way, because I wanted his vocabulary, his hesitations, for him to be completely spontaneous. There was, of course, a certain parallel between what I knew were the problems he was going through in real life and my questions. All I did was to ask him to think about the screenplay and never say anything that contradicted the story in the film (at one point, however, he introduced into his responses a grandmother who had never been part of the scenario until that moment). For the shoot itself, I made absolutely everyone leave, so that only Jean-Pierre, Decaë the cameraman, and I were left on the set. When we had seen the rushes, it was Decaë himself who said to me, "It would be madness to shoot reverse shots. We have to leave it like that." That's what we did, except that whereas we filmed for twenty minutes, we only kept three minutes of the footage in the film.

By the time you undertook your film, you had a remarkable background in cinema culture. It was thus inevitable that influences would creep in when you were filming The 400 Blows. *Which ones?*

There are two films dealing with childhood that I greatly like, and I recognize their influence on my own: *Zero for Conduct*, by Jean Vigo, and *Germany Year Zero*, by Rossellini.[7] I think that films about childhood are often unsuccessful for either of two reasons. First, more often than not, it is not really the child who is at the center of the film. He is pushed aside in order to highlight a character whose role is being acted by an adult star. For example, the presence of Gabin in *The Little Rebels* turns it into a film that is more about the judges who deal with children's cases than about juvenile delinquency itself. From this point of view, one might very well say that there are no genuine films about childhood due to the absence of child stars.

As far as child actors are concerned, I think that one should absolutely avoid young girls between five and twelve years old. At that age girls turn on their charm, seeking to flirt, don't utter a sincere sentence, intentionally tell lies, and act like a present-day Manon.[8] Furthermore, I was struck to see how Brigitte Fossey made one think of Cécile Aubry at a certain point in *Forbidden Games*.[9] People say that Clément achieved amazing results with his young actors, but I think this is overrated, owing to the fact that he forced children of seven or eight years old to act as if they were adults—certainly a very difficult thing to do, but doesn't equate with a triumph.

Then, it can happen that a child is let down by some weakness in the screenplay. Frequently, the child gets whisked away so as to foreground some object or an animal. Such films simply set out in pursuit of a dramatic or artistic idea without trying to enter into the world of childhood, or to capture the reality of it. The biggest mistake is to want to be poetic from the outset. A film is poetic after it has been finished, not before. You may be able to make "poetic" films about red balloons, white horses, and kites, but not about children.

One must always remember that when a child is used as a subject, he or she has an innate power to move the spectator simply by virtue of being a child, and that the audience is very sensitive and susceptible to this. Also, one must be careful never to be cutesy or indulgent . . . A close-up shot of a child smiling on the screen, and the field is won. But, what is striking, when one knows them, is the seriousness of children compared with the frivolity of adults.

Rossellini demonstrated this magnificently in *Paisan*, in which it is the child who behaves like an adult, and the black soldier like a child. He showed it again in *Europe '51*, in which a child commits suicide while the parents are playing with an electric train, and in *Germany Year Zero*, in which all the characters are unstable in comparison with the child who, in the end, is going to pay the price for their failings.[10]

There were certain indulgences in my film that I took out. For example, when we saw the rushes for the scene with the children at the Guignol,[11] it was truly magnificent, and we were absolutely bowled over. There was a half hour of it, but despite the temptation, I only left in the strict minimum. Even so, I think there is still a moment of indulgence in the film: it's the shot in which the children have just stolen the typewriter and are moving along the street behind pigeons that are flying away. It is very pretty, but somewhat gratuitous. The justification for this shot is, first, that I am aware it is an indulgence... second, that it is very brief, and, finally, that it represents a pretty impressive feat of shooting as far as Decaë was concerned, given that it was filmed in the middle of the Champs-Élysées, without anyone seeing us—that is a real achievement.

The moment when they arrive at the house of René's parents makes one think of Cocteau. Was this intentional?

Yes, we knew when we were shooting in that apartment that it was "à la Cocteau." We were highly aware of it, and there were actually some passages reflecting Jean Cocteau's type of atmosphere even more strongly that I cut from the film because they were not very good. One example: the children smoking the cigar, who then try to disperse the smoke by using the blankets. We brought in this horse and thus created a Cocteau-like atmosphere, without especially wanting to do so. I suspect, moreover, that it was from that moment that Jean Cocteau really loved the film, because it was close to him on account of the strangeness of the decor and, to some degree, the situation as well.

How long did it take you to make The 400 Blows, *and in what way did you shoot it?*

It was made in eight weeks. I shot a lot of it on location, in real apartments that we had rented, diverging a bit from the usual way of doing things, because there were fewer of us than is the case with a normal film. It cost a lot less money because we were not in a studio. We didn't shoot in a studio at all. We economized in areas that usually cost the most, for obvious reasons: stars and studios.

The film was shot without any mishaps?

One very sad thing happened: André Bazin died on the evening of the first day of shooting. I was shattered by this, having been so proud of making a big film at last, especially with regard to him, to whom I owed so much... Several days earlier, he had read the screenplay and loved it. I dedicated the film to him.

How did you approach the problems involved in directing it?

You might imagine that people associated with the *Cahiers du cinéma* would make very intellectual films, deliberately contriving clever framings and camera movements. However, as far as I am concerned, I am not at all an intellectual, and my first film, *Les Mistons*, was not "intellectual." No one should suppose that *The 400 Blows* is "classically" written. For the most part, it is very clumsy. I didn't pass through a film school. I have never been an assistant. That was a handicap, but also an advantage: I had to invent a way of doing things.

If I had been an expert, in the final sequence in which my young hero is running toward the sea, filmed in a long tracking shot, I would have inserted some preliminary shots of running feet, sweating faces. I had thought of having this editing effect at the Festival because I had been told about it. What interested me in this long shot was the way the landscape changed behind the boy as he was running through the Normandy countryside toward the mouth of the Seine, the sea.

One struggles with technique, and even if your intentions are clear, the results are often blurred, and variable. Fortunately for *Les Mistons* and *The 400 Blows* I had the help of a friend, Philippe de Broca, a professional assistant.[12] Eventually he would go on to direct his own films. He warned me, often with his silent presence, against committing serious mistakes that would have caused problems at the editing stage.

As far as *The 400 Blows* was concerned, without my cameraman, I would have struggled to make my film in a very small apartment. Decaë is an adventurous type. He succeeded in resolving the impossible, in a very constrained space. In a studio, to shoot in a narrow kitchen, all he would need to do would be to remove a wall. In a real setting, he had to perch outside a window, suspended in the air, with his camera in his hand . . . Similarly, we took shots of the Place Clichy and in the Franklin-Roosevelt metro with the camera hidden under a paper that we raised at the last moment, without the passers-by having time to realize that we were making a film . . .

I would not be capable of preparing a film with a very detailed storyboard, worked out in advance, shot by shot, as very accomplished people are able to do. I am neither a visual artist nor a mathematician, and one has to work with what one is endowed, otherwise one makes a mess of things. My imagination works spontaneously in response to reality, not abstract preplanning. I believe in improvisation.

> *You talk of a lack of financial means, but in spite of that you shot* The 400 Blows *in CinemaScope.*

But CinemaScope is not a luxury. It only requires the renting of a special lens, that is, around a million francs per film. On the other hand, it allows one to achieve important economies by filming fewer shots that are longer.

Moreover, thanks to it, I was able to achieve an effect that I thought was essential. The decor in my film is grim and shabby, and so I was worried about creating a disagreeable feeling. Thanks to CinemaScope, I attained a stylized effect, by showing real life in a broader perspective. Thus, at one particular moment, my character goes to empty a bucket of rubbish; owing to CinemaScope, the scene appears less grimy than it would have appeared in a normal framing. Nevertheless, it remains just as realistic. Similarly, it allowed my film to end neither on an optimistic nor a pessimistic note. I avoided the need to present a definitive solution by dramatizing the situation through the use of a wide screen, and by freezing the image of my hero, whose face remains motionless against a backdrop provided by the sea.

One detail: why do you have shots filmed around the Eiffel Tower in the credit sequence?

Basically, it constitutes a scene of relaxation in the film: the two truants decide to visit the Eiffel Tower; they go there in a taxi, but the chauffeur, a novice Algerian, drives around the tower without ever being able to find it. I had been aiming to generate some comic effects from the way the size of the tower varied depending on the place from which it was viewed—in accordance with the lenses I had when filming it . . . But, the film was already too long, eight weeks had elapsed, the general tone had become sadder, the reverse shots of the boys in the taxi had not been filmed, I gave up on this scene and the shots that had already been filmed were used as the credit sequence.

And color?

I would have loved to make the film in color, but color virtually precludes cinematic experimentation, whereas I believe that one can make films that are fairly risky, fairly courageous, and fairly pure for less than fifty million francs. With estimates of more than fifty million, one has to weigh up everything; and with color, all estimates are over fifty million. No matter how much one may calculate and ponder, one is obliged to make concessions, and to take fewer risks. As for my film, even though it may end up bringing in five or six times what it cost, there were, nevertheless, considerable risks at the beginning. It was risky to make a film without a known actor. My film cost thirty-seven million.

Do you feel that you personally achieved the goal you had set for yourself?

When I had finished the film, I was quite depressed as far as my sense of its quality was concerned, and so the first screenings were a big surprise for me, given that people were very enthusiastic, much more so than they are now. Today, the film has a good reputation, but initially, the only reputation it had was the one I fostered, and I gave it a bad reputation, given that I am always very depressed between the last turn of the crank and the sound mixing. Accordingly, I was spreading the word that it was a catastrophe.

Consequently, people were very surprised when they saw the film for the first time, and I was surprised by their surprise. That being said, I believe that the concerns one has during the making of a film and subsequently relate only to the details, and that the essential things come through unscathed. In the making of a film, unless one has been subjected to a lot of bullying, so long as the film is fairly close to what one wanted, without any constraints—that is, if no one made you change the dialogue, the screenplay, or imposed certain actors on you—the result will be fairly close to the original intentions, even if the difference appears rather large to the person who made the film. I note that people are now talking about the film to me in terms of the thoughts I myself had before making it. I am very surprised when they say to me that it is about a child's loneliness. That's exactly what I wanted to depict in the film. I say to myself, "So, that's come through!" Nevertheless, I still feel as if I failed with a certain number of things—for example, the night spent in Paris: that's a failure, in my opinion. Or else one of the ideas I entertained before the screenplay was finished: I was thinking that the film would be a kind of documentary on truancy. That aspect of it also failed, and in the end it disappeared from the film. Apart from that, I think that the main things I wanted to get across have indeed come across. The general idea that childhood is a difficult time to pass through is not something for which people have much empathy. I can see that as a result of the discussions I have already had with those around me. People don't know whether the film is pessimistic or optimistic. We don't all deal with troublesome issues in the same way, but I wanted to show in some detail parents confronting problems involving education, the relationships between parents and children, and the relations between generations. At this level, the film attained its goal.

> *What experience have you gained from this first film, and have you modified any of your critical opinions?*

I have become more tolerant, meaning that I have given up any ambition to reform cinema. Bad films don't annoy me like they used to. All I want to do is make good films. I have lost a bit of my purism as a cinephile. I have become selfish, like all directors. I am trying to fight against this tendency, and I am slightly scared about the future.

1962

After the Cannes Festival, this film took on a life of its own because of its unanticipated success, and I didn't like it all anymore. However, I saw it again in Nice recently, and it rekindled my interest. I was very moved by its purity. If I were to make it again now (you know, by the way, that I would love to redo the editing), I would make it more objective. The boys would appear more devious and sneaky. The parents would be less blameworthy. I would show the teacher overloaded with work, trying to cope with a class that was too big, with rows of benches alongside his lectern . . .

You should understand that it's really a film that was made during a particular time in my life. Had I made it three years earlier, it would have been more "rebellious." Now, to the contrary, I find that it seems too much like a relentless "cycle of abuse." When I was shooting it, I allowed myself to be unduly influenced; I was scared that the boy was too unpleasant, and I gave up the idea of shooting scenes that showed him stealing things from display windows, and his insolence. These days, it's the opposite: I would try to find scenes like that to give the film a fairer balance between the responsibilities of adults and those of adolescents.

Nevertheless, when all is said and done, I like *The 400 Blows* immensely, because I know that I would never be able to remake a film that was so effective. Everything in it was stripped down, every gesture was the only one possible: Antoine sets the table, fills the stove, empties the rubbish—each detail corresponds exactly to reality, and that is what I was trying to achieve. I see it as being like a documentary record, and it is presented in that spirit.

1962

I have realized, four years later, that the film is Hitchcockian. Why? Because from the very first image, we identify with the boy, and continue to do so right to the end. At the time, people heaped a lot of praise on a stupid film by Robert Montgomery, *Lady in the Lake*.[13] However, a subjective camera is the opposite of subjective cinema. When it occupies the place of the character, it is impossible to identify with him. We get subjective cinema when the gaze of the actor intersects with that of the spectator. Then, if the members of the audience feel a need to identify with it (even if this happens with a film that is shot without any specific approach on the part of the director), they will automatically identify with the face that has most frequently intersected the gaze of the film, with the actor who has most often been shot in close-up, and from the front. That's what happened with Jean-Pierre Léaud. In making a documentary about him, I thought I was being objective, but the more

I filmed him from the front, the more I emphasized his presence, the more people became him.

It was, then, a film that was completely naïve, made in complete ignorance about certain laws of cinematic practice. At the same time, it was unwittingly crafty, more so than with anything I've made since.

1962

I would never have been able to bring off *The 400 Blows* had I not been thinking of Hitchcock during the scene in which the mother comes to find her son during class. It was very difficult to do, because, at first, I didn't know how I ought to depict the mother, the glass window, the principal, the teacher, or the boy. It was by thinking about it, and by analyzing the scene, that I found the solution. The whole sequence of shots is composed of glances. There is the teacher who notices something behind the glazed door, then a new shot of the teacher going to meet the principal. At this moment there is a mid-shot of Jean-Pierre, who is a bit worried because he thinks that they are talking about him. Then there is a silent exchange between the principal and the teacher; a close-up shot of Jean-Pierre and his friends who are beginning to suspect something's up when they see him grow pale. Then a shot in which the framing doesn't do the work, but instead is very Hitchcockian in its conception—the principal summons the boy with his finger. It's presented in a very sinister way, closely observed by the boy who points his finger to his chest—"Who, me?"—and, finally, we see the mother arrive behind the window, throwing a distracted glance toward the classroom. This is where we can see Hitchcock's talent: the ability to judge the moment at which we no longer need to be realistic. Logically, a mother who has just arrived at a classroom doesn't know where to locate her son, and therefore her gaze should roam around the class. But if her gaze seems hesitant, then it is not effective, and it's because of this that I made her look straight at the boy, as if she knew where he was seated in the class. In this way, her gaze is chilling, because it looks at us, it looks at the camera. I have often checked how effective this scene is in cinemas, and I have heard people cry out. This is the only scene that I felt should be made in this way. If it has succeeded, I owe my thanks to Hitchcock, whose cutting I imitated. That doesn't mean to say that one should imitate this all the time. And so the preceding scene in which the child says that his mother "is dead" is very personal. I had a deep sense of how it should be acted, and I was confident that I would not screw it up. The boy's friend had said to him, "Since you don't have an excuse, you have to invent something catastrophic." That is all that the boy knows when he arrives. One might think that he had prepared his lie, and that it was always in the cards that he would be found out—that's the idea behind the scene. Then the teacher said to him, "Show me your letter of excuse." The boy replies, "I don't have anything." The teacher then becomes very angry: "You don't have anything . . . you're not going to get away with that!" and the boy then utters his tremendous lie, as if he couldn't bring himself to say it. "It's my mother, sir, my mother . . . ," and then—this is what provokes the lie—the teacher has to be completely odious: "Your mother, your mother, all right then, what's up with your mother?" And it's because he provokes him that the boy has the courage to reply, "She is dead," while looking him straight in the eye. In the course of my three films, I don't think that I have directed anyone with as much precision as I did Jean-Pierre in this scene, owing to the fact that I knew exactly what I wanted. I even told him to think, "That's going to annoy you, eh!" when he was saying it, and to keep it in his head. It often helps an actor if one tells him what to think immediately before or after his utterance. The lie that he tells is so monstrous that the only way to tell it is for it to have been forced by events. After the episode with his mother behind the window and the slap his father gives him in the face, we see that the boy again decides not to go home. At that moment there is some rather problematic dialogue, because it is a bit unrealistic with respect to the language children use—but it shouldn't make people laugh. It's the moment when the boy says, "After that slap, I don't want to go home; I'm going to disappear; I'm going to live my own life." This is a somewhat excessive reaction. We have to think of the mentality of a child in order to understand something like that, because, for a child, everything is out of proportion. It's difficult to act; if it is overacted, it becomes ridiculous. I came away from it thinking of Renoir, because it is a problem pertaining to the acting, and not to cinematic technique.

I thought of the scene in *La Bête Humaine*[14] in which, early in the morning, Gabin, after having killed Simone Simon, goes to work and stands next to the locomotive. Then he says to Carette in complete despair, and with an extraordinary simplicity, "Oh well! That's it, I won't see her again. I've killed her, you know . . . I will have to keep on working . . ." What's marvelous here, is the fact he has said so simply something that is so far beyond anything that's ordinary. At this point in my film, I made Jean-Pierre act like Gabin to help him find his expression.

These influences are invisible, subterranean; they are the things that really influence one's work. But no one would think of *La Bête Humaine* when watching this scene from *The 400 Blows*.

1967

I myself didn't have a very good idea of where the film was going. I was recreating experiences. They asked me if I was trying to make a social critique. In spite of anything I intended, the film took on a general relevance. When Jean Renoir saw it, he was going back to America, he said, "Basically, it's a portrait of France at this point," whereas I had never had any such thought. For me, it was a very particular case, but because of staying close to things, the atmosphere of the Place Clichy, Gaumont-Palace, it's when things take on a special ambiance that is very particular, that they become somewhat general. Now I would be inclined to say, "There's a French family, and I know some people will think it is very exaggerated, but, in the end, a great number of families in France are like that." The scene I like the best is the scene where they are coming back from the Gaumont-Palace, because it is normal: suddenly, they are getting along with the boy. I love this scene, because it shows the audience that if they thought they were dealing up to that point with unusual people, that's only an impression, and that these are people who are, basically, very normal.

The mother is a little bit . . . she's played by an actress who I asked to do something very different from what she was used to, and the result was not perfect. Later I found an actress who I thought would have been ideal for this role—but it was already too late—and I gave her the role of Jean Desailly's wife in *The Soft Skin* (Nelly Benedetti). She would not have given such a forced impression in everything, and it would have suited her perfectly.

1974

Why do they shut up the three young girls in the reform center?

In fact, it is not very well explained. They are not shut up. When the boys go out, the young girls are "lined up." They are "lined up" rather than imprisoned. Obviously, they are not delinquents. These images have always provoked uneasiness. In principle, everything is clear in the film, with the exception of two or three details like that one: they are the guard's daughters.

At a professional level, is it easy or difficult to get children to act?

Children are fantastic! They have an extraordinary sense of reality. But if you ask them to do mundane things, then they get bored, and they do it badly. You really have to work in collaboration with children. You have to change the pace. When someone is not used to something, he is surprised. It is another way of working.

Are you under the impression that you have avoided introducing melodramatic elements?

Oh! Because I am sentimental, I love stories that involve feelings. Many people are scared of melodrama. Not me. I am not scared of the scene with the judge in which she [i.e., Antoine's mother] explains that he is not her husband's son. To the contrary, I really like to have a melodramatic foundation in my films.

There was a time when it was fashionable to say that Dickens was ridiculous. I have always loved Dickens. I have fairly specific tastes in which snobbery has no part.

I have some rather stubborn traits that mean I do what I want. If Chaplin had not been so successful in *The Kid*,[15] I would have really liked to tell the story of a child that someone found in a rubbish tin. I would not be afraid to be anti-sentimental. The subject matter is sentimental, but the treatment is a bit dry, by choice, like a documentary. One has to proceed with a degree of distance. Antoine does not move us greatly, except when he is in the police station. Our sympathy comes from what has always been the empathic feeling for a child. I have spent a long time coming to that understanding. We might wish it for Antoine when he is shoveling coal and drying his hands on the curtain. I get the impression that some notion of innocence is involved in all that.

Do you remember your first meeting with Jean-Pierre Léaud?

Before that, I had received mug shots in which he had very long, blond hair. I remember writing down on a piece of paper: "interesting, but the face is too feminine." And then, when he turned up, his hair was almost shaved off, and he was the opposite: all of a sudden, he seemed too rough to me. But right from the very first screen tests, as soon as he spoke in front of the camera, he was the most interesting one of all. He gave an impression of great intensity, of nervousness; he pretended to be a very relaxed type, but he wasn't at all. There was some kind of violence about him, and a great desire to win the role, compared with the other children, for whom it was their mothers who wanted it, or who were coming out of curiosity. A number of elimination rounds were involved, because I would have the children come back each Thursday; on the second Thursday, he stood out, and it was obvious that it would be him. But there were some mismatches between him and the screenplay: his was a more aggressive, less submissive character. Mine was rather humble, and pulled his punches. His was more arrogant, even insolent! I saw, then, that the character was shifting slightly, but he gave it such life that I liked and accepted what he was doing. With this idea that I had perhaps picked up from Renoir's films, that the actor is more important than the character.

What influence has Rossellini had on your work?

He was very anti-Hollywood, very anti-American, and *The 400 Blows* probably wouldn't have been made without him. He favored an almost documentary-type approach to things, a very realistic approach... The fact that, after all the time I spent being detached from French cinema, I ended up making a film as French as *The 400 Blows*, was probably because Rossellini's influence was the strongest of all. That is what gave me the urge to make a film in which, in the end, very little happens. There are very few events in *The 400 Blows*! Apart from the theft of the typewriter and the sequence in which Doinel says that his mother is dead when actually she isn't... The rest consists of scenes that are bordering on documentary... I often say, and sometimes this is misunderstood, that I have a hatred of documentary; when I say that, what I mean is that it was fiction that led me to cinema, and I feel no inclination to change my view in that regard. When I made *The Wild Child*, it was also with a loathing for documentary! And yet, the temptation is sometimes to make films with the fewest possible plot developments, but absorbing films nevertheless. And on such occasions, the fiction resides not in the invention of extravagant scenes but in the way things are laid out, in the presentation of the story as a narrative, a tale, and not simply as a neutral account of something. So, this dislike of documentary that guided me at the time, and still does today, nevertheless meant that I wanted to make a film that resembles a documentary without actually being one. During the shooting, what happened was that the team had a feeling that I was not being very kind to the character of Antoine Doinel, and that I was making him do many disagreeable things. That was the reaction of Jacqueline Decaë, in particular, who was the continuity girl for the film. She would say, "The only thing that makes me uncomfortable is that the boy is going to come across as unbearable!" Claire Maurier, who played the part of the mother, and who was frustrated because I would not allow her to call Antoine by his first name, had the same impression. In the film she says "the kid," never "Antoine!" There were some things that I was very stubborn about, which made everyone anxious. Once the film had been finished, the big surprise, obviously, was the immense surge of fondness that it aroused for Jean-Pierre Léaud. It was seen as an issue of Doinel against his parents! This showed me that it is impossible to compare things that cannot be compared! One cannot compare the behavior of a child to that of adults, because the idea of innocence is inseparably linked to the idea of childhood, whether one wants it or not. This is true even in a book like Sartre's *The Words*,[16] in which he attempts to dissect in minute detail, without any compassion and without any kindness, the child that he had once been. In spite of everything, we side with him against the family, against his Uncle Schweitzer! I think this is inevitable.

Following on from that, how do you gauge the scenes in a story so as to achieve the desired effect on a spectator?

That's a question that greatly preoccupied me, given that in my attacks on French cinema, against the whole system of Aurenche and Bost, I wanted—and still do!—to fight against discrimination on the screen. In other words, I have always detested the kind of servility that consists of making stars glamorous and the secondary roles ridiculous, even if people tell me that such a practice goes back to Molière! It's something I have always been very concerned about. Even a contemporary film like *Family Life* shocks me.[17] Notwithstanding the fact that it is presented in a much more refined way, we are still shown a character who we are made to think is completely right and a family circle that is made excessively responsible for her troubles. With me, there is always the idea of a large degree of equality, of giving everyone a chance. And, moreover, to come back to *The 400 Blows*, I realized that I had been unjust as far as the parents were concerned, and too indulgent with regard to Jean-Pierre Léaud. And given that I always react from one film to the next, my reaction is probably found in *Shoot the Piano Player*, in which I blackened Aznavour so as to avoid replicating the same effect. Furthermore, that was bound to hurt the reception of the film, because people found it very disconcerting. All of my films, I think, show this kind of alternation. At one time I used to say, "After a sad film, I wanted to make a happy film!" That is not quite true, first, because sad films contain happy elements and vice versa. There is also another idea, which came to me recently because of *A Gorgeous Girl Like Me*: when I idealize something in a film, I feel a need to put quite a lot of sordid things in the next one, so as to forgive myself for having indulged in idealization. That's the difference between *Shoot the Piano Player* and *The Four Hundred Blows*, between *The Soft Skin* and *Jules and Jim* . . . There is always the thought that after one film, there's some kind of reverberation involving a need to correct the preceding film as a result of this echo! *The Soft Skin* was a film that said to intellectuals, "You liked *Jules and Jim* too much, it made you think that love is like that, but actually love is also sordid, appalling, with this or that . . ." Just as *A Gorgeous Girl Like Me* was made in reaction to *Two English Girls*!

When it was released, what was the response to The 400 Blows?

Unanimously praised . . . very good everywhere, as far as I know, except perhaps for some jangling notes here and there! A view that was sometimes expressed was, "After having insulted French cinema so much, how could he have made such a French film!" One would need to go back and read the reviews from that time. Probably *Positif* was against it, but I don't remember on what grounds. Criticism was less politicized than it is nowadays, but it was a film that pleased both leftists and those who frequented Catholic associations. There was even a time when it became a film of those associations; there was no longer a gala of any sort without a screening of *The 400 Blows*. That annoyed me. It's a film that's relevant to the whole world. What happened, was that in certain countries it was somewhat "tampered with"—by which I mean that the last shot, that of the boy running on the beach, was ruined in Russia and Spain by the addition of an optimistic voiceover commentary. I can't exactly describe this commentary, but in those two countries it must have amounted to much the same thing—that the child would be rehabilitated by institutions, or I don't know what. When all is said and done, what's the use of fighting against ambiguity for the sake of giving an optimistic social message!

Notes

1. Truffaut is referring to Dargelos, a feminine-looking boy in Cocteau's novel *Les Enfants terribles* (1929) with whom one of two siblings, Paul, is obsessed during their schooldays. Later, when they are adults, Dargelos sends a gift of opium to Paul, most of which Paul takes, in despair, which leads to his death.

2. "*On fait les quatre cents coups*," a colloquial French expression from which the film takes its title, which means literally "to deliver the 400 blows." The expression originates in an incident during the war waged by Louis XIII against the Protestants in 1621, in which the king ordered 400 canon shots to be fired simultaneously at the walls of the town of Montauban to terrify the city into surrendering (*Projet Voltaire*, http://www.projet-voltaire.fr/blog/actualite/lorigine-de-ces-fameuses-expressions-faire-les-quatre-cents-coups, August 27, 2015).

3. Marcel Bluwal (1925–), a French director, together with Marcel Moussy (1924–1995), a French novelist and filmmaker, introduced a new kind of television series focusing on social problems, *Si c'était vous* (four episodes, 1957–1958), which was praised by the likes of Claude Mauriac and André Bazin for its realism. The first episode, "*Délinquance juvénile*" (October 1957) depicted a father's gradual discovery of his son's delinquent behavior; see Gilles Delavaud, "*Un art de la réalité: Les premières fictions de 'télé-vérité' ou la télévision par excellence*,"

MEI "Médiation et information" 16 (2002), http://www.mei-info.com/wp-content/uploads/revue16/ilovepdf.com_split_7.pdf.

    4. *La Tour, prends garde!* (*King on Horseback*, Georges Lampin, 1958).

    5. *Chiens perdus sans collier* (*The Little Rebels*, Jean Delannoy, 1955), an adaptation of the eponymous novel by Gilbert Cesbron centering on three teenage delinquents.

    6. Annette Wademant, born in Brussels in 1928, was a screenwriter known for her work on the scripts of such movies as *Madame de . . .* (Max Ophüls, 1953), *Edward and Caroline* (Jacques Becker, 1951), and *La Parisienne* (Michel Boisrond, 1957).

    7. *Zero for Conduct* (*Zéro de conduite*, Jean Vigo, 1933); *Germany Year Zero* (*Allemagne année zéro*, Roberto Rossellini, 1948).

    8. Truffaut is referring to the central character in the Abbé Prevost's *L'Histoire du chevalier des Grieux et de Manon Lescaut*, a novel about a flirtatious courtesan published in 1731 that was subsequently given operatic treatments by, respectively, Daniel François Esprit Auber (1856), Jules Massenet (1884), and Giacomo Puccini (1893).

    9. *Jeux interdits* (*Forbidden Games*, René Clément, 1952). Brigitte Fossey is a French actress who was five years old when she was cast by Clément to play the role of an orphaned child during World War II in the film. Cécile Aubry (1928–2010) was a French actress, author, screenwriter, and director known for her roles in *Manon* (Henri-Georges Clouzot, 1949), *The Black Rose* (1950), and *Barbe-Bleue* (Christian-Jacque, 1951).

    10. *Paisà* (*Paisan*, Roberto Rossellini, 1946); *Europa '51* (*Europe '51*, Roberto Rossellini, 1952).

    11. Le Théâtre du Grand-Guignol (which translates literally as "The Theater of the Big Puppet"), is a theater in the Pigalle area of Paris.

    12. Philippe de Broca (1933–2004) was a director, trained at the Paris Photography and Cinematography School, who began working as an intern with Henri Decoin, before becoming an assistant to Chabrol, Truffaut, and Peirre Schœndœrffer, and eventually a filmmaker in his own right.

    13. *Lady in the Lake* (*La Dame du lac*, Robert Montgomery, 1947), a film-noir crime mystery.

    14. *La Bête humaine* (*La Bête Humaine*, Jean Renoir, 1938).

    15. *The Kid* (*Le Kid*, Charles Chaplin, 1921).

    16. Jean-Paul Sartre, *Les Mots* (1963), his autobiography, the first part of which gives the "prehistory" of himself as a child.

    17. *Family Life* (Ken Loach, 1971), a film about a teenage girl suffering a nervous breakdown.

CHAPTER 6

1960: *SHOOT THE PIANO PLAYER*

> I think I made *The Piano Player* because of one image. At the end of the novel by Goodis, there is a little house in the snow, fir trees, and a small sloping road, and you could say that the car was sliding on this road without one hearing the sound of the motor. I wanted to stage this image . . . I have the shot of it in the film. It is possible that I made the film for this shot—for this ambiance, for these love relationships.
>
> La Leçon de cinéma, *broadcast on French television during Spring, 1983. Text reprinted by Michèle Régnier,* Révolution, *August 12, 1983*

What problems did you face after the making of The 400 Blows?

The success of *The 400 Blows* took me completely by surprise, and I attributed it to a number of rather extraordinary coincidences: its selection for the Cannes Film Festival (what would have happened to this film if it had been finished in November of the preceding year?), the birth of the New Wave (I benefited from *The Lovers*, *Hiroshima*, and *Cousins*),[1] a crisis that occurred in French film production that year, et cetera. I witnessed, then, this modest little family affair suddenly turn into a big international film.

The film escaped from my control and became something academic that I no longer recognized. It was appropriated by the audience that doesn't genuinely love cinema, to the spectator who goes to the cinema twice a year—the audience of René Clair and *The Bridge on the River Kwai* that I dread most of all.[2] With my second film, I felt myself under scrutiny, with expectations on the part of this audience, and I wanted to send everyone and their grandmother packing. I had many projects for films involving children, and I put them to one side, so as not to look as if I were simply exploiting something that had been successful. This time I wanted to please the real film devotees, and them alone, even if it meant disconcerting a large number of people who had liked *The 400 Blows*.

I refused to be a prisoner of an initial success, I resisted the temptation to repeat it by choosing a "big subject"; I turned my back on what everyone was waiting for, and I adopted *my own inclination* as the only rule of conduct I would follow (nothing utilitarian; everything is there to satisfy my pleasure as a filmmaker, and, I hope, your pleasure as a spectator).

I was as free as the air, and so I chose a constraint so as not to go crazy. I put myself into the situation of a filmmaker who has to obey a command: to transpose an American novel in the *Série noire* into a French context.[3] In any case, I chose *Shoot the Piano Player*[4] out of admiration for the author of this novel, David Goodis, whose *Dark Passage* might be familiar to cinephiles through its cinematic adaptation by Delmer Daves (with Humphrey Bogart and Lauren Bacall),[5] and his *The Burglar* through its film adaptation by Paul Wendkos (with Jane Mansfield and Dan Durya).[6] Given that I had very much wanted to make a film with Aznavour ever since seeing *The Keepers*,[7] I could kill two birds with one stone by bringing together Goodis and Aznavour.

I know the result seems ill-assorted, and that this film seems to contain four or five different ones, but that is exactly what I wanted, because I was aiming, above all, to explode a genre (the crime film) by mixing in other genres (comedy, drama, melodrama, the psychological film, the thriller, the love film, etc.). I know that there is nothing an audience hates more than changes of tone, but nevertheless I hugely enjoy changing the tone.

What is the real theme of the film?

It's love; the men in it only talk about women, and the women only talk about men. Even in the midst of fighting, the settling of scores, kidnapping, pursuits, people only talk about love: sexual, romantic, physical, moral, social, conjugal, extramarital, et cetera.

Despite the burlesque aspect of certain scenes, the film is never a parody (because I hate parody except when it successfully emulates the beauty of what it is parodying); for me, it involves something very precise that I would call a *respectful pastiche* of the Hollywood B film with which I am so familiar. For example, the scene in which Nicole Berger throws herself out of the window is a melodramatic, respectful pastiche of certain American films. In this way, I pay homage to the work of Nicholas Ray and Samuel Fuller, to mention only two of them, and to American B movies more generally.

I was wanting—it's a structural idea—to treat the subject in the manner of a story by Perrault.[8] I had already been struck by the tone of Goodis's novels, which, at a certain point, move beyond the usual gangster novel to become fairy tales. *The Piano Player* was not made to be crude, but to entertain, amuse.

Is the film more comic than tragic?

Both. With *The Piano Player*, I wanted to make women cry and men laugh.

Why did you use an unknown actress for the main part?

French cinema has at its disposal a whole bevy of young actresses—not yet thirty years old—who worry me on account of their lack of authenticity. These Mylènes, these Danys, these Pierettes, these Luciles, these Danicks are neither "real" young women, nor "real" women, but "chicks," "babes," pin-ups; one gets the feeling that they have been created by cinema for the cinema, and that they wouldn't exist if cinema didn't exist.

That's why I wanted to choose an unknown actress for the principal female lead in *The Piano Player*. Marie Dubois (this pseudonym is the title of a novel by Jacques Audiberti) is neither "spicy" nor "impish," but a pure and dignified young woman with whom one might "realistically" fall in love and be loved in return. One wouldn't be bowled over by her in the street, but she is fresh and gracious, a bit boyish, and very childlike; she is vehement and passionate, shy and tender.

Why did you want to work with Aznavour?

Aznavour is dynamite because there is an incredible contradiction between his puny physique and his strong voice. His glance conveys the sense of barely contained violence that could erupt. He has the gaze of a saint, humble and powerful. When I saw him in his first film, Franju's *The Keepers*,[9] he made me think of Saint Francis of Assisi, and I immediately wanted him for *The Piano Player*.

I wanted to try and make a film that doesn't take place in a precise location. A kind of imaginary country, and Aznavour perfectly typifies the émigré and the artist. He is socially indestructible. One doesn't see him as a workman, or as the manager of a factory, or as a civil servant. When he plays the part of a baker, as in *Tomorrow Is My Turn*,[10] he seems unconvincing. He's a man from nowhere. The only French artist aged between thirty and forty years old. There are those who are younger than thirty, and those who are older than forty, but he is the only one who drags the weight of ten years of adult life behind him.

Aznavour is vulnerable, without being a victim. His fragility allows the audience to identify with him. American filmmakers know the point at which that is indispensable, since they always manage to weaken their heroes. The more prestigious the roles and the stars are, the more one has to invent snags for them. In Westerns you have them get wounded in the course of the action. They have to be made to limp in one way or another. Hitchcock obviously did it best in *Rear Window* by leaving the superman seated in a wheelchair during the whole film.[11] Aznavour has two completely different sides . . . Reserved, calm, measured, reasonable, with no need to show his emotions—his Gabin side—and the other side of him, which is strange, pathological, unusual, a bit wild-eyed and lunatic—his Vigan side.[12] Charles often says to me, "The day you need a real crazy type for a film, I'm the one you should telephone."

Finally, what is not obvious on the surface but is perceived unconsciously, is that he is a poetic character.

I didn't make very good use of him in *The Piano Player*, because I didn't suspect that he had this reserve of violence. Aznavour possesses a certitude about himself that impresses one in private and fascinates in public. It's from that that he draws his magnetism.

The construction of The Piano Player *is very different from that of* The 400 Blows. *Was this intentional?*

In *The Piano Player* I wanted to break free of the unity of *The 400 Blows*. When the film is moving in one direction, I intercept it and send it down another route. I wanted to get rid of clichés, glamorous characters, and preconceptions. As soon as one interpretation seems to be taking over, I destroy it, so as to forestall the possibility of any intellectual comfort, both on the part of the spectator, and also of myself. I try to be objective, and so I show a thousand facets of reality. One constantly has to put oneself in the place of others, because "everyone has their reasons" . . .

Isn't this an admission of weakness? Isn't it a cop-out to avoid making a judgment, rather than proof of moral integrity? What is your opinion of the "classics," and of the serenity of their "conformist" view of the world?

I admire them and, besides, I am not unaware of the dangers of my "objective" attitude. Along with Moravia, however, I think that an artist has to live with paradox. In my opinion, a man can and even must judge—an artist, never.

Does that risk provoking misunderstandings?

Obviously, there is no other reason for the failure of *The Piano Player*. Aznavour's character was capturing too much sympathy. So then, I made him kill the atrocious Serge Davri. At that moment, Davri seems like a poet, an idealist, confronted by an Aznavour who is a cunning bastard, who then immediately becomes antipathetic. The audience switches off, and from that moment on the film is lost as far as its spectators are concerned.

All the scenes with gangsters depend upon this kind of seesaw oscillation. I made them talk about various kinds of things that made it seem as if they weren't gangsters. The ending is constructed in the same way: there is a playful atmosphere, it's unreal, and then suddenly death arrives . . .

That is because I like to disguise appearances with their opposite. I have no fear of false modesty, neutrality, straightforwardness, or even vulgarity, nor, above all, of melodramatic situations.

What would be the verdict of François Truffaut the critic concerning your films?

You know, I always think that a film could have been better, that I should have omitted one scene or another, that the editing should have been different. For example, I was thinking the other day that I should have made *The Piano Player* without any flashbacks, just telling the story as it happens. Having said that, it is very difficult to see these things objectively. In the viewing room, it is only with a lot of effort that I am able to make myself look at a film with new eyes, to empty my head and mind so as to judge my images as if they were made by someone else.

There is one thing I firmly believe: a finished film is exactly what it was meant to be, what one had in mind right from the beginning. I tell myself that to reassure myself, because during the shooting I am always very worried that the film will veer off course, collapse, and become reduced. It seems as if what you are left with is only one tenth of what you wanted to say—to the point where, reflecting on what had already been shot, I would say to myself, "The first half is useless, but I still have the second half to redeem myself." I don't believe in a precisely laid-out screenplay as practiced by Spaak,[13] in which one shoots word for word what the screenwriter has written; it seems to me that one has to adjust things to get them right at every moment, and the sum total of all these efforts ends up producing a result that is very close to what one was anticipating.

Much of the criticism directed at the New Wave concerns the insignificance of the subjects chosen. Why dodge the big problems of our age?

You can think that my film is useless, a failure, worthless, anything you want, but I don't grant you the right to tell me that I should have made something else in its place, or have dealt with this or that subject. You have to evaluate the film that I show you, that's all. I detest those generalizing articles, which are appearing more and more in magazines, that condemn a number of New Wave films en masse simply because of the themes they tackle. The major problems of our times? I don't know the answers to them; people who are much more intelligent, cultivated, and competent than me rack their brains over them—how do you think that I could meddle with them? I only deal with what I know from my own experience, or things I want to find out about. To be realistic, I could undertake a film on the war in Algeria whenever I want, but I don't want to do that because I would not be able to make a negative film, purely negative, that would simply add to the turmoil. Apart from Algeria, I'm also interested in Hitler, in the concentration camps, in racism—I read all the books that come out on that subject. When a journalist asks why the young filmmakers don't make films on Algeria, I feel like replying to him, "Why don't you write a book on Algeria? Because you wouldn't know what to write? Well then, figure out for yourself why I wouldn't know what to film."

Deportation fascinates me. How does one get deported? Isn't it complicated? What is even more mysterious is how one becomes a "deporter," how and why *everyone* can find it normal to deport someone else, or witness their deportation. I have read so many books on the camps that I could make a film on that subject, but then I start to think for a moment: what is a deported person? A man who weighs thirty kilos. But then, you can't make anyone act the role of someone who weighs thirty kilos; to choose thin people, as they did for *The Young Lions*, is simply insulting;[14] the degree of cheating inherent in the difference between a thin person and a deportee makes this expedient blasphemous, inadmissible. The only solution is a documentary film, and in that regard, Resnais has made the film that needs to be made, the only one possible, the greatest film that I have seen.[15] One imbecile wrote that *The 400 Blows* was a film against secularity, because the teacher skipped over current events. If I had been raised by Jesuits, I would have won the "prize of the Bureau for Secularity," if such a thing existed!

1962

Why did you speed up the pace of Boby Lapointe's song?

When I knew him, he used to sing like that. These days he sings a little more slowly because he has become a professional. He is a man who is hugely shy, one who had a terrible time deciding he would sing in public. I liked the rhythm a lot because I found it so disconcerting.

There is a scene in The Piano Player *that people have found hard to understand—when Aznavour goes to attend an audition and a young woman comes out. What is she doing in the story?*

It's indeed a scene that isn't clear, but it means a lot to me. I didn't want to show the end of the audition because that is a stereotype in American cinema. There is a parody of American cinema in the novel version of *The Piano Player*, but there are some scenes I refused to make. Aznavour goes to the audition—it's important for him, and he wants to be successful. I wanted him to stay outside the door, and at first I thought I would have people pass him in the corridor and make them pause. But the idea of having so many people bothered me, and so, bit by bit I decided that it would be more effective to replace a group with just one woman. She plays the violin, stops, comes out . . . thus opening the door whose bell Aznavour could probably never have brought himself to ring, and never would have entered. This man encounters this woman. They should have been able to fall in love. They should have been able to live together, he a pianist and she a violinist. It's the meeting of a piano and a violin, of a man and a woman. The camera rests on the woman, she continues walking normally, hears him playing, and stops to listen to him. Immediately after this we see her in a close-up shot, then we pull away, and we see her silhouette in the hall. I wanted this scene to be fascinating, and I chose a very beautiful woman for it.

What's amusing is how this scene can be interpreted in a number of ways. Those who see the shot for the second time, now that they know the impresario is a bastard, all say that he has made fun of her, and that's why she seems rather distracted. Others think that she has failed her audition and believe that Charles is going to succeed.

In fact, it all began because of the fact that in the screenplay there was an audition that I wanted to keep and a young woman whom I wanted to act the part, but who was incapable of reciting the dialogue. I reused this girl in *Jules and Jim*; someone remarked on this subject that "she is not completely crazy, she is merely shallow . . . it's sex in a pure state . . ." This scene, slightly extraneous to the plot, is built around the strangeness of this girl, who you will certainly see again in my future films because she has become one of my favorite actresses.

1962

To a certain extent, I made *Shoot the Piano Player* as a reaction against *The 400 Blows*, because the success of the earlier film, the giddiness that surrounded it, which I encountered all of a sudden, so bewildered me that I said to myself, "I have to be careful, I must not fall into demagoguery." But I don't have a very good explanation for what happened with *The Piano Player*. In the end, I must have remained too faithful to the book. I was also too sure of myself on account of the success of *The 400 Blows*. But it also owes something, I think, to the law of the second film. *A Woman Is a Woman* (because of the banning of *Le Petit Soldat*—I am treating this as Godard's second film) was similarly made in the euphoria generated by *Breathless*. *My Life to Live* is a regaining of control.[16]

With a first film, one takes a plunge: "Here we go, I'm going to risk everything; after this, I probably won't be making any more films, but for the time being, I want to see what is going to come out of it." The reaction to one's first film is very important. One is always surprised if it is successful. The second one suffers from the first one's success. *Marienbad* similarly displayed great self-confidence, born from the success of a first film—one in which the filmmaker had shown an initiation into life, wanting to say everything. The second is deliberately more modest in its aims. The third is the most interesting, being made in response to the other two, and marking the starting point of a real career.

If you think about *The Piano Player*, you can see that the screenplay doesn't stand up to scrutiny. Most obviously, it lacks a controlling idea. Even so, there is one in each of my two other films. In *The 400 Blows*, it consists of the depiction of a child as honestly as possible, informed by a particular moral position. The same is true of *Jules and Jim*: were it to be done in a certain way, it would be pornographic, in another way, shocking, and in yet another way, conventional—and so it had to be done in the way I did it. My mistake, in *The Piano Player*, was that I could do anything, given that it involved material that didn't impose any particular form. Aznavour has a tremendous comic gift, and so I could have made it as a comedy. He also projects great authority: I could have made his character ferocious. I myself didn't have any particular preference one way or the other at the beginning, merely a crazy desire to have Aznavour, because of *The Keepers*, but it would have been better if I had known him for a long time. The courageous thing about *The Piano Player* is that I used flashbacks, knowing that they are never forgiving. I said to Braunberger, "You recall *Bad Liaisons*? And *Lola Montès*? And *The Barefoot Contessa*?"[17] They didn't work because of flashbacks—well, we're going to treat ourselves to two of them, one within the other." In the event, that screwed everything up.

There's a golden rule: you can't mix things up. You cannot be fully immersed in one story and fully engaged with another. With a bit of work, one could certainly present *The Piano Player* in a chronological fashion. It would need some work. There are some good things in the film, but we can't say it's because we did better with such and such a theme. There is no theme.

> *Another thing must have upset the audience about* The Piano Player: *the rupture in tone. That is something that has characterized several other films that have not done well—including* A Woman Is a Woman—*and it's something that the French audience never accepts.*

Yes, that's the most difficult thing to get to work. In spite of this, people understood *The Piano Player* in America, but in a different way: they laughed the whole way through, even in the tragic passages. The first song was comic; they laughed right through the second one, which, inherently, is not comic.

The Piano Player needs a month of work. If you mix together two or three reels from films you love, you won't end up with a film that interests people, even if what it contains is good. It is true that the changes in tone are also something to work on: it's a gamble you sometimes have to make—Renoir succeeded in doing it.

1966

I have seen 1,500 American films. What I love about these films is their atmosphere; I wanted to reuse these elements, recreating them in "a French manner," to pay a certain kind of homage to them. There's a light hint of irony, never of mockery, and at the same time a desire to take them seriously. Tonally, it's very unusual—it would be better to say "subtle"—but in the end . . . There's one thing I remember, for example. When Aznavour stabs the owner of the bar, women turn up to remove the corpse, Aznavour himself being about to faint, and then some musicians join with the women to carry the body, and in the rear, there is one musician who has kept his instruments, carrying a cello in one hand and a violin in the other. All that is accompanied by a funereal march, slightly baroque, zany, and then people appear at their window, and one of the women says to the people, "Go home, there's been an accident." I have often watched the film from among the audience, and people laugh at this passage, thinking that it springs from the director's naïveté. Not so. It's a tribute to American cinema. It's a key line. In almost all American films, someone says, "Go home, there's been an accident," just as all children say, "Daddy, you are the best dad in the world." It was a cliché. This utterance just had to be put there.

With *The Piano Player*, I haven't entirely paid off the debt I owe to American cinema; I still want to make films that are a bit more extravagant. I have a project with Jeanne Moreau that will be based on an American source, and it's going to be very eccentric. Now that I know myself, that I know I am very much a realist, who, when all is said and done, is somewhat dull and not far from being boring, I say to myself that I am interested in tackling some very eccentric material, since, whatever happens, I will end up giving it maximum plausibility and normality along the way. So right now, I want to take a wide detour in order to get back to a documentary style—because, if I were to leave the documentary altogether, I would end up making films in which nothing happens.

1967

In watching the film again, I remembered that quite a lot of the relationship involving Nicole Berger was influenced by Moravia's *Contempt*. Part of this story, about a woman, focuses on her husband's success; also, in the first scenes with Nicole Berger, he thinks she despises him. That's why this kind of film can be described as an amalgam of different ingredients, containing many references, just like the American films I loved, the strongest influence being that of *Johnny Guitar* by Nicholas Ray.

Audiberti was another influence.[18] I was rather sad that he didn't like *The 400 Blows*. As a rule, he liked everything, and never rejected anything. One day he said to me, "There is a Simenon aspect to it that bothers me. There is something missing, the idea that it was simply a story." I thought of Audiberti during the shooting of *The Piano Player*, and part of Plyne's character is clearly influenced by him. I said to myself, "He has to be a character like Audiberti, who has a view of women as completely magical." At that moment there is a reversal in the film: we notice that the little, shy, likeable guy is not so timid after all, that he can fend for himself quite well, and that the real victim of society is the person who places women too high, on a pedestal, as Audiberti did, and like the boss of the bar. The film is more influenced by the personality of Audiberti himself than by his books.

1974

> Shoot the Piano Player. *One day, you said that Cocteau was a big influence on the film . . .*

Cocteau is behind everything! Rivette says—and he's right—that we have all been influenced by Cocteau. What else, for instance, is the common point of reference between Godard, Demy, and me! And now the height of this influence is seen in Philippe Garrel. I don't know if Garrel knows Cocteau's films, but he is truly Cocteau's son, that's for sure. I think that Cocteau, who loved everything, spoke well of everything, and defended everything, would have had a real shock when he saw Garrel's films. No matter who you are, everyone has been influenced by him, whether by the style of his dialogue, like Demy and me, or visually, like Godard, particularly in *Alphaville*. These days I can't really tell, because there has also been the influence of Roché.[19] At the same time, Roché and Cocteau shared points in common . . . One day while I was in a military hospital, I was sent ten or twelve novels from the *Série noire* collection, which I read one after the other, and I realized that they were very fairy-tale-like. Even more, certain things in these *Série noire* books made me think of *L'Aigle à deux têtes* and *Les Enfants terribles*.[20] I discovered a relation between Cocteau and the freedom exercised by the writers of these books in which no one is judged, who would let themselves follow wherever their imagination led them, and who were prepared to push everything towards the tragic. I found that very striking. *Shoot the Piano Player* was probably motivated by the idea of taking a *Série noire*—even something already poetic, because Goodis isn't just anyone—and of pushing it to the limit of extravagance in order to bring out its fairy-tale quality for adults: by emphasizing the business with the car, the house under the snow, et cetera. Even so, I had some misgivings when making *Shoot the Piano Player*—not a great malaise, but a malaise nevertheless—which sprang from a sudden realization that I hated gangster movies. I was helpless, cornered: I was disabled. And just as I always react against things, I didn't want to fall into the cliché you find in French cinema whereby gangsters are depicted as likeable and sentimental. The kind of gangsters who gaze into one's eyes, who promise their buddy to look after their wife and children, et cetera, as in all the literature I hated.

Such clichés annoyed me, and I didn't want to reproduce them! On the other hand, I didn't want to play the moralist. So I said to myself, "I am going to veer toward the comic, I'm going to push the characters in a comic direction!" But by doing that, by pushing them toward the comic, I was scared of lapsing into further clichés, this time British ones, as seen in the idiotic kind of gangsters of which there are always many in English films. As a result, this was the aspect of the film that I felt least confident about. In contrast, I felt at ease with Aznavour's character, the three women associated with him, the character of the boss of the bar... And then, compared with *The 400 Blows*, *Shoot the Piano Player* gave me a chance to show that I had been formed by American cinema! There was also the pleasure of having limited responsibility, a pleasure that I have enjoyed a bit since as a result of acting in *The Wild Child* and *Day for Night*—given my belief that actors derive pleasure from not having any responsibility for the film as a whole, from only having to be involved with a part of it, while others around them are preoccupied with the rest. There is also pleasure in shooting a film that doesn't have to deal with a big subject, because it is very oppressive to shoot a film like *The 400 Blows*: you have a feeling of responsibility, the feeling that you are responsible with respect to children in general... Whereas if you make *Shoot the Piano Player*, which is about nothing at all, you experience more pleasure because one has fewer scruples, fewer problems with one's conscience—you know that you are simply being guided by your own pleasure. You tell yourself, "This scene is going to be fun to make... there, we've made it!" As for grand causes, I have confronted them in *Fahrenheit 451* and *The Wild Child*... and each time I have had a feeling of being oppressed; whereas each time I've made films that gave me the feeling they had nothing to say—like *Stolen Kisses* or *Shoot the Piano Player*—they have left me with a feeling of relief. This is without taking into account the fact that people always experience more pleasure from films that are made in an offhand manner.

Notes

1. Truffaut is referring, respectively, to *Les Amants* (*The Lovers*, Louis Malle, 1958); *Hiroshima mon amour* (*Hiroshima Mon Amour*, Alain Resnais, 1959); and *Les Cousins* (Claude Chabrol, 1959).

2. *The Bridge on the River Kwai* (*Le Pont de la rivière Kwai*, David Lean, 1957), a war film dealing with the situation of British prisoners of war in Burma during World War II.

3. The *Série noire* was a series of crime fiction novels, founded by Éditions Gallimard in 1945, and published in paperback, that included works by many Anglo-American authors, such as Raymond Chandler, Dashiell Hammett, and James Hadley Chase, not to mention the

authors adapted by Truffaut: David Goodis, Cornell Woolrich, and Charles Williams. The term "*Série noire*" originally referred to the black cover, edged with white, with yellow lettering.

4. David Goodis, *Down There* (1956), known in France by its French title, *Tirez sur le pianiste* (Shoot the Piano Player).

5. David Goodis, *Dark Passage* (1946), adapted as *Dark Passage* (Delmer Daves, 1947). The French titles for the novel and film are, respectively, *Cauchemar* and *Les Passagers de la nuit*.

6. David Goodis, *The Burglar* (1953), adapted as *The Burglar* (Paul Wendkos, 1957). The French titles are, respectively, *Le Casse* and *Le Cambrioleur*.

7. *La Tête contre les murs* (*The Keepers*, Georges Franju, 1959).

8. Charles Perrault (1628–1703) was a French writer of fairy tales, derived from traditional folk tales, which included *Little Red Riding Hood*, *Cinderella*, *Puss in Boots*, *The Sleeping Beauty*, and *Bluebeard*.

9. *La Tête contre les murs* (*The Keepers*, Georges Franju, 1959).

10. *Le Passage du Rhin* (*Tomorrow Is My Turn*, André Cayatte, 1960).

11. *Rear Window* (*Fenêtre sur cour*, Alfred Hitchcock, 1954).

12. Truffaut is comparing Aznavour to two French film stars: Jean Gabin (real name Jean-Alexis Moncorgé), renowned for his deadpan look and his roles as crooks and policemen; and Robert le Vigan (real name Robert Charles Alexandre Coquillard), who was known for his work in supporting roles, for example, that of Michel Krauss, a painter, in *Port of Shadows* (*Quai des brumes*, Marcel Carnet, 1938), a film starring Gabin in the lead.

13. Charles Spaak, a Belgian screenwriter who occupied an important place in French cinema during the 1930s, writing scripts for such filmmakers as Jacques Feyder, Julien Duvivier, Jean Grémillon, and Jean Renoir, and was associated with the "quality cinema" of the 1950s, writing the scripts for *Thérèse Raquin* (Marcel Carné, 1953) and *Crime et Châtiment* (Stellio Lorenzi, 1956).

14. *The Young Lions* (*Le Bal des maudits*, Edward Dymytryk, 1958).

15. Truffaut is referring to *Nuit et brouillard* (*Night and Fog*, Alain Resnais, 1955).

16. Truffaut is referring to, in order, *Une Femme est une femme* (*A Woman Is a Woman*, 1961), *Le Petit Soldat* (*Le Petit soldat*, 1963), *À bout de souffle* (*Breathless*, 1960), and *Vivre sa vie* (*My Life to Live*, 1962), all directed by Jean-Luc Godard. *Le Petit Soldat*, made in 1960, was banned by the French Government until 1963 on account of its depiction of torture during the Algerian War.

17. *Bad Liaisons* (*Les Mauvaises Rencontres*, Alexandre Astruc, 1955); *Lola Montès* (Max Ophüls, 1955); and *The Barefoot Contessa* (*La Comtesse aux pieds nus*, Joseph L. Mankiewicz, 1954).

18. Jacques Audiberti (1899–1965), a French novelist and playwright, most active during the 1940s and 1950s.

19. Henri-Pierre Roché (1879–1959), whose two novels *Jules et Jim* and *Les Deux Anglaises et le continent*, which he wrote in his sixties, were adapted by Truffaut.

20. *L'Aigle à deux têtes* (Jean Cocteau, 1943) is a play about a queen in seclusion who veils her face for the ten years since her husband's assassination. Cocteau directed a film based on the play in 1948. *Les Enfants terribles* is a novel written by Cocteau in 1929, which was subsequently adapted into a film by Jean-Pierre Melville in 1950.

CHAPTER 7

1962: *JULES AND JIM*

> Because there was no guarantee that the film would be a success, I was rather anxious during the shoot. *Jules and Jim* was made at a time in my life when I was constantly afraid I was going to die. I handled everything gently, in a state of panic, telling myself that if there were an accident, it would be impossible to find anyone who could edit the film. There was so much improvisation in it that it was very difficult to know the order in which things should be put together. It certainly required the longest editing process in my career.
>
> *Interview with Jean-Claude Marti,* La Suisse, *March 9, 1973*

Jules and Jim *is a novel—how long had you been acquainted with it?*

The book had been out for two years when I discovered it; I found it in a secondhand bookstore at the Place du Palais-Royal. Actually, it was the title that I liked, and the blurb, which revealed that it was the first novel by a sixty-six-year-old man. I was greatly intrigued by that.

I like "real-life" stories—memoirs, recollections, people who recount the story of their life. I thought the book was wonderful, and was struck both by the risqué nature of the events he describes, and also the purity of the whole thing. I thought that it couldn't be turned into a cinematic equivalent until I saw Ulmer's *Naked Dawn*.[1] It was a Western without merit, but for a quarter of an hour it showed—as in *Jules and Jim*, and with the same freshness—a woman wavering between two men who were equally likeable.

In my film criticism for *Arts* I mentioned *Jules et Jim*, saying, "Yes, we think, all things considered, that certain books are incapable of being turned into films; however, *Naked Dawn* proves that it should be possible to make an effective adaptation of one of the most beautiful modern novels that exist, one of the most neglected: Henri-Pierre Roché's *Jules et Jim* . . ."

I received a note from the author who was very happy about this, given that no one had paid much attention to his book. We started up a correspondence. One day I went to see him at Orsay, and I said to him, "If I eventually end up making films, it would be my dream to make a film based on this book." Later I showed him *Les Mistons*, which he liked a lot, and he published a second novel called *Two English Girls and the Continent*.[2] When I shot *The 400 Blows*, I sent him a small note saying, "I had thought that my first film would be *Jules and Jim*, but I realized that it's actually very difficult to make. *Jules and Jim* is going to be my second film. I'll show you *The 400 Blows* as soon as it is finished." But he was already fairly old, being nearly eighty. In *The 400 Blows*, Jeanne Moreau makes an appearance with Jean-Claude Brialy, and I gave her the book; she said to me, "That's what I want to do the most, whenever you want!" At that point, I gathered some photos that had appeared in *Cahiers* of Jeanne Moreau in her most recent films and sent them to Roché, who wrote back to me, "I absolutely have to meet her, bring her to me . . ."— but he died five days after having sent me this letter!

How did you tackle the adaptation?

In the book, which I knew by heart, I marked the parts that pleased me most with one or more crosses, wrote several comments, and sent all that to Jean Gruault, the coadapter and dialogue writer for the film. He prepared a text of two hundred pages that I then took over, working with scissors and paste, leaving myself room to improvise the scenes that struck me as the most important at the last moment, during the shooting.

Throughout the film I inserted a voice-over commentary for each place where I thought that the text was impossible to transform into dialogue, or too beautiful to allow it to be amputated. I prefer an intermediate form of adaptation alternating dialogue with passages read out loud, which corresponds to some degree to a filmed novel, rather than a classical adaptation, which transforms a book into a theatrical play come what may. I also think that *Jules and Jim* is more of a cinematic book than the pretext for a literary film.

It is a book that contains a great many things. Do you approach it as a whole, or pick out different elements, such as a friendship, a love affair, the evocation of a period? Are there some things in it you are more attached to than others, and to which you have given preference, either because of your own inclination or else dramatic necessity?

No, I believe that both the book and the film are governed by the characters. More than anything else, it is a film about characters. Besides, if the characters are not interesting, a film is not interesting either. The period is entirely secondary. I began it without knowing how to make a period film. I am happy with this lack of awareness, because without it I would have given up making the film, or else I would have modernized it. As it was, I launched into the film without knowing that it would take half an hour to put on a false moustache, and an hour to do a woman's hair in the style of 1910.

However, you did not exclude a certain degree of stylization. In twenty years, the characters don't age.

I wanted to avoid physical aging, graying hair. Gruault came up with something to mark the passing of time that greatly pleased me, which was to place Picasso's masterpieces in the decor. There is a real progression: we see the advent of impressionism, the cubist period, the collages.

What is the theme of Jules and Jim?

There's a song in the film: it's called "The Whirlwind of life"; it reflects the tone of, and reveals the key to, the film. Perhaps because it was an old man who wrote it, I consider that *Jules et Jim* is a hymn to life. For this reason, I wanted to create the impression of a great lapse of time through the birth of children, but also interrupted by war, by death—all of which give a more complete meaning to one's whole existence.

Perhaps it was ambitious to make an old man's film, but this retrospective view fascinated me, allowing me to attain a certain degree of detachment. The film seemed easier for me to achieve, owing to the fact that both the action and the period were foreign to me. Refusing to take sides, I wanted to lead the audience to be as objective as I was. It is also a story about love, based on the idea that, because living in a couple does not always prove successful or satisfying, it seems legitimate to look for a different morality, other ways of living, even though all such arrangements may be destined to fail. Nevertheless, and despite its "modern" appearance, this film is not at all polemical. There is no doubt that the young woman in *Jules and Jim* wants to live in the same manner as a man, but that is only a particularity of her personality, and doesn't represent a feminist attitude or a form of protest.

Are you satisfied with your heroine?

It's true to say that this female character is made up of clichés and non-clichés. Also, when she becomes too much like Scarlett O'Hara,[3] I put glasses on her, I try to make her more human, more realistic. I wanted to do well by Jeanne Moreau as an actress, and it seemed to me that I needed to prevent her from becoming too glamorous, that it was necessary to shield her from being put on display. I wanted to make her likeable but, at the same time, I was afraid of making her the kind of "exquisite pain in the neck" you find in American comedy. As always, there was a heap of things to avoid in this instance. I sought to "dis-intellectualize" her in relation to her preceding films and make both her role and her acting more physical and more dynamic. I had already worked in this way with Jean-Pierre Léaud for *The 400 Blows* and Charles Aznavour for *Shoot the Piano Player*.

Are there any points in common between those two films and Jules and Jim?

At the end of each film—and I include my short film *Les Mistons*—I try to draw out some kind of "lesson." That's why I have a feeling that *Jules and Jim* is a synthesis of my previous work. Like *Les Mistons*, it has the importance of nature, a return to voice-over, and the introduction of scenes that are aesthetically constructed. As in *The 400 Blows*, there is also a spiraling chain of events, the description of a difficult situation from which it becomes more and more impossible for the characters to extricate themselves. I also tried in each of the two films to make the audience accept a character—an adolescent and a young woman, respectively—who habitually acts in a manner frowned upon by conventional morality. Finally, *Jules and Jim* is an extension of *Shoot the Piano Player* in that, in both of them, I wanted to equalize the characters so that they elicited the same degree of sympathy, and so that one would feel tempted to like them equally.

Why did you choose two unknown actors for the characters of Jules and Jim?

For a start, because of my awareness that in certain films is it provocative to create a confrontation between stars. The audience doesn't believe in the story, it goes to watch a sparring match: it goes to see if Michèle Morgan is stronger than Bourvil.[4] As far as I am concerned, I think that you should surround the star with new faces. The impact will be greater. I needed new faces opposite Jeanne Moreau, so that the audience wouldn't go to see a "match," but a "film."

I knew Oscar Werner from *Lola Montès*, and I had seen Henri Serre in small roles in the theater—he had never done any cinema previously. The casting was done like that. It is truly a film about characters, to the extent that the whole crew became Jules and Jim. Everyone knew that the reactions of each of the characters to each of the others were important. The technicians felt they learned a little bit more about them with each scene. The characters took on an incredible existence, especially on location. The fact of living together, particularly during the final month, was rather exhilarating.

You didn't worry that Jeanne Moreau would eclipse her partners?

No, the role was perfect for her. Of all the women who have a name in cinema, she was the only one capable of acting a role that demanded both authority and humility at the same time. Given that it concerned a delicate subject, often bordering on bad taste, I had to choose a very intelligent actress to make certain things work. It's often because of her that the film didn't turn out to be a failure. There are scenes that would have made people laugh, had they been acted by anyone else but her. There are, in fact, things that have to be said forcefully to intimidate the audience in a movie theater. In a film, as soon as one starts to speak about carnal love, the audience suddenly becomes very infantile, like children when they are at an awkward age, and one has to take that into account. You know all too well that a certain retort risks making people laugh. For that reason, the next line has to follow on very quickly. In the same way, certain things provoke laughter if characters say them while in bed, for example; and if the remark gets sensitive, I quickly move on to an exterior shot, the chalet seen in a tracking shot taken from a helicopter, so that the beauty of the countryside throttles the laughter in people's throats. In general, after the public screenings I have watched, I found I was not wrong. I enjoy playing this risky game a lot. I sense that people are going to be very irritated at a particular moment—they are going to hate the film—and so, I win them back over again in the scene that follows . . . except for certain spectators who drop out completely during the final twenty minutes, in particular when Catherine hooks up with Albert again, with her pajamas.

In your opinion, is there as much of you in The 400 Blows *as in* Jules and Jim?

Frankly, yes. In both cases, I was constrained as much as guided by a mass of scruples, but they were not the same ones on each occasion. Regarding *The*

400 Blows, the problem was my feeling that "no one will be interested in my personal story—I am mad to be making a film about it." As far as *Jules and Jim* was concerned, I was thinking, "Look out, I've got a masterpiece in my hands, one that is unknown, for sure, but a masterpiece none the less—I must not betray Roché; it is essential that his old friends who are going to see the film recognize the book in it. It's written in an invisible style, one that doesn't seem like much, so the film has to be the same." Georges Delerue, for example, liked the film so much that he wanted to compose some very ambitious music for it. I spent a long time explaining to him that his music must not be ostentatious, that if anyone became aware of the beauty of an image for a single moment, the film would be ruined. The same thing applied to the reading of the commentary spoken by Michel Subor in a very neutral and quick way, without expressive intonations.

And you didn't worry that this accumulation of self-imposed constraints and neutrality would end up making a neutral film?

That is precisely what had to "make" the film; I was certain that a single error of this kind would throw the whole film off balance. I believe strongly in maintaining modest appearances. Even if one were to label it "false modesty," I really like "false modesty." It is very important to pretend to be like everyone else; one shouldn't distinguish oneself through outward things. I was very happy with the title of *The 400 Blows* because it was almost vulgar. While it was being shot, I heard rumors of provincial magazines that were saying "M. F. T., having insulted the whole of French cinema, is shooting a film whose title speaks for itself." It made them anticipate something very vulgar, and one of the reasons I made *Shoot the Piano Player* was that its title pleased me also.

Do you think when making a film that one's work has to be determined by considerations of the effect that you want to produce in the audience? Is it possible to imagine that simply being happy to make what one wants, so long as the desire is deep and genuine, is initially a risk worth the taking, which can then result in something valuable, in the case of people who have a coherent and fully developed personality?

Yes, but it is a question of temperament. If one is very sure of oneself, one can make anything one wants, and after that it is up to people to join in, but that is not the case with me: I am not sure of myself, and apart from that, I am almost ashamed to make films. It's difficult to explain—I don't entirely know why—but perhaps because a film involves the mobilization of capital, capital for hiring people. The only way of making this activity meaningful is to regard it as an entertainment, and an entertainment that has to succeed. I feel as if—it's stupid, though, since the props man, the makeup artist, et cetera, get paid the same whether the film succeeds or fails—that I would be embarrassed to meet them three months later if the film hadn't been a success. I would have the feeling of having dragged them into a useless venture, of having caused them to lose two months out of their lives, I would be ashamed with regard to them. It's truly stupid to say it, but we all set off on the same adventure. For me, the only justification for this craft is that others should find it interesting.

Frankly, with *The Piano Player*, I suffered (and not because of Braunberger, since he broke even). One time, I went into the provinces with the film, and I saw that the audience wasn't responding; I stopped at once—I didn't have the courage to fight for it. I couldn't say, "It's me who's right and you who are wrong; if people are disconcerted, it's because they lack something." Even if friends and cinephiles found the film interesting, there was still something that wasn't working. It's a question of time—I am always very pressed—I believe greatly in keeping the pace up, in the value of people's time. I don't want to make them lose an hour and a half—that's important in life. I wouldn't at all make the same argument about television: people are at home, they can turn the set off, switch it back on later. Cinema, however, requires a trip.

The other day I saw *North by Northwest* again,[5] and half an hour before the end I heard a guy behind me say to the woman next to him, "It's not a bad film." That's an extraordinary utterance because it reflects the mentality of viewers who only occasionally go to the movies, as distinct from cinephiles; after all, a film is only celluloid! This fellow was a difficult, skeptical spectator, and here he was saying "Not bad for a film," which made me happy for Hitchcock. *North by Northwest* lasts for two hours, half the shots are faked in a lab or during the photography, there are dummies, astonishing moments of virtuosity, a love of the craft, and extraordinary knowledge. It's a film that is completely personal, intimate, involving Hitchcock's obsessions, his investigations; but this fellow, who had gone there by chance, was obliged to go with it, he was conquered. That was good. For me, that's cinema. I believe in this kind of challenge. One carries an immense responsibility. I also think that people enter a cinema by chance, and that there should not be several categories of spectator. The informed spectator, the one who sees a hundred films a year, the cinephile, will discover more things in a film than someone who only goes to the cinema once a year—that's normal. Nevertheless, the film must present itself outwardly in the same way for both of them.

> *You were saying just now that you wanted to avoid giving the character played by Jeanne Moreau a glamorous aspect. There are, however, characters who are more favored in screenplays than others, principal characters and secondary characters.*

In films about love there is often a notion that annoys me—that love is reserved for certain people. *Seven Days . . . Seven Nights* upset me.[6] You have the Jeanne Moreau–Belmondo couple in a small provincial town. A glamorous couple, surrounded by bourgeois and imbeciles, the husband being a perfect idiot, the piano teacher perfectly dried up. What interests me is the love story between the teacher and the husband. One had to imagine the married couple as unattractive, because it is a work that is built around recrimination. *Seven Days* was crucial for *Jules and Jim*. It was absolutely essential that I did *not* have any unlikeable characters of this sort in the background. Normally, the lover is a glamorous character, and the husband an unattractive one. I moved that so far in the opposite direction that a spectator who confuses a character with the actor prefers Oscar Werner to Henri Serre.

In order to achieve this degree of equality I had to avoid everything that could split them. I deeply mistrust anything that separates the world into two: the good and the bad, bourgeois and artists, policemen and shady types.

Now, at the present time, there is a whole artistic vein beyond cinema that is fed by these kinds of oppositions. Take songs, for example: the way Brassens has of opposing lovers to bourgeois types, cops to prostitutes.[7] Now, everyone has a need to be loved, everyone has a right to love, starting with bourgeois people and cops. One encounters the same kind of facile effect in Prévert,[8] and in all the songs of Juliette Greco: "Les imbéciles et les méchants," for example.[9]

> *But what happens when you have to create a scene with an imbecile!*

That happened to me, and I blamed myself for it afterwards. You remember the teacher in *The 400 Blows*? I think that spectators found this character off-putting, and that's a shame. I would do it differently today. I would like my characters to be as really alive as possible. It's through the degree of life they have that characters make an impression on the spectator. It's necessary for this life to escape from all the preconceived notions that the spectator may have been able to entertain about a particular character. One has to be able to make things that could seem to be exceptional seem natural. It's important that people no longer want to judge characters according to their own moral system. One has to prevent the spectator—and thus first refrain oneself—from controlling the characters. You have to let the characters retain all their chances for salvation along with all their inconsistencies.

How can a director attain this degree of generosity with respect to his characters?

I don't know if it's generosity, but at any rate it is an ethical position. In my eyes, it is the foundation of an author's morality. He reveals himself in the attitude he adopts with respect to his characters.

To illustrate this, I'll take *Touch of Evil*, a film that attests to the natural goodness of Orson Welles.[10] In *Touch of Evil*, there is a policeman who seems to be an exemplary type. However, he's a corrupt cop. When he is dealing with a suspect, he fabricates evidence to confound him. At the beginning of the film he has a young Mexican arrested. In the end, in spite of everything, the Mexican confesses to the murder. You can see here that we don't have a simplistic opposition between the good and the bad: the Mexican who seemed innocent to us is guilty, in spite of appearances. Similarly, the corrupt policeman has a certain flair, in spite of his corruption. His evidence may well be false, but it turns out to be true. Orson Welles does not judge these two people, but allows them to reveal themselves in the full complexity of their personalities.

If this is the ethical stance a filmmaker ought to take, in your view, what is it that defines an immoral auteur, in your opinion?

A filmmaker can be immoral at any stage in the creation of his film—in the screenplay, in the shooting, and even in the editing. In screenplays, the attitude that I most dislike is having important people make fun of inferior people. In real life, that has a name: subservience. Well, this subservience, this baseness became the golden rule for boulevard theater. We encounter this convention again in cinema, in all the films with dialogue written by Michel Audiard (*The Lions Are Loose*, *The President*, etc.).[11] In them, we witness one star flattening all the other characters: for example, Gabin, who seems to be as infallible as a pope, giving lessons in morality to younger people. The scenes where he is angry are contrived to impress the spectator. He has a great role. The others are there to serve him. They act like idiots so as to throw him into the spotlight.

What then, in your opinion, would be the ideal attitude for a filmmaker to adopt with regard to the spectator?

He should never try to make the spectator laugh or cry over anything that has not made him laugh or cry himself. That pretty well sums up my moral position as a director.

You revealed just before that you refuse to judge people, to create a contrast between ones who are good and ones who are bad, and that for you there is a mixture of good and bad in every human being. Do you believe in original sin?

Yes, I believe in original sin. In this respect, one film has been a landmark for me: it's *Night and Fog*.[12] When I discovered this film, I realized that you cannot reduce all problems to social or political issues. It's man who is the cause, each individual man. The idea that emerges out of *Night and Fog* is not "We could all end up being deported tomorrow," but "We are all capable, tomorrow, of deporting others and thinking of that as normal." And suddenly we become guilty, we feel that there is some guilt in every man from the outset, an original faultiness.

There is another film that rounded out this experience for me. It is perhaps the film that best reflects my own political position—Rossellini's *Europe '51*,[13] which, as far as I am concerned, says all there is to say about work, justice, religion, communism, education, and modern life.

In Shoot the Piano Player, *we see that the "pure" characters are led into an adventure that forces them to leave their usual self behind. Why?*

In making *Shoot the Piano Player* I wanted to do the exact opposite of what one finds in a certain genre of films. Convention requires, in this genre, that the baddies are killed at the end. In my film, it was necessary that the innocent should be killed, specifically, the young woman, Marie Dubois.

In your eyes, is this reversal simply meant to convey a sense that evil is all-powerful, that unhappiness is inevitable, as in melodrama?

I noticed, when I was making *Jules and Jim*, that the common denominator in my three films was precisely this construction around a melodramatic theme. Fundamentally, *The 400 Blows* is the story of an unloved child. *Shoot the Piano Player* is the story of a great piano player who has fallen. *Jules and Jim* is about a woman who loves two men, and dies from it.

Have you asked yourself why this inevitability of unhappiness is found in all your films?

I think that it comes from my desire to elaborate very simple plot outlines, ones that are accessible to everyone and not out of the ordinary. I find that a film needs to display originality at the point where it ends up, but not in its point of departure. I don't like the kind of clever plots that please producers, as when one tells them over a drink, "After the nuclear explosion, there are only three men left on earth, et cetera."

Your last two films also involve a love story. Is that an important theme for you?

Yes, it's *the* most important subject. It's the subject of subjects. It's well worth devoting half of one's career to it (like Bergman), or three-quarters (like Renoir). Because each story has its own value, just as each love relation is unique. One can very well imagine the kind of person who, during his life, would only read novels about love, or would only go to see love films. I believe that such a man would attain a certain kind of culture, a very valuable form of knowledge. Personally, a love story interests me when it has something very distinctive about it, even exceptional, never when it involves a generalized case in this domain, packed with contrived, artificial problems. Thus every film is a wager, a gamble: how to get the spectator to accept this distinctive case as if it were something perfectly natural? How to make him accept situations that are simultaneously extremely seamy and extremely pure? That's the question I asked myself with respect to *Jules and Jim*.

And how do you reconcile these extremes: the exceptional and the natural, the scabrous and the pure, within the same film?

Cinema, like life, feeds off its contradictions. I always try to approach my characters through the inclusion of small, contradictory observations. That's a strategy that is dear to Renoir, and it's a method of creation that really suits me. Because, you know, when one has an idea for a film, one can envisage a scene, for example, or a particular moment very precisely. For *The 400 Blows*, I could see perfectly in my head the scene in which the boy makes people believe his mother is dead. After that, there are many other moments in which a character lives and moves. And it's necessary to continue to discover him, even if he eludes you somewhat in those moments.

That's when I use a trick. To shed light on moments that I no longer see very well, I rely on something that everyone knows: I attempt to introduce something old from French culture into the film, little observations that I borrow from Perrault or La Fontaine because everyone knows them;[14] the character is thus enriched from contact with something universal.

In *Jules and Jim*, for example, when we were writing the dialogue with Gruault, there was a moment when one of the characters had to describe Catherine, how she became who she was. Gruault wrote, "I find her less Shakespeare, more Goethe." I, however, was acutely aware that the spectator might find such a statement pretentious, and so, during shooting, I amended the sentence to read, "I find her less like a grasshopper, more like an ant." I think this makes the meaning clearer for everyone. These are the kinds of discrepancies that I find interesting, and which I seek to translate into simple, common language.

Jules and Jim is an immoral film. Why?

Even though it transgresses against prevailing morality, it is not devoid of morality. I greatly liked Vadim's first film, . . . *And God Created Woman*,[15] which was an amoral film, destroying morality without substituting anything in its place. *Jules and Jim*, because the characters are all very pure, but, above all, dissatisfied, because they are always seeking ways of being reconciled to their own nature, Catherine especially, is a moral film. Catherine's morality is different, but it is very firm.

Nevertheless, the film displeased certain viewers.

Many rejected the character of Catherine. She is annoying. I recaptured them with one scene, because she breaks down weeping in Jules's room. Then I lost them again. Catherine is much more admired than loved. In order to make her loved, I would have needed to be dishonest, popularity-seeking. I hated *The Misfits* in this regard.[16] They contrived to have a woman moved by animals so that spectators would accept the scene in which she sleeps with some guy. For me, that amounts to an attempt to rehabilitate a "tart." One has to think of the spectators when one writes a screenplay. It is not a question of making concessions, but of knowing how to impose a particular idea, otherwise it's like a speech no one is listening to.

In a novel, one has more scope.

With cinema, one is rather cramped—you have to move along quickly. I had to cut some scenes because they were not embedded in others.

One morning the little girl was coming to join Jim and Catherine in their bed, to join them for breakfast. This scene would have outraged everyone.

Jules's daughter in the same bed as Jim and Catherine! If I had had half an hour more, I could have made the life of my characters up to that point acceptable.

Is it true to say that Jules and Jim *is a film that asserts a claim? In this case, for happiness against loneliness, for friendship against violence and war?*

Yes, and that's why I think that all films are commitments. They resemble their authors. One cannot disguise oneself—even when one is making a spy film. That's why the problem of choosing a subject is a false problem.

I would like my film to mark the end of an epoch. It's the end of people like Jules and Jim, the end of intellectuals. Books are being burnt. I am suspicious of films in which something is added, a little "trick," to show that one is nevertheless "involved" despite appearances: a small allusion to the war in Algeria. No . . . I was well acquainted with Max Ophüls, who left Germany the day after the burning of the Reichstag. He said to himself, "I have nothing more to do here," and left. He often told me that. I have always associated Oscar Werner a bit with Max Ophüls.

Do you think that the expression "modern film, modern cinema," has any meaning? Is it a concept that corresponds to anything, and if so, to what?

It surely corresponds to something, but this notion of modernity doesn't affect me at all.

Have you asked yourself whether what you are doing is modern or not?

I think that temperamentally I am not modern. I am more interested in the notion of recovering the ideas of the past—I would take greater pride in being able to make *Picratt, roi du rail* [*Fuzzy, King of the Railway*] than *Marienbad*.[17] I get the impression that there were a number of years in which cinema was incredibly alive and spontaneous: I'm chasing that, to recapture a lost secret, rather than heading toward future innovations.

1966

It is always from actual life or books that I draw powerful material; my imagination is ineffectual in suggesting it to me. I love everything that confuses the issue, which sows doubts; my bedside book is André Gide's *La Séquestrée de Poitiers*;[18] I only like things that are unanticipated, and hence prove nothing. I like anything that demonstrates the vulnerability of man.

In *Jules and Jim*, what engaged me was the idea that I was going to take a situation that was extremely original and provocative, and then make it plausible and acceptable for everybody, and that within a framework that was already well known—that of pre-War MGM films, in which couples are shown aging peacefully in country houses, in the company of their children, who are growing up. It's simply that, in this case, instead of one husband, there are two of them; that might not seem like anything, but in actuality it is an enormous change, and that is what I found pleasing. I don't like things to be completely original, entirely offbeat: I find that it is necessary to have strong links with tradition, with what exists already.

When I was a critic, I was fairly vicious in attacking the adaptations by Aurenche and Bost because their adaptations consisted of taking a novel like *Le Diable au corps*, or like *Le Rouge et le Noir*,[19] and saying, "Well, then. We have an hour and a half, so we will divide it into twenty-eight scenes," and then they make twenty-eight scenes. That has the effect of transforming the novel into something resembling a theatrical play. When the main focus is on the facts, then it's very good. But when it is on the prose or on the poetry, as in *Le Diable au corps*, which is full of extraordinary images, I found that it distorted the book. The approach that seems good, to me, which had already been tried out by Melville and Cocteau in *Les Enfants terribles*,[20] consisted instead of a kind of filmed reading, involving an alternation between scenes that one could effectively construct as scenes, acted out with dialogue, and passages that were simply narrative, designed to convey a commentary. After having used freeze-frames in *Jules and Jim*, I noticed that it was a device I was allowing myself to use a lot, and that it was running the risk of becoming a mannerism. I saw it again, in a number of films, and I decided to stop using freeze-frames for the sake of achieving visual effects. I use them only to achieve a dramatic end, and I think that freeze-frames are only interesting when they are invisible to the spectator. It takes around eight images for one to register a shot in cinema. A shot of fewer than eight images is scarcely visible, with the possible exception of a close-up of a face. What I do now, which I have done in *The Soft Skin*, is to arrest the image, but only during eight images, instead of thirty to thirty-five images, as in *Jules and Jim*. These days, I am interested in special effects that are invisible.

1975

I confess that I would be very embarrassed to have made *Jules and Jim* today—because I would be troubled by the similarities that have eventuated between its story, in which a woman is queen, and the actions promoted at present by the MLF [Women's Liberation Movement]. You know, I launched into making *Jules and Jim* with a certain degree of innocence. And, afterwards, I spent years, ten years even, coming to understand what it meant: that has only become clear to me in the last two years.

I understood much later that the reason I had wanted to make *Jules and Jim* so badly was that the subject had very deeply hidden roots in my own childhood, and that doing so allowed me to make a complete break with all the things that I had resented as abnormal around me, during the time of the Occupation when I was living in Pigalle, in the middle of trafficking, the black market, the settling of scores involving passionate relationships, adultery, and everything that was linked to the Collaboration, the Resistance, and the Purification...

What made Henri-Pierre Roché's *Jules et Jim* my bedside book was not only its style, remarkably refined in its simplicity—"an airy, tight style," as Cocteau described it—but also the message of tolerance that was "immanent" behind each line. Through her whole life, the heroine of the film, Catherine, would love two men, and these two men would succeed in remaining friends, without ceasing to love her. One of these men is German, Jules; the other, Jim, is French. In the chalet where they live together, we also find Sabine, the only daughter of Jules and Catherine. Because of that, the whole film bathes in an atmosphere that is familial and gentle—and that's what pleased me: "to make a subversive film that was completely gentle," without assaulting the audience, but, to the contrary, enveloping it in tenderness, forcing it to accept on the screen situations that it would have condemned in real life... It's indeed true that the film was very well received in cinemas around the whole world, but also that the day it was broadcast on Belgian television it provoked a scandal, with hundreds of protest letters!... That meant that Belgian television had to cancel the broadcast of *À bout de souffle*, scheduled for the week following! This film, which was acceptable in the eyes of an audience who had to go out to see it, became scandalous when it was shown in living rooms, in a family context.

Jules and Jim is a dream; in real life, we all suffer from the provisional aspect of our love relationships, but this film allows us to dream precisely of loves that would be definitive. There you have it.

1978

When you are working on a screenplay, do you begin with a consideration, an analysis of the ideas inherent in the subject, or do you preoccupy yourself with the story and characters through which you express your opinions?

With the story and the characters. I am never aware of the larger significance of a subject when I select it, or when I treat it. Usually, I understand it long after I have made the film. I had a very difficult relationship with my family, with my mother in particular, and several years ago I came to understand that I had made *Jules and Jim* to please her, and to gain her approval. Love played a big role in her life, and given that *The 400 Blows* had been like a stab in the back for her, I made *Jules and Jim* in the hope of showing her that I understood her.

Notes

1. *Naked Dawn* (Edgar G. Ulmer, 1955) is a film about a trio involving a farmer, his wife, and a stranger who undertake a train robbery, with the wife then plotting to murder her husband so that she can run off with the stranger.
2. Henri-Pierre Roché, *Deux Anglaises et le continent* (1956).
3. Truffaut is referring to the heroine in *Gone with the Wind* (Victor Fleming, George Cukor, Sam Wood, 1939), a beautiful, but spoiled and selfish, southern belle, played by Vivien Leigh.
4. Michèle Morgan, born Simone Renée Roussel (1920–), was a French actress famous for her roles in such films as *Le Quai des brumes*, *Remorques*, and *La Symphonie pastorale*; André Bourvil, born André Robert Raimbourg (1917–1970), was a French actor and singer best known for his roles in comedy films. He acted with Michèle Morgan in *Fortunat* (Fortunate, Alex Joffé, 1960), which tells the story of a lazy poacher who helps an elegant woman and her children escape from the Nazis during the Occupation.
5. *North by Northwest* (*La Mort aux trousses*, Alfred Hitchcock, 1959).
6. *Moderato cantabile* (*Seven Days . . . Seven Nights*, Peter Brook, 1960), based on a novel of the same name by Marguerite Duras.
7. Georges Brassens was a French singer-songwriter, mainly active between 1951 and 1981.
8. Jacques Prévert (1900–1977), a French poet and screenwriter, many of whose poems were set to music and sung by prominent French vocalists such as Yves Montand and Édith Piaf.
9. Juliette Gréco (1927–), a popular singer of *chansons* known as "the Muse of existentialism." The song cannot be identified with certainty, but may refer to "Imbeciles."
10. *Touch of Evil* (*La Soif du mal*, Orson Welles, 1958).
11. *Les Lions sont lâchés* (*The Lions Are Loose*, Henri Verneuil, 1961); *Le Président* (*The President*, Henri Verneuil, 1961).
12. *Night and Fog* (*Nuit et Brouillard*, Alain Resnais, 1955).
13. *Europe '51* (Roberto Rossellini, 1952).
14. For Perrault, see chapter 6, note 8; Jean de La Fontaine (1621–1695) was a poet, best known for his *Fables*, issued in several volumes between 1668 and 1694.
15. *. . . And God Created Woman* (*Et Dieu . . . créa la femme*, Roger Vadim, 1956), the film that launched Brigitte Bardot, making her an overnight sensation.
16. *The Misfits* (*Les Misfits*, John Huston, 1961), starring Marilyn Monroe, Clark Gable, and Montgomery Clift.
17. *Picratt, roi du rail* [*Fuzzy, King of the Railway*] was a silent short film, starring Al St. John, alias "Fuzzy" (Picratt in French), made by Mack Sennett, a burlesque comedian known as "The King of Comedy," in 1919. Almost all of Al St. John's films are now lost. For his part, Sennett had been instrumental, through his Keystone Studios, in establishing silent-film

comedy, introducing stars like Fatty Arbuckle, Mack Swain, and Charlie Chaplin. "Marienbad" refers to *L'Année dernière à Marienbad* by Alain Resnais (1961).

18. *La Séquestrée de Poitiers* (1930) is a crime story, based on real events, telling the story of Mélanie Bastian, who lived as a recluse for 24 years, forced by her mother to live naked among the filth of a room that was never cleaned, with the windows boarded up. When she was discovered and liberated by police, she weighed a mere 25 kg (Jean-Marie Augustin, *L'Histoire véridique de la séquestrée de Poitiers* [Paris: Fayard, 2001]).

19. *Le Diable au corps* (*The Devil in the Flesh*, 1923) is a novel by Raymond Radiquet telling the story of a married woman who has an affair with a 16-year-old boy while her fiancé is away fighting at the front during the First World War; *Le Rouge et le Noir* (*The Red and the Black*, 1830) is a novel by Stendhal tracing the attempt of a young man from the provinces to rise in society, but who, undone by passion, commits a crime and ends up being guillotined.

20. *Les Enfants terribles* (Jean-Pierre Melville, 1950), based on the novel of the same name by Jean Cocteau.

CHAPTER 8

1962: *ANTOINE AND COLETTE*

> Marie-France Pisier had the casualness of girls born after the war who would enter places without saying either "Monsieur" or "Madame." She displayed less humility than her elders, but more courage, more bravery, and expected more from life. Marie-France Pisier was very interesting; her voice irritated many people, but I liked her because she seemed very real. She is one of the most real characters that I have ever put on a screen.
>
> *Interview with Agathe Godard,* Vingt Ans, *January 3, 1973*

This sketch gave me another occasion to work with Jean-Pierre Léaud, and to make a project that I had stupidly, and regretfully, abandoned. I had thought at one point of making a sequel to *The 400 Blows*, depicting the same character a little bit further on in his life, no longer an adolescent, but engaged in his professional activities, but I didn't do it, for a stupid reason—because *The 400 Blows* had been so successful, I was scared to look as if I was profiting from its success. Well, I have since learnt that one should never give up an idea for such superficial and secondary reasons as those that relate to appearances. One should question one's choices and work, but never one's vocation. Also, I had imagined I would present the same character, Antoine Doinel, by following him in the same way as in *The 400 Blows*, that is, in a documentary fashion, while he is experiencing his first romance, his first love story.

This film was really very improvised. We only had the framework for it. I knew that I would make him a music lover who would meet a girl who was also a music lover, and that he would share a failed love affair with her.

Within this sketchy outline, each day I would invent things with Jean-Pierre Léaud, Marie-France Pisier, and two actors that I like a lot: Rosy Varte and François Darbon. This time I showed a different family, a family that was functional. That's probably why I like this film more: because it is lighter in tone, while at the same time being simpler, closer to real life, I believe. I made it in a moment of carefreeness: *Jules and Jim* had just come out and had been very well received, which meant that I plunged into work on *Love at Twenty* in a very cheerful mood.

For the encounter in *Love at Twenty* of my two young protagonists at the concert in the Salle Pleyel, I wanted to create a scene that would progress at the same pace as the music. Because of this, I did not know at what point the audience was going to notice what I wanted them to notice, namely, the presence of the young woman.

To achieve a certain degree of intensity, we used tighter and tighter frames. This scene is fairly long; for me, the main interest is the counterpoint between the music and the action. That is linked to my own memories, because earlier in my life, my aunt was a violinist, and I went to listen to a concert in which she was playing.

It is a scene that could have been very salacious, but it works well owing to the innocence of Jean-Pierre Léaud and the youthfulness of his character. In the end, there is nothing seamy—but put in two different actors and all that could have come across as much more lascivious. At the end of the day, a director's struggle to handle time is something very personal, something that continues throughout his life. I find it encouraging that Hitchcock, in his fifty-second film, should still have problems with duration, which is a significant phenomenon in cinema.

1974

Love at Twenty was a gamble: when they asked me to contribute a sketch, I had no ideas for how to illustrate this theme. Then I said to myself that I would use Jean-Pierre again, who was a bit lost in his life at that moment. After *The 400 Blows*, he had nevertheless made one or two films: an appearance in *The Testament of Orpheus*, and then a film with Duvivier, *Boulevard*.[1] Basically, however, he had lost interest in cinema. With this little sketch, I thought

I could make him "come back!" At the same time, shooting it turned out to be a very pleasant experience, and that made me regret not having made it into a full-length feature film. I could certainly have filled up an hour and a half on love at twenty! Anyhow, we improvised a lot, but there was a basic situation in the film, and the improvisation worked very well in the context of this situation. That's what gave rise to *Stolen Kisses* several years later.

NOTE

1. *Testament of Orpheus* (*Le testament d'Orphée, ou ne me demandez pas pourquoi*, Jean Cocteau, 1960); *Boulevard* (Jean Duvivier, 1960), which presents the story of a 16-year-old living in a block of flats in Pigalle.

CHAPTER 9

1964: *THE SOFT SKIN*

> I am more interested in Jaccoud than Rosenberg. I have never been able to empathize with the unhappiness of an innocent person. I need a minimum element of guilt. My characters are excluded from society and I want to show how they can occupy a place in it, in spite of everything.
>
> Interview with Raymond Bellour and Jean Michaud, Les Lettres françaises, *no. 1000, October 24–30, 1973*

It has been said that had you been asked to write a critique of The Soft Skin *several years ago, you would have torn it to pieces.*

That's wrong. I would have loved this film much more than I like it as its director. As it is, I see all its faults, everything that doesn't hold together. Previously, I wasn't in the habit of looking closely at details. I liked a film or I didn't like it, and I would have liked this one because it is packed with subject matter that I love, things that I would have liked to see at the cinema. For example, I wanted to see a man and a woman in an elevator—how they look at one another, how they fantasize, how they are curious about one another. I don't know if I have done a good job of depicting it, but of course I like it, since I filmed the episode. I have made a film about adultery, but by attempting to shoot scenes that are not usually shown—the coincidences, the ways in which one is caught in the middle. What I liked was to start a scene with a cliché, and then transcend it.

It is not necessary to eschew categories. *The Soft Skin* belongs to the category of French psychological films dealing with adultery. In this sort of film, the mistress displays her breasts, and the woman is Edwige Feuillère.[1] Here, Françoise Dorléac says, "I like to make love a lot, but I can do very nicely without it." She is in no way a teaser. And the wife is violent, beautiful, and attractive. In my opinion, she lacks a sufficient sense of humor, and is not smart.

After Jules and Jim, *you were working on the adaptation of a novel by Ray Bradbury for which you wrote the screenplay with Jean-Louis Richard:* Fahrenheit 451. *Why have you given up this project for the time being?*

It failed because of a moment of excessive optimism. After *Jules and Jim* came out, I went to America to promote the film, and I bought the rights to *Fahrenheit 451*. Bradbury was very kind. The screenplay required an enormous amount of work—it has been through three successive versions. In France, no producer, coproducer, or distributor has dared to take on the venture. It is an expensive film (being in color) that I can't produce all by myself. I am thinking of filming it in America next year. Lewis Allen, the producer of Peter Brooks's last film, has bought back the rights and the screenplay in order to make the film with me. Owing to this last-minute "rescue," I have been able to shoot *The Soft Skin* while waiting to do *Fahrenheit*.

Have you been thinking about it for a long time?

Yes, I had most of the subject in my head. *The Soft Skin* is part of a glimpse I had caught several years earlier, or at least imagined, of a couple in a taxi. It was around 7;30 p.m. when I saw them. They had to go home for dinner; they weren't married, or if they were married, they were each married to someone else, with children, and it was a terribly carnal kiss they were having in this taxi, in a big city.

When you have an image like this that sticks in your head, you say to yourself, "Even a subject like adultery has never been dealt with properly," and you have a feeling that you are going to say a whole lot of new things. It took off from there. In the film, this scene does not actually exist, because the heroine, an air hostess, is unmarried, and has no child. But the film derived from it, from an image, from an image and a sound, because I was imagining that during the kiss one could hear their teeth colliding . . .

Are you putting adultery on trial here?

I don't put anything on trial. I portray a rather weak masculine character. I think that he is very good at what he does, in his profession: so he is able to talk about Balzac, but he is clumsy, crippled, in other respects...

Are there any particular things you were wanting to say?

In general, I only become aware of them afterwards. I became aware that I was rejecting screenplays every time they showed a strong character, and that they attracted me when they involved a fragile character. That must come from the influence of Jean Renoir, and it's what has prevented me from making films according to American criteria.

What do you mean by "fragile characters"?

They are characters who are initially antisocial. The job of the film is to make them register in people's awareness as a result of the way it is shot. One has to line up the evidence, convince people—it's a task that depends upon arousing sympathy.

I have noticed one peculiar thing that separates me a bit from the audience, which differentiates me from the average spectator—the fact that I identify with weak characters, and never with strong ones. That explains why I didn't like the films with Errol Flynn,[2] or the Tarzan films.[3] I couldn't identify myself with strength. I would go even further: if there is a character who toes the line, who is goodness personified, and another who disobeys the rules and represents badness, I even identify with the character who represents badness. I can't tell you where that comes from. I would need to psychoanalyze myself, but...

The average member of the audience identifies with a representation of himself, but ameliorated; in other words, a spectator identifies with Cary Grant experiencing difficulties because Cary Grant is him, only a better version, James Stewart is him, only better. But the spectator doesn't identify with a character who is worse than he himself is. The audience won't be able to identify with a beggar, with a man who is too much of a hypocrite, with a man who is too morally blackened. That's the impediment. If I try now to work out the reasons for my reaction... it's because I used to go to the cinema on the sly; I would watch films in a state of guilt, and it's perhaps that fact that encouraged this identification with guiltiness. Furthermore, it's just the same with books.

I hated Jules Verne, and I hated children's books. When I read *Madame Bovary*, I identified completely with Emma.[4] She was a woman who had problems in her love life. It was perhaps too soon for me to read it, but even so, it interested me. I need to feel some sense of identification, to say to myself, "I've been in situations like that, or I could find myself in situations like that." I need this as a criterion in order to work. I work a lot with real material, but it is 20 percent autobiographical, 20 percent drawn from newspapers, 20 percent taken from the lives of people around me whom I know, and 40 percent pure fiction. The part reserved for pure fiction is relatively slender because I prefer to start with facts that are reported in newspapers, or which have actually happened to me, or which are reported to me by people I know. I like to see things verified in real life.

Do you like your characters?

I have lived with them for a long time. Obviously, they are flawed, but I am moved by the unhappiness of this man. I would like to make him be loved. I would not want to make films in which I could not get the audience to sympathize with a character, because it would be impossible for me to live for several months with characters over whom I would exercise too much control. What fascinates me in newspaper reports are people's weaknesses. Each week I read *Détective*, which amounts to an anthology of human weaknesses.[5]

Did you find the subject for The Soft Skin *in* Détective?

The screenplay was developed around several different factors relating to love stories that turned out badly, from which I compiled a single story.

The film is meant to seem like the kind of local news that everyone reads about in the press. Local news is both disturbing and fascinating because it contains a mixture of fact and fiction.

Above all, my aim was to make a film about adultery inspired by the personality of Pierre Jaccoud—based on the impression of him we gain from accounts of his trial.[6]

Why Jaccoud?

I was very moved by him, and I thought that through him I could show a man who displayed strength in his social life, but was weak as far as love was concerned, and who, at forty-four, found himself facing an acute dilemma, which left him more and more caught in a web. *The Soft Skin* is the portrait of such a man.

What is he, exactly?

A grand bourgeois, but with something juvenile about him, which creates an impression of innocence and extreme clumsiness when he attempts to be furtive. He experiences something that has happened to others, but which has never happened to him before. From that moment on, everything he does is the worst thing he could do. He leaves for a trip, taking her with him, then puts her in a second-class hotel; he commits nothing but blunders, that's the idea. The film was criticized for something that I was deliberately trying to achieve. He doesn't say to Ceccaldi, "I've brought a girl with me." Like Jaccoud, Desailly is the kind of man who wouldn't be able to bring himself to do that.

When Jaccoud went to a restaurant with Linda Baud, he would leave her in the car, enter into the restaurant, and start by looking to see if there was anyone he knew. If there was someone, he would get back into the car, go to a second restaurant, where he would choose a table at the back, and make her sit facing the door. Each time the door opened, he would ask her, "Who is it?" I liked this character, as someone who is emotional and a man who, each time he is presented with a problem, chooses the worst solution. He is a blunderer. The key to the film is probably that men who have a fascinating job are constantly thinking about it, whereas women only think about love. Love is the preoccupation of women.

And you make films about love . . .

Yes, other subjects don't interest me. Every case deserves a film, and I could shoot the same scene twenty-five times with different characters.

Films about love—I have about thirty of them in my head, and I shall make these thirty films in the next forty-five years.

Love is the subject of subjects. It occupies such a huge place in life—in apartments, in streets, in offices, in newspapers, in politics, in war, in factories, in success, in failure, in carnivals, in squares, in schools, in barracks, and also in airplanes—that even if one were to concede to me that nine out of ten films are films about love, I would reply that that doesn't go far enough. A sixty-year-old man and a girl of fifteen, that's *Lolita*. A woman of forty and a youth of twenty, that's *Adolphe*. A boy and a girl of sixteen, that's *Romeo and Juliet*. A woman in the provinces gets bored, that's *Madame Bovary*. The woman's husband is a brute, that's *Le Lys dans la vallée*. She is too flirtatious, that's *Wicked Duchess*. She takes money out of men, that's *Nana*. Her husband goes to war and she falls in love with a youth, that's *Devil in the Flesh*. She dies horribly, that's *Madame Bovary* again.[7] In life, certain men succeed, others don't. Certain ones are more handsome than others, or richer, or more intelligent. Men are equal, for sure, but especially before God! With love, there are no paupers. This great moving force in human life is also our unique common denominator.

> *There is a certain rigor, a classicism, a desire to show weak, flawed beings who seem to contrast with* Jules and Jim, *a film in which the characters are rather "privileged."*

"Privileged" is the word. They live outside of society. They are bohemians, romantics. Those of *The Soft Skin* are more ordinary, real, not romantics.

It's less original than *Jules and Jim*, the story is more traditional; it is closer to *The 400 Blows* in the sense that Audiberti, who didn't like *The 400 Blows*, said that it could be out of Simenon.[8] *The Soft Skin* is a story about adultery, very realistic, that gives love antipoetic images, the inverse in certain respects to what is in *Jules and Jim*, being a polemical response to the earlier film. The most interesting aspect of it is the character of the betrayed woman: people usually turn her into an unlikeable character, but here she is treated in the most unconventional way possible—she is the equivalent of Jules in *Jules and Jim*.

> *Why does he want to leave her?*

I wanted that to be the real question, the mystery at the heart of the film—something that weighs heavily on the three characters. Inexorably. But, three equal characters.

I thus wanted to be very fair, very truthful, in retelling this story, this case.

For the first time, I abandoned the wide screen. It's a film that is divided into many fragments, like those of Becker,[9] or *Muriel*.[10] A film made with a scalpel.

> *Why did you make Françoise Dorléac an air hostess?*

I preferred to have a younger woman—a love story involving a secretary of Linda Baud's age seemed too difficult. I wanted to film an affair that began on a journey, with scenes in a plane—one never sees airplanes during flight at the cinema. The rest is a succession of coincidences, of seized opportunities—a Brazilian company gave me assistance.

The majority of scenes in the film are shot in interiors. Did you work in a studio?

Not at any time. All the settings in the film are natural. Only, every scene in the screenplay required a very precise setting. It was necessary to find them all. For example, a whole part of the film takes place in a hotel in Lisbon. One sees the hall, the elevator, the corridor, the rooms. We shot the rooms at Orly, the hall in Lisbon, and the elevator at the Lutétia Hotel in Paris.

Fortunately, sometimes things happened more conveniently. During the filming, Jean Desailly continued to act at the Odéon in the evenings. In the film, he is the editor of a major literary journal. We simply used the administrative office of the Théâtre de France. He had a dressing room on the floor below. He didn't lose a single minute.

I also made use of my own apartment. This meant we lacked a bit of space, for sure, but our film crew was reduced to the minimum.

What was difficult about the film?

Above everything else, the need to avoid anything "sordid." To achieve this, I conjured up a dreamlike atmosphere for the scenes between the lovers—which corresponds to the state of being in love—and presented the marital scenes with an almost excessive violence capable of imparting a tragic dimension to the mundane.

Such as at the end of the film?

Yes. It was inspired by a local event, which I read about in a newspaper. In the reported event it was even more cruel: having discovered that he had cheated on her, the wife ordered her husband to clear out his things, among which there was a shotgun she had given him. He replied, "I don't need your presents," and it was with that gun that she killed him!

In reality, there were several possible endings for the film. A novelist would undoubtedly have finished it in the way things tend to happen in ordinary life, without any violent drama. His wife doesn't want him any more; his young mistress leaves him for a more dependable man, less disabled, also younger . . .

You didn't think of stopping at the moment she says to his lover, when learning that he is going to get a divorce, "You have made a stupid mistake"?

No, I imagined two endings: to have the legal couple reconcile, which struck me as a hypocritical solution, especially given that my depiction of the drama was pessimistic; or rather to form a new couple, as an act of rebellion, which seemed an improper solution, to me, because it would initiate a new tragedy. In any case, I felt with certitude that it was necessary to take the entanglement to an extreme point, and that death should be the outcome. What matters here is the documentary-style meticulousness of every detail and a certain way of exploring the issue in depth so as to remain close to reality, while escaping from convention.

There is no humor at all in The Soft Skin.

It is the subject that always determines the tone. Here it involves terrible things. It is absolutely impossible to have digressions. The character played by Jean Desailly finds himself cornered, the trap closes on him. No smile is possible.

Desailly's role is an unrewarding one. On the other hand, I was fairly critical of this character. I didn't want to be vicious, but somewhat critical, with the result that the film is full of annotations, mockeries. There is a left-wing Italian filmmaker, De Bosi,[11] who has said that it is a film characterized by black humor. That is quite true.

With The Soft Skin, *was there any way in which the work developed?*

Yes, because the unit in my films up to this point, including *Jules and Jim*, had been the scene. I could control each scene fairly well, but to tell the truth, I also had very few shots in each scene, and the work consisted of avoiding disharmony between one scene and the next.

Now, in *The Soft Skin*, the unit is really the shot, and therefore the film as a whole. For the first time I left scenes unfinished in the evening, which had never happened with me before. I spoke about it with Godard, who told me that it had never happened with him either, and that he couldn't bear to do it. Ah well, with *The Soft Skin* that happened to me frequently, and I wasn't too concerned about it. I even had scenes that took four days to shoot, interspersed across the whole film. I would have never dared to attempt that previously. With this film, the editing work was very interesting because everything depends on glances; there was really a lot of material to edit, and I discovered interesting principles of montage as I went along.

If you want to engage interest, it's necessary that the first glance of someone toward something should be fairly long, the glances that follow can be fairly short, the length of the first one being meant to alert the viewer, to put the emphasis on what the character is going to look at. One might think that it is the shot of the thing being looked at that should last the longest, but that is not so: it is the gaze that precedes it.

This was also the first time that I was greatly interested in what is "off"; often it is fairly mechanical in films, and one hardly cares about it. The usual way of approaching it is to show the people who are speaking, then the people who are responding. There is another, more subtle way, one that consists of establishing a kind of balance, and of placing replies "off," but often it happens haphazardly, whereas in actuality, if one thinks about it, a sentence uttered "off" creates a feeling that is complementary to the meaning of the sentence, and that has to be exploited dramatically. This was the first time that I had taken any care with that, and that I had a good sense, in each scene, of which is the character that one should see only when he is speaking, and which is the one that one should also see while he is listening.

Were you seeking to obtain certain effects specifically through the montage? Does the montage play a dramatic role in your films? Are there any situations that end up being transformed by the montage?

Yes, ones that are dramatized by expanding the length they take, by insisting on them—it's an interesting thing to do, and I attempted it for the first time. I took great delight in revealing the cheating. I have a scene in an elevator in *The Soft Skin*. It takes place between Jean Desailly and Françoise Dorléac who are looking at one another while the cage ascends to the eighth floor. The actual duration of the elevator's movement is fifteen seconds in real time; however, filmed in around twenty-five shots, the scene, in the film, lasts five times as long, about sixty-five seconds.

We now arrive at the eighth floor, Françoise Dorléac gets out of the elevator and we stay with Jean Desailly, who presses the button to go back down. This time, the same trajectory lasts only fifteen seconds, because it is filmed in a single shot, and therefore in real time.

Here is proof that cinema can be used to play around with time exactly as one wishes, using expansion or contraction.

Your taste for realism is going to shock people?

Ah well, no, because it's realistic. In life there are moments in which things are expanded, in which one experiences a feeling of time being stretched out, for example, when one falls in love. If one films actions in real time, they have no cinematic interest.

From the moment one makes use of fragments of images, and fragments of space, well then, notions of time and space are inevitably overturned, equally.

1966

The Soft Skin. I suffered afterwards, and even during the shooting, from the unattractive aspect of the film. It was the least sentimental of all my films, but it was also the driest. There is a kind of autopsy, of aridity, and I suffered from it during the shooting because it prevented me from being warm and from introducing warmth into the film.

It had to be cold. And once one has started something, you have to stay with it. I believe that the worst thing that can happen to a filmmaker is to change the concept, change the approach. That's unforgiveable. So, right to the end, I pursued my idea, but I suffered from it because the characters on the screen are ones that I don't like very much, and there was nothing else I could do about it.

Because you think that it is necessary to like the characters you create?

Yes, you have to like the actor a lot, and like the characters a lot. That helps in one's work—otherwise it's demoralizing. There is something juvenile about working on cinema, like something that you get obsessed with as a child for two, three years, and then reach a moment when you feel you've had enough of it; you need other more powerful underlying motives, otherwise one has the impression of engaging in a kid's game, of running around in a playground, of accumulating one shot after another. There is a side to it that is not very serious, especially if one doesn't like to be in charge, if one doesn't like to control grown-ups. Then, at a certain moment, one says to oneself, "What good is this serving?" You are tempted to give it up. There is something about the exercise of this craft that is lacking in maturity, at least which is a bit incompatible with maturity.

1967

What I wanted to do in *The Soft Skin* was to depict an anachronistic character. In fact, all the time I was thinking, "I have to show a character from the 19th century, and what is furthest from a character from the 19th century is an air hostess, since she is on a Boeing. It's this contrast that pleased me. That's why, when he is talking about Balzac in the restaurant, he speaks of him in the present tense. He says, "We are in Tours, Honoré does this . . ." I was inspired by a man that one sees from time to time on television, who is fascinating and totally gripped by his passion, Henri Guillemin, who has written books on

Benjamin Constant, and Rousseau—I was inspired by a man who felt more at ease with dead people and former glories than with the world of today.

Neither Jean-Louis Richard nor I could decide whether to choose between the story of a madman and that of a man like you, me, and other people. When you are writing a screenplay, one must never vacillate over an important point without finding a solution for it. We never resolved this temptation. We should have chosen one or the other. For example, at one point I wanted to make him faint in Reims, when he saw the girl on the other side of the plate glass window—Ceccaldi drinks his half pint, and then he would have got up and fallen over backwards. Then I said to myself, "That is going to turn it into a film about a madman, people are going to think that it is the story of someone who is mentally ill." So we abandoned the idea, which ended up in *Fahrenheit*. The story of a madman could have been fascinating; the story of a normal man was a different film. In the end, we made neither one nor the other.

1967

The other fault concerns the ending, even though it derives from a real event, because spectators are surprised by it, and, when all is said and done, they have every reason to be. In the course of the story, there should have been elements that tie it to ordinary, everyday events . . .

But don't you think that the beauty of the ending is in its abruptness?

Yes, but if someone who is not an idiot tells you that he has been led astray, it is necessary to take that into account, and say to yourself that you have been mistaken. I have no problem with the fact that people were surprised to see a shotgun when they were expecting a revolver, but so much the worse for them—I even made the film because of that shotgun: I wouldn't have bothered to shoot it had it merely involved a revolver. But the fact that she shoots at her husband shouldn't have surprised anyone: people ought to say, "Yes, it was inevitable, predictable that they would end up there." Along the way, certain elements that I shot, moreover, but then cut, would have been able to prepare them. At one moment, Desailly was reading about the explosion of a Boeing, in a newspaper, and one could infer from this that he was thinking about Françoise Dorléac. The film begins with a suicide in the Metro, a line remains blocked, and Desailly returns to his home saying, "I was delayed by a suicide in the Metro." An allusion to this remains in the dialogue. Indirectly, everything was designed to point to the ending, but I had to shorten the film.

In fact, I perhaps should have started with the ending, with Nelly Benedetti arriving at the restaurant, firing the gun, et cetera. In a newspaper, an item catches your attention because the first thing you read is the title: "He Fired a Gun at the Wedding," and then the text leads you gradually to this end point, explains why it happened, you become interested, you ask yourself how such things happen. In *The Soft Skin*, spectators don't know anything at the beginning, and they have an impression, at the end, that the dénouement is out of kilter with the rest of the story. An American film certainly would have begun with the ending.

1968

I made one film that didn't meet with the approval that I was hoping it would receive—*The Soft Skin*. But even if I were sentenced to twenty years of hard labor, to keep on remaking *The Soft Skin*, that would not displease me. One year, I would make it with Michel Bouquet, another year with Charles Denner . . . Look, there's a scene that I never succeeded in shooting, either in *The Soft Skin* or in *Shoot the Piano Player* . . . I would still attempt this scene, later . . .

What scene is that?

In *Shoot the Piano Player*, Marie Dubois asked Charles Aznavour to go and buy her a pair of stockings. Then, when we watched Aznavour going to buy the stocking, it completely misfired. I had to cut the scene. We saw him arriving at a Monoprix, there were saleswomen, and to see this man buying stockings was making them smile, and that was it. It was a scene about nothing at all, but it was difficult to do. In any case, it was a failure. When I made *The Soft Skin*, I said to myself, "This time, it has to succeed." And so, Françoise Dorléac says to Jean Desailly, "Don't forget to bring me back a pair of stockings." This time, instead of having the scene occur in the morning, I placed it at night, and I added the idea that, when he approaches the store, it is on the point of closing. The saleswoman is pulling across the grill, and we see that she lets him go in just the same. Then it was the same scene. I filmed two saleswomen who were exchanging smiles, Desailly disconcerted at having to buy a pair of stockings. And then . . .

And then?

Yet again, it was bad. I cut it. But the next time, I got it right. It's a matter of luck.

1968

I knew fairly quickly that *The Soft Skin* was going to be a flop—as soon as I had finished the sound mixing. I looked at the film very clinically, as if someone else had made it, and I saw that it was depressing, that it was a film that "descends." I then understood that it would be disagreeable to watch.

A film that "descends" is rarely liked: I mean a film that presents a situation that deteriorates—it is the opposite of the idea of exaltation that one is looking for in an entertainment. It's a law that is seldom proven wrong.

Did you find its failure very demoralizing?

No. To the contrary, it is rather stimulating. I have experienced more periods of emptiness and sadness after successes than after failures. I had violent bouts of depression after *The 400 Blows* and *Jules and Jim*, for example.

Notes

1. Edwige Feuillère (1907–1998) considered one of the most important French actresses of her generation, scored major successes in roles such as Evelyn Morin in *There's No Tomorrow* (*Sans lendemain*, Max Ophüls, 1939), Sophie in *Sarajevo* (*De Mayerling à Sarajevo*, Max Ophüls, 1940), and the Queen in *The Eagle with Two Heads* (*L'Aigle à deux têtes*, Jean Cocteau, 1946).

2. Errol Flynn (1909–1959) was an Australian-American actor who specialized in romantic swashbuckler roles, such as *The Adventures of Robin Hood* (Michael Curtiz, 1938), and *The Sea Hawk* (Michael Curtiz, 1940).

3. For example, *Tarzan the Ape Man* (W. S. Van Dyke, 1932), *Tarzan's Peril* (Byron Haskin, 1951), and *Tarzan's Greatest Adventure* (John Guillermin, 1959), among many others.

4. *Madame Bovary* (1856) was the debut novel by Gustave Flaubert (1821–1880), describing the adulterous affairs of its heroine, Emma Bovary.

5. Truffaut is referring to *Le Nouveau Détective*, a French weekly tabloid, founded in 1928, dealing with crime stories, reports of trials, and victims' stories.

6. Pierre Jaccoud was a prominent Geneva lawyer who had an eight-year relationship with Linda Baud, who had had an affair with another man, André Zumbach, and wanted to leave Jaccoud for another man. In 1958, Jaccoud was accused and convicted of murdering André Zumbach's 70-year-old father in his home, after a verdict that aroused great controversy throughout Europe, being widely perceived as perpetrating a miscarriage of justice.

7. *Lolita* (Stanley Kubrick, 1962); *Adolphe, ou l'âge tendre* (Bernard Toublanc-Michel, 1968); *Romeo and Juliet* (Franco Zeffirelli, 1968); *Madame Bovary* (Jean Renoir, 1934), although Truffaut may also have had Vincente Minnelli's film adaptation of Flaubert's novel in mind (1949); *Le Lys dans la vallée* (Marcel Cravenne, 1970); *Wicked Duchess* (*La Duchesse de Langeais*, Jacques de Baroncelli, 1942); *Nana* (Jean Renoir, 1926); *Devil in the Flesh* (*Le Diable au corps*, Claude Autant-Lara, 1947).

8. Georges Simenon (1903–1989) was a Belgian writer of crime fiction who lived much of his life in France.

9. Jacques Becker (1906–1960), a French filmmaker known for his "découpé" (chopped-up) style and his use of a very mobile camera in films such as *Dernier Atout* (1942), *It Happened at the Inn* (*Goupi Mains Rouges*, 1943), *Paris Frills* (*Falbalas*, 1945), and *Casque d'or* (1952).

10. *Muriel, or The Time of Return* (*Muriel ou Le temps d'un retour*, Alain Resnais, 1963).

11. Gianfranco De Bosio (1924–), a leader of the fight against Nazi-fascism during the Resistance at Verona, and best known for his films *The Terrorist* (*Il terrorista*, 1963), *In Love, Every Pleasure Has Its Pain* (*La betia ovvero in amore per ogni gaudenza ci vuole sofferenza*, 1971), and *Moses the Lawgiver* (1974).

CHAPTER 10
1966: *FAHRENHEIT 451*

> When I was in London for *Fahrenheit*, it was like being in prison—I lived for six months at the Hilton without taking a single meal outside my room. A car would come to pick me up to go to the studio. When I returned to Paris, everyone said to me, "Well then, London, eh, I hear it is great, is there a lot going on?" I didn't dare say, "I've just been released from the Hilton." Six months...
>
> *Interview with Pierre Billard, Christiane Collange, and Claude Veillot, L'Express, no. 883, May 20–26, 1968*

When you discovered Ray Bradbury's Fahrenheit 451, *what was your attitude toward science fiction literature?*

I was against it, out of some kind of aversion. I didn't read it. I was also against science fiction films, and I had written, during the time I had a column in *Arts*, an article against "S-F" films. I thundered, "Down with science fiction!"[1] Moreover, I was criticized in the magazine *Fiction* for this. I only had one soft spot, for *The Thing from Another World*, to the extent that Hawks had been involved in the affair.[2]

How, then, did you come to read Bradbury's novel?

At first, I hadn't even read it! It was Raoul Lévy who told me about it near the end of 1960.[3] Furthermore, he had forgotten the title, and recounted the story to me in three sentences.

These three sentences could not fail to be magical: a country in which people are forbidden to read, in which books are burned, and in which those who do engage in reading are being condemned to opprobrium, prison, and, if need be, death. A man who is a member of the brigades charged with the destruction of books through fire discovers reading, and ends up joining those who are resisting this decree by osmosis. They have become human books. So that books and their content don't die, they have learned one book by heart and entrust it to a child, a friend, on the day of their death.

From that moment, my mind was made up: I would make *Fahrenheit 451*. In 1962 I met the author in New York. I had secured the rights to his book, and I started to work with my scriptwriter, Jean-Louis Richard. We were disappointed to discover that it was very difficult to get this project off the ground in France, even if we enlisted Jean-Paul Belmondo to act the role of Montag, which he liked a lot. I had to wait for four years before it was financially possible to make the film, in England. The setting, however, wasn't important; we could shoot *Fahrenheit* in London, just as easily as in Stockholm or Toronto.

When you went to see Ray Bradbury in America, what kind of man did you find him to be?

Whether you like or dislike science fiction, one has to acknowledge that Ray Bradbury is a genuine writer, and Aldous Huxley, an expert in the field, had said of him, "He's one of the greatest visionaries in the whole of contemporary literature." As for the man who greeted me in April 1962, in New York... You know, I am always scared of meeting people. I first saw a man of forty, very youthful, extremely kind—he had come expressly from Los Angeles—who wore glasses with the thickest lenses I had ever seen. A man who quickly became enthusiastic, warm, and who immediately adopted me. For my part, I had completely adopted Ray Bradbury, the author, a year earlier. I set about reading all of Bradbury's works, at least all of them that had appeared in French. In the airplane during the trip, I read more of them!

What part did Ray Bradbury play in the screenplay relative to your own, in terms of what we see on the screen?

I consider that 60 percent of the film comes from Bradbury. The remaining 40 percent was invented, but I believe that it includes things that are consistent with the thought of the American writer. It's a book that I adored as soon as I discovered it. Censorship of books, in fact, is a current issue, and not simply a theme in science fiction: books are being burned every day across the world, and *Fahrenheit* interested me because it pushed this book-burning tragedy to an extreme degree. Sweden is the only country, as far as I know, that has no censorship; however, in South Africa there is a list of twenty-one thousand books that are proscribed, and books have been burned again recently in Indonesia and China; in Italy, there was the business over *Zanzara*.[4] I thought that it was necessary to denounce this state of affairs; but I had no pretensions about making a useful film. I wanted the film to seem casual. *Fahrenheit 451* is a fable, a moral tale. But, for me, a fable does not prove anything, nor has it anything to prove.

Why did you suppress everything that could constitute a defense of books in your film?

Because it was sufficient to show a book burning to make it valued. I didn't want to include a single sentence explicitly in favor of books, and that allowed me to create a film without making a speech. For this reason, I omitted the character of Faber, who defended books in the original; he was an old, talkative philosopher, and that risked boring the spectator. I have often noticed that when something "good" is on the screen, the audience is impatiently waiting for something "bad" to return, because, generally, it is less boring. Note that all the characters in the film are likeable, even the pyromaniac captain of the firemen; but I retained only people who speak ill of books—this was because I believe they are capable of mounting their own defense. All kinds of books are burned, and I arranged it so that one can see the titles of several of them: that's the most important aspect of the film, the reason I was so keen to make it—because I had been dreaming of making a film about books for a long time. The fire scenes are great! I love fire! I've always been something of a pyromaniac myself.

Were the fire scenes dangerous to film?

Yes, on occasions; for example, *Fahrenheit 451* ends with a fire in which we see a captain of the firemen burning things up like crazy. Gas manifolds were producing flames across a huge set. I positioned three cameras so I could film the fire from three different angles, and then choose the best. By opening a door, the firemen created a current of air that drew the flames towards the third camera, the highest one, the one behind which I found myself. The cameraman and I were so hot that our hair got singed. In the middle of the fire, one man suffocated: he was the "captain of the firemen." He was protected by an asbestos mask and fire-retardant clothing, but he had put his protective mask on so tightly that he was suffocating. His simulated agony could not have been more spectacular!

You were saying that you had been dreaming for a long time of making a film about books?

Yes, ever since *The 400 Blows*, I had wanted to make a film about books. A film in which books would be the hero of my argument. Initially, I thought of adapting a novel by Jean-René Clot for the screen—*Bleu d'outre-tombe*, which I like a lot.[5] I wanted a film that took place entirely in a classroom, with children. Little by little, however, in the course of developing the screenplay, I started to realize how adults were invading the story. I gave it up.

With *Fahrenheit 451*, I have been influenced by certain articles that Roger Caillois wrote in the *NRF* about books and reading.[6] He claimed that books assume a different order of value according to the individual concerned. He was talking about people who regard a book as an object, with all that that implies as far as memories and sentimentality are concerned, rather than university scholars or autodidacts. In this context, which is that of my film, the book becomes an object that one cherishes increasingly over time—even the binding, the cover, the smell of the pages acquire great sentimental value. The film is attempting to appeal to those—of whom I am one—for whom books have a great sentimental value.

The books chosen for *Fahrenheit* do not comprise a catalogue of my favorites. In a number of cases I have tried to provoke an emotion by arousing memories: for instance, by showing an example from the series *Le Livre de demain*, published by Arthème Fayard with very popular woodcuts, which, for any French reader, would evoke the time before the War.[7] And the reason we spent such a long time filming the pages of an album by Dalí being turned under our very eyes by a current of air, was because he is the only great artist who declared himself in favor of all forms of censorship . . .

You have suppressed almost all the elements of science fiction proper. The spying robot, which, in the book, pursues Montag with spine-chilling menace, has completely disappeared in the film. Why?

I feel incapable of bringing off things like that. I would have been able to have the robot constructed, but it would have been a super-gadget, which would have produced an effect that I did not want. I replaced the robot by forty glances of another fireman, Fabian, who we see throughout the film, spying on Montag.

There is practically only one science fiction scene, that of the flying men who are searching for Montag as he is trying to escape: it occurs as a deliberate contrast to the last sequence, that of the "human books." Science fiction effects are very difficult to create, and often risk appearing ridiculous. For instance, at one point Bradbury wrote "the town was buzzing"—well, then, it's very difficult to make a town buzz. I wanted to avoid anything that was systematically disorienting, and that is why I asked Bernard Herrmann, the composer of the scores for *Citizen Kane* and the *Ambersons*, whose work I greatly admire, to give me some dramatic music of a traditional kind, without futuristic overtones. You know, I strongly believe in the necessity of presenting one thing at a time on the screen: that's why I wanted spectators to see nothing else on the screen apart from books burning.

What are the problems you encountered with this film?

With respect to the audience, the film was a kind of gamble. Because, given that everything in it was very simple, the premise is very eccentric, and I had to make it plausible without losing the fantasy dimension. Basically, the problem was to decide upon the right mix between the everyday and the extraordinary, and it was necessary, constantly, to shift from one to the other, mingling them together.

At any point where the screenplay was proving difficult to film convincingly, we would say to ourselves, "This is a story about the Resistance, Montag (the fireman) is a member of the Gestapo, and Clarisse (the young woman) is working undercover." In this way, we sought to progress everything while preventing *Fahrenheit* from being co-opted to a political purpose, or resembling a left-wing American film. With Montag, for the first time, I show a "positive hero"; but nevertheless, I didn't want him to seem like a hero from American cinema.

The screenplay was designed to be harrowing, to arouse fear. But during the shooting I wasn't able to take it completely seriously. I had fun. The scene in which the old lady dies, burnt in the middle of her books, would have been too overwhelming had I chosen a scrawny woman as the actress—a pathetic guardian of culture. To the contrary, I chose a short, fat, jocular woman. The pathos isn't present at the outset, but is generated by the outcome.

The actors wanted to read poems. I was against that. To read a poem, in a film, seems like a tautology. A film can be poetic, but on the condition that no one ever talks about poetry. We don't see poems being burned, or the Bible. The Bible?—it goes without saying.

Is there any relation between Fahrenheit *and your earlier films?*

Montag (Oscar Werner) closely resembles Jean-Pierre Léaud, the adolescent in *The 400 Blows*. He exists in his normal world until all of a sudden a small thing goes wrong. From the moment he takes a book home and begins to read it, he is caught in a trap. He even ends up skipping the barracks, just like one skips school.

My main impulse compared with that in *The Soft Skin* was to give the two female roles to a single actress in order to get rid of, once and for all, the idea of a duality, or contrast, between the brunette and the blonde, et cetera. Because these roles were not very entertaining, I avoided the pitfall of having a performance by a star, all the more because Julie Christie interpreted them without showing a preference either for one or the other, with an equal degree of moderation.

This time, I tried to be realistic in the screenplay and oneiric in the shooting—by creating in each scene, even normal ones, the kind of imbalance, uneasiness, and instability of which Hitchcock is the master, and the secret he taught me. The dream of every artist is to succeed in realizing whatever the overarching concept may be, whether it is simultaneously tragic and comic, true or false.

Has your style changed?

In my other films, priority was given either to the characters or to the story. This time I paid attention to all the visual elements that Bradbury's book suggested. Thus, toward the end of the film, we have a police car entering into a drive, the people who appear in their doorway, and the panoramic shot that shows Montag fleeing in a stairwell . . . I used fewer camera movements at first because of shooting in color.

Did the fact that you kept a shooting diary of the film for the Cahiers du cinéma *have any influence on your work?*

I had tried to keep a diary for *Jules and Jim*, but perhaps that didn't eventuate because I was shooting in France with a French crew. But, in London, to compensate for the feeling of being in exile, every evening, in my hotel room, I would write two pages about what had happened during the day. I noticed that doing this helped me a lot to understand my work, and to see things that one usually doesn't realize until much later, especially in the editing. Similarly, in the past, the need to summarize the plot of films each week in *Arts* helped me to learn a bit about the craft of a scriptwriter.

What is the origin of the conflict you had with Oscar Werner? Did you encounter the same problems during the shooting of Jules and Jim?

Absolutely not. We were even great friends. It's a pity. I don't think that I am responsible. In fact, Oscar is a marvelous actor. He has extraordinary charm, but he had gotten ideas into his head about his role in *Fahrenheit* that were far too definitive, even before shooting began. Perhaps there was also the fact that he had only an imperfect knowledge of French? The entire text of his part [in *Jules and Jim*] had been written on large panels, which, in certain sequences, explains the way he moves his head . . . so suggestive, you remember . . . when he is singing *La Marseillaise*, for example.

Your quarrel wasn't resolved by the end of the film?

No, to tell the truth, it still isn't. We were no longer speaking to one another by the end. I would give my directions to his stand-in, who in turn would pass them on. It was fairly exhausting. I would always wonder what he was going to do. If I wanted him in wrinkled trousers, I was fearful he would show up in ironed trousers . . . and so it went on! Fortunately, in one of the most important scenes, when he has to faint in front of his captain, he agreed to do it. That fainting spell was important to me—in a way, it was the key to the whole film, as far as I was concerned.

Why?

Because fainting is the best way of escaping . . . the ideal ruse. In a kind of way, *Fahrenheit 451* is a eulogy of craftiness—employing a ruse—the ideal means of resistance. It's an ingenious form of ruse, is it not, to burn books in order to obey the law, but having learned them by heart so that one can pass them on at one's death, thus ensuring their immortality?

Your film, then, is also a praise of clandestine methods, of resisting from the shadows? But against whom, against what? Antifascist, antitotalitarian, or more simply antiadministrative?

I did not want to convey a political message. I loved to show a form of struggle against authority. *Fahrenheit* is against power in general, to the extent that power, alternately, underestimates culture, or else imputes an exaggerated importance to it by pretending to believe that a film, a play, a novel—for example *La Religieuse, Les Paravents, Marat-Sade*—can be really dangerous.[8]

You know, people are going to detect a plethora of big ideas in *Fahrenheit* . . . they're going to say that it is a film about culture and liberty, a social critique, or perhaps even a diatribe against countries in which books are burned. But I couldn't care less about that—it doesn't interest me at all. These big ideas are perhaps in the book, but I am not personally interested in big ideas, in the solemn side of things. I believe that one should deal with things—as I always handle my subjects—with a certain lightness. I am not gripped by big ideas. Godard, yes, he's the kind of man who is interested in the big problems of our time, but as for me, I can only make a film out of ideas that are personal to me.

1967

In your interview with Hitchcock, you talked about an almost inherent incompatibility between cinema and England. How, then, did you come to make your film over there?

With *Fahrenheit*, wherever I filmed it, the danger was that it would resemble a film from a country in Eastern Europe. I knew that my determination to shoot in color would reduce this danger. That said, in England one risks ending up needing to use visual material that is unattractive—but I think I would have encountered the same kind of drawbacks no matter where I shot the film. At one point I scouted exteriors in Toronto, and there were places that corresponded point for point to those in the book. The shots of the flight, I believe, would have been more beautiful had they been filmed there. But the drawbacks of England would have been much the same anywhere else, even if I had filmed in a suburb of Paris, at Meudon, for example. No, to be honest, I didn't suffer from having to shoot in England, where everyone was so kind.

I cast certain third-rank actors in the film, whom I would probably have eliminated if I'd had the patience to see more of them. An English actor has something sad about him: it's his "solidity," and the only thing he cares about is realism. I noticed that at all stages in the making of the film; with the sound engineer, for example, if we had eight firemen on the screen, well, he would make the noise of exactly eight! The result is a porridge of noise that is inaudible, and the thought of selectively choosing sounds is unknown over there. They include everything, absolutely everything, even the rubbing of the garment if the actor has placed his hand in his pocket, and while that may create an amazingly realistic sound, it is completely wrong, because it is not anything interesting for those who are listening to a film. Everything depends upon what you like, and there is a degree of realism that I, personally, don't like.

I remember that Rossellini, in contrast, loved English actors. He always wanted to make films with Jack Hawkins and, in *Europe 51*, he cast an English actor whom I have always found to be gloomy in other films. Rossellini finds that English actors don't give the impression of being actors, and that if one uses them to play fire chiefs or factory directors, they really resemble them. That's true. But, when you say this to the English, you find that they themselves are not aware of it. So there were even some issues of tact that arose. When I asked for people who did not have a *British* physical appearance, they asked me, "But what *is* a British physical appearance?" I was tempted to reply, "It's when one has a crooked face." And that is so true: the English all have crooked, asymmetrical faces, whereas Hollywood actors have symmetrical faces—they ended up in Hollywood precisely because of that, the fact that both sides of their face were the same. The only English actors who have been successful in Hollywood are people like Cary Grant. As soon as an Englishman is idealized, stylized, he leaves for Hollywood. And so, in London, only realists are left, Peter Finch will be there forever... This English phenomenon is very strange; one could talk about it endlessly. However, it's getting better—the young English actors are much better than their elders.

But weren't you bothered by the problem of language, given that this is a film in which books, and therefore texts, play an essential role?

Yes, if I suffered in England, that was obviously because of the language problem. I regretted not being able to modify or adjust the dialogue during the shooting. When people are talking about films, one underestimates the importance of words, and I can well understand why Astruc made *The Pit and the Pendulum* as a means, in the first instance, of understanding Baudelaire's text.[9] From the image alone of a film one gains a partial satisfaction, perhaps amounting to 70 percent or 80 percent of what one dreamt of achieving. With the addition of dialogue, you can get to 100 percent. With *The Soft Skin*, for example, I was 60 percent happy with the images, but 100 percent with the spoken words: I believe that they were totally right. Even if one doesn't like the film, I know that it is "singing in tune," but I wouldn't say the same about *Fahrenheit*, which has left me feeling somewhat frustrated. Basically, I came to cinema through the dialogue: I learned the lines by heart. It was only much later that I heard talk about "mise-en-scène"—from Rivette. My nature was to get drunk on films in order to get to know both the dialogue and the music of their soundtrack by heart. That is why I never align myself with those who oppose dubbing. I can point to *Johnny Guitar*, which probably had a greater importance in my life than in that of its creator, Nicholas Ray: the fact is, I almost like the dubbed version of *Johnny Guitar* better than his original version, and I can even tell you that certain things in *The Piano Player*, for example, were influenced by the tone of the dubbing for *Johnny Guitar*: "Play us something, mister Guitar . . ."

1970

I am not against violence out of idealism, because of a commitment to the idea of nonviolence. I oppose it because violence signifies a confrontation. It is like disputation, which I also oppose. When I want something, I want it so badly that I cannot bear to hear any discussion of it. If I have to leave, I leave—I don't talk about it, because I tell myself that if I do so, they are going to prevent me from leaving. I've been like that from childhood, with good reason. For me, what replaces violence is flight, not flight away from the essential, but flight in order to obtain what is essential. I think that this is what I have illustrated in *Fahrenheit*. There is one aspect of the film that has escaped everyone's attention, yet which, for me, is the most important: it's a defense of adopting a ruse. "OK! Books are forbidden? Very well, we're going to learn them by heart!" That's a supreme ruse.

No one could ever persuade me to join with other filmmakers in signing a paper against censorship, because I believe there are fifty ways of circumventing, of triumphing over, censorship, and of distributing to all the other countries a film in the exact form one wants it to have. For me, that's better than violence.

I will not engage in contention on the grounds of principle; my view of society is completely pessimistic.

Notes

1. How to account for the instinctive mistrust that science fiction fanatics arouse in me? I can't help thinking that one would need to be arid, lacking in sensitivity, and with a poverty of imagination to go to Martians in the search for fantasy, poetry, emotions—all of which we have here, on earth, right at hand, in our gaze and our hearts, every day, constantly. I consider the belief of certain intellectuals that subjects can be renewed through science fiction to be stupid. A plot involving a young Martian who falls in love with a pretty human woman is merely a weaker version of one in which a young man from the country arrives in Paris and

becomes hopelessly in love with a young woman from Passy, who gives him an initiation. The reason I maintain that there is a weakening of a subject when it is converted into science fiction is because everything becomes invaded by a facile colorfulness, which dissolves the things that should be most important: the dictates of the heart and body. [Truffaut's note.]

2. *The Thing from Another World* (*La Chose d'un autre monde*, Christian Nyby and Howard Hawks, 1951).

3. Raoul Lévy (1922–1966) was a French film producer who made a number of movies with Brigitte Bardot, including . . . *And God Created Woman* (*Et Dieu créa . . . la femme*," Roger Vadim, 1956).

4. *La Zanzara* was a school magazine that ran a survey among the girls and boys at the school about the use of birth control pills, resulting in the three student editors being put on trial, although they were eventually acquitted. See Guido Nozzoli and P. Maria Paoletti, *La zanzara cronaca e documenti di uno scandalo* (Rome: Feltrinelli, 1966).

5. Jean-René Clot (1913–1996) was an Algerian-born French painter-engraver and writer who produced a string of novels between 1948 and 1965. *Le Bleu d'outre-tombe*, published by Gallimard in 1956, is about a schoolteacher who does not conform to conventional pedagogical methods and is persecuted by an entire town.

6. Roger Caillois (1913–1978) was a French intellectual with a background in anthropology and sociology, known primarily for his influential book *Le Jeux et les Hommes*, published in 1958. The *NRF* (*La Nouvelle Revue Française*) is a French literary magazine founded in 1909 by a group of intellectuals, including André Gide.

7. *Le Livre de demain* was a collection of novels, illustrated with original engravings, published between 1923 and 1947 by the French publishing house Arthème Fayard, with the aim of democratizing access to these works by producing them in a cheap, small format.

8. *La Religieuse* (1796) is a novel by Denis Diderot presenting the cruelty and intolerable conditions experienced by a girl committed to a convent against her will (it was adapted as a film of the same name by Jacques Rivette in 1966); *Les Paravents* is a play written by Jean Genet in 1961, set in Algeria, which attacked the army and provoked a scandal; *Marat-Sade* (*Die Verfolgung und Ermordung Jean Paul Marats dargestellt durch die Schauspielgruppe des Hospizes zu Charenton unter Anleitung des Herrn de Sade*) is a play by Peter Weiss produced in 1963, depicting class struggle and human suffering.

9. *The Pit and the Pendulum* is a short story written by Edgar Allan Poe and adapted for film by Alexandre Astruc in 1964 as *Le Puits et le Pendule*. Truffaut is referring to the French text of Poe's story that was translated by Charles Baudelaire.

CHAPTER 11

1967: *THE BRIDE WORE BLACK*

> I have always thought that Cocteau establishes a bridge between Renoir and Hitchcock. Wasn't he talking a long time before *The Bride* about "filming death at work"?
>
> Interview with Yvonne Baby, Le Monde, *no. 7236, April 18, 1968*

Now, can you tell us how and when you got the idea of adapting Irish's novel, The Bride Wore Black?

It's one of the books that I have known for a long time. I read this novel after the Liberation, probably in 1946, without the knowledge of my mother, who used to devour all the American noir novels. Four years ago I described it to Jeanne Moreau with the aim of getting her to help me find it again. I couldn't remember the title any more, only several scenes. Then, in one of the strange accidents that occur in life, the novel was republished.

I was then worried that it wasn't the same book; I reread it, and it was this reading that made me decide to make the film. The love story sprang from events that preceded the time of the story, and this allowed me to shoot with an exclusive emphasis on Jeanne Moreau, and also not to have any scenes that could resemble those in *Jules and Jim*. As soon as I wanted to work with Jeanne Moreau, everything would tend to take us back to *Jules and Jim*—except, as it happens, this particular story. As well, there was also my admiration for this book, the atmosphere of which I liked a lot.

How would you describe it?

Irish was a writer typical of the *Série blême* that competed, for a few years, with the *Série noire* collection.[1]

Instead of having gangsters in a well-defined social milieu, we encounter stories that are like nightmares. Irish almost always writes stories that deal with love that is frustrated, terrifying stories that revolve around the idea of fate.

William Irish has often been adapted to cinema under his real name, which is Cornell Woolrich. He is a poet, just like Goodis. He's also, perhaps, a bit sick: the kind of people who can write noir novels are not completely normal.

The Bride is the second crime novel that you have adapted. You are probably anticipating questions about Hitchcock in this regard, especially in the light of the book that you have published about him during the past year?

I have an idea, you know, that is interesting, like all ideas are—one that is a bit crazy, like ideas that are too theoretical: namely, that a reconciliation is possible between Renoir and Hitchcock, between the height of cinema about characters, which is Renoir, and the height of cinema focusing on situations, which is Hitchcock. I believe in a mixture of the two. I like the experimental side of what we've done, and in *The Bride* I tried to create a story that was not Hitchcockian—because Hitchcock is more interested in innocent people than guilty ones—but which accords with a narrative principle observed by Hitchcock. The progression goes something like this: with the first man, Claude Rich, we ask ourselves, "What does she want with him?" "Hold on, she has killed him!"; with the second man, Michel Bouquet, we think, "Good Heavens, she is going to kill him!"; with the third, Daniel Boulanger, "Wait, that is not going to happen in the way we anticipated"; at the end, "She is going to get caught, but no, we thought that . . ." All the time, one takes account of what the audience is going to think, and I had fun playing around with that. You say to yourself, "I'm going to make them believe that . . ."—that she is going to fall in love with Charles Denner, for example.

The big advantage of using an outline based on a crime thriller is that while the story is very simple, and the situations very obvious, I can make use of dialogue in a way that is completely independent of the plot. The plot moves on by itself, and so one is able to create two parallel films that advance simultaneously.

This desire to make characters speak about things other than the intrigue is an attitude that is not at all Hitchcockian, but is more characteristic of a European mindset.

Many films have been made in France based on the novels of James Hadley Chase, with the story transposed to the Côte d'Azur. That has never worked. Why, in your view?

I get the impression that it is because they have always tried to make a French product out of an American or an English product. I see these things from a different perspective. Because this is a novel that is not very realistic, I have ensured that none of the locations are recognizable; I have not Frenchified the book, preferring instead to create a kind of imaginary country. This is because I see these books—the novels by Irish, and those by Goodis, which I like also—as fairy stories for grown-ups. And I adapt them in the same spirit as Cocteau filmed *Beauty and the Beast*, but by playing a game that is less overtly magical. For me, this is what's important: "appearance," "disappearance," "there were five of them," "what has happened to the five?" That's the aspect that gives me a lot of pleasure.

I am sure that Americans would not have made *The Bride* in the same spirit; they would have tried to make her more likeable. At the beginning, when United Artists, for example, were worried about the screenplay, I had fun imagining how the Americans would have made the film in Hollywood. And I saw the first scene as being set in a clinic, then the front gate of the clinic, from which one would have seen Jeanne Moreau come out with her mother and the doctor. And the doctor would have given Jeanne back to her mother, saying, "It's worked, she's going to be all right now, but take good care of her." Then they would have gone home; Jeanne Moreau would have packed her bags and left secretly with her mother! I don't know if you realize that a simple scene like that changes almost the whole film: "She has a whole lot of reasons for being the way she is—she is mad! . . ." The French mind-set is to handle this American material without introducing mad or evil people into it. In the end, I made the various men almost likeable, one by one, and never hateful, not even the father of the little boy. The European attitude is to smooth things over, rather than to heighten the tragedy, and always to alleviate it. The effect? That is the very subject of the film.

You mention two parallel films. How would you define them?

One thing, in fact, really fascinated me: to try and make a love film without having a love scene. You won't find a single kiss in the film, nothing. The action on the screen is tragic, like that of a crime film, and yet the dialogue has nothing to do with this action. The dialogue deals exclusively with the relationships between men and women.

If you look at the images in *The Bride*, you see a woman who goes from one place to another, meets various men, and kills them. If you listen to the sound track, you hear conversations about love, about the way men look at women. There is never any mention of killing. If the sound track were to be broadcast on the radio, people would be astonished. They wouldn't be able even to imagine the murders. This continuously sustained gap allows me to have two completely different films that move forward simultaneously. It's a very interesting thing to do. Each man represents a different way of seeing women, given that *The Bride* allowed me to use six actors with whom I had dreamed of working for a long time—"six at one blow," as the little tailor in Grimm might have said.[2] Recently, I noticed that *The Bride* even resembles *Les Mistons*: the men whom Jeanne Moreau encounters are *les mistons*, now grown up.

Once again, you have made a film about love . . .

Yes. I don't think that there is any better subject. I believe that if one asked two filmmakers to make *The Bridge on the River Kwai*, they would both make the same film. But if one offered them the subject of *Brief Encounter*, they would each make a different film.[3] To speak about love requires a greater giving of oneself, and obliges one to transcend the confines of mere storytelling.

The Bride is actually a film about love that is grounded in a pure feeling, because, for Julie, it involves a love from the past. She herself, on the screen, incarnates a kind of living death. She lives on after her husband only for the sake of avenging him.

Around her, the men represent a range of different types, but whether they are shy or bold, collectors of women or romantics, to Julie they all seem terribly relative compared to the absolute that her husband of five minutes, David, embodied.

For them, Julie is not ordinary—and all of them, one by one, dream, to a greater or lesser extent, of entering her life.

Are there any links between her and the other female characters in your films?

As usual, it's the woman who takes the initiatives, and who, without losing any of her femininity, manipulates men who share a common vulnerability. In this case, Julie's mission, which seems inhuman and extravagant in our eyes, is, for her, merely a task to accomplish. And it is not difficult to imagine that there will be nothing left for her to do except die, once her mission has been accomplished.

In contrast to Catherine in *Jules and Jim*, who lived in a state of sexual liberation, Julie is probably still a virgin. But the two heroines come together, of course, in their moral intransigence because, in both cases, it is always a question of morality, even if I am increasingly inclined to mask the presence of this concern in filmed entertainments. There is no need to disguise the fact that such an enterprise constitutes a game: a game played by the filmmaker with his film, and a game played by his film with the audience.

The Bride might seem simplistic and mechanical to anyone who refuses to believe that a film for adults can start with "Once upon a time..." For me, however, and also for my actors, *The Bride* is a serious film—because one cannot film death for forty-six days on end without being affected by it.

Finally, I would like to say that the five men Julie meets on her journey bring us back to the device of enumeration, which is one of the things that makes the reading of fairy stories so fascinating.

How do you evoke this fairy-tale atmosphere?

By constantly seeking to achieve visual simplification and stylization. For example, at the end of the only scene where all five men are together, the script reads, "They decide to separate and never seek to see one another again." And the image shows, flouting all verisimilitude, the five friends hurtling down a metal staircase and, when they arrive at the bottom, leaving in all directions.

On the other hand, even though the film is in color, Julie is dressed only in black and white, and rather than entering into the setting or leaving from it, one would say that she simply appears or disappears.

You were saying that you wanted Jeanne Moreau to be very different from Catherine in Jules and Jim. *How?*

I wanted to make a film with Jeanne Moreau that would have no relation to *Jules and Jim*. I didn't want any love scenes, no hugging and kissing... We never see her in the arms of a man. No laugh, no smile, no sulking, no bitter expression. I wanted her face to be neither open, nor closed, but normal, determined. I asked her to act without any flirtatiousness, like a man, a man who is thinking about a job he needs to get done.

I said to her, "I want you to act like Coutard, the cinematographer—Raoul Coutard, whose face is generally expressionless, still, and knowledgeable."

Nothing is more satisfying to an audience than to watch a character who sees something through right to the end. So I reached an agreement with her that we would pursue this forward movement in a straight line, without any artifice, affectation, very seriously, but with a light touch. In *The Bride*, I wanted Jeanne Moreau to remind one less of a goddess of revenge than someone who is purposeful and efficient. I asked her to act like a skilled craftsman.

This is a very heavy role.

Oh! She says it is the most difficult role she has ever had, and I can well believe her. She constantly had to maintain a double line of thought: it was very hard for her not to react in response to the men—they were giving themselves over to her sincerely, and she had to listen to them while having her own ulterior motive. She was depressed during the shooting of the film, in contrast to *Jules and Jim*, which had been a delightful experience for her. She suffered from a feeling that she was totally alone when she was acting, of not being able to discuss things with her partners. That might appear naïve to some people, but actors, in fact, are influenced by what they play. *The Bride* is a film about destruction, and this left her feeling very dejected: the episode in the cubbyhole, in particular, as well as the rifle shot at the marriage, which we had to do over again, because it is used several times in the film.

She is not really a character, but rather a symbol. The men, for their part, really do have a character to defend, but not her, whose character merely serves as a vehicle to take us from one to the other, like a kind of medium between the male characters (who confide in her) and the spectators who are sitting in the darkness.

Can you give a few details about your treatment of The Bride Wore Black, *its characteristics?*

With its four hundred shots, it is my least fragmented film. I felt it in that way. The form of a film generally presents itself to your mind at the same time as the idea of it consolidates. There are many long takes, because each one of the six male characters in the film only requires a quarter of an hour's projection time to be put before us. Now, one exists much more realistically within a long take containing several deliberately drawn-out periods of time than in a sequence of very fragmented montage images. The use of long takes is fairly unusual for me, but I really like to force myself to do things that I am not used to doing.

In fact, the technical principle underlying *The Bride Wore Black* consists of deriving a series of extremely powerful situations from these periods of protracted time. I tried to give quite a lot of life to a lot of tragedy—that's the main thing.

And then, because I had made *Fahrenheit* in English, I felt a lot of frustration as far as the dialogue was concerned; this time, I made up for it; the dialogue is important—rich, and very familiar, in every instance.

> *Your films seem very different from each other, embodying contrasting approaches, but in the end, they resemble one another—because* Jules and Jim *is also a fairy story.*

The way I think about it is this: since my films are inevitably going to resemble one another in terms of the finished product, they should be commensurately different at the point of departure. And then I have a need, from one film to another, to have a change of what I require from myself. The common point of all my films is that women direct events, in the face of men who are weaker. I like to have characters for whom life is absolute, and others for whom it is relative. It is very stimulating to create certain kinds of scenes: with someone like Jeanne Moreau, for example, you don't feel any desire to create a character who behaves in a small-minded manner. One feels that there is so much energy in her! You are obliged to write striking dialogue for her. For example, in *The Bride*, Michel Bouquet is about to drink out of her glass and says, "I want to know what you're thinking." She takes back the glass from him, saying, "My thoughts are none of your concern." There, that's a statement that is truly worthy of Jeanne Moreau.

> *In* The Bride, *you have set the first scene by the sea, the second in the mountains, and the third in the countryside. Previously, in* Shoot the Piano Player *and* Jules and Jim, *there was an alternation between town and mountain settings. Why?*

Again, it arises because it is a fairy story. In all such tales, the story is based on enumeration. Goldilocks invites herself into the house of three bears. She sees three bowls. The porridge of Father Bear is very hot. That of Mother Bear is too cold. That of Baby Bear is just right. This is a narrative principle that I like a lot. It is also convenient each time one finds oneself at a loss.

The first time this happened to me was in *The 400 Blows*, during the scene at the police station. They sent me extras who looked like cops. There is nothing sadder-looking than cops in French films. They are completely redundant. As a result, I called Jacques Demy to the rescue, because he has the look of an angel. He is the opposite of a cop. Then I had the cops play a game of *petits chevaux*[4]—rather than a card game! And when the three prostitutes enter the police station, I said to myself, "There you are, we are still in a disgusting French film"—and so I made them speak the kind of lines you would find in a fairy story.

The first one says—something that is completely false, given that she is accustomed to being arrested at least twice a week, "I've already seen a police station in a film—it was cleaner than this." The second says, "I have seen bigger ones." The third one says, "I have seen more cheerful ones." I did this again in *Shoot the Piano Player* to escape from sordidness, from making merely a gangster film. I created dialogue of a sort that one would find in a child's book.

In *The Bride*, when they are in the mountains, there is a scene at a concert in which Michel Bouquet has a rendezvous with Jeanne Moreau. And I placed a violinist and a pianist on the stage. I wanted a man and a woman as in *Shoot the Piano Player*: the piano was associated with the male character and the violin was feminine. At the beginning, Aznavour encounters a young woman who is a violinist, with whom he could have become intimately involved.

My dream is to elicit unconscious persuasion. I would like people to feel they have seen shots that are not there, that they think again about their own past, that they delve back into their past. I would like to arouse associations of ideas, make coincidences rise up, facilitate encounters that are more or less collaborative.

Is it true to say that this movement toward the past, toward a poetry that is always more or less linked to childhood, is also a common element uniting all your films?

I am not someone who regrets his childhood. When I was a child, I was very impatient to become an adult. I had the impression that adults could allow themselves to do everything. They lived in a world of complete impunity. For example, when I would hear friends of my parents describing car accidents, I would say to myself, "That's terrific, you can talk about that while having a good laugh, and you won't get chewed out ... Being a child is awful—you always feel as if you are guilty." On becoming an adult, I didn't change. For example, for me to demonstrate in front of the Cinémathèque, to go and sit on a board of directors, to go down the same street, is astounding. I realize that I haven't crossed to the other side. When I demonstrate, I find myself back in my childhood. Afterwards, I get the feeling of having secretly pried into someone's world, and I say "Good morning, sir" ten times more than is necessary, to everyone!

> *Doesn't this kind of fear run through all your films? Fear, anxiety—as in Hitchcock. And you have the courage to speak of this fear. That's actually very rare. In* Les Mots, *Sartre talks about his childhood, without ever giving the impression that he has experienced this kind of anxiety.*

I think that book is horrible, monstrous. To see childhood spoken of like that really shocked me. The truth does not lie in tenderizing it, but it is no more in judging it according to adult criteria. For me, it's as if he had written a book attacking someone I like a lot. This book gives the impression that when he is defending men, it is as artificial as Malraux or General De Gaulle. They espouse generous ideas, but they themselves are not generous. That creates an impression of appalling hardness. One says to oneself, "He defends the Guadeloupeans, because et cetera, but he will not defend the average guy (Toto)."[5] There's something terribly arid in that.

Basically, I require a filmmaker—or a writer—to really feel personally what he is filming. The criterion that determines the beauty of a film is nothing other than that: to feel love, to feel fear. That is probably what drew me to Hitchcock. Basically, I think that anyone who has no problems in life finds it difficult to be an artist.

1977

> *At the beginning of this interview, you said that* The Bride Wore Black *was certainly, of all your films, the one that you like the least ...*

It is a film that would have been much better in black and white, because color has taken away all its mystery. I realized this when the film was shown on television, because the reactions of people who saw it are not the same. And then, it was a bad idea to choose a subject like that for Jeanne Moreau, who is at her best when she is able to talk, when she is animated, when she is laughing, when she is moving, and when she is living. The role of the woman in the film was that of a statue, more of a role for Ursula Andress, or the type of women Cocteau used in his films. There is no point in going into details; these two errors affect the whole film—let's forget it!

NOTES

1. "William Irish" was a pseudonym used by Cornell Woolrich (1903–1968), an American crime writer. *Série blême* was a collection of detective fiction and suspense thrillers founded in 1949 that competed with the *Série noire* collection, founded in 1945 and also publishing crime fiction, until the *Série blême* was suspended in 1951.

2. Truffaut is referring to *Grimm's Fairy Tales* (*Kinder- und Hausmärchen*), a collection of German fairy tales first published in 1812 by two brothers, Jacob and Wilhelm Grimm.

3. Truffaut is alluding to two films by David Lean: *The Bridge on the River Kwai* (*Le Pont de la rivière Kwai*, 1957), an epic war film based on the novel of the same name by the French writer Pierre Boulle, and *Brief Encounter* (*Brève rencontre*, 1945), an intimate romantic melodrama based on Noël Coward's one-act play *Still Life* (1936).

4. *Jeux des petits chevaux* is a French board game, resembling Ludo.

5. "Toto" in French is a slang expression referring to an ordinary person. It is also the name of the fictional dog in L. Frank Baum's Oz series of children's books, which furnished the source for the Hollywood movie, *The Wizard of Oz* (Victor Fleming and George Cukor, 1939).

CHAPTER 12

1968: *STOLEN KISSES*

> I almost abandoned *Stolen Kisses* fifteen days before shooting began, I was so ashamed, and felt so uncomfortable about it. I had already written the script for *The Wild Child*, and that for *Mississippi Mermaid*. I said to myself, "Hell, I have two good scripts to shoot; there are magnificent novels to do, and in fifteen days I'm going to make a film that deals with nothing at all!" I was aghast.
>
> Interview with Noël Simsolo, Image et son, revue du cinéma, no. 245, December 1970

You began making Stolen Kisses *three months before May 1968 and right in the middle of demonstrations in support of Henri Langlois, who had just been sacked from the Cinémathèque. The shooting was disrupted. What happened?*

I started shooting *Stolen Kisses* on Monday, February 5, and on February 9 I arrived on the set two hours late because I had come out of a board meeting of the Cinémathèque, during which Henri Langlois had been replaced by Pierre Barbin. From that moment I led a double life as a filmmaker and as a militant, making telephone calls between each shot, giving interviews to foreign radio shows to try and compensate for the silence of the ORTF,[1] writing hurried, indignant articles in *Combat*,[2] and helping with all the meetings of the committee formed to defend Langlois—as a result of which, occupying the position of treasurer, I had to endorse around fifty supporters' cheques every evening, even if that meant I had to miss the screenings of my rushes!

The actors improvised their lines; everyone distanced themselves from the film, which became a game one played when one had enough time. Fortunately, the thrust of the screenplay lent itself to this state of mind and, in any case, we quite quickly adopted a slogan for the film that was dedicated to the Cinémathèque: "If *Stolen Kisses* turns out to be a good film, it will be because of Langlois, and, if it is bad, it will be because of Barbin."[3]

Is it based on an original screenplay?

I wrote the screenplay with Claude de Givray and Bernard Revon. Givray has often worked with me, and he himself collaborated with Revon on *L'Amour à la chaîne*.[4] Putting our heads together, we came up with the idea that Jean-Pierre Léaud would undertake various jobs. At his age, I was a journalist, and I wanted to distance myself from autobiography. A private detective indirectly linked up with journalism—that worked very well. Givray and Revon wrote a whole lot that didn't have any input from me: the journalistic bit, the part about the investigation. They went to interview shoemakers, the managers of shoe shops, private detectives—in short, all those who were involved in the situations to which I exposed Léaud. They thus spent hours with a tape recorder, from which we kept everything we could extract gags from, or comical, funny scenes. From this documentary stage, all three of us selected general situations, without filling in too many of the details, given that the details were supplied at the last moment.

I asked Claude de Givray and Bernard Revon to write everything that related to the jobs Jean-Pierre undertook, and to leave me to do the whole part relating to his love life. In the love scenes, I used a lot of improvisation.

It is a sequel to The 400 Blows?

That was the original idea. But the tone of the film is so teasing and playful that it is not really accurate to talk in terms of a sequel to *The 400 Blows*. It's a lot more like the atmosphere of the sketch I made in *Love at Twenty*, which makes one think of *Stolen Kisses*. It begins with the last day of Antoine's military service, and ends just before his marriage. The style of *Stolen Kisses* is realistic and lighthearted; the action is motivated merely by very simple, inconsequential events. The title is drawn from a song by Charles Trenet—"*Que reste-t-il de nos amours?*" Obviously, I wanted the film to resemble this song. It's the first time I made a film with comic pretensions.

I noticed that when I thought I was making a film with 50 percent comedy and 50 percent sadness, I actually ended up with a film that was 80 percent sadness and 20 percent comedy. When I work in an improvised way, it always tends to move in the direction of seriousness. So I said to myself, "This time, I'm going to try and be humorous, and we'll see what the end result will be." So it's right to think, therefore, that this is a film that is half comedy, and half sadness.

Does this mean that we are at the opposite extreme to Fahrenheit?

Yes. It's a modest production: at the beginning, there was no screenplay, just twenty pages—the screenplay was conjured up a few days before the shooting. Furthermore, it had been difficult to persuade Artistes Associés to do it.[5] And that was the reason I made the film in Paris. Otherwise, my project would have been made in the provinces.

Did that change the way you saw things?

Oh yes, completely. I followed other leads, the characters took priority over other things—such as the situations, the settings, the theme—they are more important than the structure, the execution, even though those things had to be done properly. We did very long takes. This was like nothing I had done previously, like *Fahrenheit*, for example, in which the settings took priority, or in *The Bride Wore Black*—I had come to the point of being interested in things that were too abstract, and I needed to return to concrete things.

Is it this desire to return to what is concrete that makes you inclined to speak of a certain kind of contemporary reality?

No, I'm not at all interested in depicting our current era for its own sake. There is the same difference, if you like, between *Masculin Féminin* and this film as exists between the twist and a waltz.[6] I am a nostalgic person, completely turned toward the past. I work with material drawn from my own past experience, or that of others. Again, that's one of the reasons I chose a song by Trenet dating from 1942 as the musical theme for the film. I think that this melody will arouse memories in spectators. I deal only with feelings, with things that have already been experienced. That's partly why my films are full of memories of youth. In preparing for this one, I noticed, moreover, and at each stage, that everything had changed—the caps of the soldiers, the pawnshop, everything. At that moment, I decided to cheat, to be old-fashioned, but within the setting of the Paris of today. *Stolen Kisses* is rather as if one had made a film that took place in 1945, but without saying so. There, you have it.

You said just now that in Stolen Kisses *the characters are the most important. How did you choose your actors?*

I feel more and more the need to cast intelligent actors in my films, even (and especially) if I have given them characters to play in whom this is not the most obvious trait. For this reason, I chose all my actors for *Stolen Kisses*, several days before the film was shot, by going to the theater; this was why I cast a duo from the Théâtre Antoine (Delphine Seyrig and Michael Lonsdale), a trio from the Théâtre Moderne (Claude Jade, André Falcon, and Harry Max), a defector from La Puce à l'Oreille (Daniel Ceccaldi), an actor from the Théâtre Lutèce (Jacques Rispal); Claire Duhamel came from the Centre dramatique d'art d'Aix-en-Provence, François Darbon from the Athéné, Martine Ferrière from the TNP,[7] and the conjurer Delord from Galerie 55.[8]

But the linchpin of the film, its reason for being, is obviously Jean-Pierre Léaud. Jean-Pierre interests me because of his anachronism and his romanticism: he is a young man from the nineteenth century. Basically, he is a character out of Dickens or from Jack London, endowed with such a romantic purity in *Masculin Féminin*, for example, that one ends up supporting him against all the others. In *Masculin Féminin* he seems a lot like Godard, like Skolimowski in *The Departure*;[9] and I think that he is not unlike me in this film, as well.

Playing opposite Léaud, you have Delphine Seyrig...

Yes, that's somewhat amusing. I used Delphine Seyrig on account of her high reputation, but in a comic way. Seyrig has never attempted comic roles, but she is perfectly capable of doing so, and besides, she found it amusing to do so. In actual fact, moreover, she doesn't perform her role in a comic manner. She acts just like she normally acts, but in the context of a comedy. It is the Léaud-Seyrig couple that makes one laugh: the contrast between her and him—because, in truth, the gap is enormous. She plays the wife of a shoe seller, and Jean-Pierre joins the shop as a warehouseman. Once there, he falls in love with her, like a madman, owing to his reading of *The Lily of the Valley*![10]

It's also the first role in a film for Claude Jade.

When I hired Claude Jade, I gave her the screenplay, and she trusted me: there was very little written down and she didn't know what kind of character she was going to play. For many scenes, I sent the script to the actors the night before via the pneumatic system, and if I wasn't able to send it, they got it just before shooting. I was very worried about the whole scene with Delphine Seyrig in Jean-Pierre Léaud's room. I held it back until the last possible minute. Delphine Seyrig had not had the time to learn her script. So we had to multiply the number of takes. In the end, we had very fragmented scenes. I worked in a very nervous manner, but this nervousness also manifested itself in laughter and amusement. We had a lot of fun while making this film. This was probably because the Langlois business was making me very worried during this time. I was concerned about the Cinémathèque, and those worries carried over to the film: it was as if the film had to be sacrificed for the sake of it. This was the first time I had worked with such a carefree attitude.

> Stolen Kisses *is a film that tells a story. At a time when many filmmakers were sneering at storytelling, you attempted to tell yours like Hitchcock or Renoir.*

Yes. I had discovered what I call the theory of "privileged scenes" while I was making *Fahrenheit*. When I do the timing of the screenplay with the script, I immediately spot the scenes that ought to be "privileged." During the shoot, I know that the more one extends the timing of these scenes, the better it is. With the other scenes, the more one can reduce the anticipating timing, the better it is. I know, for example, that René Clair's approach is wholly aimed at acceleration. There is a danger that characters will end up being puppets. There are some scenes that it is not good to accelerate. So I search for an alternation of scenes that need to be accelerated—scenes giving information, for example—with moments in which one shouldn't be afraid to linger—like Delphine Seyrig in Jean-Pierre Léaud's bedroom, for instance. She can take her time, allow silences to occur—I know that we are going to listen to her. On the other hand, when the older detective presents Jean-Pierre Léaud with work to do, it is pointless shooting the scene as written. It's sufficient to see the two talking behind the window of a bar, for a moment, and everyone understands what's going on.

> *How did you discover these techniques?*

All of this is precisely what I learnt at the Cinémathèque. You learn these kinds of things from watching old Lubitsch movies. For me, the real influence doesn't come from contemporaries, but from the filmmakers of the silent era . . . And we French filmmakers have many opportunities to learn, constantly, at the Cinémathèque.

You were saying that the subject matter of your films is not modern, and that your way of filming is not modern either. Your storytelling is very classical.

I believe that cinema is making progress, and that spectators, especially, understand more and more. But I continue to believe that cinema has to respect chronology and ought to be simple. For many people, for example, Godard represents complete freedom. If one looks closely at his films, however, one notices that they, too, impose a very strict discipline. In the course of making fifteen films, he has never used a slow motion, nor a speeded-up motion, nor a flashback. He has almost never reversed the chronology of a story. People often say, with regard to a film that scrambles everything up, "It is made à la Godard"—whereas it is actually full of things that Godard did not allow himself to do.

I think that it is very dangerous to throw perplexity into the cinema theater. When a spectator asks himself, "Hang on, is that something happening in the past or the present?" he stops watching the screen for five minutes. Now, I feel as if I am in the situation of a singer—it's the film that is on the stage, not me—and it is disastrous if people stop listening to what I am singing. I have never been an actor, but I feel that the film, the entertainment, is rich in potential catastrophes. Among these catastrophes, that of not being watched, of not being heard, is terrible. A filmmaker, like an actor, has to make himself interesting.

On the other hand, I am not at all displeased if one viewer finds one scene funny, and another finds it sad. For example, the guy one glimpses in *Stolen Kisses* delivering the television screenplays—I imagined him before the events of May. That was something funny. Now, it becomes sadder after the dismissals. It doesn't bother me if one spectator is moved, or troubled by this scene, while the person sitting next to him is laughing.

You have made sad films, and funny films. Have you ever thought of making a politically engaged film?

That would be absolutely impossible for me, because I am disengagement personified—owing to the fact that I have a very intense streak of contrariness.

You were saying just now that you always want to distance yourself from autobiography. Yet those who like your films find that they resemble you.

I think that one can function more easily in disguise. For example, the writers in the Série Noire speak more freely than Steinbeck or Dos Passos. I have always dreamed of making a film that would be anonymous—like Italian filmmakers who take an American name. That's a freedom that Buñuel must have enjoyed with his first Mexican films, before the success of *Los Olvidados*.[11] He was not yet a target for critics.

> *Critics and spectators are going to wonder about a mysterious character in* Stolen Kisses: *the man who follows Claude Jade until the end, and abuptly declares his love to her.*

For me, he is not so mysterious. The idea came to me in a restaurant. There was a couple and, at another table, a man who was constantly looking at the woman as if she were not accompanied. For me, this man is a madman, but like all madmen, he says important things. He says that feelings are temporary, that everyone betrays everyone else. He is mad, because he believes he is different. The whole film is founded on the idea of the temporary, and, suddenly, we get someone who claims to be unchanging.

> *One feels that the ending of this film poses a threat to the couple of Jean-Pierre Léaud and Claude Jade.*

Yes, yes, there's a threat. Langlois wants me to make a sequel; he's waiting to see the married life of this couple.

1970

At the time of *Stolen Kisses*, a private detective said to us. "In this business, we are at the heart of the human heart." The sentence isn't in the film, but I have remembered it. He also told us the story of a homosexual who had not wanted to believe that his friend was married: to control him, he had to call the dentist on the floor above. I liked this story. What is great about a news item is that it is both true and baroque; we are no longer in the realms of psychology, nor of a well-constructed drama—as it turns out, there is a dentist on the floor above, and not a judo teacher.

> *In relation to other films,—let's say, broadly speaking, adaptations from novels—*Stolen Kisses *gives the impression of having been very free in its construction, a bit like an amateur film.*

I think, however, that what holds *Stolen Kisses* together is technique. The screenplay is so slight . . . Had it been my first film, I think that it would not have held up. There is a lot of craftiness in the mise-en-scène: at the moment of shooting I constantly invented a number of things, brought together two or three elements, consolidated a scene in which nothing happened ... But it is accurate to say that the success of *Stolen Kisses* depends on its unpredictability: one never knows what scene is going to follow the one you're watching on the screen. This success is also owing, I believe, to the actors. Thanks to them, the curve of interest never weakens. After an hour into the film, one has a chance to bring on Michael Lonsdale, a terrific actor, and, ten minutes later, his wife, Delphine Seyrig. The admirable performances of all the actors strengthened the line of interest.

1970

I was thinking of Delphine Seyrig for *Stolen Kisses*. The role was written for her. However, I lived in a state of anxiety for several days, because the role was so small and had a salacious aspect to it ... I said to myself, "She's going to refuse." I did not sleep because of it. I was preparing for other contingencies. And then I realized that it would be a catastrophe: she was irreplaceable! I had so completely devised this role with her in mind! Part of the role depended upon the glamor she had gained from her role in *Last Year at Marienbad*; my film had to have an actress who had made that earlier film—it couldn't be anyone else. I sent her the screenplay, but the dialogue had not yet been written. I was ashamed; I said to myself, "Oh! Là, là! It's a catastrophe." So I said to her, "I am sure that you are going to ask me a question I won't be able to answer: why did Madame Tabard marry Monsieur Tabard?"

She replied to me that that this question had not occurred to her, and that she would act like a woman who was overjoyed to have married such a man—it was an intelligent response.

Why is there the scene in which Antoine repeats the names of Fabienne Tabard and Christine Darbon in front of a mirror?

The problem was that I wanted to avoid, at all costs, a scene with a confidant to whom Antoine explains his indecisions regarding the two women in his life. He repeats his name constantly to assure himself about his own identity, as if he were trying to clarify some thoughts.

1970

For *Stolen Kisses*, I used Jean-Pierre Léaud as the sole point of departure. I needed to improvise. That forced me to break from the academic construction of my earlier screenplays. I remember having to improvise a scene as a result of the decor, because the façade of the parents' house had two exits. I was very happy with this, because it allowed me to do something I would never have dared to do several years earlier. This scene completely contradicted the psychology of the characters. One saw Jean-Pierre arrive at the girl's parents' house; the mother on the doorstep tells him that Christine has left, but she insists that Antoine go into the house. On the right of the image, we see the door of the cellar open. Claude Jade comes out of it, and creeps past the level of the windows. This unexplained little episode is not linked to anything else; it implies a number of things—a silent understanding between the mother and her daughter; that Antoine is not well regarded in this household; that Christine has another life apart from him . . . In short, it was a red herring and certain spectators even thought that the girl was going to meet the man who walks after her—the man in a raincoat following her that ends the film . . .

In truth, in the case of *Stolen Kisses*, each spectator "conjured up" his own subject: for some, it was *L'Éducation sentimentale*;[12] for others, it involved a rite of initiation; still others were reminded of picaresque adventures. Each brought to it whatever he wanted, but nevertheless it was genuinely contained in it. I had packed the film with all kinds of things linked to the theme that Balzac calls "A beginning in life."

1974

I have often thought about the problem of endings. An ending, for me, should balance the whole film, meaning that if the film has a predominantly comic tonality, the ending needs to be tragic; and if, to the contrary, it has been very tragic and pessimistic, the ending should compensate for that by being happier, more optimistic. And I find this duality very interesting: we know that life is moving toward death, decline. The life of a man descends. For this reason, I always try to have an ending that respects the purpose of an entertainment; I always have two final reels that are fairly lively and frenetic, and at the same time, I try to respect the way life progresses, which is to move toward death, regardless. This means that there is always an idea of things cracking, of tearing up, of breaking.

> *I think that this is felt in all your films; whatever the final eventuality may be, there is always something in the background . . .*

That's the ambiguity; I shoot optimistic endings that respect the law of life. These are endings that try to respect the law of entertainment and the law of life. An entertainment, in fact, fights against death.

My contrivance of the final, enigmatic character in *Stolen Kisses* was a bit theoretical, but at the same time it reflects an idea to which I adhere closely . . . He is a madman for whom things have to be definitive, and he says to Claude

Jade, "That guy you are with is only temporary, I am permanent, I will never leave you, I will be with you all the time and I have no need to make a living, and so I will never be absent, I will always be there." It's terrifying, and at the same time one no longer knows whether love should be like that, or like what Doinel offers . . .

1975

With the passing years, I think that the final scene in *Stolen Kisses*, which was made with a great deal of innocence, without me myself knowing what I was wanting to say in it, becomes a key to what I am doing in all the stories I tell.

Notes

1. *Office de radiodiffusion-télévision française*, the former French broadcasting corporation.
2. *Combat* was a French newspaper created during World War II for the Resistance, which served as a mouthpiece for the left in the decades following the War, until it ceased publication in 1974.
3. Pierre Barbin (1926–2014) was the founder of an association for the distribution of cinematic short films and animated films. Between February and April 1968, he replaced Henri Langlois as director of the Cinémathèque française, as a result of the intervention of André Malraux, a minister in the government of the day.
4. *L'Amour à la chaîne* (*Tight Skirts, Loose Pleasures*, Claude de Givray, 1965).
5. Artistes Associés is a French production company.
6. Truffaut is referring to *Masculin Féminin* (Jean-Luc Godard, 1966), about a young man, also played by Jean-Paul Léard, who is similarly discharged from national service in the French army, and who, in contrast to Antoine Doinel, becomes disillusioned with civilian life as his girlfriend builds a career as a pop singer.
7. Théâtre National Populaire, founded in 1920, in Paris.
8. Jacques Delord (1928–2006), a French magician who performed in cabarets and music halls.
9. Jerzy Klolimowski (1938–) is a Polish film director who directed *The Departure* (*Le Départ*, 1967), starring Jean-Pierre Léaud.
10. *The Lily of the Valley* (*Le Lys dans la vallée*) is a novel by Honoré de Balzac, published in 1835, about the unconsummated love between a younger man and a woman 20 years his senior.
11. *Los Olvidados* (*Los olvidados*, Luis Buñuel, 1950), a film about a group of juvenile delinquents in the slums of Mexico City.
12. *L'Éducation sentimentale* (*A Sentimental Education*, 1869), is a novel by Gustave Flaubert.

CHAPTER 13
MAY 1968

> For me, De Gaulle's only virtue was to oblige technicians in television to create good framings. Whereas television cameramen could not film a singer or a writer without zooming into their nostrils, when they framed De Gaulle, it was impeccable; they always left a bit of space above his head, one could always see the knot of his tie—it was like Dreyer.
>
> *Interview with Monique Sobieski,* Journal du show-business, no. 118, April 30, 1971

The "Cinémathèque affair" was a kind of prologue to the events of May. Of course, I didn't realize that until later, in the light of May—but, in fact, in microcosm, there was somewhat of the same kind of situation: "intellectuals" who were contesting decisions (the government's decision to get rid of Henri Langlois, the founder and soul of the Cinémathèque), and who were demonstrating in the streets and being bludgeoned. What the government officials did at the Cinémathèque is what they did across the whole of France: they subsidized organizations, and then they infiltrated them. During the demonstration at the Palais de Chaillot, I was bludgeoned, for the first time in my life, and I found that it was not as painful as all that. The clubs were made of rubber, or out of some sort of plastic material that was unknown to me, and, at one particular moment, I actually broke one. The experience "warmed up" my head, but I wasn't bleeding. At the next demonstration, in the rue de Courcelles, the police had been replaced by the CRS,[1] and this brought with it the appearance of new "gizmos," the clubs of Charonne.[2] This took place on March 19, and, for me, the Cinémathèque represents a prologue because I saw Daniel Cohn-Bendit there for the first time on that occasion.[3] Moreover, I think he came to two out of three of the demonstrations. To be honest, I formed a very bad impression of him. Several of us wanted to maintain a semblance of impartiality, to ensure that the fight we were leading would remain apolitical, because we thought that if we politicized things, Langlois would have no chance of being reinstated as head of the Cinémathèque.

When we saw this red-headed youth who climbed up a street lamp and was calling us "comrades," we all asked who he was and what he was doing there. Afterwards, he ensconced himself at a window. I found him very methodical, very professional. He waited for the crowd—of young people "from the western world"—to be silent, and it was particularly with them that he engaged in debate, because there was the danger of a confrontation. I think that Cohn-Bendit was interested in all forms of contestation, and so he came to the rue de Courcelles because of that, and then he got caught up in the action, showing all of us things to do that we hadn't known before—but always calmly, and very articulately. One youth had been arrested by the police, and, at the end of the demonstration, as we were preparing to leave quietly, Cohn-Bendit seized the moment to harangue us. He said, "We are not going to leave until our comrade has been set free." I myself thought that the poor lad had already been taken away to a police station somewhere. But Cohn-Bendit, as he would later do on a much larger scale in the streets of the Latin Quarter, immediately decided to stay and obtain his release, deciding that the struggle would take form there, on the spot. He said something like this: "In Britain, farmers spent six hours waiting for one of their comrades to be freed. How long are Parisians prepared to wait?" He was very clever, in fact. Because of him, with several other filmmakers, we went to negotiate with the police, and we succeeded in obtaining the release of the boy—he was a high-school student, I believe. I didn't even know it was possible to achieve that kind of thing. When I asked who this red-haired youth was who had taught us how to defend ourselves, someone replied to me, "He's a guy from Nanterre..."

The government realized quite quickly what a monumental gaffe it had made over Langlois—and they backed down. Obviously, today, one can see that it was an object lesson ... Cynically, one could say that it confirmed the need to demand in the street the things that one could not obtain from government offices.

To return to Cannes and to the month of May . . . I followed all the events on the radio, up until the 17th. On that day I had to go down to Cannes to participate in a press conference specifically on the Cinémathèque. At Orly the planes had already stopped flying. So I rented a vehicle and drove across France by car, and I remember having turned on the radio and hearing, every half hour, news flashes that announced the shutting down or occupation of one factory after another. That was the day everything stopped in the country, resulting in the complete paralysis of Sunday the 19th. When I arrived at the Hôtel Martinez they told me that they had received phone calls for me from Jacques Rivette all day long. He was at the "États généraux du cinéma" at Vaugirard, in which I had not participated.[4] I ended up joining it, either because of him or a friend, I no longer know the reason, and they told me, "Hey, we've decided to shut down the Cannes Festival." And to me, that seemed a completely logical and obvious thing to do. I reported this to one or two other friends, but no one else. It was essential to present everyone with a *fait accompli*. I saw Louis Malle, who was a member of the jury, and he explored the possibility of obtaining resignations from others in the jury (Monica Vitti, Terence Young, Roman Polanski), and we approached directors to find out whether they would withdraw their films from the competition.

The following day, around 11:00 a.m., Jean-Luc (Godard) arrived. We had had no time to coordinate our actions. The Jean Cocteau Theater was full of journalists and cinema professionals. I read out a text of five or six lines explaining that the États généraux were demanding that the festival be shut down, and were asking everyone who was participating to join in this action. The thought was that it was necessary to show solidarity in everything that was happening, at that moment, across the country. Cannes is a sealed-off place during the festival, in which people talk about nothing but cinema. No one listens to transistor radios, no one reads any newspaper apart from *Le Bulletin du film*. Everyone is conducting business, that's all. So people were rather dismayed. They hardly understood anything of what was happening in the rest of France. And then, you know, during May 13, 1958, the Cannes Festival had continued as if nothing were going on.[5] So there was a certain amount of amazement, of surprise. No protests. I explained that, because of the films that had been withdrawn (Resnais had decided to withdraw his, along with Lelouch and Cournot), and the resignation of the jury members, the festival was finished anyway. Jean-Luc, who arrived from Paris, where he had lived through the whole affair much closer than I had, said at one point, "Good, let's go into the big theater to deliberate." That led to the Sorbonne aspect of the story. It was 11:30 in the morning. We occupied the theater. There was Claude Berri, Claude Rich, Lelouch, a heap of journalists, and everyone began to speak. Foreign filmmakers arrived: Richart Lester came to say, "I am withdrawing my film," also Saura, et cetera. Then, Favre Le Bret came to negotiate.[6] We were asked to evacuate the place. That all got drawn out, protracted, and turned ugly. And then there was a spiraling chain of events: once you are somewhere and you are asked to leave, you decide to stay. It became ridiculous, but that is how it was. And a number of increasingly stupid remarks ended up being said over the microphone. At 2:30 p.m., the hall was empty. We were on the stage. There were big bouquets of flowers—very Cannes Festival—between the audience and us ... In the theater, the audience was made up of Cannes inhabitants. One always forgets that all the theaters are filled with locals from the town during the festival: people who are "in the business" have, as a rule, already seen the film. In this case, the members of the audience present were less well informed about cinema matters, but felt at home and regarded the festival as their thing. So they found our whole circus unacceptable. They hurled abuse at us. One or two producers arrived and yelled at both Lelouch and me. They said to us, "This is absurd—so this is how you welcome strangers! Don't forget that you owe everything to the Cannes Festival ..." People went out and came back in. The officials arrived at 3:00 p.m. Favret-Lebret, annoyed, gave an order for the projection to begin. They started the opening credits of Saura's film, and then there was simply bedlam. It was dark on the platform and in the hall, and only the beam from the projector lit up the incredible mêlée that started up on stage. As I recall, that was the only successful moment of this confused day—a rather ridiculous one.

Someone cried, "Everyone to the curtain!" There were fifteen or twenty people who tried to prevent the electric curtain from opening. Saura and Geraldine Chaplin were on our side, and it was their film that was being projected, the first images of which fell on us. And we saw Saura fighting to prevent the film from being shown! That was a pretty good moment ... Someone must have seized the wires of the loud-speaker because the sound was cut and we could no longer see the images. Finally, the lights went on and the film ceased. So there was a big skirmish, a kind of brawl. There were people from Nice, and from Cannes, who climbed on to the stage; I must have received a punch, and straight after, one of my friends struck the guy who had hit me and flung him into the bouquets of flowers. It was grotesque ... This state of confusion lasted for the whole day. We heard just about every point of view—there were people who absolutely insisted that the festival should continue, and I realized that we were really hated when I walked from the festival palace to the Hôtel Martinez. People waved their fists at us ... No one seemed to want to understand that the country was paralyzed and that it was, realistically, merely logical to close down this celebration. I left . . . It stopped by itself the next day. Certain rumors scared the officials. People were saying that a stock of cobblestones had been amassed behind the Palace, that "students" were going to arrive. Someone even came to tell me, "Three hundred students are waiting for you at Nice—go and meet them." This was really not my thing. I remember that Claude Berri called me on the telephone. He said two things that were amusing: "You realize that we are in the toughest town in France." He meant the money people, and the "business" side of things. And then he said to me, "You know that we're hated." I said, "Yes," laughing, and he said to me, "Yes, but in-ter-na-tion-al-ly!" . . .

Seriously, today I realize that we could not have done otherwise. We didn't do it very well, but we stopped it. For me, and I am no longer speaking of the festival, I'm talking about everything that happened in Paris, and in France generally, it was fantastic. There are times when one has to take sides. So, obviously, that year I ended up giving interviews in which I explained that I had not become involved to support a political cause, that I didn't believe in doing that, that I was completely cynical and antisocial . . . And it's true—I've always been an individualist. I have always regarded people in the game of politics as adversaries, with myself being an observer of the combat between them. Perhaps there are autobiographical reasons for this: the cops knocked me about when I was a kid; I have never liked political parties, and I have always felt that people never pay any attention to the only thing that I am concerned about in life: social misfits. Thus, earlier on, what had moved me about the students was that they were returning the blows that the police inflicted on them. And after that I followed everything they did. On my return from Cannes, I even marched on the first of June, something that I had never done before . . . On the other hand, I never went to the Sorbonne, I didn't want to act like a tourist, a "complete Parisian." At a deeper lever, however, I noticed, thanks to the students, that my petty cynicism was no longer legal tender . . . In the face of stupidity, intolerance, people's narrow-mindedness (political or otherwise), I had always had an attitude that consisted of saying, "That's not worth discussing." Now, rightly, the students had shown me that I could no longer spout that kind of sentiment, that those things were indeed worthy of discussion . . .

I feel great admiration for the young people who were capable of marching while singing "We are all German Jews." I had never thought it possible to see intelligence, humor, strength, and justice marching together in the streets at the same time. That's what moved me. It was difficult not to choose between the "toot-tooting" of the motorists in the Champs-Élysées and this slogan.

Notes

1. The Compagnies Républicaines de Sécurité (CRS)—the riot control forces of the French National Police.

2. "Clubs of Charonne" were long (85 cm x 4 cm in diameter) combat truncheons made of wood, and were notorious for having been used by police in their charge against demonstrators protesting against the Algerian War at the Charonne Metro station in 1962, which had left eight people dead from fractures to the skull.

3. Daniel Cohn-Bendit, a student studying sociology at the University of Nanterre, was a student leader during the unrest of May 1968.

4. The "États generaux du cinéma" was a gathering of film technicians and professionals who met at the Vaugirard film school in Paris to discuss and pass resolutions on a variety of issues, declaring themselves the "États généraux du cinéma" (General Estates of Cinema) on 17 May 1968.

5. Truffaut is referring to the May 1958 political crisis that began as a coup attempt in Algiers during the Algerian War of Independence, and led to the return of Charles de Gaulle to political affairs and the establishment of the Fifth Republic on October 4, 1958.

6. Robert Favre Le Bret (1904–1987) was the Director General of the Cannes Festival from 1952 to 1972, and subsequently its president from 1972 to 1984.

CHAPTER 14
1959–1968: OVERVIEW 1

You have almost always, at one stage or another, worked in collaboration?

Always, yes.

With Marcel Moussy and with Jean-Louis Richard. Is this a necessity for you, and, if so, why?

It is a necessity, because I have a great belief in the value of discussing things. I find that one keeps on improving an idea when you discuss it with someone else. You throw out an idea that you like a lot. Your partner doesn't like it. He explains that he doesn't like it because it presents this or that difficulty. Once you have been alerted to this difficulty, you say, "Ah! Yes, that's true," and then you both work together to find a way of salvaging the idea, keeping the advantages while avoiding the difficulties—it's a great way of working, often exhilarating. I can't imagine proceeding in any other way. It's necessary to do it with someone who genuinely shares your ideas. One needs to be able to read between the lines.

There has to be some kind of intellectual sympathy between the two of you?

Ah! Yes. That can vary with the subject. One should probably change the screenwriter to suit the genre of the film, but at present, after three screenplays written with Jean-Louis Richard, we have got the hang of it, to the extent that I believe we can keep on working together. We have written together an adaptation of *Fahrenheit 451*, a screenplay about *Mata Hari* that he is going to film,[1] *The Soft Skin*, and things have gone really well each time.

And you don't think that passing through this stage of relatively collaborative work imposes any kind of limitation on your individual expression?

No, frankly, I don't. Even though it might give that impression, I don't care, because I will always put the interests of the film before anything else; even if that means I do not seem like a genuine auteur, too bad. We are in the domain of entertainment; but even if directing is necessarily a solitary mode of expression, why should we reinforce this solitude? Similarly, I am never annoyed if an actor asks me to change a piece of dialogue. This is not the way I think. I don't invest a lot of ego in issues relating to authority or paternity; all that matters to me is the result.

When you write a screenplay, or an adaptation, is there something in particular that interests you more than anything else—namely, the story, or the characters, or the tone, the atmosphere, the dramatic progression?

All of those, absolutely all of them. The characters are very important, because I don't want to have unrealistic or stereotypical characters on the screen—and so I insist that the characters should be realistic.

Do you identify with characters?

Yes, completely. I act out scenes when I am writing them. That usually takes place in hotel rooms. I do a lot of my work there, and it is fun to mime the scenes. The difficult thing about paying a lot of attention to the characters is that one risks ending up with limp scenes because of all the nuances—this is the real dilemma. The dilemma of situation versus characters, which, in Hitchcock's case, he has always resolved by favoring the situation over the characters; this is the only criticism one could make of his films—it's the only area in which he encountered problems. Indeed, in Hitchcock's films, the situation is so tightly woven, so strong, that sometimes his characters don't have much of an existence. It's a dilemma from which I suffer also, but in a somewhat different sense: I often have a situation that is a bit too lax.

My concerns are different in each film. For *Fahrenheit 451*, thanks to the framework provided by the novel, I ended up with a very tightly constructed plot. When you're making an adaptation, everything becomes important. You must not lose sight of the reason for which you chose the book—that's essential. I think that it is good to have one or two personal positions, and to stick to them obstinately. These preoccupations become threads that connect each film, each enterprise. They can involve a conception that is adopted at the moment of writing the screenplay, or at the moment of shooting, but I greatly believe in having one. When I see a film, I always sense whether the auteur has adopted a position of one sort or another, or whether he does not have one. Sometimes, I also sense that the auteur has changed his position along the way, and that is always harmful. I think that sticking to one's guns pays off. An idea, even a far-fetched one, if it is pursued very energetically through the whole course of the film, represents such a lot of effort, over several months, that in the end this conviction generates an allure, it imparts a style. This can be moral, it can be aesthetic . . . I don't know. For *The 400 Blows*, I think that the approach I adopted was one of neutrality—it was necessary to be very documentary-like, very cold, and not to try and find strategies for moving the audience, given that the subject matter of the film was already intrinsically moving. With *Shoot the Piano Player* it involved never allowing a scene to end up where one was anticipating it would lead. The spectator thinks that such and such a character is going to die, and it turns out to be the other one, et cetera.

If one thinks that it is going to be tragic, it turns out to be comic!

That's it, exactly. One needs constantly, constantly, to change direction, precisely at the moment where things are veering towards conventionality. *Jules and Jim* is a film that was made very much with the audience in mind—that is to say, I didn't know whether they would accept this or that, or whether sad things might make them laugh; in this instance, it was necessary to introduce them regardless and then immediately to prevent laughter by inserting a sentence or an idea, the seriousness of which was immediately apparent.

And so you think of the audience when you are writing a film?

Yes, all the time. You may like a particular idea, but you sense that people won't find it acceptable; and so, you have to find a way of making them accept it. There is always a way, there is always some strategy you can adopt to sway them. I think that one is obliged to think of the audience. I don't believe any longer in the notion that I used to favor—it was Preminger, by the way, who told me this in an interview, and other filmmakers have a similar view—namely, that you don't need to worry about the audience: "If I like something, I know that the audience will like it too." This is not true. It is more complicated than that, and I now hold the very opposite opinion: I think that an idea that pleases an artist, by definition, is going to displease the audience. Why? Because an artist is someone outside ordinary society who is addressing himself to people within society. Accordingly, it's a matter of imposing one's own original perspective on the members of the audience, and not of surrendering to their ordinariness; yes, indeed, you have to be honest about it. And so, these days, I strongly believe in working to impose one's own originality. It's work that needs to be informed by one's convictions, and the enterprise becomes a contest with other people. I sense this repeatedly every time I see one of my films while sitting among the members of an audience. I can sense when they find one idea outrageous, and the next one acceptable, and when they respond to the one after that as scandalous, and so on . . . Even with a film like *The 400 Blows*, which you might think was accepted by everyone, if one watches it from among the members of an audience, one notices that there are some scenes that shock people deeply, and that the scene after that obliges them to accept it. I very much enjoy this feeling that a contest is taking place between me and the spectators, in spite of everything that might appear disagreeable about it—I mean the degree of calculation involved and, in all likelihood, the ruse one needs to employ; it seems to me that this is part of our job.

Do you enrich a screenplay or a film with personal observations? Do you find yourself living your life in a state of alertness, saying to yourself, "Hold on, that's not bad . . . I'll see if I can use it somewhere?"—or is it more spontaneous than that?

Yes, it's just like that; that's the enjoyable thing about writing with a co-scriptwriter. In the end, the most important thing is probably not what ends up on the screen, but everything that one says about oneself during the work of making the film, everything that is confided, everything that one reports about one's earlier life: "Look, one day, this happened to me, I met someone who did that . . ." In a span of eight hours, you only work effectively for two hours, but during the other six hours you muse about incredibly significant things. And at that moment, I think that such reflections influence the film in a very important way, unquestionably.

At the editing stage, during the technical preparation, do you prepare everything down to the last detail, or do you leave some scope for improvisation?

In the beginning I used to leave a lot of latitude, but now the scope has diminished. It has grown less because I am visualizing more. I know in advance if I am going to find a particular scene boring to make, and so I simplify it on paper rather than simplifying it during the shooting. I get the impression that what I write now increasingly resembles what will appear in the actual film.

Do you visualize the film when you are writing it? When you are working on it in advance?

It's a question of the percentage. You could say that 30 percent is visualized, and the rest is not. You says to yourself, "That will depend on the location in which the film will be shot—let's hope that we are lucky." Sometimes it happens that scenes that one has visualized clearly turn out to be disappointing, simply because one has idealized them in the course of visualizing them; and, in contrast, those that one didn't visualize precisely often result in something really surprising.

Is it the case that concerns relating to distribution and the choice of actors have an impact on the way in which you write a film? Do you write for the actors? Do you want to get to know them in advance?

Ah! Yes, I do want to know them in advance. For *The Soft Skin*, I thought initially of François Perier. When I found out that he was not free, I immediately looked for someone else. I hired Jean Desailly, then two women, but only after we had written the screenplay. Furthermore, the degree to which the actors can improvise during the shooting is almost always a function of the reaction of the actors.

What problems have you encountered when you try to force a particular subject on a producer? On one hand, you are your own producer, and so you have been able to make films that would have encountered difficulties had they been made in other circumstances, but when you are dealing with foreign producers, what kinds of problems have you faced? Do they merely involve difficulties in obtaining finance for your project, or do they cause you to modify the project itself?

No, none, apart from *Fahrenheit 451*, where I met with such resistance that I had to postpone the film and make *The Soft Skin* while I was waiting for something to happen. I always manage it so that I present things when it is too late to put them up for debate. This can also be problematic. When I approach distributors, I always turn up with a finished screenplay, with the actors already having been given their parts. Sometimes that annoys distributors and coproducers. All I require from them is their money!

Although this may be good in terms of your artistic freedom, doesn't it hamper you in your efforts to win over a producer?

That's for sure. I can't tell you how frustrating my experience of coproductions has been. The screenplay is finished, and then you realize that it is impossible to incorporate an Italian actress or actor—that happened with *Jules and Jim*, and again with *The Soft Skin*. I couldn't entrust the main roles to an Italian, and the secondary roles were too slight; and so, at the last moment, the coproduction idea collapsed. That's typical of the kind of frustration I have encountered. As a result, I have had to take bigger risks as far as coproducers are concerned.

Do you change many things during the course of shooting compared with what you have written?

That depends. I changed a lot in my first three films, but not much in *The Soft Skin*. But I think that the others were not reworked to the same degree. I suspect that the screenplay for *The 400 Blows*, if it had been filmed exactly as it was, would have presented serious difficulties. The same with *Shoot the Piano Player* and *Jules and Jim*. Some improvisation during the filming is really necessary. In the case of *The Soft Skin*, the problems were resolved at the screenplay stage. Improvisation was responsible for the way the air hostess came across; this role was very skimpy in the screenplay, it lacked realism. I had decided to include an air hostess simply because I wanted to create the atmosphere of flying in a plane, and there really was no tangible character defined in the screenplay. Gradually, without adding a single scene, simply by shooting a number of slightly different endings to a scene, by adding a sentence or a glance, here or there, the character, I believe, became interesting.

I am under the impression that you have almost always shot in real exteriors. I don't know how many days you spent in an actual studio, but the hours must have been very few?

None. Zero. I have never shot anything in a studio.

For you, is that a matter of principle, economic considerations, or aesthetic ones?

Not of principle, but of both economic and aesthetic considerations, because to have in a studio the equivalent of what I have been able to find up until now in natural settings would require the expenditure of sums that exceed what is possible in terms of French cost estimates. The satisfaction that the real chalet in *Jules and Jim* gave me is inestimable compared with what a studio budget could have provided. Quite apart from the impossibility of moving from the exterior to the interior in a single shot, from the ground floor to the upper floor, a studio would have deprived us of all kinds of chance events and coincidences, such as the sequence in the mist.

Doesn't this practice present you with technical and practical limitations?

It's true. That began with *The Soft Skin*. Up until then I had done things as best I could, and in *The Soft Skin*, for the first time, I shot scenes knowing that they should not be done in that manner. That happened to me in the air hostess's small studio apartment. There I was in a very confined setting that I had liked when I had seen it fleetingly. At the moment of shooting, however, I realized that it was not going to work.

A studio is ideal, but a studio like the one in *The Last Laugh*, or in *L'Aurore*[2]—that is to say, with the main square of a town, with a thousand extras walking past, with trams, police agents, buildings which light up. That's when a studio begins to be interesting; that is when it truly competes with reality.

Let us talk about the film after shooting has wrapped. At that moment, do you still have important creative work to do?

The editing is a very important stage in my films because I am still not able to shoot films in such a professional way that I can say in advance that there will be shots of four seconds, shots of seven seconds, and shots of two seconds—all that is needed is for them to be put end-to-end and that will be the film. This is not the case. I am able to shoot more and more precisely, with a better idea in advance of how the film is going to be edited, but even when one anticipates how the shots will be put together, the editing process absolutely does not lose any of its importance; to the contrary—I don't know why.

Does this mean you are becoming more exacting regarding issues of pace?

That's it, and then thinking about the editing while I am shooting also makes me use a lot more cuts. Thus, at last, I am becoming much less hesitant during the editing: there are fewer solutions that need to be sought out, fewer things to shift, but there are also a greater number of shots to adjust, and I am more careful to adjust them "musically."

Les Mistons, for example, is a film that owes everything to the editing, because I didn't really have much sense of what I was shooting, and how. There was no screenplay, only the novella by Maurice Pons. Each day I would film whatever came into my head, and often episodes that were extraneous to the subject. I didn't have a very good notion of what I was doing—I merely tried hard not to shoot anything ugly, or anything that was too slow. I was preoccupied with speed, but the editing made the film—it was during this part of the process that I decided in what order I would put the shots; there was a lot lacking, as with all first films.

I started to become really interested in the editing with *Shoot the Piano Player*, because it was a rather special film, in which improvisation played a big part. At the end of the shoot, after the first end-to-end showing, it gave the impression of not being fit to be seen, because of a storyline that seemed too jerky and uneven, especially when compared to that in *The 400 Blows*, which was simple and linear. I spent several months editing *Shoot the Piano Player*, and I realized that the process was fascinating—for the first time, I began to alter the film stock a bit, to play around with it.

In the course of editing, one checks for continuity of emotion, and, because of the fragmented, nonchronological nature of the shooting, one notices mistakes that have crept in, and the fact that the emotion is interrupted here and there. You then have to fix that, compensate for it, fill in the gaps.

In *The 400 Blows* the emotion was interrupted each time the boy was not on the screen. If there was a scene that took place between adults and one lost sight of the young boy for three minutes, the emotion disappeared and it was necessary to cut the scene; I kept some of them, but it is obvious that this is a serious fault, and one that arises, or runs the risk of arising, whenever you have a main character on the screen whom the story has followed since the beginning of the film; it is extremely dangerous to let go of him, and yet it can happen that one does let go of him while still preserving a certain degree of emotion—for example, if a scene concerns him, if people are speaking about him; when he comes back, in the next scene, he will be enhanced with additional prestige, and that is preferable to contriving a fancy scene that actually shows the actor.

I encountered this kind of situation in *Jules and Jim*; at a certain moment, I felt that it was necessary to have Jeanne Moreau disappear, to not have her come to the station when Jim returns from Paris after a long absence. In the screenplay, Catherine comes to the station and she looks sullen. Jules and Jim, a short way from her, are engaged in discussion, and Jim wonders why she is sulking. I thought that by removing Catherine from the scene and having Jules say that she has disappeared, that one would not know where she was, or when she was going to return, and by making the two of them talk about her, I achieved something that was missing in the screenplay, something very useful: one now noticed that Jules's feelings with regard to Catherine were much stronger than those of Jim. At the end of their discussion, Jim was ready to give up, to go back to Paris, and then, abruptly, Catherine reappears. This arbitrary disappearance and abrupt return constituted a great improvement to the character of Jeanne and also renewed the emotion.

In *The Soft Skin*, I had only one scene without Desailly, and I was obliged to remove it—it turned out to be impossible; he *had* to be on the screen throughout the whole film, and so I cut this scene, to which no one would have paid any attention, and which would have broken the audience's interest.

You don't have any preconceptions? You don't apply any theories to your filmmaking?

Yes, every time I notice a flaw and find a solution for it, I tend to say, "Well then, that must be a rule," whereas it turns out to be not necessarily a rule.

The music . . .

Music is almost sacrificed in all films and this continues to be a scandal, except in the rare cases of certain filmmakers who pay a lot of attention to it.

Producers have never understood that work on a film continues after the shooting. It is necessary to spend at least three months on the editing. Normally, one should have a first editing of the images, fairly rough, to which one applies certain sounds, dubbing, and then one should have a second edit based on this first soundtrack. Following that, one should work with the composer, then one should record the music, and after the recording of the music, one should arrange for a final stage of editing, but that never happens; the music is recorded several days before the sound mixing and all that is left is to place it. Fifteen days in advance one gives the tedious parts to the composer, having shown him the film two or three times, but without having listened to his advice sufficiently. The composer ought to have the power to say, "I need to have this image prolonged a little." Specialists go even further, since Maurice Le Roux maintains that the composer ought to be on the set during the shooting and even give his opinion in the choice of actors, based on the timbre of their voice.[3]

How does that happen for you in practice? Georges Delerue has written the music for all your films, I believe?

For *The 400 Blows*, I made the mistake of using a songwriter, Jean Constantin;[4] everyone said, "Ah! The music for *The 400 Blows* is marvelous," whereas people who knew something about it, especially musicians, were outraged—and they were absolutely right. Whenever I see the film again, I hear all the wrong notes, all the clashes—it's flippant, quickly dashed-off music that often ruins the effect of the image. The theft of the typewriter is accompanied by jazz music that is completely inappropriate. Besides, jazz is almost always inadequate in films, because it distorts the duration of a scene; in the absence of a melodic line, your image doubles its length; I am convinced that all improvised music is fatal to the effect of an image, to be rejected, unless the film is purely decorative, as in the case of *No Sun in Venice*.[5] Every time I hear jazz in a film that aspires to be moving, I feel acutely that the emotion disappears. Moreover, with films of this kind, it often happens that the director realizes his mistake after the event, when it is too late.

Music should always be created not with the intent of illustrating the image, but to assist it, reinforce it. So much so that the old debate as to whether one should have music that *highlights* or music that *counterpoints* is, in my view, outmoded; the issue is more important than that.

Georges Delerue is a very interesting man because he is the greatest cinephile among musicians; he is one of the only ones to understand perfectly what one is trying to do in a film. I am very grateful to him because, for *Shoot the Piano Player*, all the composers I asked to supply the music refused after having been shown the film. Georges Delerue watched the film and was the first to see what it was really about, being able to see the reference to American films, and the fact that it was a pastiche rather than a parody, that there were successively ironic elements followed by others that were meant to be moving, and he very quickly wrote a score that I think is splendid. So I owed him a film that offered more comfortable working conditions, *Jules and Jim*, which he did very well also, and now he's going to do *The Soft Skin*.

One day, in the course of an interview, you talked about how people were criticizing you for your moderation, your "classicism," in contrast with certain aesthetic developments that have occurred in cinema during the past few years. What do you think about that?

I fully intend to keep clear of these aesthetic developments, because I'm completely incapable of making anything that I don't feel deeply. Up until now, I've been lucky enough to make only projects that interested me, and to make them with a free hand. I have the reputation of liking a lot of very different films, and, indeed, I can understand—a bit like Rivette—all kinds of films and enjoy them as well—films that don't have any relation to what I want to make; what I don't like, however, are films that are contrived—I profoundly detest snobbery and its twin brother, bluffing, and that extends from *Modesty Blaise* to *Trans-Europ-Express*.⁶ This is miserable cinema, because the director, by being determined to confuse the issue, hopes to escape from being judged critically. The motto of the contrivers might as well be the saying from *Thomas the Imposter*: "Since this mess is getting out of hand, let's pretend to have organized it."⁷

This attitude resembles that of New Yorkers who, by buying rolls of toilet paper printed with fake dollar bills think that they are demonstrating their contempt for money. Since no one, in reality, wipes their backside with real dollars, it is pointless to pretend to do so—let us buy blank paper and tell our stories normally, and risk having them analyzed, dissected, and criticized. I hope to stay away from all that pseudo-fantasy.

The danger that threatens me, of course, is to be "out"; no one wants that, but I have absolutely no desire to be "in." When I see a film like Claude Berri's *The Two of Us*, it gives me immense pleasure, because I feel as if I am less alone, I feel that my family has grown larger, I say to myself, "There's someone who is happy to deal with human material that affects me, which speaks to me about things I know and recognize, and which I would like to tackle.⁸ There will come a time when I, too, will feel a need to deal with the Occupation, which I experienced in the city and not in the countryside. It stimulates me and gives me great joy to see it depicted in Berri's film. And yet, it has been made in a normal way—the Michel Simon of *Boudu* thirty years later,⁹ events from twenty years ago that had not previously been depicted, something that is the opposite of *Is Paris Burning?*,¹⁰ France as it really was between 1940 and 1944, with people who were singing "Marshall, here we are . . ." and yet, despite this, were happy to see the arrival of the FFI.¹¹

I think that Rohmer's definition was right when he made a distinction between films in which characters are dominant, and those in which cinema is made to serve the story. However, I haven't yet come to the point of classifying myself, since I am still navigating the waters. *Fahrenheit* is somewhere between the two. For the audience, it's the story that prevails, whereas for me, it was the cinematic qualities of the film. Generally, however, I am one of those who use cinema as a means of telling a story, as in *The 400 Blows* and *The Soft Skin*.

From this point of view, the best storyteller, in fact, is Eric Rohmer himself. In *The Collector*,¹² cinema is used to present a narrative that is both extraordinarily subtle and yet completely simple. The film moves forward with a tranquil assurance that one rarely finds in French cinema: one has to go back to *A Man Escaped* in order to find this sort of domination, this level of control imposed simultaneously on every shot in the film and on the work as a whole.[13]

There are films that are beautiful, or moving, or enjoyable on account of their lack of certainty, their experimentation, the way they have of seeking to create cinema by wandering around (for example, *Law of Survival*),[14] but *The Collector* seems magnificent to me because of the very certainty one senses behind each framing, each change of shot—the feeling you get that "it could not be done in any other way."

Visually, *The Collector* is also beautiful, with a beauty that is as neutral and discreet as the series of films Hitchcock made in VistaVision.[15] Instead of alternating day scenes with night scenes, Rohmer, as with all his films, succeeded in making us aware of each hour of the day, harnessing the sun, light, shadows—and all of that without using any "effects" that are extraneous to the story being told.

With his *Joan of Arc*, one might think that Bresson was trying to achieve something that would be fascinating—a style that was invisible, absolute neutrality, perfect, anonymous narrative—but after watching *Balthazar* and *Mouchette*, I no longer think that.[16] In contrast, I think that *The Collector*, which is as conventional in its structuring logic as any film in the world could be, succeeds in attaining this anonymity of execution I dream about, because of its precision and simplicity.

Does this mean it is a fault to adopt a particular style in excess of what the subject necessarily requires?

Yes. I have never really known what "style" was, nor a style; the form of a film comes into my mind *at the same time* as the idea for the film; if I think I am going to film a couple who are kissing, I don't ask myself a month later whether I am going to have them kiss in sunlight or in rain—no, all of that is in my head from the moment the idea comes, completely formed: they are going to kiss . . . in the rain . . . this will occur at knocking-off time . . . people will be passing in front of, and behind them . . . one will hear their teeth collide . . . her scarf will have the look of a floor-cloth, et cetera—even if it means doing the opposite at the last moment: sunshine, no one in the street . . . But, if I haven't visualized the scene from the outset, I exclude it from the screenplay.

In *The Bride Wore Black*, I am going to have to depict five guys who have just done something bloody stupid; they decide to separate, and not to seek to see one another again. To avoid having reams of dialogue, I am going to have an absolutely vertical high-angle shot looking down on a sunlit square, and

I'm going to show the group of five breaking up, with each one departing in a different direction—I am hoping the idea will work.

The work involved in making cinema is so specific that I don't enjoy talking about cinema with writers, or, often, even with journalists; I like to speak with Rivette, with Aurel, obviously with Hitchcock, but I think that a person like Robbe-Grillet still doesn't understand anything at all about it. Currently, I never go out to dinners, so as not to have to answer questions about cinema.

I believe that a film imposes an approach on us that is both formal and moral, one that guides us at every stage of shooting; this conception can influence the way an actor performs—one knows that one is not going to let him smile once in the film (Montgomery Clift in *I Confess*), that he is going to wear a hat even in bed and even when he is taking a bath (Michel Piccoli in *Contempt*), perhaps that he will never be seen walking or sitting down . . .[17] It can also affect the camera—there will not be a single dolly shot (Eisenstein), no reverse shot (*Citizen Kane*), sixty sequence shots in motion (*La Longue Marche*), et cetera.[18]

> *Do you have this kind of bias when you begin making your films?*

In *The 400 Blows*, it was obviously necessary to prevent Jean-Pierre Léaud from smiling. One never smiles when one is alone. In *Shoot the Piano Player*, it was a matter of finishing each scene in a mood that contrasted with the one at its beginning: more than a bias, it was a kind of gamble, an experience. In *Jules and Jim*, it was necessary to be sparing, to preserve the moralistic side of Roché, and so to offset the situation constantly with contrasting material—by integrating nature, the surroundings into the story, hence all those 360-degree panoramic shots. There was no question of showing the chalet without showing fields, nor the fields without the forest. In contrast, *The Soft Skin* was surgical, there could be no panoramas—the camera did not have any license to stroll around. Critics said, "He's changed his style"—no, I had merely changed the subject!

> *Members of the audience often confuse the notions of author and style. That is why they sometimes seem to be annoyed by your films which, subordinating themselves to the nature of the subject, to the story, do not have a single identifiable "style" . . .*

Yes, I'm aware of that, and it doesn't bother me. In the end, people who watched all my films one after another, at Annecy, found hidden continuities in them. Whatever the case, I never feel unsure before making a film as to what look it ought to have. The continuities are secret; for example, the central character in my films must never say what he is thinking explicitly—things cannot be conveyed directly. I think there has never been a single "I love you" in my films. That's something I can't envisage; I am going to have one in *The Bride Wore Black*, but it will be uttered instrumentally, to trigger an event in the story.

The situations from one film to another may differ, but I think that the characters I show and their outlook on life remain constant.

> *You once said that you were against an "anything goes" type of cinema—one example of which would be the cartoon film—because, in your opinion, one quickly reaches a kind of saturation point, meaning that surprise, interest are no longer possible. In this regard, you separate yourself from a certain tendency, not only in cinema, but also in modern art, which plays precisely with a whole range of possibilities, in which the meaning is never fixed, in which ambiguity reigns, but without anything of an arbitrary nature being put in place. For us, one recent, very powerful example is* The Man Who Had His Hair Cut Short.[19]

That's right, when a work of this kind is successful, it's very impressive. But I was very troubled by Delvaux's film, which I liked a lot, on account of this approach. I realized that this film was overturning the ideas that govern my approach, with my desire to say everything, to follow a character as he is getting up, having his breakfast, leaving his home, arriving at his office, with my concern to leave nothing out. All the same, I would have liked *The Man Who Had His Hair Cut Short* even more had I been able to follow its chronology, which was too complicated for me. I appreciated the actors, the style, the ellipses. I myself am tempted to use ellipses, of course, but they are very hard to control. As for mixing up time and space, I don't think I will risk it any time soon. Jeanne Moreau was telling me that if she were to direct a film, she would like to shoot scenes that were supposed to take place in the same spot at different moments, because, according to her, when one returns to locations, they never resemble what they were the first time you visited them. That's a very worthy idea, but one that, in my opinion, is impossible to translate into cinema, in which it is already very difficult to convey the sense of an actual reality. Unwanted confusion often eventuates. All it takes is for the filmmaker to shoot a house in sunlight at one moment, and then in shadow at another time, for spectators not to be able to recognize it; and so, if one starts to play around with the uncertainties of life, everything on the screen becomes arbitrary, and that can only ever be acceptable if there is a very powerful element of charm involved. Anyhow, I agree with Rohmer when he says that things have an inherent reality that it is pointless to try and attack.

At the beginning of such projects, there is always a "spurious good idea." For me, one filmmaker who always starts with these "bad ideas," but who succeeds in imposing them, is Resnais; with him, there is a determination to force cinema into his corner, to not allow it to take second place behind literature. The most striking instance of this is *The War Is Over*.[20] We have an activist in it who is not very heroic, he has lost faith, he is tired, his activities are slightly dangerous, but not excessively so. He loves his wife but is involved with many others, there are images of the past, images of the future, and even "imaginary" images; at the end, he will perhaps find himself being arrested at the frontier, but perhaps not! . . . One after another, all of Hitchcock's principles are overturned in this story, which is nevertheless filmed in his manner. In fact, the whole movie is filmed in a way that works against the screenplay, but because it involves a contradiction that is intentional and skillfully contrived, the film as a whole is coherent, logical. Basically, what I like in Resnais' work is the critical attitude he adopts toward the screenplay: one senses that the script is never a positive thing for him. This attitude contrasts with that of Richardson when the latter shot *Mademoiselle* without realizing that it wasn't enough to coax the script as it was, but rather to seize it with both hands and wrestle with it.[21]

> *But, in the end, doesn't this notion of "everything is possible" disappear once the film is made, given that the film has consisted of giving such weight to surprising things that they no longer appear to be what they are?*

Yes, indeed, everything depends upon the authority of the director. He has to contrive things in such a way that issues of realism, verisimilitude, and plausibility are effaced as a result of the power of the image, its weight. What is bad in the "all is possible" approach is when you get a composite mixture. The mixture of elements in Resnais' films does not interfere with the unity of inspiration, which is essential, just as in *The Man Who Had His Hair Cut Short*, or in *8½*.[22] These films are entirely different from rash or risky films, because they are controlled, and I would even say designed to be cunning [*rusés*], in the good sense of the word.

> *In* Fahrenheit, *there are many things that make one think of Hitchcock. In what way do you think you have reconciled these references with your initial project?*

It is a bit like what Resnais did with *Muriel*, a film that resembles *The Crime of Monsieur Lange* crossed with Hitchcock.[23] I am attracted by the same kind of mixture, to meld together things that seem contradictory—for example, to place characters from Renoir in a Hitchcockian situation. Furthermore, I am also interested in inserting references to American films into a typically European context in which they are going to appear strange, as in *The Piano Player* and now *The Bride*.

Basically, I have a studious side, a Becker side, which makes me want to improve, to make progress. For example, I have sufficient confidence in myself to make my characters live, move, and speak, and so I would now like to focus my attention on the construction of my screenplays and the poignant aspect of the plots; currently, there is only one man to whom I can turn for this, and that is Hitchcock. To those who question the originality of a cinema that is so heavily influenced by other films, the cinema of a cinephile, I would remind them that the young Hitchcock watched the films of Fritz Lang with the same passion and profit as the young Renoir watched the films of Chaplin. Obviously, when one speaks of Renoir, everyone sees his genius for what it is, whereas with Hitchcock, it's a bit of a potluck dinner, and what interests me about him is not necessarily what interests Resnais, or Chabrol, or Douchet. For me, it's the fairy-tale dimension of his work that fascinates me in the first instance.

Do you think, then, that the mistake people make in borrowing a style is to try and borrow both the technique and the emotion it arouses in a spectator, an emotion that, by definition, can only be obtained by one person . . . ?

Absolutely. If Hitchcock obtains this or that emotion, it's because he has felt it first. He is the only filmmaker in the world who has been able to film adultery as a scandal, and the only one, even, to have the right to film it thus . . . And then the instinctive part of the process is very strong in him, but reflection is always on high alert.

I increasingly prefer filmmakers whom I recognize as having felt that there were several different ways in which a particular scene could be shot, and who have known how to choose between them. For example, I was very happy to learn that Ingmar Bergman had already finished the screenplay for *Winter Light* when he had the idea of including the Chinese atomic bomb, a decision that strengthened the whole film.[24] Even while shooting *The 400 Blows*, I realized at certain moments that neither instinct, nor sincerity, nor faith would be enough to ensure that I would be understood in the way I wanted, so that each time I encountered a problem with the mise-en-scène or the narrative, it helped me to think of Hitchcock, or of Renoir if the problem concerned words or acting. For a long time, I had believed that when something is close to you, instinct would be enough to render it, but I quickly realized that even to express something sincere, it was necessary to make a detour through a lie, and the more I rewatched Hitchcock's films, the more I felt that he was the strongest in this domain. Almost all the other Americans disappointed me.

Even Hawks?

No, not him—he is remarkable, his mise-en-scène is prodigiously clear and simple; I loved *Red Line*, which was screened in London to empty theaters, and also *El Dorado*, which is fairly wild, and which will be successful, I hope. Hawks and Hitchcock remain the two solid pillars of Hollywood, and also Billy Wilder, whom I like more now, especially *Kiss Me, Stupid*.[25]

There is one filmmaker whom you don't seem to like very much, and whom you have even attacked—I mean John Ford . . .

I know that I have been unfair. It was his material that I didn't like: the familiarity with which he portrayed women, bellyaching sergeants, and slaps on the backside. But then, I re-watched *The Quiet Man* on television and I was amazed. It's a film that I had hated, and, in fact, it is like an American Renoir. *7 Women* is also magnificent, simple and neat.[26] Yes, I admit it, my mistrust of Ford was unjust, but even so, I prefer other subject matter—that of Hawks, for example, with its impertinence, the curious relationships his heroes have with women. I firmly believe that Hawks is the greatest intelligence in Hollywood—so there you have it!

You are very concerned with ensuring that you have a strong foundation for your films—in other words, to supply yourself with very strong trump cards at the stage of the screenplay. If there is improvisation in your films, at what level does it generally take place?

Effectively, I am very concerned with coherence and consistency, and I have to have a firm guiding principle. Improvisation only slips in within a very tight framework. Generally, this happens in the middle of the shoot, when I form a new idea of what the film is going to be. At that moment, I tend to strengthen whatever aspects seem to be becoming most important, and it is then that improvisation can enter into it: perhaps a modification of the scenes, by grouping several together, by omitting certain ones—anything is possible. The Italians are stronger for doing without the screenplay. Jean-Luc also; he depends upon the impact of one moment, then of another, and the coherence of the whole materializes at the end, but with the risk of having a slack stretch in the middle of the film, which happens to him from time to time.[27] Personally, I like to have an ascending movement; in this regard, I am similar to Hitchcock, and it is what takes me back to entertainment, since I believe, as do Fellini and Welles, that achieving the goal of entertainment is linked to the way the mise-en-scène is managed.

Significantly, my favorite filmmakers are all directors who write their own screenplays, because what, exactly, is mise-en-scène? It is *the whole collection of decisions taken* in the course of the preparation, shooting, and completion of a film. I think that all the choices available to a director—the choice of screenplay, of ellipses, of locations, of actors, of collaborators, of angles, of lenses, of shots to adopt, of sounds, of music—lead him to *decide*, and what one calls "mise-en-scène" is obviously the common direction toward which the thousands of decisions taken during these six, nine, twelve, or sixteen months of work tend. That is why "partial" directors, those who are only involved in one stage of the process, even if they are talented, interest me less than Bergman, Buñuel, Hitchcock, and Welles, who are responsible for everything that occurs in their films.

One example of a director who is a screenwriter, however, is John Huston, whom you do not like very much . . .

Huston, in particular, is an example of a charlatan. He lends substance to the myth that Hollywood martyrs the pure artist. In reality, he is one of those types who, finding mise-en-scène difficult, pretends to prefer real life; this attitude allows such directors to go hunting while others do their job, and then to dissociate themselves from the result. If you read the book by Lillian Ross, *Picture*, devoted to the shooting of *The Red Badge of Courage*,[28] you will see that contrary to what Beaucourt or Braucourt, the idiot working at *Cinéma 67*, said,[29] Louis B. Mayer conducted himself correctly in this business, giving carte blanche to the producer, Gottfried Reinhardt, and to Huston, while at the same time warning them that he did not believe in the film.

At the beginning of the shoot, Gottfried Reinhardt sent Huston an amazingly kind and lucid letter with five excellent pieces of advice that the latter would not follow—concerning, for example, the topography of locations, indispensable to a sound understanding of the action. At a projection of rushes, Reinhardt criticized the execution of one scene, involving the regiment coming across a dead soldier, which Huston had said was superb: "This scene does not serve its purpose, which is to show the youth's first frightening impression of war."

Annoyed, Huston backed off, claiming merely that "the body is too brightly lit." Later, Reinhardt gave Huston a three-page memorandum that was incontrovertible in the soundness of its observations: "You are right, Gottfried," said Huston, and the shooting continued, with results that were more and more disappointing. One day, Reinhardt said to Lillian Ross, "There is no story, because we are never showing what the young man is thinking about. It is not in the storyboard. John has said that he would put it on the screen. It is not on the screen." Immediately after the shoot, Huston went away to do *The African Queen* without leaving any instructions.[30] Reinhardt continued to be preoccupied with the film, writing to Huston without receiving any response. He fought with Dore Schary to impose an unobtrusive musical score, and he was there when it was recorded, and then again at the sound editing. One evening, Huston came to see the finished film, receiving compliments. Then, it turned out to be a flop. After a disastrous preview, Huston left for Africa shrugging his shoulders and, as usual, without making any suggestions. Reinhardt continued to struggle like a devil—for example, by returning a credit sequence showing that the film had been adapted from the novel by Stephen Crane, and MGM let him incur supplementary expenses without complaining; a commentary was added expressing the ideas that Huston had not known how to put on the screen. Then, Reinhardt was obliged to give up—the film escaped from his control, but he sent another long, friendly letter to Huston, who responded with a very offhand telegram. The film was released, and was a failure. What becomes clear from this book is that it was Reinhardt who identified with the film, suffered for it, while Huston had adopted the same attitude of a gilded slave that would lead him blithely to spoil other great subjects—*Moby Dick*, *The Roots of Heaven*—or accept lamentable assignments like *The Bible*, all the time giving the impression that what he did was infinitely better than it actually was.[31]

It will be obvious that the reason I published the interviews with Hitchcock was to counter the likes of filmmakers like Huston, Stevens, Wyler, Zinnemann—in other words, the story of a filmmaker who was able to claim his freedom, and to preserve it. Hitchcock has never made, and never will make, one of those immense turkeys meant to bail out the big studios; he only films what inspires him, and no one has the right to interfere with his films because he does everything himself from A to Z. His success protects him against professional advisors, and he owes that to his patient pride and his pitiless sense of self-criticism. Hollywood has never bestowed on him one of those Oscars that are often used to reward servility.

Hitchcock has succeeded in Hollywood, but what about Welles . . . ?

Welles, in spite of everything, has always remained himself, whether he is making *The Stranger* for Sam Spiegel, *The Lady from Shanghai* for Columbia, *Macbeth* in twenty-one days, or *Mr. Arkadin* without a dime.[32] Orson Welles can make mistakes, but he is incapable of making a dud, even if all the elements are against him, and I think the same is true of Godard.

You were talking just now of the degree of satisfaction that an author derives from his film. How high would you rate your own?

Sometimes, in my films, I am not happy with certain details—and they can be numerous—but for some time now, I have gained confidence from my realization that I rarely make mistakes at the stage when I am deciding to make a film, the stage when I get the preliminary idea, at the point of departure. Afterwards, I always have a feeling of dissatisfaction, because I am a perfectionist and would always like things to be better; on the other hand, given that I am fairly careless and absent-minded, I don't lay into myself when things don't go well, but I have never felt I had a 100 percent failure. I have never made any film that made me say that I had been wrong to undertake it, even if it didn't succeed at the box office. That gives me confidence in the choice of films I want to make in the future. The only thing that worries me is, as I've said to you, the prospect of being "out"—but, frankly, I don't want to be "in." Were it to happen by coincidence, yes, but the idea of wanting to be "in" is unbearable for me. I could never bring myself to decide to film only what is modern. I approve of it in the case of Godard because it is instinctual with him. In a dozen films, Godard has never alluded to the past, not even in the dialogue. Think about it: never once has one of Godard's characters ever spoken about his parents or his childhood—it's extraordinary. In fact, a study of what is absent in the films of Godard would be as fascinating as one that looked at what he puts in them. He is someone who is profoundly modern, and the fact that he is Swiss is important. One day, someone will have to study the Swiss aspect of Godard's films—the Switzerland that enjoys formatting, monsters, modern materials, secret accounts, and all that.

But almost all the films that imitate Godard are unbearable because they lack the essential thing. People imitate his casualness, but they forget, and for a good reason, his despair. They imitate his play with words, but not their cruelty.

My distrust of what is fashionable extends even to daily language: for example, I can not bring myself to use an expression that pops up in *Cahiers* from one end to the other: "with respect to . . ."

It is always *L'Express* that launches these horrors and, in the domain of cinema, it is Marcorelles.[33] Six years ago, it was "in human terms," and ten years ago "valid" . . . or "not valid . . ." On the Left Bank, one would finish it thus: "valid . . . in itself." When I have a literary problem, a comparison I want to establish, a quotation to make, I turn to Grimm, Perrault, or La Fontaine.

For me, cinema is an art that uses prose. Beyond question. It is all about filming beauty, but without seeming to do so, and without any fuss. I adhere to that intensely, which is why I cannot rise to the bait of Antonioni, which is too indecent. Poetry exasperates me, and when people send me poems in letters, I throw them straight into the rubbish bin. I love poetic prose, Cocteau, Audiberti, Genet, and Queneau, but only prose. The filmmakers I like all share a modesty that makes them resemble one another, at least on this point—Buñuel who refuses to make two takes, Welles who shortens "beautiful" shots to the point where they become illegible, Bergman and Godard who work assiduously to diminish any portentousness, Rohmer who imitates documentaries, Hitchcock so emotional that he pretends to think only of money, Renoir who feigns that he is leaving things to chance—all of them instinctively reject a "poetic" attitude. To finish talking about modernity, I don't know whether I am reactionary, but I don't go along with the critical tendency that consists of saying, "After such a film, one will no longer be able to bear seeing stories that are neatly resolved, et cetera." I think that if *The Magnificent Ambersons*, *The Golden Coach*, or *Red River* were released now in 1967, they would be the best films of the year.[34] So I have decided to continue with the same cinema that consists either of telling a story, or of pretending to tell a story—it's the same thing. In a profound way, I am not modern, and if I pretended to be so, it would be artificial. In any case, I would not be happy with it, and that is a good enough reason for me not to do it.

NOTES

1. The film that resulted was *Mata Hari, agent H21* (Jean-Louis Richard, 1964), starring Jeanne Moreau and Jean-Louis Trintignant.

2. *The Last Laugh* (*Le Dernier des hommes*, F. W. Murnau, 1924); *Sunrise: A Song of Two Humans* (*L'Aurore*, F. W. Murnau, 1927).

3. Maurice Le Roux (1923–1992) was a French composer and conductor who wrote 19 film scores, including that for Truffaut's early film *Les Mistons*.

4. Jean Constantin (1923–1997) was a self-taught songwriter and composer who wrote the lyrics for one of Édith Piaf's hits, *Mon manège à moi*, and the music for many films during the 1950s.

5. *Sait-on jamais* (*No Sun in Venice*, Roger Vadim, 1957).

6. *Modesty Blaise* (Joseph Losey, 1966); *Trans-Europ-Express* (Alain Robbe-Grillet, 1966).

7. *Thomas l'Imposteur* (*Thomas the Imposter*, Georges Franju, 1965).

8. *Le Vieil Homme and l'enfant* (*The Two of Us*, Claude Berri, 1967), about a Jewish boy who is sent to live with an elderly couple in the countryside to avoid him being sent to a concentration camp.

9. *Boudu sauvé des eaux* (*Boudu Saved from Drowning*, Jean Renoir, 1932). Michel Simon was the actor who played Priape Boudu.

10. *Paris brûle-t-il?* (*Is Paris Burning?*, René Clément, 1966), which deals with the liberation of Paris by the French Resistance and the Free French forces in 1944.

11. "*Maréchal, nous voilà!*" was a French song, with lyrics composed by André Montagnard and set to music plagiarized from the Polish Jewish composer Kazimierz Oberfeld (murdered in Auschwitz in 1945), that served as the official anthem of Vichy France. The FFI (*Forces Françaises de l'Intérieur*) were resistance fighters organized into light infantry units, who played a significant role in the liberation of France.

12. *La Collectionneuse* (*The Collector*, Eric Rohmer, 1967).

13. *Un condamné à mort s'est échappé ou Le vent souffle où il veut* (*A Man Escaped*, Robert Bresson, 1956).

14. *Law of Survival* (*La Loi du survivant*, José Giovanni, 1967).

15. VistaVision was a higher resolution, widescreen variant (with an aspect ratio of 5 x 3) of the 35mm film format. It was introduced by Paramount Studios in 1954, and was used by Alfred Hitchcock to film *To Catch a Thief* (1955), *The Man Who Knew Too Much* (1956), *Vertigo* (1958), and *North by Northwest* (1959).

16. *The Trial of Joan of Arc* (*Le Procès de Jeanne d'Arc*, Robert Bresson, 1962); *Au Hasard Balthazar* (Robert Bresson, 1966); *Mouchette*, Robert Bresson, 1967).

17. *I Confess* (*La Loi du silence*, Alfred Hitchcock, 1953); *Le Mépris* (*Contempt*, Jean-Luc Godard, 1963).

18. *La Longue Marche*, Alexandre Astruc, 1966.

19. *De Man die zijn haar kort liet knippen* (*The Man Who Had His Hair Cut Short*, André Delvaux, 1966)—a study of obsession involving a fragmented narrative, together with a mixture of realism, surrealism, and allegory.

20. *La guerre est finie* (*The War Is Over*, Alain Resnais, 1966).

21. *Mademoiselle* (Tony Richardson, 1966), with a script written by Marguerite Duras based on a story by Jean Genet.

22. *8½* (*Huit et demi*, Federico Fellini, 1963).

23. *Muriel ou Le temps d'un retour* (*Muriel, or The Time of Return*, Alain Resnais, 1963); *Le Crime de M. Lange* (*The Crime of Monsieur Lange*, Jean Renoir, 1936).

24. *Nattvardsgästerna* (*Winter Light*, Ingmar Bergman, 1963).

25. *Red Line 7000* (*Ligne rouge 7000*, Howard Hawks, 1965); *El Dorado* (Howard Hawks, 1966); *Kiss Me, Stupid* (*Embrasse-moi, idiot*, Billy Wilder, 1964).

26. *The Quiet Man* (*L'Homme tranquille*, John Ford, 1952); *7 Women* (*Frontière chinoise*, John Ford, 1966).

27. Truffaut is referring to Jean-Luc Godard.

28. Lillian Ross's *Picture* (1952was translated into French as *Un Film est un film*, and published by NRF-Gallimard in 1966. It discusses *The Red Badge of Courage* (*La Charge victorieuse*, John Huston, 1951).

29. Truffaut is referring to Guy Braucourt, who conducted interviews with various filmmakers and wrote for a variety of journals during the 1970s and 1980s.

30. *The African Queen* (John Huston, 1951).

31. *Moby Dick* (John Huston, 1956); *The Roots of Heaven* (*Les Racines du ciel*, John Huston, 1958).

32. *The Stranger* (*Le Criminel*, Orson Welles, 1946); *The Lady from Shanghai* (*La Dame de Shanghai*, Orson Welles, 1947); *Macbeth* (Orson Welles, 1948); *Mr. Arkadin* (*Monsieur Arkidin*, Orson Welles, 1955).

33. Louis Marcorelles (1922–1990), a French journalist and cinema critic.

34. *The Magnificent Ambersons* (*La Spendeur des Amberson*, Orson Welles, 1942); *The Golden Coach* (*Le Carrosse d'or*, Jean Renoir, 1952); *Red River* (Howard Hawks, 1948).

CHAPTER 15

1969: *MISSISSIPPI MERMAID*

> It was the first time that I depicted a genuine couple. In *Jules and Jim* and in *The Soft Skin*, scenes involving two people are always presented with reference to a third figure, to someone who is not there. In this film, when the man and the woman are in harmony, or when they hurt each other, it arises solely from within themselves.
>
> Interview with Claude-Marie Trémois, Télérama, no. 1013, June 15, 1969

Of all your films, Mississippi Mermaid *is without doubt the one that has attracted the most criticism: people have criticized you for the scale of the resources, the fact you chose "A-list" French stars as actors (Belmondo and Deneuve)—in short, of having sold your soul for a grand Hollywood-style operation.*

As far as I am concerned, I think that this is because of certain received notions that the French have—ones they find difficult to let go. Shortly before the shooting of *The Mermaid*, I was talking about my project in New York, and someone said to me, "Ah, that's very good—Belmondo-Deneuve, they will make a good couple." Across there, as you know, it's the land of Cary Grant and Marilyn Monroe! The French have always had a prejudice against the "big" film, always clinging to the idea that "small" actors are better than "big" ones. I don't take any account of that. For me, one kind of film needs

Jean-Pierre Léaud, while another needs Belmondo. I would feel dashed by these criticisms if I had made the film cynically, using a combination of stars for the sake of making money: if, for example, after having been turned down by Belmondo and Deneuve, I had then made the film with Delon and Bardot. That is not the case!

Having said that, I am one of the few directors who love criticism. Currently, I find that publicists, press officers, and certain directors themselves exert too much pressure on critics. One should allow the critics to do their work in peace. It is childish to attack criticism when it is hostile to us, because it is also necessary to contest it when it incenses us. Besides, I never find criticism too severe, whether of me, or of others. Criticism that is excessively laudatory during the course of a career can discomfort an artist considerably; we all know cases of that, such as René Clair, whose creative faculties were destroyed by an exaggerated reputation.

Why did you come back to an adaptation after the original screenplay of Stolen Kisses?

With films like *The 400 Blows* or *Stolen Kisses*, films where you start from scratch, from a feeling, an emotion, and where you draw everything from yourself, at every moment, the process empties you. Between times, it is necessary to recharge one's batteries. And so, I feel a need to lean upon a novel.

When did you read this novel?

I read *Waltz into Darkness* while I was making the adaptation of *The Bride Wore Black*.[1] In addition, at that time, I read everything that William Irish had written so as to be steeped in his work and to be as close to the novel as possible, despite the inevitability of cinematic infidelity. I really like to know the writer whose book I am transposing on to the screen. Thus, when I had to confront an "Irish problem," I had the opportunity to find an "Irish solution." This is the way I proceeded with David Goodis for *Shoot the Piano Player*, and with Ray Bradbury for *Fahrenheit 451*.

Irish is one of the American authors who has been influenced by cinema. This influence became obvious to me in a very palpable way while I was adapting *The Mermaid*, when I was working with the book in my hand as if it were already the screenplay. In the novel, Irish says that the detective "had the most direct stare that anyone had ever encountered." That's the only instruction I gave to the actor playing the role, Michel Bouquet, and it was enough to inform his interpretation.

But the screenplay is very different from the novel.

My final screenplay turned out to be less an adaptation in the traditional sense than a choice of scenes. In the novel, I had especially admired the way events were arranged—the appearances, disappearances, and reappearances of the main characters. I therefore respected this construction for the film, attempting to preserve all of its proportions. But, whereas I was faithful to the novel in *The Bride*, in this instance I altered it. Certain people who liked the book were surprised. New Orleans became the island of Réunion. There is none of the period charm of the 1880s, given that I transposed the story to our own time.

Why? You had already made a period film with Jules and Jim?

If I had made it as a costume film, I would have had to give up any improvisation. That was a constraint that I didn't want. Moreover, New Orleans would have obliged me to shoot it in English, which I don't yet think I am capable of doing, despite the experience of *Fahrenheit*. I write my lines of dialogue in the evening for the next day. I like to be able to make changes up until the last moment. In *The Mermaid*, I didn't even want to write them out anymore. I dictated them to avoid any literary flavor. The actors had hardly enough time to learn the scripts that I handed them at the last moment, so that their surprise then immediately fed into the scene and they confirmed the intensity of it by seeing the reactions of the technical team who encountered the incidents together with them. I would never have been able to proceed like this in English.

Why do you place so much value on improvisation?

I do not like actors to arrive on set knowing their dialogue by heart. I want them to learn their lines in the heat of the moment. I think that when one is feverish, in the medical sense of the word, one is much more vibrant, and I want my films to give the impression that they have been shot with a fever of forty degrees. Certain actors find it hard to adjust to this. In *The Mermaid*, Michel Bouquet, one of my good friends and a great actor, arrived at the location for the shooting in Aix-en-Provence one Monday, the only day on which he was not performing in the theater, and I gave him his script when he got out of the airplane, which only left him the time to learn it between the airport and the set. He came to see me in a state of panic and said, "François, I would do anything for you, I have complete confidence in you, but, I beg you, don't ask me to do that!" And so I told him to come back on the following Monday.

What did you like about the novel?

What appealed to me about *Waltz into Darkness* was the fact that in it William Irish dealt with a subject that had been traditional in cinema before the War. It is found in *The Woman and the Puppet*, *The Blue Angel*, *La Chienne* . . .[2] The theme of the vamp, the femme fatale who subjugates an honest man to the point where he becomes a puppet—all of the filmmakers I admire have tackled it. I said to myself: it has to be done . . . And then, I realized that I could not do it.

The scene in *Nana* in which the baron demeans himself to the point where he begs for *marrons glacés* like a puppy,[3] or the one in *The Blue Angel* in which Emil Jannings cries "cocorico" are scenes that I admire. But I myself am incapable of shooting them. Perhaps that is another reason I transposed *The Mermaid* to our own time—because, in our days, things are no longer like that. A girl, today, is no longer a vamp, a slut. She is a character who is much more understandable. And the victim is no longer entirely a victim. What used to be black and white has now become gray. Therefore, in spite of myself, I reduced the contrasts between the characters, at the risk of downplaying the dramatic quality of the subject.

In contrast to your other films, The Mermaid *includes many shifts of location. How did the shooting take place?*

With this film, I was able to realize the dream of all filmmakers: to shoot in chronological order a chronological story that depicts an itinerary.

And what is this itinerary?

It followed the course of the story: the shooting began in the island of Réunion, continued successively in Nice, Antibes, Aix-en-Provence, Lyons, and ended in the snow near Grenoble. The fact I could respect the chronology allowed me to "build" the relationship between the couple with precision. Given that the story had originally been full of romantic elements from the previous century, I thought that I should parallel the sentimental trajectory of the novel (which we followed) with a physical trajectory. This means that, at each stage, the spectator has to know precisely where the characters are in their physical relationship as well as in their emotional relationship. It is perhaps because of this that the film, which could be classified in the category of "films of love and adventure," ended up describing a contemporary couple.

Why did you choose Catherine Deneuve and Jean-Paul Belmondo?

Jean-Paul Belmondo, along with Jean-Pierre Léaud, is my favorite actor. As far as Catherine Deneuve was concerned, it was impossible not to think of her. Indeed, her role in *The Mermaid* brings together various aspects of her that we have been able to see recently. I think that many girls who have had a difficult adolescence will recognize themselves in the antisocial character she plays in *Mississippi Mermaid*.

Finally, and because he is the most complete actor in Europe, Belmondo has alternated between three characters during his career: one who descends from Sganarelle;[4] one who is inspired by the heroes of American gangster films; and one who could be the son of Gabin in *La Bête humaine*.[5] It is this third possibility that I asked him to explore by drawing on his seriousness, which allowed him to say the lines in which he expresses love so well.

Because, yet again, you have made a film about love?

Yes. But in *The Mermaid* there is no second man, nor a second woman, and I was thus able to focus exclusively on the intimacy between a couple: the transition from using "vous" (as Gide used to say) to "tu," with returns to "vous," confidences, long silences, and that which, through trials and deceptions, leads two people to become indispensable to each other.

Above all, *The Mermaid* is the story of the deterioration of a passion, brought about by love. I believe that most of my films are built around the principle of a web in which the protagonist finds himself caught, always weaker than his partner. Usually, it is the heroine who takes the initiatives; in addition, the story is usually, if not recounted, at the least visibly experienced from the perspective of the hero.

In sum, once again you eschewed striking situations in order to focus on characters depicted in half-tones.

I include romantic adventures at the beginning. But afterwards, I cut them out. I want people to behave normally in a situation that is not normal. Undoubtedly, the reason I do this is because I identify myself with the character. When Louis catches up with Julia, he pulls out his revolver and says to her, "I have come to kill you." But no sooner has he done this than I realize that if were I in his place, I would not know how to use a revolver. And Louis says, "A revolver is not a magical object. I can not pull the trigger."

These are the kind of discrepancies I find interesting. To put very real characters in very intense situations—by that, I mean uncomfortable. Because an intense situation is always an uncomfortable situation, in which people are trapped, caught in a web. And in awkward situations, they react in a genuine way. In the end, *The Mermaid* is the story of a guy who marries a woman who is the exact opposite of what he wanted. But he fell in love, and he accepts her as she is. At the same time, through her, he, who knew nothing about life, becomes a man.

Why did you include a reference to Johnny Guitar *in your film?*

Because *Johnny Guitar* is a fake Western, just as *The Mermaid* is a fake adventure film. My personal taste inclines me to pretend to submit to the laws of Hollywood genres (melodramas, thrillers, comedies, etc.). Within a constraint of this sort, I experience a great freedom of action in all my work. In this business, one has to try and make progress, and, with the passing of time, when I reflect on my most recent films, I get the feeling that I rather neglected their aesthetic appearance—which is all the more serious now that color has become almost obligatory. I am therefore trying hard to pay greater attention to the photography, helped in that by the sensitivity of my cinematographer, Denys Clerval. It seems to me that a great deal of particularly fine talent has been marshaled for *The Mermaid*, especially that of Antoine Duhamel, responsible for the music, and Yves Saint-Laurent, who, as far as I know, is the greatest cinephile among the fashion designers. Yves Saint-Laurent really understood what cinema costumes had to be like, and he designed them both for their movement and style. The little feather coat at the end, which caused me a lot of worry as far as its execution was concerned, thanks to him, turned out to be a character in the film.

You have dedicated The Mermaid *to Jean Renoir . . .*

Stolen Kisses was dedicated to Henri Langlois, owing to the fact I made it when the Cinémathèque business was taking place; this one is dedicated to Renoir because I always think of him when doing my improvisation work. When any difficulty arises, I ask myself, "How would Renoir sort this out?"

1975

With *The Mermaid*, I wanted to make a film that is sincere, but one that would nevertheless look like a photo-novel. And I think that the reason it has received a fairly glacial reception (it has been booed everywhere, except in Japan, a totally unpredictable country) is not because it is poorly executed, but because it is unquestionably a bit perverse. It was a cinephile's film . . . I sought to introduce both a "cliché" and a genuine emotion into the same sequence; spectators mainly noticed the "clichés," but did not pick up the sincerity to the same extent. Many people thought I was having fun at their expense; however, I wouldn't be capable of this kind of mockery, I couldn't remain so cynical for a whole year—the time needed for the conception, the making, and the editing of the film. It is very difficult for the French mind to grasp the fact that a middle way between seriousness and pastiche can arise from genuine emotion. The French can't handle this *"entre-deux"* [between-two] very well. I would call this approach (already present in *The Piano Player* and *The Bride Wore Black*) an affectionate homage to American cinema. I don't like parody, it bores me; the notion of *affectionate homage* means to take something you love, mock it a bit, but without ceasing to love it—in sum, to create a warm kind of irony, an element of sympathy . . . *The Mermaid*, I realize, was not a very easy film to receive; in the final scene, there is also an allusion to *La Grande Illusion* by Jean Renoir.[6] You remember the snow into which Deneuve and Belmondo sink—it evokes this recollection of a frontier to cross, of freedom nearby: one could almost say that, as at the end of *La Grande Illusion*, they are arriving in Switzerland at this point. But there were also allusions to *Pierrot le Fou*, *The Blue Angel*, *Snow White and the Seven Dwarfs*, *The Naked Jungle*, Balzac . . .[7]

It is fairly easy to imagine what shocked audiences in the Western world. *Mississippi Mermaid* depicts a weak man (despite the way he looks) who is spellbound by a strong woman (despite appearances). My work during the making of the film was informed by a secret approach: for me, Catherine was a boy, a hooligan who had had a hard time, and Jean-Paul a girl who was expecting everything from her marriage. He gets married through the classified ads; I nearly made him say in the credits, "Young man, twenty-nine years old, Island of Réunion, *virgin*, is wanting to get married, et cetera." He doesn't actually say so, but, when it comes down to it, for me, Belmondo is a virgin!

1977

With *The Mermaid*, I said to myself, "I have made films about the physical relationships between people, but without showing feelings; I have also made sentimental films, but which deny the characters any sexual life." So I focused my efforts on trying to ensure that the audience knew at every point where the characters were in their emotional life, their sexual life, and also their money problems! However, this was not fully appreciated. It would have been more so had I used actors who had been less mythologized. Belmondo had already been classified as a virile strongman, and I tried to turn him into Antoine Doinel's brother. As for Catherine Deneuve, she had just achieved a series of successes as a suave character, and suddenly I was making her a wicked person. The role of a bitch is marvelous for launching the career of an unknown actress, but if the actress is well known and loved, people begrudge it if she undertakes such a part. So, for sure, I made a few errors of judgment.

NOTES

1. *Mississippi Mermaid* is based on William Irish's novel *Waltz into Darkness* (1947), which was published in a French translation by Georges Belmont as *La Sirène du Mississipi* (Paris: Le Livre de poche, 1964).

2. Truffaut is referring to either *La Femme et le Pantin* (*The Woman and the Puppet*, Jacques de Baroncelli, 1929), or *The Devil Is a Woman* (*La Femme et le Pantin*, Josef von Sternberg, 1935), both adaptations of the novel by Pierre Louÿs; *Der blaue Engel* (*The Blue Angel*, *L'Ange bleu*, Josef von Sternberg, 1930); and *La Chienne* (Jean Renoir, 1931).

3. *Nana* (Jean Renoir, 1926), based on the story by Émile Zola.

4. "Sganarelle" (derived from the Italian verb *sgannare*, which means "to open one's eyes to what one would like to ignore") is a name that recurs in the plays of Moliére.

5. *La Bête humaine* (Jean Renoir, 1938), in which Jean Gabin plays a tortured train driver who falls in love with a troubled married woman who has helped her husband commit murder.

6. *La Grande illusion* (*La Grand Illusion*, Jean Renoir, 1937).

7. *Pierrot le Fou* (Jean-Luc Godard, 1965); *Snow White and the Seven Dwarfs* (*Blanche-Neige et les sept nains*, William Cottrell, David Hand, 1937); *The Naked Jungle* (*Quand la marabunta gronde*, Byron Haskin, 1954).

CHAPTER 16
1970: *THE WILD CHILD*

> Basically, I always tell a story about something lacking, some frustration. *The 400 Blows* concerned a lack of tenderness; *Fahrenheit 451*, a lack of culture. *The Wild Child* is about the frustration of lacking knowledge, together with Itard's stubborn determination to try and remedy this lack. He himself wrote in his memoir, "Without civilization, man would be one of the weakest and least intelligent of the animals." This is a film about communication, exchange, language, and culture.
>
> Interview with Claude Veillot, L'Express, no. 945, August 18–24, 1969

The Wild Child begins with a hunt for the child—a child pursued in a forest by a bunch of adults. When you rewatch this scene, don't you get the impression of having created a Truffauldian pastiche?

Not really; in all the books that recount this true story—about a child of eleven to twelve years old, in a wild state, discovered by peasants in 1798 in a forest in Aveyron—the beginning is almost always the same: "A naked child, nearly deaf and dumb, with tousled hair, fleeing at the approach of men." At the time he was captured, people had known of his existence for two or three years: some peasants had noticed him while talking together. He had become a myth. I think that he was not happy in the forest during winter: the cold was unbearable, and he began to prowl around the village . . .

This is the first time you have worked with historical documents. Did this present you with any particular problems?

Ever since I read this story as it was related in *Rapports et Mémoires du Dr Itard*, in Lucien Malson's book *Les Enfants sauvages*, published by 10/18,[1] it fascinated me, but I was undecided as to whether I would make a film about it. There were too many technical difficulties; it was necessary to rework the text as written by Itard (a doctor who had taken in and "raised" the child), which consisted of two medical reports written four years apart. The first dated from 1801, probably being intended for the Academy of Medicine; the second, written in 1806, was aimed at getting the Ministry of the Interior to renew the pension of Madame Guérin, who was looking after the child. I had to imagine that Itard was keeping his journal, and then turn these reports into a chronicle—but at the same time preserve his text, which is superb, consisting of writing that is simultaneously scientific, philosophical, moralizing, humanistic, by turns lyrical and familiar. It was a bit like the problem I encountered with *Jules and Jim*, in which the interest is both literary and cinematic. I adore phrases like "Il était arrivé à supporter le séjour dans nos appartements" [he managed to endure a stay in our apartments]—to omit them was out of the question . . .

But there is one scene I could visualize from my reading of the *Rapports*, and it made me determined to make the film. Moreover, it is the only theatrical scene: the unjust punishment Itard inflicts on his pupil in order to provoke him into rebellion; it was the only way he could discover whether this child, with whom it was impossible to communicate, was endowed with a moral conscience. Together with Jean Gruault, I therefore created a screenplay that "worked" fairly well, but which was too neatly divided into two equal parts. The first was the "variety show," that is, the forest, the moment of capture, the Institute for the Deaf and Dumb, the curiosity shown by the Parisians, the boy's various attempts to escape, Itard's assumption of custody of the child; the second was his reeducation, and the exercises it involved. I preferred to go to the essential things—to what is essential for me—and to considerably reduce the "variety show" dimension, turning it into a sort of prologue to what follows; the film, I gradually started to realize, would only really begin with the exercises, with the relationship between Victor, the child, and Itard . . .

How did you tackle the problems posed by the reeducation and the exercises?

I conducted research, but not systematically; I simply read a few books on deaf-mutes, such as the book by Maria Montessori.[2] I have always been scared that an excessive amount of background information would make me give up an idea, by making the subject seem too vast for me; I try to limit myself from the outset in terms of what I read.

Similarly, I didn't want to consult a medical advisor during the shooting; I didn't want anyone preventing me from doing certain things. I was content to take some advice, sometimes even during the shoot itself; for example, because I had to deal with tuning forks, I didn't want to do it in any old way. I invited an "ear, nose, and throat specialist" to dinner, and he gave me two or three precise instructions on how to do it.

Before the filming, I watched several medical films on autistic children, and I noticed that they exhibit a very wide range of behaviors: you have children who are very gentle, very slow, who do something insistently, who knock on a table all day long; you have others who are very frenetic; you have those who really look like animals, and others whose gaze is not focused on anything. You have some who live in slow motion. So, I thought, this gave me plenty of scope to invent things.

You decided to act the part of Itard . . . For a director like yourself, who has a reputation for shyness, this is a bit surprising . . .

That's a decision I came to gradually. At any rate, I knew straight away that it was important not to cast a well-known actor; then I thought of television actors; then of journalists I had met in the provinces. This went on until the day I decided that the essential work of the film would be to move the child, to manipulate him—given that one couldn't speak to him—and that doing all that would be much more important than deciding on camera positions. I was still not entirely resolved to play the role, but I was already jealous of the actor who would be the intermediary between the child and me. Moreover, with an actor, there is always some degree of timidity: you say to him, "Move from this door to that window," and what happens?—He never really leaves the door, and never goes all the way to the window; I have never fully understood why this is the case. Perhaps actors worry about taking up too much space; they always try to reduce it . . . But it was particularly after having spent several days shooting a broadcast for Janine Bazin, *Cinéastes de notre temps*,[3] that I felt that I could undertake the role. On the first day, I was nervous, shy, like you said; on the second, I was very happy, and then, on the third, I was so confident I may as well have asked, "Do you want me to make my entrance jumping?"

I don't know whether I was right or wrong to act the part myself; I don't know whether I am a good actor or a bad actor, but I don't regret my decision:

I feel that if I had entrusted the role of Dr. Itard to a professional actor, of all my films, it would have been the one from which I derived the least satisfaction, because I would only have had technical work to do. I would have spent all day saying to some gentleman, "Now, take the child, make him do this, lead him there," and I wanted to do all that myself. From the day I decided to play Itard, for me, the film acquired a real purpose and justification that remained with me. I don't feel as if I acted a role during this experience, but simply that I directed the film from in front of the camera rather than from behind as I normally do.

Some might say that your acting lacked a degree of naturalness, that it is rather severe, stiff.

It was very important that Itard didn't do anything sentimental. Madame Guérin is sentimental. Obviously, since he devotes all his time to the child, he feels something. But there is also in his character the egoism of a man who has found his mission. Of course, that operates at an unconscious level.

How did you choose Jean-Pierre Cargol?

As for choosing the young boy who was going to interpret the main role, I thought of two kinds of children: at first, of the highly educated children who are studying dance at the Opéra. It was seeing photos of Nureyev that led me to this idea. I often think of Nureyev as someone who would be terrific in a film in which he would appear not as a dancer, but as a wild man.

And so, I set off with the idea of finding a child version of Nureyev, but then I abandoned this idea because the young dancers I saw were really too sweet. Secondly, I moved to the opposite idea, which was to repeat what I had done in *Les Mistons*, my first film, in which I had directed five children from Nîmes, one or two of whom really had something very wild about them. I wanted to find a small boy of this sort. I sent my assistant on trips to schools: at Arles, Nîmes, Marseilles, etc. It was in a street at Montpellier that she noticed, questioned, and photographed a small Gypsy boy, Jean-Pierre Cargol, among a group of others.

The role of Victor is a part that could seem very hard for a child. In giving Jean-Pierre directions, I would constantly try and come up with comparisons. For glances, I would tell him "like a dog"; for head movements, "like a horse." I mimed Harpo Marx when it was necessary to express wide-eyed amazement. But nervous laughter and pathological laughter were difficult because he was a very gentle child, being very happy and well balanced, who could only do calm things. Difficult scenes like nosebleeds, nervous crises could only be sketched. We stopped fairly quickly. I avoided anything spectacular: there was no question of arousing fear or of trying to impress with this film, but simply of telling a story.

> *Yet, you were saying that the scene that made you decide to make* The Wild Child *was that in which the child, who has just been punished unjustly, rebels against his teacher . . .*

Indeed. In this scene, which is a duel between the child and the teacher, what interested me most—more than whether or not the child would revolt—was the fact that the teacher mistreats him for his own good. Does he have the right to do that? At any rate, there is no scene in the film that is stronger than that one.

Here is another example, if you like, of the same situation that is just as phenomenal: it is the true story of a Jew during the War who was waiting to be deported. He had an only daughter. He adored her. When he knew that it was only a matter of days before he would be arrested, he became very strict, hard, unjust toward the little girl so that she would be less sad when he was taken away. For me, that is the height of heroism . . . One day, perhaps I will make a film about it.

> *The first spectators who saw your film were surprised by the unequivocally optimistic ending, which also diverges from your usual approach.*

It's true. Generally, my films have rather ambiguous, pessimistic endings whenever they involve stories with characters who are, shall we say, "romantic." I do this so as not to betray the truth about real life, which is not a bundle of fun. And then there is an issue concerning the relative mix of happiness and sadness in a film. If a joyous tonality has been dominant, in order to restore the balance, I try to have an ending that is somewhat melancholic . . .

I think that the power of this story resides in the situation: this child has grown up removed from civilization, so much so that everything he does in the film, he is doing for the first time. When he agrees to sleep in a bed instead of on the ground, it is for the first time; when he eats at a table, it is for the first time. He sneezes for the first time, he weeps for the first time. In my opinion, each step forward already constitutes a great opportunity, and the film draws its power from the accumulation of all these steps forward.

When you have a theme in which you believe, it is impossible to be pessimistic. In *Fahrenheit*, which was a film about the need for books, I also had an optimistic ending, an ending that I like a lot: people who are learning books by heart, who are reciting them in the countryside. For *The Wild Child*, it is quite similar: even if the child has not succeeded in speaking, some form of communication has nevertheless been established—it exists.

You are sure about that?

Yes, certain. And one of the reasons I wanted to make this film is because of my irritation at a notion people have been talking about for some time: that of "incommunicability." "It is the same language, but we do not understand each other." I find that people have become overly sophisticated concerning this issue—Antonioni, in particular.[4] I often say of him that he is the only good filmmaker I don't like! What I value about *The Wild Child* is that all these new "received" ideas are cleared away in order to get back to what is essential: it is wonderful to be able to make yourself understood, it is wonderful to stand upright, it is wonderful to walk in shoes. Elementary? That doesn't bother me one bit. I wanted to go against all the fashionable sophisticates who say that it is better not to read at all than to read paperbacks . . .

Of course, the original "wound" this child has suffered is irreparable. The creation of sounds is the most complex phenomenon involved in being human, and at the same time, it is tied to early childhood. There are theories on this subject, most certainly true, according to which a child raised in the absence of any spoken or sung expression runs the risk of dying. Being deprived of speech is a critical frustration. That is the painful point of this story. Other "wild children" have succeeded in speaking. In the case of the one with whom we are concerned, the question is to know whether he was abandoned before having uttered his first word, or afterwards.

Whatever the truth of the matter, I believe that the end of the film contains positive events (the flight of the child and his voluntary return) that are authentic. Of course, I could have eliminated them. The fact that I preferred to finish the way I did was not, I believe, to reassure the audience. This film contains nothing that is disturbing—it is made like that, in a way that is completely natural.

But I also don't like the idea of a film that "bites its own tail" because, when it is released, it leaves you feeling as if you have wasted an hour and a half. Once again, this reflects my reticence about loading a film with irony and paradox. During a certain period, one could see a series of films by Huston that were all built around a failure. Many critics found that very good, but it irritated me enormously. For an hour and a half we are shown men constructing a tunnel and, at the end of the film, the big trick is the discovery that the tunnel was all for nothing. I have always felt tempted to say: in such circumstances, I want my money back!

When someone says to me, "That which was gold is no more than sand," I am bothered, I feel uneasy, experiencing a sensation of something bogus in the spectacle, an impression of having been manipulated. I know very well that one is always manipulated, but I prefer to be manipulated by Hitchcock rather than Huston.

The fact is, however, that your hero never becomes a normal person . . .

That depends on what you mean by "normal" . . . He lived until he was forty, at the rue des Feuillantines, with the same Madame Guérin who had been his governess in Itard's house (the latter lost interest in him when he was nineteen, having made as much progress as was possible). He led a domestic life. Imagine a person from the country who found it difficult to get used to Paris, who went out very seldom. All he would do is eat, and sleep: Paris is full of people like that. I have tried to include a character like this in the film I am shooting at the moment, *Bed and Board*. He is a type who sits at a window, not having gone out since the Liberation. As I needed some kind of motive, I imagined that he had sworn not to place a foot in the street so long as Pétain remained unburied at Douaumont.[5] I am sure people like that exist. Every time I have had to shoot scenes from a balcony and I have gone back into people's houses through a window, I have seen extraordinary things!

So, you find adults interesting! People say of you that the only characters you believe in are children and adolescents . . .

Especially after *Mississippi Mermaid*, because that film did not do very well! It's rather a blunt summary. That said, it is true that each time my films revolve around a child, a young man, or a woman, they have been received well by the audience, and that my failures, *Shoot the Piano Player, The Soft Skin, Fahrenheit*, all had adult men as heroes. Every time I depict a guy of thirty-five, people don't like it, they say, "No, that's ridiculous, infantile behavior." Jean-Pierre Léaud in *Stolen Kisses* was still acceptable because he was an adolescent.

People accuse you of putting children on the screen because it is a surefire recipe for moving the audience . . .

But films about children aren't always successful. Look at *Naked Childhood*,[6] a film I think is excellent, about a child in state care, in which I participated as coproducer; we lost everything! I can list heaps of films with children that, each year, don't even get to be released, on account of the distributors.

Do you really think that children are little scared animals, pursued by a pack of adults?

I have never said that! But I think that in France children have a hard time. It's worse than hostility, it is a result of hypocrisy, of narrow-mindedness. *The 400 Blows* is a critique of the French way of raising children. I only realized that after having made the film, because, before shooting it, I had never been out of France. It was only afterwards, in traveling, that I was struck to see that the happiness of children had nothing to do with the material situation of their parents, or of their country. In Turkey, a poor country, a child is sacred. In Japan, it is inconceivable that a mother could display indifference toward her son; Audiberti dreamed a lot about Japanese mothers . . .

Here, parent-child relationships are always lousy, narrow-minded . . . When I showed *The 400 Blows* to Renoir, he said to me, "It's a portrait of France." I was pleased with that remark, but I didn't really know why. It was only by going overseas that I came to understand.

All the same, there are happy children, even in France . . .

Yes, in Jewish families . . .

Antoine Doinel, in The 400 Blows, *was a certain kind of "wild" child because he was maladjusted. The theme of* Fahrenheit 451 *hinges on the idea of a certain humanism that it is necessary to safeguard. Would it be too arbitrary to link these two films to* The Wild Child?

From the outset, it concerns a child who is deprived of any education, and therefore of any culture. Currently, and especially since the events of May 1968, people are voicing fashionable ideas that don't sit well with me, undoubtedly because I am self-taught . . . How to express that? Suffice it to say that, as far as the essential things in life are concerned, I have no sense of the paradoxical—I don't enjoy it. I have ideas that are very basic, very simple, and very firm on a certain number of essential points. For example, sometimes people cast ironic aspersions on *Le Livre de Poche*.[7] They refer to it as an object of the consumer society, they are critical of the fact that it is sold in Monoprix supermarkets. I find these arguments completely ridiculous and pretentious.

You alluded just now to ideas that have been in vogue since May 1968. Isn't one of them precisely the idea of a return to a primitive state, or, at any rate, a natural one?

Perhaps, but I am unable to adopt this point of view. I have always preferred the reflection of life to life itself. The reason I chose books and cinema, from the age of eleven or twelve, was because I preferred to see life through books and films. If someone were to ask me which places I have liked best during my life, I would answer that it is the countryside in Murnau's *Sunrise*, and the town in the same film,[8] but I would never identify any place that I had actually visited, because I never visit anywhere. I am aware that this is a bit abnormal, but that's the way it is. I don't like landscapes or things; I like people, I'm interested in ideas, in feelings.

1981

One other aspect of your stylistic work seems, to me, to be apparent in the taste you have for scenes filmed in doorways or windows.

Decisions that relate to the mise-en-scène and imaging are often instinctive. Good solutions are instinctive. When something lacks plausibility, truthfulness, if one places it within a frame, it seems to me that the theatricality of the scene works better. I realized that while shooting *The Wild Child*. As a result of seeing the rushes, I said to myself, "Why did I feel a need to place the camera in the neighboring room and not in the room in which the action was taking place?" And I think that it was because there was a hiatus in *The Wild Child* between the almost scientific material in the film (the manner in which the doctor deals with the child) and scenes that are presented as if they are taking place in the present (I don't speak in the past tense—the narration is a journal written in the present). Ordinarily, deep down, I would find it shocking to treat a 19th-century story as if it were in the present. And so, my unconscious way of excusing myself was to turn it into a *representation*, with the *representation* being signaled by the fact that, on both sides of the screen, we have the surrounds of doors, or the frames of windows. The more disturbing a scene was, the further away the camera was, as when the doctor says, "You are going to be called Victor." I needed this drawing-back. In fact, everything is seen as if it is taking place in a little theater. There, it's because of the period. There are always reasons for these things.

Notes

1. Truffaut is referring to Lucien Malson and Jean Marc Itard, *Les Enfants sauvages, mythe et réalité, par Lucien Mason, . . . Suivi de Mémoire et rapport sur Victor de l'Aveyron, par Jean Itard* (Paris: Union générale d'éditions, Saint-Amand impr. Bussière, 1964), in which Itard's *Mémoire* (1801) and *Rapport sur Victor de l'Aveyron* (1806) were reprinted. 10/18 is a French publishing house that was established in 1962, issuing books only in paperback format.

2. Maria Montessori (1870–1952) was an Italian physician and educator who is known for her book *Il Metodo della Pedagogia Scientifica applicato all'educazione infantile nelle Case dei Bambini* (*The Montessori Method: Scientific Pedagogy as Applied to Child Education in the Children's Houses*), first published in 1909.

3. *Cinéastes de notre temps* was a series of documentaries produced by Janine Bazin, the wife of André Bazin, and André S. Labarthe, a former editor of the *Cahiers du cinéma*, between 1964 and 1972. The tenth episode was titled *François Truffaut ou l'esprit critique* (directed by Jean-Pierre Charlier, 1965).

4. Michelangelo Antonioni (1912–2007), an Italian filmmaker, best known for *L'Avventura* (1960), *La Notte* (1961), and *L'Eclisse* (1962), which eschew traditional narrative realism in favor of evocative images and ellipses.

5. Douaumont is a village destroyed during World War I that contains the remains of over 100,000 unknown soldiers.

6. *L'Enfance nue* (*Naked Childhood*, Maurice Pialat, 1968), a film about an unwanted boy who is put into a foster home.

7. *Le Livre de Poche* is the name of a collection of literary works, begun in 1953, that have been published in a small format that could fit into a pocket. By 1969, sales had reached 28 million copies.

8. *Sunrise: A Song of Two Humans* (*L'Aurore*, F. W. Murnau, 1927).

CHAPTER 17

1970: *BED AND BOARD*

> I am about to turn thirty-eight, and I feel as if I am fifty. I began to live actively at the age of twelve and, what's more, around 1944 and 1945, I watched many films and read many pre-War plays, meaning that my personal folklore focuses on France during the 1930s and 1940s. I would have loved to go to the dress rehearsals for *Amphitryon*, *La guerre de Troie n'aura pas lieu*, *Le Soulier de satin*.[1] I feel as if I belong to that generation.
>
> Interview with Pierre Loubière and Gilbert Salachas,
> Télé-Ciné 23, no. 160, March 1971

Currently, a new categorization is emerging in cinema: people are placing "bourgeois filmmakers" on one side, and "nonbourgeois filmmakers" on the other. Your detractors put you in the first category. What do you think about that?

Frankly, I don't know what to say . . . That is not a perspective with which I am familiar, either in my life or my work. Almost everyone feels insulted if someone refers to them as bourgeois, but I myself do not take this as an insult. In fact, I don't feel at all concerned, probably because I participate so little in ordinary life. In general, the designation "bourgeois" is an attack on a certain way of living. I have no particular lifestyle (I don't live outside of cinema), and so I don't feel as if that is addressed to me; if it arises because of some misunderstanding, I am not concerned to dispel it.

Nevertheless, I am not merely someone who works purely by instinct. Before filming, all I can think about is how to improve the skeleton of the screenplay; but once the film is finished, I once again become a spectator of my own work, and the character of Antoine Doinel, for example, provides me with material for reflection. I say to myself, "The character is like this, or like that." The strangest reaction has been that of Jean-Pierre Léaud, which is fairly similar to my own. As soon as he had watched the first cut of *Bed and Board*, he came to me and said, "You know, I realized near the end of the shoot that this film was not going to be very funny. I felt that it was going to be rather sad . . . Now, I am going to have to change, I am going to have to behave better towards girls." It was futile for me to tell him, "But it's not you, it's Doinel." He remained shocked and kept on repeating, "No, no, I really have to make an effort to behave differently . . ."

Having said that, I can see that Antoine Doinel is certainly not an antisocial type. He is definitely asocial, but he is not a revolutionary of the sort that is fashionable today. In that regard, I do admit that my films are condemned politically. Doinel is not the type who wants to change the world; he despises society, he protects himself from it, but he is full of good will, and I think he really wants to be "accepted."

Is there any difference between Antoine Doinel in Stolen Kisses *and in* Bed and Board?

In *Bed and Board*, I feel as if I blackened Antoine Doinel somewhat, a bit like Pierre Lachenay in *The Soft Skin* . . . I was telling you that the revolutionaries reject Antoine Doinel because he is not fighting against society. Rightly so, because Antoine wants to be on good terms with everyone; he never clashes with anyone; when things are not working out, he simply goes away . . . The other day, a friend said to me. "Doinel never gets into an argument." I had never thought about that, but it is true. Conversely, I have noticed that there is not a single reel in a single film by Clouzot without a quarrel.[2] All of his films present two characters who are never on equal terms: there is always one who bawls out the other. Clouzot sees life in terms of power relations. For him, there are those who are superior, and those who are inferior. This hierarchical vision must derive from his experiences as an assistant director to particularly odious types. I think that he sees life as a settling of scores. I, on the other hand, see life as an attempt to make oneself be accepted. That must be a theme that affects me, because one finds it in *The Wild Child*. You can see, then, why I place so little store in the word "bourgeois," or the fact that people have said the wild child was better off living in the forest, and that it was stupid to have brought him into the town. This argument is the opposite of the reasons for which I made the film. I don't defend the particular society in which we are living, but I like civilization, and I believe in it. My life, my experiences, and my ideas all tend in that direction.

That's where your conception of art contrasts with that of Godard, for example. Have you nevertheless remained on good terms with him?

I have not seen Godard for a year and a half. That's normal. I don't think he wants to see me. The last conversation I had with him was by telephone. He asked me for money to fund a rather adventurous history of production he wanted to embark on: a twelve-hour film in 16mm, made by workers, whom he would have supervised. He thought I would go with it, but I didn't. He said to me, "You can't do it?" I replied to him, "No, I don't want to do it." Put like that, at least there was no ambiguity. I felt that we wouldn't see each other again. He is making a different kind of cinema; he believes that after May one cannot make the same sort of cinema, and he holds it against anyone who continues to do so. As far as I am concerned, I have made my choice, I am very clear in my mind, I want to make normal films—that's my life.

Once again, Bed and Board *is a chronicle about Antoine Doinel. Do you intend to follow this chronicle right to the end?*

Oh, no. I think that this will be the last one. I will make another film with Jean-Pierre Léaud, but he will no longer be playing Antoine. I cannot follow him throughout his life, because I don't want to end up making, as it were, "the story of a filmmaker." I don't want to settle him into society. Indeed, I have not even thought of that. In making *Stolen Kisses*, I wasn't thinking about what would come after it. It was Henri Langlois who said to me, "You absolutely have to portray them once they are married." I am not thinking of making a film about Antoine Doinel every three or four years. Perhaps . . . I can't see what I could add. I get the impression, on the other hand, that the continuation already exists. It is in *Shoot the Piano Player*, *The Soft Skin*, and if one could incorporate it into a dream, in *Fahrenheit*. I think that I have always filmed the same main character, and that I have asked everyone to act like Léaud. I even think that he is the character in *The Mermaid*.

Would you agree that in Bed and Board *there is distinctive approach that draws upon the spirit of a certain kind of American comedy?*

Certainly, because for some years now I have been influenced by Lubitsch, whose films I look at very closely, being fascinated by a very particular form of wit that has been lost after having exerted an enormous influence at the time, especially on Leo McCarey and Hitchcock. It consists of arriving at things through a circuitous route—of wondering, "Given that I have to get the audience to understand a particular situation, what will be the most indirect, the most interesting, the most intriguing way of presenting it?" This oblique way of working (which is also Hitchcock's way, except in his case it is directed toward, uneasiness, suspense—"What is it that will make this scene dramatic?") provided me with a strategy in *Bed and Board* for handling the plot with the Japanese girl. When Jean-Pierre Léaud has an affair with a Japanese woman, his wife knows about it, and when he returns to the house, he opens the door and his wife is at the back of the apartment dressed in Japanese clothes. I knew that people would laugh, and so as I had him advance into the room, I did a tracking shot on to her and, when it ends in a close-up, we see that there is a tear on her face, and the laughter is arrested—people are ashamed of having laughed. This effect was something I had fully foreseen would be achieved by making it in this way, because I knew that once the girl was dressed as a Japanese, the scene would not be any good if she were then to continue and serve him a meal . . . So I knew that it had to end at the moment we see her, but I was looking for a final "effect," and thought that this tear could serve as the high point, because it would have the impact of a cold shower. And it worked well, I think. These things are somewhat experimental on my part—I am thinking about Lubitsch when I do them: "What are people expecting?" How to give them what they are expecting, and then give them the opposite of what they are expecting at the same time. You see? It is all about playing with people, but it amuses me a lot, gives me a lot of satisfaction.

Design for Living, *which has just been rereleased in Paris, is a fairly good illustration of Lubitsch's approach.*[3]

Oh yes, certainly, and there is a scene in it that is completely autobiographical with respect to Lubitsch's methods of working, the one in which the playwright, acted by Fredric March, is composing his play in a loud voice: "Bassington gets up and says: I have only one thing to say to you . . .," and Fredric March then wonders: "What is it that Bassington would be likely to say?" If you read the accounts of people who have collaborated with Lubitsch, such as Wilder, you see clearly that he himself worked in this way: a female character would step on to a diving board, open her mouth, and would say . . . and three scriptwriters were there for the purpose of working out what the heroine was going to say—it didn't have to be on any specific subject, or have any particular meaning, but it absolutely had to be funny . . . This example illustrates how an artist has nothing to say, but has to find something to say. Lubitsch had to find something funny; Hitchcock had to find something terrifying.

I think that the process you used for these last two Doinel films places you fairly close to a particular kind of realism.

Yes, that is the contribution of Claude de Givray and Bernard Revon, who like to seize upon elements of ordinary reality while examining people of the type that one finds in the film.[4] For this reason, they assembled sixty pages of conversations with florists, interviewed concierges, people working for the Americans, et cetera. I really like this way of working because it allows for brainwaves (for example, Mothers Day—an invention of the Occupation) that are very useful in the writing of dialogue and sometimes provide ideas for scenes (it was someone who patronizes a bistro who told us the story of a guy who was asked what he was looking for, and he replied "I'm looking for a fight"). But I also find this approach reassuring, given that I still lack a bit of confidence when I work from an original script. So this method of conducting interviews, of collecting small authentic details, is a kind of vetting of actual life for me. But quite apart from that, the issue of realism is not really very meaningful, given that a film involves a coming-and-going between the real and the stylized. Thus, when I ask Jean-Pierre Léaud to convey the discomfort of a Japanese meal, I tend to go for a kind of stylization that is typical of American comedy, with simplified gestures that evoke cartoons; in contrast, when the couple are speaking in the apartment, I stick with whatever is most realistic, so that one particular word is not forgotten, so that there is a silence after another one . . . There are some things that I regret not having developed more. For example, I was aiming to create a comic effect with the violin case, and I didn't succeed in achieving this. The girl uses it during the night as a suitcase; that is all. I was telling myself all the time that Lubitsch would have achieved wonders with the violin. I classify myself among a series of directors for whom cinema is an extension of youth—a cinema made by children who are sent to play in a corner, who remake the world with toys, and who continue playing games into adulthood through the making of films. This is what

I call "cinema of the back bedroom," which involves a rejection of life as it is, of the world in its actual state, and, in reaction, a need to recreate something that shares some qualities with fairy stories, a bit like the American cinema that made us dream when we were young.

> Bed and Board *is reminiscent both of Renoir and also of American comedy* . . .

Certainly of Renoir, with the courtyard that evokes *The Crime of Monsieur Lange*. But I don't really see Renoir resorting to a trick to create a gag, such as having flowers that open and release words of love in Japanese; you would be more likely to find this in films by Leo McCarey. I very much like the ending of *The Awful Truth* and the use of a Tyrolean cuckoo clock to reconcile the couple:[5] each hour, a good little wife comes out and curtseys, and, at the denouement, McCarey makes the little man and the good little woman come out together. That is exactly in the spirit of Lubitsch, of whom I was speaking just now.

> *Apart from* Lange *and Lubitsch, you allude to Tati-Hulot, and also Guitry with the sequence involving a telephone in the restaurant, which makes one think of the saying: "My God, how pretty you were tonight on the telephone"* . . .[6]

I am very surprised to hear you say that to me, and that Rivette also remarked on it—because, while I like Guitry enormously, I never thought of him while I was making this film. So the scene with the telephone is not a citation, as far as I am concerned (at least not a conscious one), but a means of redeeming certain things in *The Soft Skin* with which I was dissatisfied—the behavior of the wife, in particular—by giving Doinel's wife an amazing aura of respect in relation to the mistress . . . As for Hulot, that's a different matter. Tati, speaking of his character as if he were a real person, said in an interview, "I see Hulot when I go to a restaurant, I see Hulot when I am in an airport, I see him everywhere, but I regret not seeing him in films." In sum, I took Tati at his word! I asked him for permission, and I used the best of his stand-ins for this scene (in fact, he has several).

> *In the structure of* Bed and Board, *as in that of most of your films, there is an endless string of false leads. Are they also in the screenplay?*

At the time of *Shoot the Piano Player*, I realized that I had a tendency to be trite and unimaginative in my work as a scriptwriter. When I started to write a screenplay, it was always very laborious: darkness—in a bedroom—an alarm sounds—he gets up, he puts on a record—he lights a cigarette—after that, he goes to work. On the first day, there was always something like that described. When I introduced a new setting, it was the same: I would have the character walk around each room so that one could see the apartment. At certain moments, it was rather laborious. I lacked the courage to start scenes right in the middle. In *Shadow of a Doubt*, Hitchcock does something that always impresses me: one scene begins with Teresa Wright, who is walking with a supposedly government official; she meets some friends and they exchange jokes, they go to a bar, et cetera. Suddenly, after a drink, we go back to her, sitting on a bench, in extreme close-up, there is a tracking shot behind her, and she says, "I understand: you are from the police!" Often I have asked myself whether there is a scene missing; since I find that to be very daring. It would have taken a lot of film to show how the girl discovers the identity of the cop, and Hitchcock realized that it would have served no purpose.

The editing is very important to you.

Increasingly so—to the point where I no longer show my films before the final edit. In earlier times, people who used to see them really got a bad impression.

Agnès Guillemot says that it is fascinating to work with you, but that it is a very long process, and that there are many pre-montages.

In particular, there are many scenes that one has to invert: for example, the brothel scene at the end, where Antoine encounters his father-in-law, is a scene that could have been placed anywhere one wanted. With respect to this very scene, Agnès Guillemot's reaction was exactly that of a married woman—she would constantly change the place of the scene. She didn't want to put it after a scene with Claude Jade. However, the natural place for this scene comes after the scene with the taxi, in which Jean-Pierre says to Claude Jade, "No, no thanks, I prefer to walk . . . to be alone." And that is where we had it. But Agnès changed it and put the scene after a sequence with the Japanese woman, so that Jean-Pierre seemed to be deceiving his mistress and not his wife!

This anecdote shows once again (as with *The Soft Skin*) how the team feels implicated each time one makes a film about marital matters. There is a kind of uneasiness, a kind of dark laughter when one is shooting the film. Everyone in the team feels as if they are involved.

The character of Claude Jade has changed a lot.

I was careful to ensure that it would be like that. I wanted her to act as if she were twenty-five, and even that she would appear to be older than Antoine. There is one sequence that succeeds in doing this; remember when they are talking together in the bedroom, how the concierge climbs the stairs to look after the child and Claude Jade takes a taxi; throughout this scene, she appears much more mature than he does, more thoughtful.

This scene gives the impression of being a long-take when one recalls it.

That is very much the intention—I was very careful to keep the couple in the same sized frame and to catch them always in movement, in the middle of the image, without interrupting their dialogue . . .

Strangely enough, the menagerie you depict actually does exist in the Barbès-Clichy-Pigalle neighborhood.

Certainly, and that bears upon our discussion at the beginning on *bourgeois or not bourgeois*. That is one of the reasons such a criticism doesn't bother me. I grew up in Pigalle, and no social or political setup touches me because the German Occupation in that area, well . . . it was all about love affairs. In these neighborhoods, very posh apartment buildings sit next to poor houses and there are hotels of all sorts. It is so mixed that there is a veritable explosion. My love for this Pigalle neighborhood, for the people who live there (and those who live off it), makes me think that while it is normal to hate a society that drives one to prostitution, theft, and fraud, well, it is just as necessary to hate any society that could not tolerate them.

Since you have become a director, you sometimes intervene as a public figure, not only through films and the statements you make, but through the assistance you provide in relation to certain events: the affair at the Cinémathèque, the SOS Villages d'enfants, et cetera.[7]

Sometimes, I am asked to support a film that I like a lot (for example, *Détruire dit-elle*).[8] The SOS Villages is one of the organizations that I most believe in: the aim is to prevent brothers and sisters whose parents have died in a car accident from being separated. It is an association in which I have confidence, which I know, whereas I hardly have any faith in UNICEF, for example.

The Langlois affair was a different kind of thing: it was obvious that Langlois could not be replaced by just anyone, and that the films in the

Cinémathèque did not belong to the state. I felt very sure of myself: I am rather inclined to turn away from real life, I take refuge in cinema, and so I have to defend cinema when it is attacked.

You turn away from real life?

There's a bit of that. I like life in moderation, owing to the fact I am fearful (I admire the vitality of a Polanski or of a Claude Berri). I want to know, but not to be known.

In that case, interviews must be a torture for you?

No, not at all. Everything takes place in a small group and, in addition, for the filmmaker, it replaces psychoanalysis, as it were: everything one says in films and interviews amounts to a substantial inward clearing. Fellini says that interviews help him a lot in his work. I think that this is true. After each film, there is a period for us during which the need to formulate what one has done allows one to see more clearly, to gain a deeper understanding, and that helps us move on to the next film.

On the other hand, I regret it if the film doesn't manage to look after itself: it is necessary to accompany it, follow it, support its career, and that bothers me a bit because I don't like meeting people, at least not at first. I prefer individual contacts. I have a talent for paralyzing a dinner, it is dreadful: I peruse the guests around me, as if watching an entertainment, and that creates uneasiness.

I believe profoundly that observation is painful—primarily because one feels bad about looking at people like that, and also because you encounter words that betray snobbery, and thoughts that reveal themselves semiautomatically. Think of the things people say about a show, for example: it is not successful because it attacks the bourgeoisie, or indeed, to the contrary, it is successful because it has been "hijacked" by the bourgeoisie. To have to talk about an art, about cinema in such terms, is depressing.

1974

Because of the fact that people loved *Jules and Jim*, I felt a kind of irritation, telling myself that I was at fault because I had not made the film sufficiently pessimistic, at the very least, not hard enough; and so, I wanted to make *The Soft Skin* to show that love is something much less euphoric, less exhilarating. I thus made it as a response to *Jules and Jim*: there are lies, there is a sordid side, it involves living a double life, it is a film about a nightmare. Films respond to one another. *The Soft Skin* made me suffer because it was booed at the Cannes Festival; on top of that, it has had a difficult career. I felt very dissatisfied, and *Bed and Board* was a response to *The Soft Skin*. I said to myself, "I am going to remake the same film, and I am going to show that one can say all of that while laughing, instead of remaining too uptight." That's what explains why you find very similar scenes, strong resemblances, between the two films—because the second is a lighthearted "remake"; and then, when *Bed and Board* was finally finished, I found that it, too, was sad ... When you are dealing with adultery, it is not lighthearted, and to turn it into something lighthearted means lying, as in certain American comedies. If one is going to treat the subject with any degree of realism, it is sad by necessity.

> *The meeting of characters generally ends rather badly in your films, there is often a breakup, which allows for a glimpse of other possibilities ...*

That's true. Look at the end of *Bed and Board*, for example. I created a happy ending, but one sees that Jean-Pierre Léaud behaves just like the opera singer behaved earlier—that is, he takes his wife's coat and handbag and throws them down the stairs; he has become a husband like the latter. But I wanted to counterbalance that, to show that it is not very serious, and so I make the singer's wife say to her neighbor, "You see, dear, they are like us, now they are really in love." But I didn't want it to finish like that: I show the singer making a face that contradicts what his wife says. In other words, each shot contradicts the one before it in this final sequence, in which I show in succession four happy indications and four unhappy indications.

1979

> *You have had the opportunity to do what directors don't always do, which is to rewatch your first films, undoubtedly several times. Do you see them differently at this point in your career, and would you make* The 400 Blows *again in the same way, for example?*

There are faults in *The 400 Blows*, but they are not all that serious—I still think that the film as a whole is quite good. *Love at Twenty* was very improvised, but that lends it a certain kind of grace ... With *Stolen Kisses*, I was so pessimistic when I was making it that I was pleasantly surprised after it was released. My strongest reservations concern *Bed and Board*, which is also the one that has been the least well received by the press ... At the time, I found that very unjust, because I was very happy with the actors—I thought that they had never been better—but on watching it again, I really divided it into three parts: everything that is in the "marital home" is very good; everything that happens in the office where Jean-Pierre works is a bad joke, which makes for poor comedy; the third part, which involves adultery, the affair with the Japanese woman, is also bad because I wanted this Japanese woman to be comic, but she is so beautiful, she has such a noble face, that one cannot laugh at her. Ideally, a good Doinel scene is one that should simultaneously amuse some spectators, while making others rather sad . . .

Notes

1. Truffaut is referring to *Amphitryon 38*, a tragicomic play by Jean Giraudoux first performed in 1929; *La guerre de Troie n'aura pas lieu* (1935), another play written by Jean Giraudoux, which explores the fratricidal motivations that led to World War II; and *Le Soulier de satin*, a mystical play about an impossible love set during the Renaissance, written by Paul Claudel in 1929, but first performed in 1943.

2. Truffaut is referring to Henri-Georges Clouzot (1907–1977), a screenwriter and director best known for *Le Corbeau* (*The Raven*, 1943), one of Truffaut's favorite films.

3. *Design for Living* (*Sérénade à trois*, Ernst Lubitsch, 1933).

4. Claude de Givray (born 1933) is a French film director and screenwriter who cowrote *Stolen Kisses* and *Bed and Board* with Truffaut. Bernard Revon (1931–1997) was a French screenwriter who also contributed to the scripts of these two films.

5. *The Awful Truth* (*Cette sacrée vérité*, Leo McCarey, 1937).

6. The reference is to a character created and performed by the French comic Jacques Tati for a series of films, including *Les Vacances de Monsieur Hulot* (Jacques Tati, 1953), *Mon Oncle* (Jacques Tati, 1958), and *Trafic* (Jacques Tati, 1971).

7. The *SOS Villages d'enfants* is an international humanitarian association created in Austria in 1949 that provides a family context for orphaned brothers and sisters under the care of an SOS mother until they become self-sufficient. It was launched in France in 1956.

8. *Détruire dit-elle* (Marguerite Duras, 1969).

CHAPTER 18
1971: *TWO ENGLISH GIRLS*

> *Jules and Jim* was filmed from a distance, both in space and time, and the painful shocks were blunted. For *Two English Girls*, I wanted people to feel the emotions of the characters along with them and, if possible, for one to feel them physically. I am not ashamed to say that I was hoping people would cry when watching this film, if only because the actors genuinely cried when they were performing in it.
>
> Interview with Yvonne Baby, Le Monde, no. 8356, November 25, 1971

Each one of your films comes out of the others. It is Jules and Jim *that led you to* Two English Girls and the Continent. *Both books are by the same author, Henri-Pierre Roché, who wrote the first when he was seventy-four years old and the second when he was seventy-seven. It is the same story in reverse. Nevertheless, these two books are very different from one another. For you, what constitutes this difference? And how will it be apparent in your film?*

Since it was published, I have read and reread *Two English Girls and the Continent* several times each year, for my own enjoyment. The idea of making it into a film occurred to me quite recently. In *Jules and Jim*, I used quite a few sentences and ideas from *Two English Girls*, but this second novel struck me as less successful than *Jules and Jim*, even though it had more beautiful things in it. On top of that, an adaptation of *Two English Girls* seemed still more difficult to bring off than one of *Jules and Jim*, because this time it would need to involve three characters who are rarely together, and who communicate through letters and personal diaries.

Another important difference between the two works is that the characters of *Two English Girls* are appreciably younger; because of that, their story sounds a more painful note, more anguished.

Anyone who does not like to hear about love in cinema should not go to see *Two English Girls*. There is not a single image, not a sentence that does not relate to it. The characters experience very strong feelings. They comment on them for each other, between themselves, without respite, and at a certain point they become sick with love. That is the essential difference from *Jules and Jim*, which was a hymn to life, while this one is a film about grief.

People have been talking for some time about the physical representation of love in films. That seems a normal phenomenon to me: cinema has to make up for fifty years of hypocrisy and lying by omission in the domain of sexual relations. But for *Two English Girls*, there is something else. Rather than a film about physical love, I have tried to make a physical film about love.

There are a certain number of differences between the novel version and the film version of Two English Girls: *characters, scenes, and lines that figure in one, but which one does not find in the other.*

Indeed, and the reasons that I have brought in these changes are more or less mysterious, even to me. At the moment, I am confused about it, but there will come a time when someone will surprise me by saying, "This is in the book and not in the film," or vice versa, because, in my memory, I end up completely mixing the two. There is no doubt that I have been less faithful to Roché than I was in *Jules and Jim*.

The two brothers, for example, have been left out.

Yes, for reasons of neatness. It was the women who counted for me. If I had needed to depict a large family, I would have been very uncomfortable—because of the time it would have taken.

And Diurka, the friend we meet at the end, whom you have turned into a publisher?

We gave him a trade, probably for the simple reason that I don't like to show idle people on the screen. In *Jules and Jim*, Gruault invented the fact that

Jules would be interested in insects, drawing his inspiration for that from the personality of Roché's son. With Diurka, I elaborated his role for another reason: Claude needed a confidant, especially near the end of the film, because there was already a lot of commentary. We preferred to enlarge the role of someone people already knew. Moreover, I liked the idea of a character that one would see again, but who would elicit a change of opinion when he comes back. Claude utters this statement, which I really like: "You were getting on my nerves, I didn't like you very much . . ." after which they are going to become the best friends in the world. Things of this kind are what reinforce a sense of time passing.

Why did you make Anne die?

That is certainly a major departure from Roché. How to explain it to you? Don't forget that the story stretches out over a very long time. Jean Gruault and I had an intuition, without being entirely certain, that one of the two English girls is still alive—just as the heroine of *Jules and Jim*, the woman who inspired the character of Kate, still lives in Paris—of that we are certain, even though she has been very discreet, avoiding seeing anyone. I would like to believe that it's the same for Muriel; today, she would be between eighty-five and ninety years old. It is true that Roché, who was working from personal diaries originally written between 1903 and 1909, doesn't have anyone dying, but it seemed indispensable, to me, in the end. So as to provide answers for certain unresolved issues that remained in the book, I reread an account of the lives of the Brontë sisters, and I picked up some surprising coincidences from it: the games they played, their daily routine . . . I was extremely affected by the death of Emily, who would only agree to be seen by a doctor two hours before she died. I transposed that end on to Anne. Of course, it is not her, of the two of them, that one would expect to die—it would have been Muriel. In cinema, it is always the idealistic characters that one most readily sacrifices: I wanted to do the opposite.

Do you agree that this is a very pessimistic film?

I think that it is dark, but not pessimistic. If it were, it would be unfaithful to Roché, whose every line attests to a love of life. In the production of novels and films, most love stories involve love that is impeded, but here the impediments are almost never from the outside: they are from the inside, and even mental.

I hope that I haven't depicted *Two English Girls* from a masculine perspective—besides, I am more interested in the femininity of artists than in their masculine qualities—and I hope that in the future there are more female filmmakers.

What did you do for the scene of Muriel's deflowering? That red that invades the screen ... Roché merely wrote, "There was blood on her gold."

For this kind of scene, Jean Gruault drew patiently from the personal diary Roché kept each day from 1903, when he was 24, until his death in 1959. This journal would be about the size of that of Léautaud, amounting to around twenty volumes, and Gallimard thought that Roché was insufficiently well known to justify its publication ... Nevertheless, it is a fascinating document, as much for the insight it gives us into the man and his relations with women, and thus the genesis of his novels, as for the knowledge it provides of the period and its artistic milieu; personalities appear under pseudonyms in it, but sometimes Roché has added in the margin, or above, real names—Picasso, Apollinaire, Braque ...

For Roché, this journal was a vital necessity, and in the end it was what prevented him from turning it into a work written for the public, because he was constantly preoccupied with it. So, what was needed in the first instance was to preserve this hand-written journal, most often in notebooks and diaries, sometimes on little bits of paper, and to have all of it typed up, in order, for a second time, to give it a chance of finding a publisher ...

The fact that I made use of this personal diary, which contains the real-life human material for his novels (Jim was Roché himself; Jules was a prominent Jewish writer he met in Germany), led me to make a film that is more cruel and realistic than Roché's novel.

In his novel, Roché idealizes things, he softens the suffering of the women. In the journal, to the contrary, he doesn't flinch from any aspect of the actual reality, and it teems with intimate details, sometimes of great cruelty. On the other hand, I felt that the story was so sentimental, possibly melodramatic, that I needed to balance this element with scenes that were very physical, like the one you mention. Take note, however, that I am not scared of melodrama *per se*. I wanted this to be as physical as possible; ideally, I would have liked to have shown semen. Still, I have tears, vomit, blood—in brief, suffering (and an exaltation of the bodies as well).

This was the first time you have used Jean-Pierre Léaud outside the story of Antoine Doinel. Is it because Two English Girls *is closer to your own personal world than the other novels you have adapted to the screen up until now?*

No, not really. I don't feel a deeper affinity with Roché. Undoubtedly, this is because of one particular reason: he was born rich, and therefore he couldn't tackle life and its human problems with the same kind of attitude as people like Jean-Pierre Léaud or myself. That is the aspect of the role I constantly stressed when directing Léaud, so that he would completely erase his Antoine Doinel side—all of that "cheeky guy" aspect that he had shown us at the time of *The 400 Blows*. In this way, I forced him to achieve a real character-creation.

Roc, like Roché, is an intellectual motivated by curiosity, someone who knows practically everyone in the artistic circles of his time, but also someone whom the others don't know, or only slightly know. Thus, Cocteau, to whom I showed *Jules and Jim*, didn't remember until ten days later that he had met Roché . . . In that respect, Roché reminds me of the young Proust; like him, he frequented society, he observed, he listened, and, like him, he had to suffer being regarded as a frivolous man, a dilettante, owing to the fact that he wasn't creative. But in Proust's case, this period of apparent dilettantism lasted only a short time, and he went on to make a masterpiece out of it, whereas Roché appeared to prolong it throughout his whole life, while concealing a different work that was entirely personal.

And in the end, I realized that I am closest to Roché in the degree of happiness we each gain from the act of writing. He had a kind of innocence in the richness of his use of language that made me think of a version of Cocteau from the countryside—for example, when he puts into the mouth of one of his English girls the words: "Love, love, the dogs are unleashed and are running at full speed in my heart . . ."

Is it true to say that you have pushed Claude in the direction of a certain intellectual dryness, in contrast to the much more emotional, more sustained playfulness of the two women?

For Claude, the key word is "curiosity." Jean-Pierre Léaud conveys that idea when he speaks; in these instances he is perfect, and all I needed was to leave him free to do it. When he listens to, or observes something without saying anything, I find him less convincing. So I asked him to adopt a neutral expression, so that no one could impute discernible emotions to him at those moments. What matters is that Claude always looks on his love affairs with an aesthetic eye, even when he is leaving women gasping for breath, broken. Take, for example, his intention to publish Muriel's confession as a book—a reaction that, displaying intellectual curiosity (which I invented), seems characteristic of his personality, to me. Let us say that he is very predisposed towards such a state of mind! He only breaks down on one occasion, and when that happens, we see him completely helpless and shattered.

The girls are completely different. Muriel conducts herself like a puritan in love. The fact that she contradicts herself from one scene to the next, and sometimes within a single scene, pleases me greatly. Remember when she says, "We will never see each other again." And then, she almost immediately adds, "If you were to come, I would open my arms to you."

One gets the impression that the feelings Claude expresses are fabricated, whereas Muriel and Anne express real feelings.

Claude is a bit like Jim in *Jules and Jim*, someone who is fairly enigmatic. This is the case in novels and films told in the first person: the narrator is always the least well-defined character.

Do you have an ironic, critical attitude toward him? Doesn't he end up becoming somewhat irritating?

Certainly. As far as I am concerned, I side with the two women, against him. Claude is less passive than Doinel was in *Bed and Board*, but he has a knack for reacting at inopportune moments (the film is full of setbacks—I really played that up). Claude does not know how to seize his opportunities when they present themselves, he shies away . . . I am not at all surprised that spectators get rather irritated by his attitude.

There is a very beautiful statement in Roché that you have retained in the film—it's this: "Life is made out of pieces that don't join up." I wonder if, for you, cinema, editing, are precisely what allows you to stick the pieces together?

Well, it's strange, but I didn't preserve this statement in the original script—I only inserted it at the last minute, during the editing. It's true that it is very beautiful. When Muriel utters it, she does so with the energy of despair. Of course, it is possible to interpret it in many different ways . . .

Why do you use iris-in shots so much?

Are there really all that many of them? I think the reason was mainly so as not to "spoil" the image. I think it is a mistake to present films that place in an old setting through means that are too modern. It's the same with color—one has to be careful. The zoom shot, for example, is a modern invention; I use it, but in a way that is invisible. I liked Pasolini's *The Gospel According to St. Matthew* as a film, but the zoom shots bothered me.[1] I don't mind pretending that cinema existed at the time of Jesus Christ, but not the zoom! Although iris-in shots, on faces, go back to Griffith, I feel that a technique that is commensurate with the times work better. Earlier, I conceived *The Wild Child* according to this principle. Jean Gruault spent some time watching old Griffith and old Chaplin movies in 8mm copies.

In Two English Girls, *there is an element of sublimated melodrama that indeed makes one think of Griffith, or of Borzage.*[2]

I don't know Borzage. I was definitely more influenced by a film such as *The Magnificent Ambersons*, which I watched as often as I could, and which is one of my favorite films. There is a scene in my film that directly references it; it occurs when Claude's mother tells him to light the gas—the light on her face at that moment . . .

How is it that in almost all of your films (including those that are taken from Roché), there is, as in Jules and Jim *and* Two English Girls, *a man caught between two—or a number of—women, or a woman caught between two men? I am thinking especially of* The Soft Skin, Fahrenheit, Stolen Kisses . . .

Frankly, I don't know what the answer is. There is, nevertheless, one exception, at least—*The Mermaid*. However, I grant you that in the case of that film, it felt very odd to me to have only a couple. During the shooting, I would say to myself, "This is the first time that I have two people without reference to a third. Is this because I hate clichés?" With Renoir, the constant configuration is not a trio, but a quartet (a man and three women, or a woman and three men)—it's his fundamental theme. But after all, for drama and conflict to exist, the intrusion of a third person is generally necessary.

In reading Roché, one finds short, dry, rather breathless sentences. Were you trying to achieve that effect through the way you edited the film?

Roché's sentences end up being very short as a result of deliberate deletions and very strict cutting: he achieves a synthetic style as a result of concentration. Roché expresses himself—he told me this himself—in a way that is unbelievably "airy and tight," and that comes, perhaps, from what he was accustomed to recording on a daily basis, in a telegraphic style—his encounters, his sexual adventures.

After an absence, he notes, for example: "I met her, I held her in my arms, she was my only lover between the age of nineteen and twenty-three." I wanted, naturally, to preserve that quality, but not through the editing. There are many tracking shots in *Two English Girls*. In that regard, *Jules and Jim* definitely moved at a quicker pace: it was meant to evoke the whirlwind of life. In this film, there is a sense of time passing, a dilation of time. There is the idea of reliving things in the present—an idea that is not present in the novel.

This is why the sound, which was almost always recorded directly, is so important. I think that this method creates a particular kind of emotion. For example, when Claude meets Muriel in the studio, the only noise we hear is the sound of his footsteps—he advances slowly toward her, as she holds out her arms, in a dreamlike manner, as if they are dancing; I never would have dared to do that earlier.

That makes me think of this statement in the commentary: "A curiosity that had something sacred about it . . ."

That's it, exactly. Rivette observed to me that the film has an incantatory and religious aspect. The precision of the soundtrack, and also the quality of the photography are definitely there for a reason. I am very happy with what Nestor Almendros, my director of photography, delivered me. Four or five years ago, I was still very afraid of color, because I am not a painter. In real life, I never pay any attention to the color of the curtains, the floors . . . Black and white was a safeguard for all of us. But these days, color has become almost obligatory, and, with color, ugliness has come to disfigure the majority of films. I would never dream of repainting nature, the walls, as Demy or Godard (in *Pierrot le Fou*) do, because I do not have their visual imagination. In order to avoid ugliness, we paid a lot of attention to the decors, the costumes, the furniture . . . This was made more complicated by the fact that a "period" film was involved. For me, color applied to the period of the 1900s—or even later: let's say the Occupation—is very anachronistic. When I recall the years of the Occupation, my memories of it are in black and white, not color. This is even more so the case if I go back further in time. I have therefore tried to recreate time in the present, terribly present.

How did this film eventuate in the context of your own life?

Although people generally think that the "Doinel" series is autobiographical, whereas the series of adaptations I have made simply attest to my literary predilections, the reality is very different. I have a great propensity to talk about myself, but a very great dislike of doing it directly. For this reason, I feel that I am projecting myself more personally and sincerely through borrowed subjects—*Mississippi Mermaid, The Wild Child, Two English Girls*—than through the Doinel films, in which I constantly dread an identification being made between Jean-Pierre Léaud and myself.

I began this film in a bad psychological state that improved as the shooting progressed. This made me whisper to Claude (he has just finished his first novel), "I am better now, I feel that the characters in the book are going to suffer in my place."

1981

Two English Girls was made as a reaction against *Jules and Jim*. I thought that there were terrific things in the novel of *Jules and Jim* that I had not dared to shoot, and that now I would do so. In the novel, there is a moment when Jim and Catherine want to have a child with each other. They make love in the countryside and, after having made love, Jim shakes Catherine by her feet so that she has a better chance of getting pregnant. This was a wonderful idea, but I was twenty-eight, twenty-nine years old, and I didn't feel I could film this scene. So I was determined to push the treatment of *Two English Girls* deliberately in the direction of crudity to compensate for what was too angelic in *Jules and Jim*.

Notes

1. *The Gospel According to St. Matthew* (*L'Évangile selon saint Matthieu*, Pier Paolo Pasolini, 1964).
2. Frank Borzage (1894–1962) was an American actor and filmmaker, known for films characterized by lush romanticism, portraying young lovers whose love triumphs over adversity, in films such as *Seventh Heaven* (1927), *Street Angel* (1928), and *Lucky Star* (1929).

CHAPTER 19

1972: A GORGEOUS GIRL LIKE ME

> I love cinema to the point that I cannot bear the company of people who do not like it. One day, I gave a ride in my car to a German who was hitchhiking. I spoke to him about Fritz Lang. He didn't even know the name, nor of Max Ophüls—and so, I made him get out of the car at Lyons, leading him to believe that I was stopping there.
>
> *Interview with Monique Sobiesky,* Le Journal du show-business, *May 21, 1971*

Could you comment on A Gorgeous Girl Like Me, *adapted from a novel by the American writer Henry Farrell, and why it has been so poorly received?*

This film was not made, as certain people assume, "to earn a crust," to make up for the commercial failure of *Two English Girls*—in fact, the script for *Gorgeous Girl* had already been written. It was simply that I was attracted by another literary form: after the beautiful language of Roché, composed of short sentences, and marked by an incredibly refined sophistication, I turned my attention to a completely invented kind of language—a very coarse form of slang, but less vulgar than the kind Queneau used in the *Adventures of Sally Mara*.[1] In addition, I wanted, in my own way, to even the score with respect to romantic love. When I was making *Two English Girls*, I knew that this would be the last time I would film a girl climbing the stairs with a candle in her hand while romantic music was playing in the background. I tried to destroy the romanticism by being very physical, which is why there is so much emphasis on illness, fever, vomiting, et cetera. *A Gorgeous Girl Like Me* was the continuation of this destruction: it is a mocking of romantic love, and an affirmation of brutal reality, of the struggle for life . . . It is a film that displays an exaggerated vitality, which I wanted to be close to the kind one finds in certain films by Billy Wilder, and I think that when you drive a film in accordance with such a desire to push things as far as they can go, the film inevitably deviates from reality, becoming somewhat abstract. I like the form of *A Gorgeous Girl Like Me*. I was probably wanting to make a movie by Audiard filmed by Jean Rouch:[2] the mad world of Audiard (which, I might add, I don't despise) as seen by an ethnologist.

The humor in this film is more American than French. How would you define it?

Yes. American humor depends on bad faith, and bad faith is a tremendous wellspring for comic effects. With regard to Camille, the young sociologist arrives at a crazy interpretation because he is madly in love. He wants to force everyone to see her as a victim of society, whereas the opposite is true. No woman, however, is duped by Camille. There is a terrific scene in the book—which, unfortunately, is omitted from the French translation: the sociologist's visit to Camille's former teacher. She says so many bad things about Camille that he ends up interrupting her indignantly: "Madame, your opinion is of no interest to me—you are not objective." "Indeed," she replies to him, "I am not objective as far as Camille is concerned. Where epidemics such as bubonic plague or cholera are concerned, I am definitely against them."

There seems to be a lot of cruelty in the comedy of this story. That hardly seems like you . . .

Yes, it is a cruel film, without an ounce of sentiment, a mocking kind of comedy in which everything is scoffed at, but I hope that it is too lighthearted to be bitter. I wanted to go further in all directions. *Two English Girls* was my first film without any humor. This one is my first film that is really comic.

How did you direct your actors?

Usually, I always ask the actors I cast to perform with restraint and realism. They are not very enthusiastic about that, and this approach also garners me criticism of this edifying sort: "Truffaut, always in half-tones . . . gentle, tender Truffaut, et cetera." With *A Gorgeous Girl Like Me*, I had a chance to film a story in which all the characters are mad, which allowed the actors to go all out in their acting—"as if their lives depended upon it," as Audiberti said with regard to Joan Crawford in *Johnny Guitar*, one of my favorite films. Furthermore, I was exploring, inventing. When a shot was neutral, I would say to myself that I needed to change it, to find some other way. With Bernadette Lafont, I was constantly adding things, all the time.

You had already made a film with her, in Les Mistons.

I laughed to myself in imagining her in this role. I must say that we both greatly enjoyed making *Les Mistons*, a film in which the two of us made our respective debuts. At that time, I was tripping over the cables and confusing the camera with the projector; as for Bernadette, who was not yet twenty, it was enough for her to enter and say "hello" to blow the fuses of three flood lamps. All that was needed to persuade Bernadette Lafont to take on this role was to let her hear the noise of the pages of Henry Farrell's book being thumbed over the telephone.

I was struck by the old-fashioned look of the sociologist's car.

The town in which this story takes place—like that in *Shoot the Piano Player*—had to be a somewhat imaginary one. You don't see any signs or notices in it. The cars there are all old, but the television set is a color one. We exploited everything. There was no need for it to be too closely associated with France. When I read a *Série noire* novel, I don't get any impression of America—let alone France—but rather of a third country, a dreamlike country. To get so much craziness across, you have to be very precise. To impose something arbitrary, you have to be rigorous.

Language plays an important part in this film, given that the comedy arises from the contrast between the language of the sociologist and that used by Camille.

There are people who will find Camille's language vulgar and be astonished that dialogue written by Truffaut is not "literary." But it is not because it is coarse that it is not literary. As far as vulgarity is concerned, that occurs when one is trying to be refined and distinguished, whereas in actual fact one is not. That is not the case with Camille.

There is also wordless comedy when Sam Holden puts on a record of the Indianapolis races each time he goes to cavort in bed with Camille.

That's an attempt on my part to achieve indirect comedy. You know that I have been greatly influenced by Lubitsch. Like him, I try to tell stories that are very simple, but in an indirect way. For example, rather than show "intimate scenes" between Camille and Sam, I let the Indianapolis record be heard. From the context, we know that this is one of Sam's obsessions. So, when the din of the cars suddenly bursts forth, even though we are in a deserted street and cannot see either Sam or Camille, we know what is happening.

To what do you attribute the failure of the film?

I think that there was one small error in the film: I made the sociologist too realistic; from time to time, the story gives the impression of being told by him. That's a pity, because the film ought to be centered solely on the girl, and the people who identify with the sociologist resent the film as being vicious: it is not vicious, but people don't understand that I sympathize with the girl. For me, she is the big sister of *The Wild Child*.

In addition, you depicted the sociologist as completely ridiculous: he doesn't understand anything about life, he always misses the point, and, worst of all, he is a sociologist.

He is ridiculous—he does not understand life at all; perhaps it was because I made the character too much of an idiot . . . Once again, this was a response to *The Wild Child*: this film is both the same and its opposite simultaneously: Bernadette is the wild child, but this time, the film is against the educator, who is a theoretical type and doesn't understand life.

Some have thought that this is an anti-intellectual film. That is not the case. But it is true that it is a film against a vision of life that is too theoretical, too academic. I loved punishing the male character, because his error is so serious. This is not because it is scandalous to be a sociologist, but because it is scandalous to adopt a strictly scientific point of view toward things that have such a living reality—for example, children in prison. Here's how I would put it: Bernadette's character in this film does not represent women as they ought to be, but real life with its drive, and, above all, what these days we would call a sense of survival. If I were politically inclined, I would have made a film in which Bernadette represented the "third world." She struggles for life throughout this film, and I am absolutely not concerned with notions of sympathy or antipathy—when people came and told me that she was a real slut, I was genuinely astounded. I said to myself that they had not watched the film very closely.

> *Since you were talking about intellectuals, what do you think about the question certain contemporary critics are raising today about André Bazin, accusing him of idealism? What do you think of the structuralist critical approach?*

That is a very difficult question for me, because not having had any university education, I am not acquainted with the vocabulary that would allow me to convey any judgment on structuralism. I can only tell you that André Bazin was an extraordinary man to know, and that what he wrote was subtle, but nevertheless accessible to everyone. Bazin understood the world through and through; he was not a doctrinaire person, but had a liberated intelligence. I don't find an equivalent clarity, logic, or power of reasoning in any film critic today: the only writer who frequently makes me think of Bazin is the Jean-Paul Sartre of *Situations* and, more recently, of *The Family Idiot*.[3]

1975

I do not consider any of my films to be atypical, even *A Gorgeous Girl Like Me*, which is perhaps the most controlled, coherent, and integrated of the others. I believe it has a great logic, a real reason for being. There are mistakes in it, but I don't regard the film in any way as a departure from what I normally do, or as making a concession of any sort. I have never made a film on demand, or a commercially motivated film, or anything that has been suggested to me from outside myself. This is not an absolute rule, but, up until now, all of my films are ones *I* have chosen to do. Because of this, I accord them absolute equality; I do not arrange them into a hierarchy.

This film has been regarded as one that projects contempt; that is a mistake, because one cannot be contemptuous of oneself. The film was made *against myself*—that is what has not been understood. The film is ambiguous in the sense that it is secretly—but no less than any of my other films—autobiographical. In *A Gorgeous Girl Like Me*, I am both of the characters: Camille Bliss and Stanislas, the sociologist. I laugh at someone who persists in seeing life from a romantic perspective: I agree with the girl, who is a kind of hoodlum, who has learned to mistrust everyone, and the need to struggle to survive. I contrast the one against the other, but I love them both.

The film's failure, in my opinion, derives from the fact that there exist two types of screenplay. There are scripts that escape from generic classification: in them, everything is permissible, so long as it maintains a certain degree of coherence. And then there are other screenplays that belong to genre cinema, like *Mississippi Mermaid* and *A Gorgeous Girl Like Me*. Now, if one is making a genre film, it is necessary to respect all its laws. In *A Gorgeous Girl Like Me*, one shouldn't approve of all the characters. To put it another way, if the projection of a "genre film" were stopped halfway through, one ought to be able to ask the spectators about what they are hoping for, and observe that they are all hoping for the same thing. In *A Gorgeous Girl Like Me* (as in *Mississippi Mermaid*), I confused the issue—the sympathy of the audience vacillated, and a certain uneasiness set in that prevented people from laughing and participating.

Notes

1. Sally Mara is fictional writer invented by the French novelist Raymond Queneau (1903–1976) to be the purported author of his novel *On est toujours trop bon avec les femmes* (*We Always Treat Women Too Well*, 1947), the salacious account of a beautiful woman caught up in the 1916 Easter Rebellion in Dublin, which was followed by a second work, *Le Journal intime de Sally Mara* (1950). Subsequently, *Les Oeuvres complètes de Sally Mara* were published in 1962 under Raymond Queneau's own name, and it is to this edition that Truffaut is probably referring.

2. Jean Rouch (1917–2004) was a French filmmaker considered to be one of the founders of cinema verité, visual anthropology, and ethnofiction.

3. *Situations* was a series of 10 volumes published by Sartre between 1947 and 1976, including *Literary Critiques* (1947) and *What Is Literature?*; *The Family Idiot* comprised three volumes, published between 1971 and 1972, about the French writer Gustave Flaubert.

CHAPTER 20

1973: *DAY FOR NIGHT*

> I dedicated *Day for Night* to the Gish sisters, Lillian and Dorothy, the first two genuine cinema actresses, but above all I was thinking of the song "Moi, j'aime le music-hall," in which Charles Trenet affectionately and humorously lists all the singers in vogue. This was the spirit in which I made *Day for Night*, out of a desire to bring the cinema world into a movie, and to make it enter through all the perforations of the film: "Moi, j'aime le cinéma."
>
> Pariscope, *no. 263, May 10, 1973*

What made you want to make Day for Night?

Why a film about cinema? Because it had been in my head for a very long time. And I felt that I had waited a long time to do it, in so far as I had, for example, made films devoted to books in general, like *Fahrenheit 451*, or a particular book, like *Two English Girls*. Everyone finds the vocation of a filmmaker mysterious. We know that because of the questions people ask us, ones that we find very hard to answer. During the War, I asked an adult, "How long does it take to make a film?" And he answered, "Three months." I learned that what takes place on the screen was made in three months. I had just discovered what people generally know. But, within those three months, everything that occurs is a mystery. To tell the truth, every time I found myself shooting a film, I would think of how interesting it would be to make a film about cinema—for the very simple reason that mind-blowing things always happen during a shoot, things that are funny, strange, or interesting, but which the audience never get to know about, since these events are part of the filming process that takes place beyond the edge of the shots.

You realize how odd the shooting of a movie can be when you have an actor who has never made a film as the main character, because you rediscover the strangeness of this craft through his or her eyes, and to an even greater extent when a child is involved. I remember paying a visit to the set of *Bay of Angels*, which Jacques Demy was shooting with Jeanne Moreau.[1] There was a young man there, Claude Mann, who had never made a film. In one scene, he had to enter a hotel room with Jeanne Moreau and turn on the light. At the moment of filming, when he was putting his hand on the switch, he realized that it was not he who was turning on the light, but an electrician off screen; he burst out laughing and it was necessary to stop filming. I remember that as a very nice incident: it exemplified the discovery of cinema. I myself had obviously experienced that with Jean-Pierre Léaud, but I have to admit that I discovered it at the same time as he did with *The 400 Blows*, and I experienced it again with young Cargol with *The Wild Child*.

In such moments, one can see clearly that there is something marvelous in the daily practices involved in this kind of work. All of that deserves a film because this craft, which is glamorous in its totality, is also, in its detail, constantly surprising.

What points would you make about it?

I made *Day for Night* like a documentary, and there is very little discrepancy between the shooting process that I depict and that of my other films. I imposed some very precise limits: I respected the unities of place, time, and action. To evoke the making of *Je vous présente Paméla*—the film within the film—I wanted to enumerate in a fairly systematic but plausible way all the pitfalls that can handicap and threaten the achievement of a good outcome for the enterprise. People have often said to me, "Aren't you scared of demythologizing cinema?" No, I have no worries on that score. I have not tried to destroy the mythology of cinema—to the contrary. Given that French cinema is rather lacking in mythology, I wanted this film to bear the imprint of Hollywood.

I also wanted to continue what I had begun with *Stolen Kisses*, which is to say that I wanted to fight against a trend in French cinema, which, since 1960, had tended to concentrate on a single character. In *Day for Night*, I tried having ten characters of equal importance. This collective, united aspect of the film expresses nostalgia for the cinema of Prévert.

Is there any other kind of nostalgia?

There is a nostalgia for films that are not scared of telling a story, which are not afraid of melodrama, and which are prepared to risk being judged adversely. In my view, a storyteller has to accept the possibility that he will be regarded as an idiot in the eyes of the disciples of Paul Valéry.[2] *Je vous présente Paméla* is the story of a young married woman who runs away with her father-in-law. I chose this story for its simplicity, because I knew that the spectator would be able to locate the reference points for the drama at any time. For the sake of intellectual comfort, I could have left the subject of *Je vous présente Paméla* completely in the shade, but I willingly took on this bourgeois tragedy; it illustrates a cinema of feelings that I first defended and then practiced, and which I would be one of the last to abandon. I can add, to "defend" the tale of *Je vous présente Paméla*, that the only "pirandellism" in the enterprise resides in it: all the conflicts of *Day for Night* and *Paméla* concern problems of identity and paternity. Because of that, I contemplated dedicating this film to Philippe Garrel, whom I admire a lot.

Your problems?

Perhaps, I don't know. From the scriptwriter who is pregnant without anyone knowing by whom, to the actress Julie Becker who (in real life) has married a doctor who could be her father, and who goes away (in the film) with her father-in-law, passing by Léaud who kills his father, Valentina Cortese who drinks because her son has leukemia . . . All that flabbergasted me belatedly, once I had registered its presence during the course of the editing.

Could one say that Day for Night, *in the context of the rest of your work, marks a new departure?*

For me, *Day for Night* is somewhat of a recapitulation film. In it, I feel, Jean-Pierre Aumont is like an echo of Pierre Lachenay in *The Soft Skin*, and given that Jean-Pierre Léaud plays the part of a young actor, obviously Doinel is also present in the film. We thus have a meeting of Pierre Lachenay and Antoine Doinel. I invested the character played by Jacqueline Bisset with many of my memories of working with Julie Christie in *Fahrenheit 451*, given that they are both Englishwomen, and English actresses project moral qualities that are very different from those of French actresses. They are very frank, very loyal, and at the same time possess a great deal of femininity. Sometimes, for example, they are very brutal in the questions they ask... Jacqueline Bisset, in this film, is a synthesis of the four Englishwomen with whom I have worked.

From this point of view, *Day for Night* is a crossroads where the main characters of my other films meet one another. That is why its tone is that of the films I have made based on original screenplays. At first sight, it is the tone of *Stolen Kisses*, but less teasing, a bit more dramatic.

Is it a farewell or a renewal?

A farewell, I think. I am certain that there are some things in it that I am depicting for the last time. The exploration of the theme: are women magical, for example?... There are several things initiated in other films that are finished off here: I am putting a full stop after them.

Certain filmmakers who also arrive at some sort of turning point—I'm thinking of Fellini and 8½, in particular—suddenly address the question of artistic creativity, as it occurs in cinema. So, it reflects a period of crisis, anxiety, questioning. What is it for you at this time?

I only dared to undertake *Day for Night* because *8½* stopped *before* the shooting, and only dealt with the preparation for a film. Mine is less inward. I knew that I would not depict the same things; I was voluntarily more anecdotal. If there are any elements in the film that are profound, I would prefer to think that they eventuated almost in spite of me. At two moments in the film, one maybe gains a glimpse into the process of creation, but I'm not even sure of that. I stuck with what one can see, and what is visually verifiable.

The fact that I acted the part of the director is because I probably would not have dared to say so many things had I engaged an actor to play this role. I feel I have said more about the characters surrounding the director than about the director himself. But in spite of this, seeing him tie up all the threads by working with the team, allows one, I think, to infer quite a lot—more than I would have wanted to reveal about the process openly—at least I hope so...

This is the second film in which you have acted. How would you compare your experience to that in The Wild Child?

I felt a special kind of emotion at finding myself "alongside" Jean-Pierre in front of the camera. I was more at ease in acting in this film that in *The Wild*

Child, probably because there was none of the stiffness of a period film—of costume and language—and also because I saw it as a form of reporting, as if one were making a television film about my work.

Why the hearing aid?

I needed to establish a small distance from real life, which is why I gave myself a hearing aid, because I am preoccupied with problems of communication (I probably wouldn't have made *The Wild Child* unless that were so), and for me it served as the equivalent of a hairpiece for an actor. I wanted to find an idea that would not depend upon makeup, so as not to lose time each morning putting on a false nose or a wig, or I don't know what. So I adopted this hearing aid which only required me to put it in my ear, and that helped me to act, because I knew that I was no longer quite myself, I was no longer really Truffaut, but Ferrand (his name in the film). Having said that, Ferrand is a director into whom I have projected many of my reactions—I depict him behaving in a way that is quite close to my own during a film: that is, trying to maintain a good atmosphere, not to show that I am concerned when I actually am, and to play the game, in the sense that a film is something that shifts enormously; one has to be ready to accept the idea that the actors are more important than the characters they play, the idea that what is living in actuality counts more that what is theoretical. This kind of approach obviously comes from Renoir, but I have always felt it myself. In the end, the idea that even the snags can lead to improvements, can serve to nourish the film instead of impoverishing it.

In Day for Night *you also pay homage to Orson Welles.*

If, in the course of *Day for Night*, I pay homage to *Citizen Kane* in particular, it is because this film changed both cinema and my life. Through the young actor played by Jean-Pierre Léaud, I am constantly pondering a question that has tormented me for thirty years: is cinema more important than real life? Perhaps that is hardly more intelligent than asking, "Do you prefer your father or your mother?" But I think of cinema for so many hours each day, and have done so for such a large number of years, that I cannot prevent myself from making films compete with life, and reproaching life for not being so well arranged, or so interesting, dense, and intense as the images that we organize. "There are no traffic jams in films," Ferrand says to Jean-Pierre Léaud, "no troughs, no dead time. Films advance like trains in the night."

Between a film and life, between an "American Night"[3] and a "French Day," what do you choose?

That's the whole question, of course. All the same, it seems to me that real life has the last word. In contrast to *The Golden Coach*, if you like, *Paméla* is perhaps a little too stylized, too "American," but that is not true of the material that surrounds *Paméla*. There is a holiday-camp, euphoric aspect to the scenes shot outdoors that I wanted to reproduce (it is the aspect to which foreigners are most responsive). The French shooting style allows more of real life to enter into films . . .

How is it that the film could have such a happy vision, and yet finally leave an impression of bitterness?

As with *Stolen Kisses*, it is always this way when one tackles life in general, and when one does so with truthfulness and a degree of familiarity. The feeling of things happening that are going to end . . . I think that people laugh more in the first part, which is descriptive, and less in the second, in which the narrative is more dominant. The break occurs approximately at the time of the first departure, that of Dani.

Isn't it the abundance of departures—and of deferred arrivals—that creates the melancholy?

Assuredly, yes.

I would like you to talk to us a bit about the interpretations of your actors, about the way in which you reconciled the scenes of the film proper and those of the film within the film . . .

The actors are a little more uptight in the film *Je vous présente Paméla* because it involves a bourgeois tragedy. I tried to include as much real life in the part dealing with real life as possible, to reinforce its normality; for instance, the dialogue is scarcely written—rather than write out the lines, I preferred to tell them to the actors before shooting, in order to procure hesitations, and so that there would be a compromise between my vocabulary and theirs. I tried to achieve dialogue that was the least literary I had ever had, in relationships, in life. But, having said that, I didn't try to create a very big contrast between the film and the film within the film.

What I can say is that when one makes a film, one struggles to make it, one makes it with suffering and joy. And then several years later, when you see it, you forget the mistakes in the mise-en-scène that caused you to suffer during the editing and the sound mixing, you forget the errors in the screenplay; you might forget the errors of production, of framing. The only thing that one cannot forget is an error in the casting of an actor, when one has selected someone that one should not have chosen; it still makes you suffer, seven years later, when you see the film; you say to yourself, "Oh no, I should not have chosen that one."

But, this time, I felt that the film had been lucky in getting a cast that worked very well, sometimes creating the impression, perhaps, that the roles are very close to the actors themselves—but that is an illusion, because in each case there is, in fact, a very big gap. In spite of this gap, however, there is a homogeneity that I was very happy to have obtained, a meeting up of very professional actors and less well known actors who act the part of technicians, who are themselves mixed in with real technicians from Nice. And if all that gives the impression of a very homogeneous family, well, I am very happy.

You were talking about dialogue being improvised—in this regard, have you ever used the words of an actress for a film in the way Ferrand does when Jacqueline Bisset has a nervous breakdown?

That has often happened to me. I realize that there is something cruel about it. This is, in fact, one of my memories of *Jules and Jim*. Jeanne Moreau had a personal problem. She was upset, she was crying (there were no scenes involving tears in the film) and three days later, I put that into a scene, the one in which she and Oscar Werner are crying together, and I gave her several lines that she had uttered when she was distraught. But in this new film, it was designed to illustrate an important aspect of a director's work, which is theft. A director is a thief.

Jean-Pierre Aumont's role in this film does not match up with his usual image.

Jean-Pierre was not happy that I gave him a boyfriend, but I needed that, and I persuaded him to do it. It is a rather noble thing that he wants to adopt the young man and give him his name. I was thinking of Jean Cocteau, who later in his life adopted Édouard Dhermit, a young painter.

People wonder a lot about the title on the poster: La Nuit américaine. *Don't you think that it risks putting them off, or at the lease not attracting them?*

I have no way of knowing. With *Stolen Kisses*, it was impossible to know whether it was a good title or not. Given that there was no one in the theaters during the first week, I said to myself that I had given it a bad title, then, all of a sudden, the film started to take off amazingly—by that I mean that people were happy and told others to go to see it; and so this title, which had seemed bad to us, became good. In the case of *The Soft Skin*, I thought I had a good title, and yet the film was not successful. Perhaps this wasn't because of the title . . .

A title is just one element, nothing more. I would not like to choose an off-putting title first off, but *La Nuit américaine* does not seem off-putting, to me. It is a title that makes me dream, even if I am not thinking about cinema. The proof is that when we were shooting the film, a book came out bearing the same title, and was awarded the Prix Renaudot. That was an occasion when I could have changed the title of the film, since it had always been a bit of a drawback, but I decided to keep my title because I like it a lot. I wouldn't be able to bring myself to call the film *Silence, We Are Shooting*, or *Camera*, or *The Red Light Is On*. *Action* was a title I liked but which would have sent the audience down the wrong track because in a film called *Action*, one expects to see Burt Lancaster, Charles Bronson—one anticipates a Raoul Walsh type of film, and here that would have been misleading. I thought of calling it *Meet Pamela*, which is the title of the "film within the film," but it was too bland. In the end, I was happy with *La Nuit américaine*.

One question that could be put to you after practically each of your films: why this loyalty to Jean-Pierre Léaud?

Because he inspires me greatly. It is enough for me to start off with an idea, to add Jean-Pierre Léaud, and already this provides me with a third of the screenplay. I can imagine instantly how one would see him in this or that situation, I know what I would make him say, I know how he will act it out, and that stimulates me a lot. I find that I work best with people I have already directed. It is not so much during the shooting that one discovers an actor, it is on the editing table. So, I think I can obtain a better result when I work with an actor for the second time, that's to say when I have looked at him for weeks on the editing table.

The ideal is Ingmar Bergman's small troupe. As for me, I love meeting the same actors in Bergman's film, I find that terrific, all the more so because these are actors who belong to him, because you cannot say that you have seen Gunnar Björnstrand except in a Bergman film, nor Bibi Andersson. That is also explained by the fact that Sweden is a small country with a small film production, and that Bergman's work involves only a small number of characters—he is like the director of a troupe of theater actors.

I know that Jean-Pierre Léaud is controversial at the moment, but he is controversial because he has begun to exist. One doesn't find mediocre people controversial—they are regarded as good throughout the length of their career. Jean-Pierre Léaud is one of those actors, like Jeanne Moreau, who are so generous that sometimes they can be led to give too much, or in the wrong way, and at the moment, people are lashing out at them. But the fact that they can give so much invests them with their richness, and as far as I am concerned, I am not worried about Jean-Pierre Léaud.

NOTES

1. *La Baie des Anges* (*Bay of Angels*, Jacques Demy, 1963).
2. Paul Valéry (1871–1945) was a French poet, essayist, and philosopher who, although admired by other modernist writers like T. S. Eliot, was often criticized as obscure, remote, and difficult.
3. A "*nuit américaine*" (American night) is the French term for a cinematic technique whereby night scenes are simulated while filming in daylight.

CHAPTER 21

1969–1974: OVERVIEW 2

In Day for Night, *you are talking directly about yourself, your love for cinema. Where does this need to speak directly about yourself come from?*

It is strange that you should define the film in this way. I don't feel as if I were talking directly about myself. Let us say that I was talking directly about cinema. There are not many allusions, or "private jokes" in my films, in contrast to those of the New Wave. I expressed my love for books in *Fahrenheit 451* and in my films that were based on novels. I felt that it was not natural to leave out the cinema side. That was missing, and I had been thinking about it for three years. While I was shooting certain scenes in other films, I decided to look at how they could be used in the context of a film about cinema.

In *Two English Girls*, the mother of the two young women says to Jean-Pierre Léaud at one particular moment, "You cannot stay here any longer because people in the district are talking. You are going to live with our neighbor, Mr. Flint." She then points out to him a house situated some distance away. In actual fact, there was no house. We only had one house, that of the two English girls. I therefore had to execute a trick and position some plants in front of the camera. I filmed the house of the English girls from an angle that had not been used before, so as to make people believe that it was Mr. Flint's house. Then we climbed higher up the hill and I asked for a fake window to be constructed with a little curtain round it. Jean-Pierre Léaud opens the curtains, then the window, and looks at the two English girls, in their garden, in the distance. In shooting this scene, I was amused to see this fake window with all the members of the technical team fussing around it. This is a scene that you find repeated in *Day for Night*.

Even before the shooting of *Two English Girls*, I would take notes, read, and listen to everything people would say to me. One day a makeup artist told me the story of poor Martine Carol who, in her last film, mistook a door during the shooting of a particular sequence.[1] I felt that this could be turned into an extraordinary scene. So I used it in *Day for Night*. I also recalled the shoots of my other films. The sequence with the little cat, for example, comes directly from a small incident that took place during the filming of *The Soft Skin*. I hadn't forgotten the tenseness of the whole team who were anxiously wondering whether or not the cat would move on to the set. The film was slowly built up from an accumulation of all these minor details.

You have been making films for fourteen years. Why did you wait so long before making a film about cinema?

I don't know. I was not ready. I was reticent. I didn't want to make either an abstruse film, or a documentary. Moreover, I do not like documentaries. I didn't want to do scenes about the preparation for making a film. Everything on that score had already been said in *8½*. Similarly, what happens after a film has been finished had been depicted many times in Hollywood films: the grand premiere in which everyone is persuaded it will be a failure, and then the film turning out to be a stunning success. I wanted to leave that aspect of it out.

I was very tired when I did the editing of *Two English Girls*. Given that it was the holiday period and I wanted to be near my children, I had hired an editing suite at the Victorine Studio, in Nice. This setup obviously fascinated me. The studio, built by the Americans, was starting to deteriorate. Storms had brought down the signs, and it was almost unusable. I felt that I could exploit all the possibilities that were inherent in this setting. Anything could happen there. It furnished me with a unity of place, of time, and of action. I said to myself, "Everything will begin on the first day of the shoot, and it will all finish when the members of the team part." At a single stroke, the ideas for it precipitated. The film was fairly easy to write.

Even though you do not like documentaries, isn't there a documentary aspect to the film in spite of that?

Yes. There had already been a documentary aspect in *The 400 Blows* and *The Wild Child*. My aim in *Day for Night* was to supply as much information on the shooting of a film as possible. But, you know, I did not come to cinema through a documentary route. It was fiction that led me to it. I like the idea that people are acting a character, and that interesting things happen to them. There is a certain kind of modern cinema that aims to kill the notion of characters and situations. I have absolutely no interest in that. I will always adhere to the form of cinema that led me to cinema. If I had to be the only one to tell a story, I would always persist in telling it. So there you have it!

In your view, however, is it more interesting to tell a story, or to be interested in the characters? Do you prefer to make a story-cinema or a character-cinema?

The characters derive from the former. They have to be true. One has to be interested in them. They have to say interesting things and act in an interesting way. In *Day for Night*, I tried to have eight characters of equal importance, to observe them at work, and to understand what they do at work. I also wanted their private life always to involve something interesting.

But why did you act the role of Ferrand, the director, yourself? Could you not have used a professional actor?

I thought of doing that. I dreamed of choosing an actor who had already had experience of directing. However, I know that I would have had to force him to have my own reactions, and that would have assuredly irritated him during the shoot. Placed in the same situations, he would probably not have had the same reactions. That would have bothered me, because I did not want the character to have any feelings other than my own. Those are the ones I know the best. For instance, when I start paying a lot of compliments, it is because things are going very badly. Those who are participating in a shoot for the first time are always very surprised by this attitude. Those who have already shot a film with me, and who know me well, say, "If he says that it is not bad, that means that he is very happy."

When things are on the brink of a catastrophe, I feel that it is necessary to reassure the people with whom one is working. The director has to be reassuring. One does not achieve anything good by terrorizing the actors. I could not invent a director's reactions. The film has the appearance of a report made by a television crew who had come to see me filming.

That is what we see at the end of the film when television intervenes directly.

Yes, that's it. I had probably also been influenced by the work done by Janine Bazin's team at the time when I was filming *The Wild Child*. They had wanted to film me at work, and I liked the gap, the contrast existing between the film I was making and the one that Janine Bazin's crew was making. On one hand, we were filming *The Wild Child* in period costumes; on the other hand, we saw Nestor Almendros, camera in hand, filming the work that I was doing. It was very good! That is why I wanted to have a period scene in *Day for Night*. I slid the scene with the period costumes into it because I was thinking that without that, the film would not be complete. I really like the contrast between the candle, the period dresses, and the camera, the music being played back.

Was it Suzanne Schiffman who took on the work of director while you were in front of the camera?

Yes. You undoubtedly know that she has been my script girl since *Shoot the Piano Player*, and production assistant since *The Wild Child*. She played a very important part in the development of *Day for Night*, which is why I wanted to give her a credit as a scriptwriter. On Sundays, when we were not shooting, we would always make general revisions to the screenplay. She collaborated very closely with me on this work. I therefore found it perfectly natural that she should be listed as a cowriter of the screenplay. In addition, to some extent she served as a model for the character of the script girl in the film. We developed a kind of mutual understanding. It was she who said to me at the end of the film, "How about finishing in the snow?" I said to her, "Ah yes! We will even put a reference to that in the dialogue."

Did you encounter any problems in editing all the material that you shot?

No. We filmed much in the order that had been initially envisaged. As had often happened before, I had some scenes that could be placed anywhere in the film. I didn't know, for example, how I would use the dream sequences and those showing the child. All I knew was that I wanted to insert them between two things that needed to be separated. At the beginning of the film, events succeed one another in a fairly chronological order. We witness the three or four first days of shooting, while at the end of the film we witness the three or four last days of shooting. I wanted to place the big shooting sequence at the very middle of the film in order to show the elapsing of time.

Before the shoot, did you have a particular visual conception of the film? Did you want it to have a certain texture?

That was more difficult. In *Two English Girls*, for instance, I worked with a very predetermined approach. It involved never showing the sky, making a film entirely in low-angle shots so as to have characters who stood out against the grass, against a dark green background. I think you only see the sky and the sea on a single occasion in the film. In *Day for Night*, I was a prisoner of what actually existed: the decor, the makeup rooms, the corridors, the dressing rooms. All of that, I have to admit, was not very appealing. All the money devoted to the settings had been gobbled up in the restoration of the Victorine Studios. I had been preoccupied with a series of small details and I had not had the time to do very much work on other aspects of the film—the color, for example. The metro exit you see in the film was completely artificial in actuality. It was a setting without any entrance, entirely blocked. To make it look real, I placed extras next to each other, squeezing them together as much as possible, so as to conceal the absence of any opening.

But were your other films made with a particular visual conception in mind?

Certain ones, yes—*Jules and Jim*, *Two English Girls*, and *The Wild Child*. I am not happy, for example, with the photography in *Jules and Jim*. The night scenes were not successful. There was a lot of carelessness in that film, many things to which I didn't pay sufficient attention, but which I am careful about these days. The light in the interior of the chalet is not really very satisfactory. You have to pay more attention now because with color, ugliness threatens to infiltrate everywhere. One must get rid of ugliness through all means possible.

You wrote the whole script of Day for Night. *Previously, you had adapted several novels to the screen. Why this marked interest in adaptation?*

Let's say first of all that *Day for Night* gave me the courage to write original screenplays. I no longer want to adapt American novels. I find that you can make yourself better understood through original screenplays. You start from an idea and you end up creating a work that has a greater internal logic. When one is making an adaptation, one has to omit a great number of things: anything that is too costly to film, things that you don't want, things that you think would be visually unrewarding, things that you think are extraneous to the action and you don't think carry much interest. Often, you keep certain scenes in the belief that they will be good and interesting without taking account of the fact that they sometimes only make sense in relation to material that has been cut. The screenplay that one ends up with is too mysterious. In the adaptations of American novels, I didn't want to say overtly that the action was taking place in France. In general, therefore, from the outset there is a mystery concerning the locations of the action itself, because I wanted to situate the experience of the characters in an imaginary country between France and the United States. This country had to have multiple characteristics that made it impossible to identify it. But I was never satisfied with the results I obtained.

The subject matter of *Mississippi Mermaid*, for example, interests me greatly, but I think I would have needed more courage simply to make a love film revolving principally around the relationship between a couple. I could just as well have written an original script instead of adapting this excessively long novel. I realize that today. The film, moreover, contains all the faults that I listed above. In novels, the dramatic and psychological progression is often very slow. In order to achieve a more rapid progression, a more lively rhythm, one systematically cuts large passages. However, as a result, the rapid progression becomes absolutely incomprehensible, completely unrealistic. When you are reading, you can skip large passages. If the long agony of Madame Bovary is boring you, you can easily leave out a few pages. People never talk about literature this way, but I am convinced that readers jump lines and pages when an author is describing in great detail an event that is almost unbearable.

In cinema, that becomes a more serious issue, because the spectator has no other choice but to watch everything that is happening on the screen. Even if he is annoyed by it, there is nothing he can do. Cinema lends itself to quick deaths, murders that are brief and efficient, but it is not well suited to poisonings, for instance. When someone is poisoned in cinema, spectators have had enough of it after four shots. Confronted with slow deaths, the audience becomes annoyed and impatient. Everyone shuffles in his or her seat: one wants the character to die quickly. That's a very real, acute problem faced by a filmmaker when he wants to portray the slow progression of a painful event.

However, Bergman in Cries and Whispers *shows us the slow death of a character without ever boring us. To the contrary, we are literally fascinated by the death throes of Agnès.*[2]

Yes, that's true, it is strangely cut. The actual death does not last twenty minutes without a break. Bergman has taken a lot of care to spread the moments that are hard to bear across the film as a whole. I think that Bergman really knew how to make us watch, how to capture our complete attention. He exercises an enormous authority over the spectator. One shouldn't forget that he is a man of the theater, and that, like all those who do a lot of theater, he is scared of being boring. People who also do theater, like Welles, Skolimowski,[3] and Bergman, are much more aware of the audience than those who are purely literary, like my friend Rivette, who makes films that are thirteen and a half hours long. I think that Rivette would have had an entirely different approach to cinema if he had had some actual experience with an audience in the theater. Bergman, although he is very austere, plans everything in a very meticulous manner. His films never last longer than an hour and a half and comprise around fifteen sequences.

Has everything been planned in advance very precisely when you begin shooting? Do you believe in the necessity of a very strong initial structure?

You need an initial structure when one is often changing locations during the shooting, and when one has many actors who are coming and going. When I shot *A Gorgeous Girl Like Me*, we were in the south of France near Béziers. I knew that I could use the actors from Monday to Friday. Everyone was on the spot. It was therefore a matter of not making mistakes, of being as exact as possible. When you are using a small troupe, as was the case with *Day for Night*, you can change the work schedule, and attempt various experiments. There were ten scenes that I really wanted to shoot, which I liked a lot. I knew that in each reel there was a shooting scene and that, between two reels, one could insert various moments of private life during work. At this level, there were not many changes. The changes all occurred at the level of dialogue and minute details.

A Gorgeous Girl Like Me seems to leave little room for improvisation, whereas the three films of the Doinel cycle seem much more free and relaxed at the level of overall structure.

Yes, that's true. In *A Gorgeous Girl*, the structure was organized around the tape recorder. Everything departed from that and came back to it. There were not many opportunities to improvise given that the girl was recounting her past in a very precise way. In the Doinel films, to the contrary, we improvised a lot more. Everything depends upon the particular film, you know. In *The Bride Wore Black*, nothing was improvised. Everything was written and planned out in advance. I was almost bored shooting it. It was very frustrating.

It has been noted that problems of structure relating to the story in several of your films are directly linked to an almost constant refusal to adopt one genre and follow it to the end. There is an enormous mixing of genres in your films. Certain scenes in Shoot the Piano Player, *for example, begin with one kind of tone and end with another.*

I admit that *The Piano Player* was the extreme instance of this. There are changes of genre that I myself didn't notice. People are used to seeing things in a univocal way—so much so that when you contradict the procedure of thousands of films they have seen, they get the impression you are mocking them. A typical example can be found in *The Mermaid*, which imitates films that had been made earlier. We have there the wicked woman and a weak guy. He is so obsessed with her that he is ready to sacrifice himself, to die for her. The unusual thing is that at the end everything turns out well, even though she poisoned him, and that at the moment he discovers the truth, she confesses to him that she loves him. Usually, films in this genre end at the moment a cordon of police surround the house in which the two lovers die. The ending that I created unmistakably breaches a long cinematic tradition, of which the ultimate manifestation was *Bonnie and Clyde*. Given that I was trying to inject a maximum of verisimilitude within a conventional frame, this ending seemed more true, to me. I liked making such an optimistic ending, but the audience was confused. Renoir used to say, with a lot of justification, that there is a real-life-truth and a cinema-truth. Cinema has created a kind of false people in which people believe. When one breaks conventions and viewers' expectations, the reactions are often violent. People get the impression that you are making fun of them.

You talk about The Mermaid *now with more detachment than several years ago.*

I have not watched it again since its commercial release. I know that many people hated it, and that several loved it. It seems to me that it was more interesting than *The Bride Wore Black*. I don't pass judgment on my films. There are times when I think more of certain ones than of others.

Are there films with which you are more satisfied than others?

I like the ones that have the least number of components, the simplest ones—*The Wild Child*, for example. There are not many faults in that film. To be sure, one can question Itard's educational methods, one can dislike the fundamental concept underlying the film, but one cannot say that the film as such has major weaknesses. I like it because I managed to make something interesting that, at the point of departure, seemed very unattractive when one recounted it. I succeeded in making an anti-documentary out of something extremely real. There was almost nothing that I made up, except for the scene in which the child is listening to the tuning forks. When you make something out of almost nothing, one is necessarily very happy with the result that is obtained.

> *This was a film with a very unified tone, in contrast to several other of your films, in which one encountered constant ruptures of genre and tone.*

The most enormous rupture of tone that I ever executed is probably in *Mississippi Mermaid* at the moment when Belmondo is poisoned by Catherine Deneuve. At one particular point, she tells him she is going to look for a doctor. She goes out of the cabin and he remains alone. He falls on to the floor and sees a cartoon of *Snow White* in the newspaper. That is a highpoint of rupture, because, at that moment, not even my friends could understand me. The good-faith audience, the popular audience which I really like, the audience that looks at the photos at the entrance of the cinema and doesn't care less about the name of the director, probably accepted the idea that Catherine Deneuve had poisoned Belmondo, and that he had let himself be poisoned by her. Belmondo realizes that he is in the process of being poisoned at the moment he sees, in the cartoon strip, Snow White biting into the apple that the witch has offered her.

I think that the audience felt I was making fun of them at that moment. That is not so. The preceding scenes were reminiscent of Renoir's cinema, and here I was, all of a sudden, passing into the mode of Hitchcock's cinema before returning to Renoir's cinema. At the end of the day, this is more or less the balance I maintain in real life. I try to reconcile two things that seem to be completely opposite, and which, moreover, are indeed opposed. In order to create such ruptures of tone, it is necessary to consider and understand seventy years of the history of cinema. A film is a film. It exists by itself and remains, in itself, its own end. Several folks who love American cinema passionately often criticize it for having this attitude, this way of conceiving of a film as a discrete entity that relates to nothing else apart from itself. Even Raoul Walsh's cinema indulges in digressions, ruptures of genre that are an integral part of his films.

> *Yes, but aren't these jokes and subtle ruptures of tone more veiled, less overtly presented and explicit than in your films? What an audience finds difficult to accept is when you confuse it in a way that is much too overt and self-aware, when you confuse the issue in a self-advertising manner.*

With the Americans, perhaps, jokes inhere more in the expression of meaning. They are incorporated into the story itself, and thus do not appear so provocative. In France, we have Lelouch who does this through the whole length of his films, as if it were a matter of driving in nails at all costs.

You don't think that several great American filmmakers constantly neutralize the story by multiplying tonal ruptures? The strength of a filmmaker like Lubitsch is to involve us constantly in this process of destruction, to make us accomplices.

Lubitsch doesn't try to make us believe in the story. He takes us by the hand and systematically disassembles all the mechanisms that he sets in motion. He tells us a story and makes a joke, every two minutes, to show us that he is telling a story. That provokes laughter, but it always concerns laughter that is generated by complicity. Lubitsch directly involves the spectator in his work of destruction. He makes us participate in it. We are his accomplices.

In American films, everything is perfectly integrated and related to the very strong conception Americans have of the story.

It is the perfection of American cinema that creates its sincerity. You have unrealistic situations, the psychology is often basic, but you always believe in the story that is being told. In American films, the actor moves as if on a kind of rail. No matter what Henry Fonda or Montgomery Clift does, you believe them. When you come out of film with Humphrey Bogart, there is no question of saying that the film is bad. The film might indeed be bad, but it is impossible to register it as such because it is so well executed.

You don't think this is tied up with a very sharp sense of dramaturgy?

I think that in Europeanizing themselves they have lost this very strong conception of dramaturgy. Now, like us, they are making films that are too long. By imitating the Europeans, they have lost the professional aspect that made their films so intense. Formerly, Hollywood was an immense factory in which each person played a very clearly defined role. The screenwriters corrected one another, and the director did not have the right to go into the editing suite. Films thus achieved a high degree of standardization that was simultaneously a form of perfection. It was admirable!

While French critics are so fascinated by American cinema, don't you think that, on the other hand, the Americans are fascinated by certain aspects of French films?

Certainly. Take the case of Jean-Pierre Léaud, for example. The Americans like Léaud a great deal. There is a shyness, a modesty about him that makes him sympathetic. There is a shyness in his relationships with women. The French prefer Lino Ventura to Jean-Pierre Léaud, because he represents for them the very image of a strong, virile, and powerful man.[4] The French still have this conception of the all-powerful male. Léaud corresponds less to their sensibility than Ventura, while it is the opposite with the Americans. Léaud represents the weaknesses of men, his timidity regarding women, life, and action.

NOTES

1. Martine Carol (1920–1967) was a French actress who was frequently cast as a blonde seductress and was regarded as a leading sex symbol of the late 1940s and 1950s, until she was superseded by Brigitte Bardot.

2. *Viskningar och rop* (*Cries and Whispers*, Ingmar Bergman, 1972), in which a woman dying of cancer is visited by her two sisters.

3. Jerzy Skolimowski (1938–), a Polish film director, dramatist, actor, and screenwriter.

4. Lino Ventura (1919–1987) was an Italian-born actor who developed his career in France, specializing in hard-boiled gangster movies, in which he often starred with Jean Gabin.

CHAPTER 22

1975: *THE STORY OF ADELE H.*

> I don't know why I would make a film like that. So sad. But an obsession has something intoxicating about it, and I think I was caught up in the intoxication. I show that it was doomed from the outset: the lieutenant is never going to love Adele. And the entire film is about her insistence that he do so. We get the feeling that we are seeing the same scene over and over again. Instead of emotion born from surprise, I wanted it to arise from repetition. Just as laughter can be generated from repetition, I hope there will be emotion from repetition.
>
> *Interview with Claude-Marie Trémois,* Télérama, *no. 1319, April 26–May 2, 1975*

Adele H. is Victor Hugo's second daughter, who was not well known. How did you come across her story?

In 1969 I read an article by Guillemin that announced the publication of her diary.[1] This diary had been dispersed around different parts of the world as a result of auction sales. Miss Frances Vernor Guillie had found part of it, decoded it, because as her rationality wavered, Adele Hugo wrote by reversing the words.

The existence of Adele, who died in 1915 in the Saint-Mandé asylum, was kept concealed as a family secret. You know, that was very unjust: everyone knows of Léopoldine Hugo, drowned in 1843, to whom her father devoted many poems, and no one knows about Adele. In making this film, I felt that I was making her take her revenge, at last, on Léopoldine. Too late, unfortunately, because I am convinced that Adele suffered a lot from being less loved. She felt too much. She didn't even have a name of her own: she bore the Christian name of her mother, and the surname Hugo crushed her. In Halifax, living in the house of her landlords, she hid her identity.

Was that the reason you gave the film the title "Adele H." and not "Adele Hugo"? And why "The Story" and not "The Life" of Adele?

The script was constructed in such a way that one doesn't learn Adele's true identity until halfway through the film. I know, you're going to say to me, "But everyone knows that it is about Adele Hugo when they enter the cinema!" I don't think so. I continue to believe that many spectators enter a cinema by chance, without having read the newspapers, or without having made a connection between what they have read and what they are watching. Given that articles on the making of a film are published six or nine months before its release, the memory of them is erased by other articles people read in the meantime. And besides, you have to remember that cinema is not restricted to the Champs-Élysées, nor to Paris, nor to France, nor to Europe. So we contrived the screenplay in the hope that the film would be seen by people who did not know what its subject was about.

For the title, I didn't like "Adele H.," by itself; I thought it seemed too much like a piece of modern theater. As for "The Life," that would not have been appropriate, given that it deals with only a few years in Adele Hugo's existence. Besides, I like the word "story," because it is an old word, and also because I like to tell stories. I am 100 percent in favor of a novelistic approach in films; Jean Gruault and I both have the same ideas in that regard.

Do you regard The Story of Adele H. *as a historical film?*

Just as with *The Wild Child*, it is a real story transformed into a work of fiction, but deriving part of its interest from the fact that it was true. The pleasure in writing such a script is to organize it into a fiction without inventing anything, and to end up with a film that doesn't resemble a documentary. I don't like documentaries, even though I need real material on which to base my work.

Did you film in the same locations found in the story?

Apart from one scene situated in Barbados, which was actually filmed at Gorée, a little island off Dakar, almost all the film was situated at Halifax, but shot at Guernsey. That gave us an Anglo-Saxon ambiance that I needed, and the advantage, because of choosing people from the island for the secondary roles, of being able to film individuals, lawyers, doctors . . . who were bilingual—meaning that they could perform scenes in two languages with a lot of realism. I would not have achieved this result had I brought in actors from London: either their French or their acting would not have been entirely suitable.

What held you up in choosing this film?

I have come to the point where I no longer remember, because so many years have now passed since I first thought of this subject—it was six years ago, I think, when I read about Adele Hugo. Her biography greatly moved me, perhaps because it presents the opposite side of the coin to *The Wild Child*. Just like the Aveyron child, Adele has a problem of identity, but here it is the reverse, given that she is the daughter of the most famous man in the world. Her father was a genius.

I am emotionally and morally drawn to characters who are on the margins of society. So, after having written a first trial draft with Jean Gruault, as I often do, I wait to see if the subject continues to engage me. If this turns out to be the case, there is a moment when I say, "Oh well, I must make this film! . . ." Generally, a complementary idea also comes into play. When this idea arrives, it means that the film definitely has to be made. With *The Wild Child*, the trigger was the idea of playing Itard myself. With *The Story of Adele H.*, the decisive factor was the opportunity to use the music of Maurice Jaubert. I had read the book on Maurice Jaubert by Francois Porcile, and I saw from the list of his works that many of them had not been published. So I made the style of the film correspond to the music he composed between 1930 and 1940. I think that for me to feel compelled to make a film, there need to be several reasons that complement one another.

By leaving a screenplay to ripen for several years, doesn't one risk losing in freshness what one might gain in construction?

No, because the first time round Jean Gruault works more than me, and after that, I don't reread the script, so I am not thinking about it constantly. It is there, in a drawer, and I do something else in the meantime. Later, when

I reread my notes, my enthusiasm rekindles, as if in response to a new script. What does happen is that certain ideas can cross over from the preceding film. Sometimes people say, "It's strange, at the end of *Jules and Jim*, books are burnt as in *Fahrenheit 451*." I had probably just read *Fahrenheit 451* before shooting *Jules and Jim*, and as I needed some documents from 1930 at a particular moment, because my mind was already preoccupied with *Fahrenheit 451*, I chose a document showing Nazis burning books in the street.

Many directors say, "I have worked so much on this subject that it feels as if I have already made it," and even that "were one to give me the opportunity to do it now, I wouldn't want to do so." That's the case with Resnais, for example, but it's not like that with me, probably because I live less intimately with the subject before the making of the film.

At the time when you're making your first films, you experience doubts. Even if the first film went well, you are very anxious about the second one. You say to yourself that the subject is too remote from you. And then, with the third film, you still find reasons to be anxious because each film presents new difficulties—you feel that they are new, and you don't believe that you are able to confront them. Everyone does that: one is fearful of one's own incompetence! I have already been through that stage, and I have decided never again to be undermined by an initial shock. If I have an initial encounter with a subject I like, I no longer question this love at first sight, I no longer say to myself, "I'll never be able to do it," or, "This isn't the right time." I have decided to brush aside such considerations and to see the making of films in a broad perspective. I have been making cinema for fifteen years, and I hope to be making it for that long again—thus, a new film takes place in the context of a thirty-year output, as one of thirty films.

What drew you to Isabelle Adjani for the part of Adele?

Isabelle Adjani had greatly impressed me in *L'École des femmes*,[2] which I had seen on television, and I had a project, with Jean-Loup Dabadie,[3] to make something with her, but I wasn't thinking at all of casting her in the role of Adele. For this character, I was considering a dossier of actresses. I wanted someone who was as strong in English as in French, who was not well known, nor too modern, plausible in the nineteenth century. Frankly, I was looking for someone ten years older than Isabelle, but who had the same emotional capacity. But, when I saw *The Slap* in a private screening, it had an enormous impact on me.[4] I watched this film as if it were a tragedy, almost trembling. When I returned home, I reread the entire script of *Adele* and I saw that Isabelle could play all the scenes. I therefore offered her the role and she immediately accepted it, even though it took some time to formalize our agreement, given her complicated situation with the Comédie-Française.

I understand that there were seven different versions of The Story of Adele H. *Could you comment on the successive modifications you made to the screenplay?*

There were probably not seven versions, but certainly five, which were influenced by the films that I made in the meantime. The first version of *The Story of Adele H.* was written by Jean Gruault before *Two English Girls* and, after that film, which was not rigorous enough, too picturesque, I said to myself that I no longer wanted to see a period film with the obligatory dance hall scene, the hackney carriage arriving at the end of the street, and thirty dressed-up extras. I therefore reworked *The Story of Adele H.* by cutting out anything that was outside Adele herself. I didn't want any longer to hear about the sun in a period film, nor the sky. The film of *Adele* became tighter and tighter, more claustrophobic, the story of a face.

Adele is entirely alone.

Up until this point, I had made films about children or love stories: love stories with two characters, sometimes three, like *Jules and Jim* and *Two English Girls*. This time, what pleased me was the possibility of telling a love story with only one character, because the lieutenant hardly counts. Adele's love is all in her mind. It is an obsession. For once, I think that the critics will not be able to claim that I have made a film in half-tones. There is a lot of weeping on the screen, and we didn't have to worry about appearing ridiculous.

The secondary characters are reduced to an extreme. We never even see Victor Hugo.

I never show Victor Hugo's face, but even so, there is a lot of talk about him, one feels his presence. We hear very moving letters he addresses to Adele being read out: "I am old. My dream is to have you all around me. My arms are open to you. Come back."

There was one unavoidable scene in which I have to introduce a new character who does not concern Adele. This is the colonel who summons Lieutenant Pinson (with whom Adele is in love). The lieutenant himself only has three or four scenes in the film, and although, in addition, I needed to show his colonel, I felt that there would be something excessive about doing this, if it were to work as cinema. So I chose to remain with the camera behind a half-opened door. Through the gap of the door, I show Pinson standing to attention, and one merely hears the colonel, whom we see passing twice behind Pinson. In this way, I avoided imposing a new character on the audience; I merely suggested him. This is a very rigorous kind of approach, very exhilarating, one that I had already enjoyed adopting in *The Wild Child*; like an electrician, I strip the wires bare, I reduce the number of elements.

Cinema, especially now that it is in color, can lose itself in diversity and variety. I agree with Bresson: you have to concentrate as much as possible. It is necessary to avoid the picturesque. Color films give too much information; we have to be careful, now that color is practically obligatory, to reduce the number of locations, the number of characters, in order to create more emotion through unity. There is an experimental aspect to *The Story of Adele H.* In actuality, a filmmaker doesn't have too many films to make—perhaps three films, or six films, and if he makes more, it is because he experiments subsequently with different combinations. *The Story of Adele H.* attempts to mix the emotional climate of *Two English Girls* with the rigor of *The Wild Child*. These three films have in common the fact that they are clear, being framed by the best cinematographer in French cinema, Nestor Almendros, who is a genuine artist. Nestor is not only a cinema technician, he is a man who reads widely, is well informed about architecture, painting. A director who is able to collaborate with him is very lucky—he is a tremendous asset.

As in The Wild Child *and* Day for Night, *and for good reason, you appear as an actor in* The Story of Adele H. *Why did you do that? For fun?*

Yes, so that this shot in *Adele*—because there is only one shot—could serve a symbolic purpose. It's a joke that is vaguely sad.

Would you comment further on the music in The Story of Adele H. *What relation do you see between Jaubert's music and the style of the film?*

The affinities between a piece of music and a subject are had to explain. I remember having asked composers, several times, to provide saxophone music for sad scenes, but in vain. They were very afraid of doing that, because, these days, the saxophone is used for comic effects, whereas for me it elicits an enormous emotion.

To the extent that I felt, while making *The Story of Adele H.*, that I was making a film without having to be concerned with contemporary preoccupations, it pleased me to use music from the 1930–1940 period, with a saxophone. I never regretted it. Maurice Jaubert's importance grew even stronger as we went along.

Actually, we recorded the music before making the film, and I used it on the set, both in silent scenes to assist Isabelle Adjani's performance, and also in the course of repeat takes to help her adjust her acting. It worked almost like a movie performed in dance. That is a very attractive thing. An actor who performs to music adopts a kind of acting that approaches dance. Carried by the music, he is not scared to use stylized gestures, something daring that he would refuse to do if one asked him to do it bluntly—like slowly extend your arm forward, or leave a room walking backwards. With an emotional actress like Isabelle, this worked very well; sometimes she would weep to the music. She is an actress who rejects artificial tears; she asked simply that she be left for several moments in silence. So, one waited; when she was ready, I played the music softly, and exactly at the right place in the music and the right place in the tracking shot, the tears would start rolling down . . .

Was this the first time you used this kind of playback?

I had adopted it with the text for certain monologues in *Two English Girls*. There was one reel that I liked a lot, which we called "Muriel's despair," a reel in which the actress Stacey Tendeter broke down after Claude informed her of their breakup. I had had the text recorded for her and she wept at the sound of it. I noticed that it helped her a lot.

One thing that shocks me greatly in cinema, especially American cinema, is when the music is lyrical, but the image is not. It's terrible. That never happens with Hitchcock who shows things more or less in the same rhythm as Herrmann, but in most American films, the music becomes heroic while the image remains pinned to the ground. That is not normal. I am scared of lyrical music and a prosaic image because it means that, at that moment, cinema is relinquishing its effectiveness. What I like about *The Story of Adele H.* is that the music and the image are proportionate; a just relationship between eye and ear should be done by instinct.

Could one regard The Story of Adele H. *as being your first harsh, violent film?*

With me, one film out of two is romantic—the other one tries to destroy this romanticism. There is a kind of emotional contradiction in this. Very often, a new film is a violent response to the preceding one; thus, *The Soft Skin* relative to *Jules and Jim*, *A Gorgeous Girl Like Me* relative to *Two English Girls*.

I am not complacent about that because there are some things that, quite frankly, I would like to settle once and for all, but from which I cannot break free. When I was making *Two English Girls*, I sincerely thought that it would be the last time I would show a woman opening doors, a kerosene lamp in her hand, with this whole world of feeling displayed like a mass. Now, in *The Story of Adele H.*, I have again gone further in this direction. In this sense, it is a film that has been made with a degree of guilty feeling. It annoys me all the same that I have not succeeded in showing love except in a religious way... People always want to divide my films in terms of original screenplays as opposed to adaptations; my personal division would be between (a) dramatic comedies and (b) liturgical films.

> Now that *The Story of Adele H.* has been finished, is there anything you regret not having been able to achieve or realize?

I often choose subjects that are only pleasing to me, and about which people are dubious when they read the script. When I make a film about children, everyone says, "Very good." With *The Story of Adele H.*, I encountered a lot of skepticism, even on the part of people who liked me. From this point of view, for me, it has been a risky film, but I think that the skepticism that one might have when reading the script will disappear when one watches the film. I hope so.

For me to be able to form a definitive opinion about a film, I need to know the extent to which it has moved people. I am not indifferent to people's opinions, since I am seeking to work on them physically—I am even trying to make them cry. One could say that the quality of a film has nothing to do with how warmly it is received, or vice versa. In the case of *The Story of Adele H.*, that remains to be seen.

1980

I don't like films that leave people looking at each other, amazed, at the end. I hate that—I am very traditional. One ought to *feel* the end. *Adele H.* is one of my favorite films, because I have this music from Jaubert's *Suite française* that rises up with the commentary in which we learn that Adele has entered a mental home: everything about this ending pleases me greatly. I made a mistake with *The Wild Child* by having the film end too abruptly. The audience felt frustrated. I had thought that to end on "This afternoon we will resume our exercises," with the child having come back to the house, would be a good way to finish but, given that the film was presented as a real-life story, the audience wanted to know more, but I deprived them of that information. So, in *Adele H.*, I took care to cover that aspect, but without needing to give too much information, thanks to this very lyrical music.

1981

If I set up four or five projects in the months ahead, perhaps one of them will be made in English. I almost did that with *Adele H*. No one realized it because in the French version a third or a quarter of the film was already in English, with subtitles. That was entirely justified by the story, because Adele H. was the only Frenchwoman in an Anglo-Saxon world. In any case, it is a film that I made with a double negative, in other words, after the French take, we did an English take.

I shall undoubtedly repeat this kind of experience in the years to come, if I have a subject that absolutely lends itself to it.

With a double negative, do the actors have to reenact each scene?

Yes! You first do the French take, and then the English take, and so that the negatives are pure, even when it involves a scene without dialogue, one shoots it twice in order to avoid shifts of color-matching, even for insertions, neutral shots, or documentary shots, in one of the copies.

Don't you find that there are enormous variations?

There are variations, yes! Nestor Almendros says that the English version is always better, because of the fact that the French take is always shot before the English take. Slow shots, camera movements have been worked out toward the end, because it is as if instead of merely doing six takes, one is doing twelve of them. Thus, the last take of the English version is likely to be impeccable from the point of view of the camerawork.

NOTES

1. Henri Guillemin (1903–1992) was a historian and literary critic known for his work, often iconoclastic, on the great figures of French history.
2. *L'École des femmes* (Raymond Rouleau, 1973), based on the play by Molière.
3. Jean-Loup Dabadie (1938–) is a French man of letters, theater director, and screenwriter.
4. *La Gifle* (*The Slap*, Claude Pinoteau, 1974), with a script cowritten with Jean-Loup Dabadie.

CHAPTER 23
1976: *SMALL CHANGE*

To make a film with children requires special methods, like making a film with a helicopter. A helicopter causes sand to blow up, and so, one needs to moisten the soil. You think you are wasting a crazy amount of time by doing that, but as soon as the camera is in the helicopter, you gain an immense amount of time. You film twenty kilometers in ten minutes. One is in a different world— that of traveling pigeons. It's the same with children. From time to time, they refuse to participate in the filming. You need to give them time to play with a balloon. And, suddenly, they give you ten times more than you expected.

Interview with Claude-Marie Trémois, Télérama, *no. 1319, April 26–May 2, 1975*

Small Change *is as different as it could be from* Adele H. *This one is as lighthearted, unbridled, and contemporary as the preceding film was dark, tight, and romantic.*

From the beginning, I thought that *Small Change* would be a restful film, in order to contrast with the oppressive aspect of the making of *Adele H. Adele H.* was a gamble: is it possible to tell a love story with only one character, one situation, without twists and turns? Here, to the contrary, I had a collective film, many characters, a succession of unanticipated scenes. I am constantly leaping from one event to another.

I understand that this was a very old project . . .

Yes, it was the realization of an old idea. At the time of *The 400 Blows*, when I spent five days filming in a classroom, I said to myself that I really would have liked to stay there for the whole length of the film, without being the prisoner of a linear storyline. Some time later, I was at the Institute for the Deaf and Dumb for *The Wild Child*—for three days—and the desire came back to me to make a film with a multitude of children. That was it, *Small Change*: to set myself up with a team, in a provincial town, for two whole months, to exploit a unity of time and place, with a whole school at my disposal, and with the whole town in the background. I would certainly not have been able to make *Small Change* had I not done *Day for Night* beforehand, in so far as the earlier film taught me how to mingle a dozen characters, and have them intersect with one another, in such a way that we are interested in each one of them. It seems to me that *Small Change* is a kind of combination of *Day for Night* and *Stolen Kisses*.

Was this collective mosaic prefabricated entirely in the screenplay, or partly in the editing?

Partly in the screenplay, partly during the shooting, and largely in the editing. With this kind of shoot, you cannot rest on Sunday. On Sunday, with Suzanne Schiffman, my assistant, we would go over everything, discussing what we were going to do the following week. I didn't want the hairdressing woman to be seen only in the interior of her hairdressing salon; so, I made her accompany her son to school; she wants to go in, but her son prevents her from entering. These are the kind of things we would sort out each Sunday.

And the editing was just as important, because the reality is that one sometimes changes the order of scenes in the editing. Thus, I had one scene that could go almost anywhere, and which is rather cruel—at least, I find it cruel: it is not the cruelty of children, but the cruelty of life—in which little Julien, because he doesn't know his lesson, is sent into the corridor, and we see him rifling through the pockets of his friends—he steals. Now, this scene could have been placed anywhere, but I had to seriously consider how it might change its meaning depending on where one put it. In the end, I positioned it at a place I had thought was insignificant, only to find that it was not insignificant; this is because in the scene that comes immediately after, we see him come out of a bar carrying bottles; he encounters Patrick; he sends him away, saying "Leave me alone!" At the time of editing, I didn't think that people would be able to see a link in all that, but now some people say to me: "He stole money from his friends to buy bottles for his mother"; but that wasn't at all what I intended. It is very difficult to control meaning in cinema; one goes to a lot of trouble, and in spite of that, there are always interpretations that one was not anticipating.

You set yourself up in a real school?

Yes, at Thiers, in the Puy-de-Dôme. They let us have the whole establishment, the teachers had left, only the school caretaker remained, whom I kept, and who plays—with a lot of naturalness—his own character.

You have said that this film was composed of genuine things, real episodes that you had gathered over a long time, perhaps including personal memories. Could you give us some examples?

What takes place at the summer camp really happened to me: word for word, image for image. That includes something that is rather out of fashion these days, which is a visit to a stadium with a race involving bikes attached to motorcycles—an element that is very anachronistic. I took a lot of trouble to find a sports team that could do that. These are personal memories. But the film is not autobiographical, because I am not precisely any one of the characters: sometimes I am Patrick, sometimes Julien, possibly the teacher, but not any particular character.

Among these disparate elements, there are nevertheless two characters who stand out: Patrick and Julien. Are you afraid that this could upset the collective nature of the chronicle you originally wanted to make? Aren't you scared that they will occupy too great a place?

I did not bring their importance completely under control because, during the shooting of the film, I became more and more interested in Julien, probably both in the boy who was acting the part and also in the character; and obviously, there are things that happened that were not planned in the screenplay: all of a sudden, I wanted to include the story of the funfair at dawn when he gathers objects that the revelers have dropped from the attractions that take them up into the air, and so that was added. Besides, I don't like to make documentaries—I like fiction, I like to create plots, to construct stories, I like to surprise, I like to give pleasure, and all those notions, for me, are always valuable and I take them to heart. So I know that one can hold the audience's attention through a good moment for half an hour without really setting a story in motion. But it doesn't surprise me that after that, little by little, two characters detach themselves, in which one becomes more interested than in the others: in this case, it's Patrick and Julien; let us say that, while others have had two or three scenes, of which one is important, theirs gradually all become important. They become two threads to follow; they don't contrast with one another in the manner of "Jean-who-cries and Jean-who-laughs,"[1] but there are nevertheless two distinct characters. Especially physically, they complement one another well... No, I think that can work.

I believe that this construction is better, because had I done the opposite—that is, begin with two characters, and then abandon them for a multitude of characters—I would have lost everyone. So I preferred to adopt the reverse strategy.

You wanted to show all the stages of childhood, from the cradle to adolescence.

That's true, one catches a glimpse of birth, on the father's face at the clinic (the teacher); then feeding the baby milk; early childhood with the scene of little Gregory and the cat; and then all gradations until around the age of twelve. This is the period just prior to adolescence treated in *The 400 Blows* (and also, in a different way, in *The Wild Child*, given that in one year Victor gains a whole education). Little Gregory, of course, at the age of two and a half, doesn't know that he is making a film, why one makes him climb the stairs when he loves going in elevators—this whole scene was very difficult to shoot, it needed a lot of patience. But, I felt a need to obtain these images, just as I needed to depict a crib, and the mixed dining hall at the holiday camp, the whole range, eventually. At the time of *The 400 Blows*, while I was filming the kids sitting at the puppet show, secretly, with a telephoto lens, I had been very struck by the fact that a collection of children's faces becomes smooth, ageless, evoking what is tantamount to a Chinese crowd. I had to show that, and I filmed the final shot to achieve an effect of this kind.

The thing that all the children shown in the film have in common is their desire for autonomy, together with an underlying need for tenderness of which they are not conscious. Julien's home, for example, is hell, his life is outside, he has to fend for himself, and he takes things to make up for what he is not given. Patrick, who lives alone with his sick father, finds himself in a situation in which he has to assume responsibilities that are above his age. No mother, a father immobilized in a wheelchair, all that matures him precociously, and at the same time, at the level of feelings, he is totally confused. In his mind, he doesn't know whether a woman is a mother, a fiancée, a mistress; probably a bit of each simultaneously. All the children have to adapt.

The fall of the little boy from the window, without his suffering the slightest harm, is rather unbelievable.

That actually occurs four or five times each year—I cut out articles from newspapers that report this kind of thing. It illustrates this wonderful statement by Bernanos in *The Diary of a Country Priest*: "I understood that youth is blessed, that it involves running a risk, and that even this risk is blessed." I made the teacher's wife say the same thing, with different words: "Children bump into everything, they bump against life, but they have grace, and they are also thick-skinned."

And that slightly crazy story about the child whistling to the news?

Ah! You are touching on the theme of the film, which is all about this need for children to be autonomous. People often quote the parable about the emperor who forbade nurses to speak or sing to children: the latter all died by the dozen. This is a good example that educationalists use to explain how the "song of the nursing mother" is vital for a baby. I therefore imagined the story of a child born of an American father and a French mother, who couldn't communicate with his parents in their respective language, and found a way out by whistling instead of speaking. Obviously, I liked the fact that he made a success of his life by whistling: he becomes a professional whistler. I have always loved such transformations of weak points into strong points. This idea is also expressed in the final speech of the teacher: "Through a strange kind of balance, those who have had a good but difficult childhood are better prepared for life than those who have been very much loved, very protected."

Isn't there a deliberate intention to inject comedy into the dialogue: "Thank you for this meager meal," "Plick and Plock," et cetera?

I think that when one is making a realistic film like *Small Change*, it is good to emphasize, whenever one can, the touches of craziness that reality contains. This can be verbal, it can be visual, like the railway poster that fascinates Patrick . . . In addition, don't forget that children have their own peculiar logic, which escapes us.

There are things that I adore in the film, like the final scene, there are others that I found amusing, and even very entertaining—as, for example, when the daughter of the police chief attracts the attention of those dwelling in the apartment building—but which seemed to me to be a bit facile.

That's a true story. Yes, it is facile. I asked people about what, in their experience, had happened to little girls between the age of six and eight, and I retained this particular story. I wouldn't have included it had it not been the story of a child who was actually maltreated, because it concerns a little girl who, for several hours, pretends to be an abandoned child martyr when in fact she is not. At the time, I had been shocked by Fernand Raynaud's sketch *Bourreau d'enfant*,[2] because I found that it made people laugh, that it took the heat out of something they ought always to be passionate about... Moreover, the story appealed to me when I heard it, because of its cinematic potential. I could immediately visualize the courtyard, the people at their windows.

What does the final scene in the holiday camp relate to?

Well, it takes us back to the prologue, in a fairly logical fashion. I was keen on this scene, because the way it is organized resembles the work of Lubitsch... doors which open and close... a crowd of children which is succeeded by shots showing empty staircases... a misunderstanding... a kids' prank and then the kiss... All of that appealed to me visually. In addition, this scene marks Patrick's passage into adult life.

Did you choose the children because of their physical appearance, or because of their affinity with the character concerned?

No, not even because of their affinities, because a character is very open... It was because of the way they appeared in front of the camera. I made them all learn Harpagon's tirade from *The Miser*[3]—that provided me with a little test—and then I asked them questions; we made some tests in the school courtyard at Thiers, and it was as a result of their liveliness, their vocabulary, of the extent of their desire to act—that came into it as well—and even their availability. I started on purpose with the classroom scenes; there was one class with thirty-five pupils, another with twenty-five younger ones; that gave me time to study them; I didn't want to have regrets, to have to say to myself, "I should have given that one a larger role..." It worked well. It was also that method that led to the importance of the two little Italians—it wasn't at all anticipated that these two little brothers would feature so prominently in the film; they didn't have much character, not much happens to them in the film; but they were so interesting, and they wanted to come every day, and so I always managed to find something for them to do.

You have admitted that you love children to the point of becoming an "idiot." Doesn't that present a certain risk, however, I mean the risk of being too "kind"... Did you have to react against that?

There is only one criticism that I have heard regularly now that the film has been released—in actual fact, one person uttered it initially and many others have picked it up—and that is that there is one thing missing from the film, the cruelty of which children are capable.

I was thinking that too—especially since it is in Les Mistons.

Yes, but in *Les Mistons*, that had disconcerted me. I realized that it was very contrived: the children were very good in *Les Mistons*, when I gave them things to do that related closely to their daily lives. But when they had to act out the main situation, that is, persecute the pair of lovers, that bothered them, and they did it badly. And it was then I said, "I am not going to make any more artificial stories with children; I will start with much more flexible material in which I can bring in their relationships, but I will no longer film a story in which children are used to illustrate something. I know that children's cruelty exists; I didn't have to suffer from it because I was an only child. I think that people who have brothers and sisters experience much more aggressive relationships. So, I have no personal experience of that side of children; and, on the other hand, I have seen the cruelty of children used in an artificial way too often in cinema and literature, to show the absurdity of war, or the cruelty of war, et cetera. People exploit childhood, and I didn't want to do that. So, that may be missing, but I don't regret it.

Yes, but is it possible that the film is too favorable in its view of children?

Many people have criticized the kindness of the film. I think that it was rather necessary given that the children were roaming around the camera, wanting to know how it worked; they were very interested in the technical side. They prowled around the sound equipment, and would speak with the sound engineer. They would come, and I would let them see the rushes at the town cinema: I was not going to block the doors to prevent them from watching the rushes! Thus, bit by bit, they entered into the film to such an extent that I felt that, in part, it had to become their film, and that I was making it for them. One doesn't use the same kind of language with children that you use with adults; you say serious things to them in a lighter tone, or by taking the sting out of it, or by making things seem less serious. That was the problem: I wanted to deal with serious things all the same, but I wanted the film to please them, to be theirs, their film. So there you have it.

It must have been very hard to make such a large troupe of children act?

To work with children is a terrible ordeal. It is much harder than with adults, but much more surprising, because when a scene succeeds, it is not merely the screenplay "made better," it is six times better than the screenplay. In contrast, when something is impossible, you simply have to abandon it. It involves another way of working; you need patience.

Working with children has made me understand certain adult actors better. I have never been a fan of Marlon Brando, but by watching children as they act, I see what people find pleasing about Marlon Brando, his unpredictability. When an actor speaks to Marlon Brando, one never knows if he is going to reply, if he is even going to deign to listen to what is being said to him, if he is going to simply open his mouth without uttering the slightest sound; moreover, one doesn't know whether he is going to look at the person who is speaking to him, or whether he is going to look at the clouds, whether he is going to turn his back to the camera to go and play football. Well then, that's children. They act like Marlon Brando. You have a child at the bottom of some stairs and you say "Action!"—you have one chance in two that he is going to climb the stairs, one chance in two that he will run away. You feel strong emotions!

What part was played by the children's improvisations, or even by chance?

Oh, that is important, because within scenes, I gave them very little dialogue: I would usually outline the ideas for them, and they would do the rest in their own words. There was no improvisation concerning the facts because the stories were already there. But, for example, in the scene in which the teacher arrives and says, "I have a baby," they asked whatever questions they wanted to ask. In this instance I adopted an approach like that of Jean Rouch: I had the camera first on the children so that they could ask the questions they wanted to ask, the continuity man noted down almost everything that was said, then the camera moved to the teacher, with the children asking questions again, offscreen, and they are almost the same ones, and the teacher answers them. Another reason that worked very well was because Jean-François Stévenin has a very good rapport with children.

Do you not find that, with the exception of Stévenin, the image of adults you present in the film is rather unflattering?

I knew in advance that I was going to be moved by the children—I don't reject the word "emotion"—and so, I didn't want to contrast them with adults, because at that moment this would have been unfair. So I didn't want any character to be negative; the adults are shown to be rather weak, sometimes a bit negligent or handicapped by something, like the disabled man, Patrick's father, but they are not portrayed negatively, as being wicked. Absolutely not. The teacher somewhat represents the other side of the coin compared with the one in *The 400 Blows*, he has an easy rapport, wants to be close to the children. He is a very fine character; he was very well acted, I think . . .

Do you think that this film can also speak to children on occasions?

Proof of that has already become apparent. The only public screening I have seen was at Thiers, because I had promised to go back there, and obviously it was an enormous pleasure to watch the film with them, all the children who had participated in the making of it. Children are the spectators for whom this film was intended. One needs to ask them what they think. That has been done on TV, in Lyons, and generally they have been interested wherever it has been shown, they have asked good questions, obviously many technical questions. This was already the case with *The Wild Child*, which attracted a large audience of children. That film, in particular, had a story that was fascinating to children: in one year, a wild child learns what children know after seven or eight years, namely, to learn how to walk, to stand upright, to wear shoes, to eat correctly, learn to read and write, to recognize objects . . . It was all gathered together. And suddenly, it gave them a shock to see that. Many people telephoned me; someone said to me, "My son has not walked on four legs for three days!"

1979

Small Change takes place during one term of the school year and each student is wearing a T-shirt of the same color at the beginning and end of the film. That goes against any notion of realism, but if I had changed the color of the characters' T-shirts, it would have been disastrous.

1980

Small Change is a film that was very successful at the box office, but one which intellectuals, generally, did not like. I imagine that they found it too cheerful, almost condescending. It's rather similar to the similar misunderstanding that attended *A Gorgeous Girl Like Me*. They said, "How does Truffaut dare to make a film like that?" I am not very concerned to clear up the misunderstanding, but, if I were minded to clarify it, I would say that it is because I have become old very quickly, so that, for me, *Small Change* is already a grandfather's film. It is a vision of children from a long distance away. The vision was a brotherly one in *The 400 Blows*, because there is very little difference between Jean-Pierre Léaud and me. The distance has already increased in *The Wild Child*, which is a father's film, and even further in *Small Change*. What's more, I was highly aware of it. There was a scene that had been shot, but which was not good, inspired by Victor Hugo's *How to be a Grandfather*.[4] It was after the day when the young girl had said "I'm hungry" from the window. Her grandfather, an old man whom I had vaguely noticed in the cinema theater, who is hardly in the final edit at all, came to her parents who said to him, "The girl has been punished, she is in her room." And at this moment, I had visualized the poem by Victor Hugo: "Jeanne was with dry bread in a black cupboard." It was filmed with the parents, the grandfather, and the little girl, in a very stylized fashion, but it was not well acted.

This is a vision of childhood that is not consistent with the tone of the period. That is not how one regards children currently. You often seem to set yourself against the dominant way of seeing things that is currently fashionable.

Yes, because I often make "period" films that do not overtly proclaim themselves as such. Basically, I only work with memories from twenty-five or thirty years ago. If someone tells me about something that happened last year, I don't completely believe it because it is too recent. It is as if I can only ever believe in things that are old.

NOTES

1. A line from a poem by Voltaire that evokes the volatility of human moods.
2. Fernand Raynaud (1926–1973) was one of the best-known standup comics in France during the 1950s and 1960s, becoming a national star thanks to television. *Bourreau d'enfant* [Child Abuser] was one of his most famous sketches in which a misbehaving child refuses to eat his meal and is harshly treated by the parent.
3. *L'Avare* (*The Miser*), a play by Molière first performed in 1668. Harpagon is the miser who, even though he is over 60, is trying to arrange a marriage between himself and a beautiful young woman.
4. *L'Art d'être grand-père*, a book of poems published by Victor Hugo in 1877.

CHAPTER 24

1977: THE MAN WHO LOVED WOMEN

> No one has ever spoken enough about the notion of sacrifice as far as cinema is concerned. One can write a great novel without sacrificing anything, but in a film one must always sacrifice something and, sometimes, this choice concerns some elements that may have been practically the point of departure for the film.
>
> *Interview with David Sterritt,* Christian Science Monitor, *November 27, 1978*

When you began preparing for The Man Who Loved Women, *what were your main sources of interest?*

With the release of each film, I get the impression that I have been repeating the same thing—it's true each time: this is a film theme I have been thinking about for a long time. Contrary to what one might think, the theme of the neurotic, frenetic, compulsive womanizer is not often dealt with. The problem resides in the choice of an actor, the mistake being to entrust a role of this kind to a young man—because either one disappoints his fans, or else one falsifies the character a bit to make it resemble the characters the young man usually plays.

The Man Who Loved Women depends entirely on Charles Denner, given that he was the actor I deliberately chose; I saw this film as an extension of the character he had played in *The Bride Wore Black*. That film was not one I particularly like (of all those I have made, it is the film I like the least), but the part with which I was happy was the one involving the painter who makes Jeanne Moreau pose, explaining to her from the outset that he is a womanizer, that he is not interested in feelings, and that she has nothing to fear from him because she is not his type. Gradually, he falls madly in love with her, and she kills him; I very much liked how Denner interpreted this character. The main character in *The Man Who Loved Women* is the opposite of the guy who sees a girl in the street and invites her to have a drink with him. He goes to enormous trouble to seduce them, but he never approaches them directly. For example, he notes the number of a license plate, and it takes him a week to track down a pair of legs he has glimpsed. I am interested in complications, detours. This guy does everything in an indirect manner. Denner works well as this character because he has a natural seriousness, he rarely smiles—he has something fierce, wild about him. He is not a young leading man. His admirers have seen him mostly in the roles of policemen or gangsters, generally in secondary roles in which he has been terrific. In this case, we progressively identify with him, even though we view him critically along the way, because one cannot pass judgment on him. This film can only elicit sympathy or hostility, a rejection of the character, or compassion toward him.

Do you get the impression in this new film that you are reencountering all the women represented by Catherine Deneuve in Mississippi Mermaid, *Isabelle Adjani in* Adele H., *Julie Christie in* Fahrenheit 451?

Not really, no! Or else it is unconscious. At the beginning, I obviously said to myself that a film like this provides a stunning vehicle for filming many women with whom I had wanted to work for a long time. Once the screenplay was finished, however, I realized that there were only five roles that were really important—that is, roles comprising several scenes, perhaps two or three further roles that included a good scene, with the rest being like an assembly of walk-on parts, which meant that I could only partially satisfy my desire to film a whole lot of women. I remember having given a very thankless role to Nelly Borgeaud in *Mississippi Mermaid*; she played the part of a shrewish woman, she was made up to be ugly, old, and that was a kind of wasteful transformation, given that she is really beautiful. Also, at the time, I said to her, "One day, I will think of you and will write you a sexy role." This doesn't mean that her role here is all that sexy, but nonetheless, it is that of a beautiful woman.

> *Your character is a collector and a diarist. This inevitably makes one think of Don Juan and Casanova, even though there is no reference to them in the dialogue. What is your position in relation to these comparisons?*

I am not conversant with the learned studies published on the myth of Don Juan. I proceeded out of a desire to contradict, as I often do: to portray the opposite of a Vilallonga, an attractive guy who was very pleased with himself.[1] I constantly tried to alter the character to suit Charles Denner. I didn't consider whether he would seem likeable or not. The risk, of course, was that people would reject the character.

> *Why do you think people might disapprove of him?*

Some people could react like the typist in the film. But, on the other hand, I know that I was not wrong in my choice of Charles Denner. I made a mistake in *The Soft Skin*, because of having a thankless character played by a good actor, but one who lacked any seductive quality. *The Soft Skin* turned into a nasty film in spite of my intentions. Instead of defending the character, I had condemned him. With Denner, his wild demeanour and his peaceful savagery prevail in spite of everything else.

> *Your character dies as it were "on the job," cruising. Is this the "destiny" of seducers?*

It was inevitable. I was working on something that was mythic. You have to respect the law of myth. The scene of his death in a hospital, while looking at the legs of the nurses, had already been recounted by the character acted by Daniel Boulanger in *Shoot the Piano Player*—when he describes the death of his father in a car. I gave it a visual representation here. His death is obviously not a punishment. It is a question of logical probability, as with the death of Père Grandet: someone comes to give him extreme unction, he sees the crucifix, it is made out of gold, and shines, he tries to grasp it, and dies.[2]

> *In this story about a great lover, there is very little nudity, and no sex scenes. Could you comment on this legendary modesty attributed to Truffaut?*

It's the problem of showing nudity on the screen. I am very interested in Henry Miller, but the nudity he describes in literature, if it were transposed to the screen, would not preserve the same value. I am for a clothed form of eroticism. The film that most moved me in this regard was Bergman's *The Silence*:[3] Gunnel Lindblom goes to the cinema, she sees a couple making love between the rows of seats, then she follows a waiter into the porch of a church—a scene that Malraux mutilated under the pretext of protecting Bergman from censorship! She enters her hotel room, puts her hand under her dress, takes off her panties, and places them in the basin to wash them. It was superb. But explicit nudity? No. With Miller, we have abstract bodies. In cinema, nudity becomes trivial, or else too pictorially alluring, and that harms the story: one wonders about the shape of the breasts, patches of redness, body hair. Nevertheless, I have to say that in *More*, Barbet Schroeder perfectly steered the movements of his naked actors—but that film remains an exception.[4]

Are the flashbacks with the mother in The Man Who Loved Women *designed to illuminate the main character?*

First, I encountered a child from Montpellier who bore a remarkable resemblance to Denner. That prompted me to improvise some short scenes showing his childhood. With women, one has the same relationship that one had with one's mother. I found it satisfying to go beyond the mere suggestion that Bertrand had simply suffered from having a detestable mother; he was also subjected to seduction, which is what he is seeking to recreate with the women he encounters.

Basically, his mother behaved like he does.

Yes, it is like Léautaud with his father, a prompter at the Comédie-Française, who would bring home a different woman each night. Léautaud led a life similar to that of his father, although a more protected one.

Is the character an extreme case?

I don't think so, if one compares him with the number of women Georges Simenon professes to have slept with: he admitted he had "known" ten thousand women in his lifetime. Ten thousand means many women behind doors, in the corridors, and between two typewriters . . . Denner is a shy little boy compared with him!

The construction of this film is fairly complex. What was your intention in doing it that way?

A particular problem presented itself that I didn't entirely resolve: how could I make the film proceed once Bertrand has finished the novel? I had two plots lines going, and I had suddenly arrested one of them. Then the episode with Brigitte Fossey begins. Normally, I establish an accelerating movement in the last two reels, but in this case I could not do that. I set off again as if I were beginning a new film: the scenes could not be synthetic—to the contrary, they had to be enriched with many small details, such as the storm in the room.

Your recent films include dreams: the child in Day for Night, *the drowning in* Adele H., *and, in this case, Denner's nightmare concerning the mannequin in the shop window.*

I have always included dreams in my films since *The 400 Blows* but, for a long time, I have found myself cutting them at the editing stage. Here, I first thought of showing a real scene, of a woman who requires a man to wear garters during their rendezvous. I gave up this gag, which I thought too contrived, opting instead for a dream that illustrated the idea of fetishism.

Are there any personal memories in this film?

I am much less autobiographical than one might think. I simply want to tell a story, and I like to choose a character who likes solitude, who has no family, no friends, who is only happy in the company of women. I didn't want him to be cynical or cruel; although there are some harsh things in the film, they only arise from the nature of certain situations. My thinking about the "womanizer" doesn't extend beyond what I show. I don't know anything about professional pickup artists. I have not spoken enough with them. I don't know. Certainly, they would not have made this film. Undoubtedly they would be critical of my interpretation of the character. That would be interesting to find out—I did not want to follow the itinerary of a womanizer merely driven by a desire to score. I deliberately chose a type of individual who is anxious, secret; who avoids conflicts, while flying irresistibly from woman to woman—perhaps out of fear of becoming too attached, out of fear of according too much space to a unique feeling. One scene in which he meets a former lover clearly shows that this fickle man has previously experienced such intense feelings that he has developed a morbid fear of ever experiencing them again . . . Because a womanizer is also someone who is scared of love. I liked that angle. And then, the manner in which he becomes hooked on women is completely visual. It's the movement of their legs, movement plain and simple. Rhythm. It's all about that. The film is constructed around this movement. Every time, he seizes upon a detail of movement here or there and allows himself to be pulled along by the rhythm of it. I don't identify in any way with my womanizer. But like him, I could say about women, and this is the most sincere way I can put it: "I love that particular one because she looks like she has come out of a Russian novel, that one because of her orphan's smile, that one . . ."

> *Your films increasingly depict groups: the crew in* Day for Night, *the children in* Small Change, *and here Charles Denner's harem.*

First of all, I like the idea that everything should be related to the subject. When you are dealing with a particular theme, you need to feed it. Here, everything relates to it: the woman with the telephone wake-up call, the laundress who has a bit of cloth in her hair . . . It's pleasing to the mind. I started depicting groups in *Stolen Kisses*. In order to bring more realism to the screen, the New Wave suppressed secondary roles. That was harmful with respect to a certain kind of cinema, that of Jacques Prévert. Deprived of good secondary roles, films became narcissistic. My awareness of this led to a shift in the number of roles in my films—it was a deliberate choice in *Stolen Kisses*, *Day for Night*, and *Small Change*.

> *Have you never been scared of being a bit cursory in your treatment of characters when a large number of them are involved?*

That's a risk you run, and if a film changes a lot during the filming, this kind of film changes to an even greater extent. One runs the risk of giving a very small role to someone one wants to see on the screen for a much longer time; one risks changing one's mind during the shooting by concluding that a particular person would have been better in such and such a role. With this type of film, the scenes also become synthetic, more concentrated. I took account of the fact that people would be going to see Charles Denner for two hours. Thus, whenever he has a scene with a woman, I almost always put the emphasis on the woman, to whom I give twice as much dialogue and twice as many shots, so as to restore some kind of balance. That is why we see Charles Denner from behind in many scenes; in many of the scenes with women, this almost creates the effect of a monologue—he does not react. He only does that later, when he is sitting in front of his typewriter.

> *Aren't you scared that by making other films based on this kind of construction, people might accuse you of adopting a "procedure"?*

That's possible. I know that in this business the use of a commentary is something that often elicits disapproval; people assume that a film that has a commentary is a film that is failing in its efforts to tell a story. Now, commentary, for me, is a form of confiding—it is like speaking in someone's ear. Cinema and theater draw a lot of people together, but in theater, one is addressing everyone, whereas in cinema, one is speaking to each individual person. I confess that I have been greatly influenced by films I saw in my youth that had a commentary, like *Diary of a Country Priest*, or *Les Enfants Terribles*. It's a form I find greatly appealing. I have gone to see certain films fifteen or sixteen times because of the spell the commentary had on me, which is the same as the effect of a piece of music. Personally, I react in the same way to films with commentaries. I like Charles Denner not only because of his physical appearance, his feverish eyes, the impression he gives of being troubled, but also because his voice is fantastic, magnificent, and one that I knew would be pleasant to listen to. To prevent the audience from growing weary, I made Denner laconic in his dialogue, but when he speaks, he only speaks for a limited amount of time. I hope no one is put off by this: I thought I had to risk it. I think that one way of expressing oneself is to display contrariness. When you are doing something that you know no one else is doing at the time, you can restore a certain forcefulness to old forms. I am interested in narrative forms that no longer interest people at the present time, because the fashion now is to have direct confession. For ten years, that generated some good films, but it is no longer the case. One should constantly ask oneself questions: is what I have to say interesting? Are there several ways of saying it, of which one is better than another? Sincerity, intelligence, and good taste are not sufficient. You have to think of the strip of film scrolling through the projector, which is the means whereby the film you are making, among all the films that are made by the dozen, delivers more enjoyment than the others. There is a striking convergence between the train you set in motion and the unreeling of the film itself. It is possible to take account of this magic in order to try and discover its laws. I believe in entertainment—even in *Adele H.*, in other words, even when it's a question of using close-ups for an hour and a half, I am still interested in entertainment.

> *With* The Man Who Loved Women, *you somewhat undermine the idea of a "cinematic genre," given that it is a film that one cannot classify as such . . .*

Pariscope definitely labeled it a "dramatic comedy" . . . The screenplay was rather funny, but the way it was shot increased the sadness of the film.

The impression of loneliness came out more. One might be led to laugh at the complicated state of Denner's mind—of his imagination, of his way of skirting around things—whereas in actual fact he takes a serious approach to his character. With this kind of film, we pass judgment more on the character than the film itself; furthermore, people respond to this theme very personally. It makes them recall someone they know, and they then feel concerned. I am hoping, furthermore, that this will generate some lively debate, that people will say the film is imbued with male chauvinism. It will be amusing when others say the opposite. It is a feminist film, made after my fashion.

Apart from deepening the loneliness of the character of Bertrand Morane, in what other ways did the shooting lead to a development of the film?

For a long time I had been wanting to depict everything that is involved in the preparation and production of a book: the book is written, then it is typeset, printed, you are given proofs to correct, you choose a cover, and then the book is there, finished, existing as an object. In fact, it involves a process that is very like the process of making a film. Unfortunately, the preoccupation of the film doesn't completely lend itself to this theme because my character only decides to start writing after a third of the film has gone by, and he finishes a bit before the ending. I was not able, therefore, to show all the stages without spoiling the screenplay. Nevertheless, my idea is present in it, without ever causing the spectator to feel confused over whether a particular scene is fictional or real. Everything is clear, I hope.

In this regard, is the film a kind of preface to Fahrenheit 451*?*

There are some things I was not conscious of when I was making the film, but which I realize now; for example, there is a competition between love and the book. That was genuinely unconscious—I did not intend it. There is an antagonism between the relations Bertrand Morane has with women and the relations he has with books, as if it were impossible for him to mix the two together. I only realized this during the process of editing. Had I been conscious of it from the beginning, I think that I would have either tried to erase it, or else reinforce it. I am happy that I have realized it too late to do anything about it. You think you can control everything you want to in a film, but there is always some important element that completely escapes your control; on the other hand, you are often led to take pains over something that doesn't present any problem.

Why do you no longer shoot any films in Paris?

I have not shot a film in Paris since *Bed and Board*, because it was a film made without passion. I remember meetings in Paris in which the technicians would arrive late; it was hard to find a place to park in order to see the rushes . . . It was a film-shoot that seemed as if I had to keep office hours—and that didn't strike me as a good thing. It's necessary for people to feel like they're experiencing an adventure; actors who come to shoot for several days in the provinces, dying from stage fright when they arrive, who find an existing team of people who adopt them and reassure them. That's more like the idea of cinema that I have. The shoot should not be a fraught undertaking, but a comfortable adventure; relations between people should not be tense, and they must not face any physical dangers. It should be an emotional adventure.

How did you handle the cinematography of The Man Who Loved Women *with Nestor Almendros, who you used again as a DOP?*

I think carefully before choosing a location, and I look at the color of the walls in order to decide whether it needs to be changed. I discussed the backgrounds with Jean-Pierre Kohut, the set designer, and Nestor Almendros, in terms of the coloring of the actors, of their faces. With black and white, there was a kind of standardization, a scene with shot / reverse shots always worked. These days, all it takes is for one person to speak against a green background and another one to speak against a red background for the scene to be ruined by presenting unnecessary sensory information. For this reason, I maintain that it is much more difficult to *listen* to dialogue in a color film, just as it is more difficult to laugh. It is almost impossible to make a comedy that takes place in sunlight; you don't have the feeling of being in a fiction if there is shadow and sunlight in the image. One has to fight against the ugliness that threatens to enter into films, unless one makes a style out of it as Alain Resnais does in *Muriel*. Now I am becoming increasingly fussy; for example, I want to have several lampshades for the same lamp because, for certain scenes, I will need a lampshade that is darker than the one that was seen earlier. I also hate everything in the image that is white, everything that is shiny. As far as color is concerned, I think that the whole sequence showing Charles Denner's apartment is very successful. From the very outset, this was a film that was less interesting for Nestor Almendros than *Adele H.*, in which everything was recomposed—but he took still greater pains with it, and I am very happy with the result.

This time, was it an advantage to be working on the screenplay with Suzanne Schiffman (as you had done with your preceding scripts), given that she is a woman?

Her input probably made the women characters more interesting and lively, although I always have female characters that are stronger than my male characters. Suzanne is very careful not to interfere with the kind of inspiration that leads me to want a particular scene against all logic. She knows that sooner or later she will accept the craziness that is implicit in the idea. It is always important to respect an urge one has to do something eccentric, otherwise you end up with a film made by a board of directors. Every Sunday (it's a ritual!) we would go over the script. It reflects her influence very strongly, because she is much more observant than I am, with a sharper eye. Sometimes I am discontent without knowing why, and her analysis helps me. In shooting *Jules and Jim*, for example, I remember thinking that Jim was good in certain scenes, and not so good in others; Suzanne realized that, viewed in profile, he had a good and a bad side: one is very sculpted, and the other is a bit slack. From that moment on, I took that into consideration when shooting the rest of the film. I have always asked Suzanne to criticize only things that can be improved, but not those that cannot be altered further, so as not to leave me feeling demoralized; it is a game we play, our rule of the game.

You are often described as a "psychological" artist. Do you want to respond to this notion?

With cinema, there is a degree of contrivance that goes on that may appear off-putting to people who are writers, someone who has only logic at his disposal. You can ask yourself a disturbing question: are film directors more successful if they are idiots and energetic, rather than intelligent and disinterested? The answer is "yes." This dilemma does not exist with literature, in which one can express oneself without ellipses, like Proust, or in a succinct manner, like Gide, or through understatements, like Queneau. A writer who encounters the manipulation inherent in our craft can only arrive at one conclusion: "Cinema is an art of compromise."

Is there a large element of truth in this belief?

Yes, with cinema, it is necessary to adopt a ruse. You can be a good writer without adopting a ruse, but not a filmmaker, except in the case of the odd film now and again. The need to manipulate time forces you to simplify. You cannot retain the same narrative approach from one end of a film to the other, except when the story resembles that of a novella, as in the case of Rohmer. Rohmer's films are slightly expanded novellas, with a very smooth unfolding of time. For all sorts of reasons, certain passages in a film can project psychology, but not the whole film. If a film is exclusively psychological, it is not a good one! With cinema, there is an entertainment logic that often prevails over the logic of the story, over psychology, over realism, et cetera. A film is balancing between literature and music, all the time. One constantly has to abandon psychological laws for musical laws.

Do you agree with the critical argument one often hears, that a film is outdated?

Does one have to make films for the present moment, like Rivette thinks, or like Clouzot thinks for different reasons? I like to make a film that resembles an object. A film that resembles an object ages better than a film that resembles a conversation. The currently fashionable notion that a film should be a dialogue with the spectator amounts to a moral con job, in my opinion. When someone is on a giant screen and people are sitting in the dark, the situation relates strongly to monologue rather than a dialogue. I believe, therefore, in a film as an object: Rohmer, Buñuel, Polanski, Fellini. I think that with this kind of film, people later come to accept any apparent naïveté that might seem dated. Moreover, the aging of films has its own life. Take *Les Dames du Bois de Boulogne*, for instance:[5] the film was meant to be timeless, but it was shot just before the Liberation and then completed after it. There were no fur coats—women were putting on three-quarter-length coats. In the absence of fabric for hats, they wrapped their hair in turbans. The whole marriage scene had an atmosphere that was redolent of the black market. Five years later, the film looked ludicrous on account of that, but now it is not embarrassing at all.

To return to the notion of an object: if the two best films from the Occupation are *Angels of Sin* and *Le Corbeau*,[6] it is because these were the two films that received the most careful attention. When I had finished *Adele H.*, I was happy to have made an unassailable object. For me, the film resembles an ivory egg—you can't cut it open; one can, at most, take it in one's hand—it is smooth, with no bumps, oval.

Currently, your cinema—and The Man Who Loved Women *proves it yet again—seems to depend upon one of two alternatives: either you eliminate as many characters as possible that are not really indispensable to what you are doing, or else you have a crowd of characters whose actions are intertwined...*

That is probably to avoid a mediocre product. In earlier times, the mere fact of going to the cinema was magical; one entered into a certain state of emotion when the film began. These days, because of television, this state is no longer possible. My position on this matter may be a bit reactionary, but if one wishes to "preserve" the magical dimension of cinema instead of accepting that it no longer exists, it is essential to fight back against the lack of style in television. If you see a historical drama on television, you get a grand salon with magnificent paneling, a splendid chandelier, and five miserable extras. To resist that, I fill the salon with so many people that one can no longer see the decor, or, alternatively, I only include one person, but filmed from such a close distance that, whatever happens, one will no longer see the decor. You also have to avoid the "gown shown in its entirety," because this idea is always uppermost in television: "the gown cost a lot, and so we have to show it!" That is why in *Adele H.* the whole film is shot in close-up, why one doesn't see either a café terrace, or a hackney carriage. One only sees a close-up shot that extends throughout the whole film, because I wanted the audience to see only this face, not to be interested in anything else but that, and not to be distracted by elements that are merely eye-catching. All my efforts are designed to ensure that things are looked at, listened to, made intriguing, and to omit everything that is merely decorative. During the time when the New Wave was at its height, there was a tendency, for example, to deliberately shoot in unusual settings; all that has passed now. Color film conveys too much information, making it necessary to have backdrops that are as neutral as possible.

If a whole film can be brown, instead of being sometimes brown, sometimes blue, sometimes red, then that is good. It also counters the effect of cinema verité, in which one simply attempts to capture life by making people speak. The New Wave was merely an attempt to get out of the studio to restore the impression of reality that had been destroyed by the films of Delannoy and Autant-Lara. The best film in this genre was definitely *Breathless*. Gradually, because of color, we have swung round to the opposite viewpoint, concluding that cinema was at its most beautiful when streets were in a studio; this kind of shift in opinion is natural. We are returning to artifice, which does not amount to a retreat into aestheticism, but for the sake of allowing films to recover some kind of form. The height of realism is the documentary, and to make a documentary with hardly any fiction is anything but art—it is of no interest. On that score, the influence of May 1968 brought about a kind of pressure to mix politics with fiction which, in fact, do not mix very well; so we have films that depict crime stories with a sprinkling of politics. The result is a bastardization. To that, you can also add the pressure exerted by feminists, which paralyzes many people. It is necessary to rediscover freedom, and for that, to go back to analyzing the things we used to like. It is only now that I understand why I liked *The Big Sleep*, or *Beauty and the Beast* so much, for example—it was because those were films that took place entirely at night.[7]

> *Quite by chance,* The Man Who Loved Women *is going to be released in France just after the two Italian films on Casanova by Fellini and Comencini, which, as it happens, could legitimately have the same title. Does this similarity annoy you?*

I would love to be able to make a film like Fellini's *Casanova*, which I think is splendid. It is a brilliant film, the most beautiful Fellini has made, which confirms that he is the greatest visual filmmaker in the sound era, along with Orson Welles. The big difference is that in the visual magic of Orson Welles, the camera plays a major part; in Fellini's case, it's what he presents in front of the camera that is phenomenal. In addition, I am carried along by the music, and when I see the film again, I experience the same emotions at the exact same places. I think that the end of the film, the court at Württemberg, is so sublime that I watch the film repeatedly for that passage. Fellini pushes a certain number of the things I have been talking about to an extreme limit; for example, there is not a single scene shot in a real exterior, there is no sky in his film. He has not even filmed a courtyard in a studio; when we are with the carriage on the bridge, it is really in an interior, with false mist. Everything is phenomenal; it is the logical joy you derive from having recreated everything. With Visconti, when you have interior scenes, they contain everything imaginable that one could put into a period film, but when the characters suddenly pass through a garden, the film collapses every time. *Death in Venice* works for me, because Venice is treated like a theater, and the big black clouds function like a backdrop.[8] Fellini clearly thought about all that, while Visconti definitely never thought about it. In contrast, Fellini was not interested in holding his audience through the way he told a story. It is only achieved through the spectacle: we sit down, and then he puts on a show for us, but involving things that are more and more astonishing and brilliantly successful.

1980

For a long time, *The Man Who Loved Women* was called *Le Cavaleur*,[9] and, secretly in my mind, I classified it in the crime film category involving men who kill women. I said to myself, "It amounts to the same thing, except he does not actually kill them." My point of reference was a series of films that began with *Shadow of a Doubt*, continuing with *Monsieur Verdoux*, *Unfaithfully Yours*, and *The Criminal Life of Archibald de la Cruz*.[10] For me, these are films that have been influenced by each other. I decided to leave out the murders, and what remained was a man, nevertheless troubling, who looks like an assassin—given that it was written for Charles Denner—and then different kinds of female reactions he elicits. But I started with almost nothing.

Notes

1. José Luis de Vilallonga y Cabeza de Vaca, 9th Marquess of Castellbell (1920–2007), was a Spanish author and actor who wrote four autobiographical books detailing his love affairs.
2. Le Père Grandet is the name of a miserly character in the novel *Eugénie Grandet*, by Honoré de Balzac, one of Truffaut's favorite authors, published in 1833.
3. *Tystnaden* (*The Silence*, Ingmar Bergman, 1963).
4. *More* (Barbet Schroeder, 1969).
5. *Les Dames du Bois de Boulogne* (Robert Bresson, 1945), the second feature film by Bresson, adapted from a story by Denis Diderot.
6. *Les Anges du péché* (*Angels of Sin*, Robert Bresson, 1943).
7. *The Big Sleep* (*Le Grand Sommeil*, Howard Hawks, 1946); *Beauty and the Beast* (*La Belle et la Bête*, Jean Cocteau, 1946).
8. *Death in Venice* (*Mort à Venise*, Luchino Visconti, 1971), adapted from the novel by Thomas Mann.
9. Literally, the "Skirt Chaser."
10. *Shadow of a Doubt* (*L'Ombre d'un doute*, Alfred Hitchcock, 1943); *Monsieur Verdoux* (Charles Chaplin, 1947); *Unfaithfully Yours* (*Infidèlement vôtre*, Preston Sturges, 1948); *Ensayo de un crimen* (*The Criminal Life of Archibald de la Cruz*, Luis Buñuel, 1955).

CHAPTER 25
1978: *THE GREEN ROOM*

> I have just turned forty-six, and I am already beginning to be surrounded by people who have died. Take a film like *The Piano Player* . . . half the actors who participated in it have gone. From time to time, I miss people I have lost—Cocteau, for example. So, I put on one of his records, and I listen to it. I listen to his voice, in the morning, in my bathroom. I miss him.
>
> Interview with Catherine Laporte and Danièle Heymann, L'Express, no. 1392, March 13–19, 1978

Why did you change from the nineteenth to the twentieth century in adapting Henry James's novella The Altar of the Dead *for the screen?*

I chose to transpose Henry James's themes to 1928 because I wanted them to be directly linked to a memory of the First World War. The idea of massacre, of millions of deaths, is not evoked with as much power by the last War. On the other hand, I decided not to preserve the atmosphere of the nineteenth century, because I didn't want to repeat the romantic setting of *Adele H.*, and it was necessary to establish a very strong contrast between the scenes of ordinary life and those in the chapel. The work of Almendros, my cinematographer, played a critical part in this—it was essential that he achieve a contrast of colors from the use of electric light for domestic life and of candlelight for the chapel, which is a fairy-tale kind of light, almost unreal.

In actual fact, there were many more cinematic references than literary references in the development of *The Green Room*. I thought a lot about certain American films from the beginning of the sound era, in particular the films from Universal Studios. Obviously, I didn't contemplate using an actor like Bela Lugosi, but before commencing work with Jean Gruault, I outlined two screenplays that could have been developed from James's themes in the manner of Universal. In the first, there was a man who only loved dead people, and who slowly kills the woman he likes in order to be able to love her. In the other, conversely, a woman meets a man who only loves dead people, and she lets herself die to please him.

That strongly reminds me of a film by Tod Browning, The Unknown, *with Lon Chaney. But the central part of* The Green Room *is a direct evocation of the atmosphere of fantasy films . . .*

Yes, it begins with a storm scene, the window that suddenly opens, and that is followed by the episode with the wax mannequin, which is a reference to Buñuel's *Archibald de la Cruz*, and by the night spent in the cemetery. These cemetery scenes, in fact, come from my memories as a child, but I didn't realize that at the time of the shooting. I had a paternal grandfather who was a stonecutter, he worked in cemeteries, and during the holidays he would often take me with him. I also went there with my grandmother, whose family had suffered from many bereavements, and had many graves to visit.

There was a whole hierarchy among her dead people. For example, she would spend much more time at the grave of a young woman who had died at the age of twenty. I remember when my grandfather died, that she slid a pair of socks into the coffin, because he would be cold.

Let us come back, however, to The Green Room. *I phrased my question clumsily: is it a film on the cult of death? Are spectators perhaps going to experience it as such . . . Or is it a cult about people one has known . . . ?*

It is not a cult of death. Effectively, it is an extension of the love for people one has known and who are no more, and the idea that they have some kind of permanence. I don't entirely identify with the main character, and sometimes I criticize him. He is half-mad, with an obsession, but what is important is his refusal to forget. For me, this refusal is important. In our cinema craft, I am amazed at how Jacques Becker, for example, has fallen into oblivion, even though *Casque d'or* has been replayed on television.[1] No broadcast about Becker, neither on the radio nor on television. I would cross the whole of Paris on foot to see *It Happened at the Inn*, but what has become of this film?² I am against forgetting, which is an enormous frivolity, the frivolity of the present day, the frivolity of "Parisianism," et cetera. I reject all of that.

> *What about the portrait of Cocteau in the pantheon of* The Green Room . . . *I get the impression that, for you, it is a retrospective.*

That's true to some degree. *Day for Night* celebrated the work of filmmakers. Here, there is a celebration of people who have counted. It is a little like a declaration of love. It is neither depressing, nor morbid, nor sad. It is the idea that the strength of remembering, of fidelity, and obsessions is more powerful than reality. This is something that must not be surrendered to whims of fate. Don't remove yourself from the things and people that one no longer talks about: continue to live with them, if you love them. I refuse to forget.

> *Why did you decide to act in* The Green Room?

To make this film more intimate. Charles Denner would have played it magnificently, but I had just made *The Man Who Loved Women* with him, in which we see him in every scene. Apart from Denner, I couldn't think of anyone else. I thought that, if I played the role, I would achieve the same effect as when, doing my mail in my office, I dictate certain letters that are typed up, as against writing others personally by hand. *The Green Room* is like a letter written by hand. If you write by hand, it will not be perfect, perhaps the writing will be shaky, but it will be you, your writing. A typewriter is very different. This doesn't imply a contemptuous attitude on my part toward actors, because there are Olivettis with marvellous characters, Underwoods, Remingtons that have a lot of personality, portable Japys. I love typewriters!

> *What is the importance of the role of the deaf-mute child?*

I invented him, he is not in Henry James. We had a story that worked through repetitions, accumulations, and which doesn't have a lot of action. I had to find a way of inhabiting the house, to find secondary characters. It was not possible to endow the hero with a male confidant, for he has very little contact with living people. The idea of the kid probably came to me as a result of the eight days of filming I spent in an institution for deaf and dumb children for *The Wild Child*. In the end, I did not choose a deaf-mute child for this film, as I was too scared that it might be too nerve-racking for a handicapped boy, but I have been struck by the abilities of these children to "super-adapt," the quickness with which they understand, size up situations, and reconstruct them. In *The Green Room*, he is to some degree a replica of Julien Davenne, but he is better adapted than him in certain respects.

> *I also want to come back to this recurrent theme: handicapped people assume a lot of importance in your works, precisely because of this need for communication.*

I have always held an optimistic view of people who are handicapped in one way or another. A handicap can and must be surmounted. I have learned that there are books printed in large letters for people who are starting to have poor vision. I have ordered these books, merely to have them at hand, and not because I have bad eyesight. Mine is good. But I want to touch these books because they represent what I want to do.

> *One of the most important characters in your film is one particular dead person: Massigny. It is he who separates the living pair, Davenne and Cécilia. Without him, would they have been able to get together?*

Without him, there would not have been a film, because it would have been too static. *The Green Room* is a fairy tale. Massigny is its villain. He symbolizes everything that prevents us from sleeping, on which all our aggression is focused. Given that Davenne loves dead people (that is even his only religion beyond any notion of God) and that he has the same relationships with them as if they were alive, he rejects the old convention that sees death as leveling everything. He is capable of hating a dead person.

In this film, Massigny is the equivalent of Victor Hugo in *The Story of Adele H.*—invisible like him, but always present. The triangle of Davenne, Cécilia, and Massigny is similar to the triangle of Adèle, Pinson, and Hugo. *The Green Room* is the story of a missed meeting, of a love that is wasted. If Massigny had not existed? Cécilia is more rational than Davenne, but she feels the temptation to join him in his madness. If they hadn't been separated because of Massigny, she probably would have become the keeper of the temple. But even so, she would not have been able to bring him back to life: another obstacle exists between them, Davenne's dead wife.

> *More than being faithful to the dead, it seems to me that fidelity plain and simple is the subject of your film. For Davenne, to reject death is only an ultimate consequence of a cult of the absolute that one encounters in many of your characters.*

Yes, it's always a matter of a contest between the absolute and the relative, between the provisional and the definitive. It is a law of life that one gradually forgets. Anyone who would experience feelings that were just as intense ten years after the death of a person would be in danger. "Friends disappear, other friends replace them, that's the law," says Cécilia.

But everything that pertains to one's affections demands to be absolute. A child wants his mother for life; lovers want to love each other for life; everything in us calls out for the definitive—whereas life teaches us that things are provisional. I wonder whether the most important thing in life may not be the moment when we change—when we consider, for example, that our children count more for us than our parents . . .

As we draw closer to death in time, it prompts us to forget our dead ones. Because, in forgetting them, it is our own death that we are forgetting. Proust also said, "It is not because others are dead that our affection for them weakens, but because we are going to die ourselves . . ."

Yes, the real heartbreak resides in the necessity that, to survive, we have to accept the provisional.

What emotion are you hoping to arouse in the spectator with The Green Room?

I imagine that certain spectators might be put off at the thought of going to see a film about death. But when a subject makes me fearful, I try harder than if it presents no problems. If it lacks any problems, I wonder about other ones. But if I am scared, I take greater pains to remain exciting, poignant, create a progression. *The Green Room* resembles a kind of fairy story, the end is like a happy ending because it is satisfying to the mind. An idea that is seen through to the end, which is taken right to its summit, is very satisfying to the mind. In *The Man Who Loved Women*, the death of Charles Denner, which occurs while he is looking at the legs of a nurse, is a death that gives me a lot of pleasure, because it was so logical that he would die as a result of his passion. It is a story that is finished off well, achieving a kind of harmony. That is what led me to James. He was obsessed with harmony—he is constantly talking about it in his works.

Finally, I believe in restrained emotion, in emotion expressed not in paroxysms, but through accumulation. I would like people to watch *The Green Room* with their mouths agape, that they go from one astonishment to another, and that emotion only grips us at the end, thanks to the lyricism of Jaubert's music alone. I have tried to unroll a thread without breaking it, and to achieve a line that is as pure as possible.

Does the phrase "it is necessary to complete the arrangement" come from James?

Yes. We are in a fairy story, in "Once upon a time." It's the kind of film in which form is very important. Everything has to be very concentrated, very tight. In fact, everything is synchronized to the music of Jaubert, the *Concert flamand*, which was recorded before the film was shot. The camera movements and those of the actors are governed by the music. *The Green Room* is constructed like a musical with no dancing or singing. In the end, there were three elements that had to be harmonized: James, the work of Almendros, and that of Jaubert. It is an anti-Hollywood film in the sense that in Hollywood, one works with a great deal of narrative expansiveness. It is more resolutely European in that it rests on the classical idea of making something with almost nothing, with small things that have to be amplified in order to bring them to the height of an event.

For me, *The Green Room* belongs to a family of films in which one finds *Fahrenheit 451*, *The Wild Child*, and *Adele H*. The dead in it are like the books in *Fahrenheit*, one is trying desperately to make something inert come to life, the living give them their own breath, their own passions.

During the past three years, you have made four films one after the other; does this mean you have a guilty conscience when you are not working?

Yes, I have a hard time going to the cinema on afternoons during the week...

You never set it aside?

No. I create projects. Especially in December... It is terrifying to see the year ending. I get very depressed at the end of a year.

When you are simultaneously the producer, director, and an actor—which of these responsibilities do you find the heaviest?

The hardest stage is the preparation. Fellini depicted it magnificently in *8½*. This is the period in which you feel like an imposter because you have to resolve many issues for which you do not yet have a solution. During the actual shoot, however, you find yourself confronted with problems that, because they are so concrete, you can really tackle them...

The really creative part, in fact, is the preparation, the writing...

Yes, there are moments of intense joy when you feel that you are improving something. It is always fantastic when you come up with an idea that was not in the screenplay. When one says, "Hold on, those two are going to meet one another in the corridor," you get the feeling that you are remaking the world. These are pleasures that are out of all proportion.

What is the ultimate aim?

To move things in the direction of fiction. This particular thing will be more poignant, more intriguing, more interesting. That is what I am looking for, in fact. Not realism—but to make it interesting. To create something that is "as if." This is the paradox that marks a filmmaker's career. A novelist prolongs his literary life with conferences and articles, whereas a filmmaker is forced to work like a novelist for his whole life, even when he is beginning to have more general views. That is why films made by old men are never understood. They are always attacked because they are symbolic. The characters are thinner, but these films are very rich. Only cinephiles like them.

You are thinking of Renoir, of Hitchcock . . .

Yes, of the last films of everyone . . . Dreyer, Hawks . . .

Do you yourself think about your own final films?

Sometimes I imagine to myself that I would be capable of stopping voluntarily, and I dream of a paradise of reading . . . All those books that are waiting to be read. But no . . . Billy Wilder says, "A director who has retired becomes president of the jury of the San Sebastián Film Festival!"

Notes

1. *Casque d'or* (Jacques Becker, 1952).
2. *Goupi mains rouges* (*It Happened at the Inn*, Jacques Becker, 1943).

CHAPTER 26

1979: *LOVE ON THE RUN*

> The end of the film was trying for everyone. It was a closing of the door, despite the ending that I had wanted to be theatrically happy. Yes, the transition had to be made. In the final scene, Léaud was shattered. Me too. I left very quickly, but I wanted everything to be accomplished like the finale of a variety show in which everyone comes back in a collective number. That marks the end of the spectacle. Now, I feel very liberated. For the first time, I don't have a project underway.
>
> *Interview with Anne de Gasperi,* Les Nouvelles littéraires, *February 11, 1979*

I think that the experience of Love on the Run *is fairly amazing insofar as it allowed you to work on basic material that is probably unique in the history of cinema: a character interpreted by the same actor on a number of occasions over a period of almost twenty years. Were there already some examples of similar kind of work?*

It exists in amateur cinema, family cinema, but I don't think there is anything comparable in the history of cinema proper.

Were you completely satisfied with the use you made of this exceptional material, or do you have some regrets, things that bother you?

No, no, it didn't totally satisfy me, but I asked collaborators like Suzanne Schiffman, Marie-France Pisier, and Jean Aurel to work with me, for good reason, because I mistrusted my own choice of extracts from the Doinel films... I was scared of making choices based merely on the quality of scenes—of selecting scenes that were well acted, well lit—whereas I knew that this was not what really counted; I needed to think, above all, of how it would work in the story... The most difficult thing was to convert shots from the two earlier films in CinemaScope (*The 400 Blows* and *Love at Twenty*) into a normal format—that is, to choose what needed to be cut on the right side, or cut on the left.

Were there any shots from the earlier films that were chosen solely on the basis of the technical solutions that they provided, and not because of the needs of the story?

There are some major tricks in the film, including a false flashback. I didn't want disgruntled souls coming out of it saying, "All the old material is good, and all that is new is awful." In actuality, there are parts of scenes that look as if they happened four or five years ago, but which were shot for *Love on the Run*. For example, in the scene when Dani and Léaud get into an argument, the "field shot" comes from a scene in *Day for Night* and the "reverse shot," in which we see Claude Jade with a hair dryer, was shot for the new film.

This trickery matches the main character's attitude, because he, too, plays tricks with his memories, tells lies in the autobiographical novel he has published...

Yes, absolutely, the jigsaw puzzle of the torn-up photo that he puts back together is also a form of montage... When I made *Love on the Run*, I was thinking of *F for Fake*, which is a film that I have examined closely for its use of lying.[1] This film shows that it is important to return to the moment in which a character is speaking. You don't authenticate a flashback at its point of departure, but after you have returned from it.

One could imagine a new Doinel film from time to time, and why not, until he is sixty years old...?

This time it is definite: this is truly the last Doinel film. Besides, I really thought I had finished with Doinel after *Bed and Board*, but one day Henning Carlsen told me something I found very interesting. In Denmark, cinemas are "allocated" like newsdealer's stores in France. Henning Carlsen had inherited the cinema that Carl Dreyer operated until his death, the Dagmar Theater in

Copenhagen. In it, Henning Carlsen indulged in the following experience. He screened all the Doinel films in the form of a cycle. *The 400 Blows* at two o'clock in the afternoon, *Love at Twenty* at four thirty, *Stolen Kisses* at six o'clock, and *Bed and Board* at eight o'clock. And there were young people who would spend the whole day watching Antoine Doinel grow up, fall in love, and age. And it was when he told me this that I felt a desire to make a final Doinel film, which eventuated as *Love on the Run*.

Why do you say that this will be the last Doinel film?

Because ... there are some things in this story that are not very comfortable. In Doinel's case, he has major limitations, because of the fact that he is a kind of dropout without even being aware of it ...

I made him evolve almost alongside society. Unconsciously, I have brought him to a state in which he suffers from multiple incapacities. He cannot control people, he cannot play sports ... With him, there are merely limitations, very few positive things ... a kind of loneliness, populated with feminine presences, obviously, but he does not have much contact with men ...

We are living in a combative age in which people who are well integrated into society criticize and want to leave it; he always tries to reenter society; he always tries hard to connect with people ...

Do you think that Doinel has reached a point where he could construct a summary of his life, a self-reflection?

Oh, one can do that at any age. In one of the early drafts of the screenplay, Marie-France Pisier was a psychoanalyst, Jean-Pierre Léaud had a nervous breakdown and went to see Marie-France, who explained to him that you can't treat someone you know. Given that she had had a relationship with him, she could only listen to him two or three times, in face-to-face sessions, before referring him to someone else. We rejected this idea, however, because an analysis is something too complex for it to be simplified in the course of a comedy, and it was Marie-France who suggested that she should be a lawyer. So we then set off in a different direction; but, in actual fact, this was my original idea: to have Jean-Pierre on an analyst's couch, with him being led into recounting the various episodes in his life.

Why did you have Marie-Pisier collaborate in the writing of the screenplay?

Through the years, I have often talked to Marie-France about this project, telling her that even though *The 400 Blows* may have been the most famous in the series, and that *Stolen Kisses* had also been successful, my favorite was the least well known, the one we had made together, the segment in *Love at Twenty*. It is less well known simply because the whole film was not distributed widely. But I really liked the duo that Marie-France formed with Jean-Pierre Léaud, that birth of love at first sight that occurs during a concert of Berlioz; that is what I want to pick up again, from another perspective. Eventually, I asked Marie-France to work with Suzanne Schiffman on the first draft. For the next stage, I completed their screenplay with Jean Aurel because he helps me with all my films, especially at the editing stage. He knew the Doinel material off by heart, and I had a lot of confidence in his judgment.

Would you say that in Love on the Run *Antoine Doinel learns a lesson from the memories evoked in the course of the film?*

Antoine Doinel never reacts intellectually to life, but always emotionally. How has he evolved? I would like to quote a saying by Scott Fitzgerald: "All life is a process of breaking down."[2] We know very well that life has its ups and downs. You always find more freshness in the face of a child . . . Nevertheless, if I had to describe the enduring quality of Antoine Doinel, I would say that he is animated by a kind of "bravery." He is only at ease in extreme situations. He is the opposite of an exceptional character, the opposite of a hero, but what distinguishes him from average people is that he never settles for a middle state. Either he is deeply disappointed and despairing to the point where one fears for him, possibly, or else he is in a total state of exhilaration and enthusiasm. That is what is amusing about him, and what makes him unpredictable.

In Love on the Run, *he falls in love with an idea you might find in a novel, he falls in love with a photo.*

Yes, he falls in love in an indirect, romantic way. Romanticism often propels us in life. People get married because they met each other on a boat. Had they met in the Metro, they wouldn't even have paid any attention to one another. That kind of thing happens constantly. Romanticism adds something. In addition, in this instance we see that Antoine, for once in his life, goes to a lot of trouble to track down the girl . . . the torn photo. But none of that is realistic—I treated it like an Arabian fairy-tale. There is a "Thousand and One Nights" aspect to the film that reflects the pleasure of telling a story. I feel as if I created a narrative experience at the heart of this film that greatly interested me: the story of the photo is told twice, the first time as something that Antoine would have made up, and a second time by reporting what really happened.

Can we believe in this couple? Can we believe in the ending?

Oh, I think one can believe in it if one wants to believe in it. This final part of the film is not treated psychologically, but theatrically. I realized, for example, that when Dorothée is listening, staring wide-eyed, to the absorbing story that Antoine is telling with such intensity, she is instinctively adopting the expressions of Sacha Guitry's heroines. Often, in Guitry's films, things are resolved theatrically at the end, and in a somewhat unforeseen way. It is a form that "eliminates" the background at that particular moment. It is his passion that creates the atmosphere rather than the words that are spoken. Doinel's lyricism often makes you forgive the rest, and it is thanks to that that he is able to charm Dorothée once more, because it is his most attractive trait, I think. So we attain a happy ending, or relatively happy. The dialogue says, "Of course this cannot last forever, but one can pretend as if—yes, that's it—let's pretend as if." There is a sense here of two people who are acting in good faith, and who are going to try to make their way together.

Did you know that the boy who comes to listen to a disk in the shop at the end of *Love on the Run* is the little boy from *Shoot the Piano Player*? But we don't recognize him because he has changed so much. I had one shot in which we see him crossing the street while clicking his fingers, as he does in *The Piano Player*, but it was too indirect for people to register the connection.

In Love on the Run, *there are extracts from earlier films that are changed or altered from their original meaning. Does this imply that there was a great deal of work to be done during the editing?*

Actually, there are only eighteen minutes borrowed from the earlier films, out of a length of an hour and a half. This was certainly the film on which I spent most time during the editing since *Fahrenheit 451*, which was also very fragmented, and in which the book burnings were played as flashbacks. The problem with *Love on the Run*, for Martine Barraqué and me, was to blend disparate material, to avoid losing the thread, not to disappoint when one returns to the present after a flashback. The more disparate the visual material is, the more you need to preserve the unity of the sound. It is the sound that establishes the bridges. In the screenplay we had obviously foreseen where the flashbacks would go, and how long they would last, but the editing, which lasted for sixteen weeks, imposed its own laws on us, certain laws that were very peculiar. Let us say that, when there are changes to an image, there must not be any change in the sound—at any rate, as little as possible.

Why did you include certain flashbacks involving women, and not just about Doinel?

Well, because that is a principle of the film: everyone is recounting things to everyone else. Doinel is not entirely frank when talking about himself. He lies. He only recounts a part of his story to Marie-France on the train. For example, as far as the affair with Dani is concerned, he does not tell the whole truth—one only learns of it from the account given by Claude Jade . . . when she found them in bed with the story of the book that had been wrapped in newspaper . . . There are flashbacks that are deliberately falsified, as when Antoine pretends that Colette's parents came to live opposite him, whereas it was he who had changed his lodgings so as to be near her . . . In short, a flashback does not automatically mean that it is presenting the truth.

Thanks to the mosaic in Love on the Run, *we discover the crucial role of the mother in* The 400 Blows, *who causes Antoine to feel so insecure. You have never spoken of your mother . . .*

I classify my books according to their author. But I would like to reserve a shelf in my library for books about mothers. They constitute the best book by each writer. Just look at Simenon, Roger Peyrefitte, Bataille, Pagnol, Albert Cohen. If one were to pick just one subject, it would be that one. For me, it is perhaps too soon.

1982

There is always a scene in the Doinel cycle in which a water cart passes by the Sacré-Coeur . . .

As far as that is concerned, it is a bit of a joke, because the small truck that is spraying water comes from the way the Americans depict Paris. It is a shot you often find in the films of Billy Wilder and Minnelli . . . So I did it to amuse myself, yes . . . All the same, it is a real shot, and the advantage of having this shot is that it indicates the time of day—when one wants to show that it is very early. I even did it in *Day for Night*. That was completely unrealistic, since in *Day for Night* we had this hotel in Nice, the Hôtel Atlantique—but, because the producer had said that journalists do not realize that actresses are women who get up early in the morning, when Jacqueline Bisset, who has spent the night with Jean-Pierre Léaud, comes out of the hotel, I had a water cart pass by, at a place that was really absurd, near the hotel, so that one could sense that it was very early in the morning.

NOTES

1. *F for Fake* (Orson Welles, 1973), a film about the art forger Elmyr de Hory, Clifford Irving, who wrote a fraudulent biography, and fakery in general.
2. A quotation from F. Scott Fitzgerald's novel, *The Great Gatsby* (1925).

CHAPTER 27

1980: *THE LAST METRO*

> Renoir's death was very distressing to me, at a personal level. He had not declined intellectually at all, since he had finished his book at Christmas and he died in February. For Hitchcock, there was no way out. I knew that he was doomed. He could no longer make films, and he did not know how to do anything else—it was unbearable. What most deeply affects me is that the generation who flourished in the silent era have all died: Chaplin, Renoir, Hitchcock. No one will ever make any more films like they did.
>
> *Interview with Anne de Gasperi,* Le Quotidien de Paris, *June 11, 1980*

Love on the Run *marked the conclusion of a series of your earlier films (*Stolen Kisses, Bed and Board, *etc.).* The Last Metro *has been compared—sometimes by you yourself—to* Day for Night; *nevertheless, is it a film that also relates to your whole oeuvre?*

After you have made nineteen films, none of the themes you tackle can be entirely new! Each element always depends slightly on what precedes it. People follow what I am doing better when I add new elements while keeping one foot in the past. *The Last Metro* not only refers to *Day for Night*, but also to *Jules and Jim*, and even *Stolen Kisses*; but, in addition, I address a subject in it that I have never attempted before: theater, against a backdrop which I am not used to treating—the War and the Occupation.

The Last Metro has been criticized for its optimism tinged with naïveté. Is the image you present of the Occupation too indulgent? In New York, the critic Andrew Sarris wrote that French people found The Last Metro *reassuring because it made them forget denunciations of the Collaboration, and because it allowed them to believe in the myth that there was a Jew hidden in all Parisian cellars.*

It is true that I didn't make a dark film, but I think that I am also speaking in it of the cruelty of everyday life. More than anything else, my film embodies a notion of compromise and tolerance. At the beginning, that made me unhappy, because I know that the best characters in cinema are characters who want to achieve something, and do achieve it. I have a hard time with that idea. Instead, my characters have obsessions. They do not necessarily achieve their goals, but they keep on pursuing them nevertheless. In *The Last Metro*, the characters cannot do everything they want to do, but constantly have to make compromises. After the film had been completed, I realized that this was probably the defining quality of the film. It was what made people identify with the film—because in real life, very often one does not fulfill one's dreams, and you have to be content with compromises.

My film is lenient toward those people who are not biased, toward those who continued on with their business as if nothing were happening. I am against people who did wrong, against those who denounced people, such as Daxiat, the critic. I don't pass judgment on France itself; I think that it was quite simply waiting. People had been told that Marshal Pétain's government was acting in good faith, and they believed it. But it is always the same old deception: we always believe that old men are honest, which is why we make them leaders of the country. Apart from the fact that this old man was a complete imbecile, he was lucid for one hour during the day, one could take nice photos of him; at school they asked us to write letters to him, it was no more serious than that. What was serious, during that period, was that people with extreme ideas had power on their side.

The world was living through a tragedy, but as far as artistic life was concerned, this was a great period, especially for theater. Television did not yet exist, people were living in solitude, cold, with restriction, anxiety. Theater could provide a rare form of escape. Authors and actors competed with one another in talent. During this time, the best plays by Sartre, Montherlant, Claudel, and Anouilh were written.

And, at the end of performances, everyone tried not to miss the last metro train?

The last metro, in fact, determined when entertainments had to finish. Actors met each other there and exchanged all kinds of impressions and information—which is why I gave the film this title. *The Last Metro* is an illustration of the famous American slogan: "The show must go on."

Why isn't the political backdrop of the film more clearly laid out?

That is not the object of the film—primarily, I wanted to sketch the relationships of a certain number of characters in an exceptional atmosphere. Given that actors are involved, they do not live through this period in quite the same way as other people. Naturally, emotions, love, friendship come into it. As in *Day for Night*, we see people in the same craft loving each other, sympathizing, confronting each other, and how they enter into passionate love affairs. The political framework necessarily exists because of the way the German Occupation constitutes the backdrop. Even though I didn't try to create a detailed reconstitution of the period, I didn't avoid showing German uniforms. Furthermore, the authorities overseeing the Occupation, the *Propagandastaffel*, required that twenty seats in each theater be reserved each night for German soldiers. As Henri Amouroux has demonstrated in *La Vie des Français sous l'Occupation*, there were pro-Nazis who were worse than the "occupiers," driven by Hitlerian zeal to the point of being anti-Vichy and anti-Pétain. These pro-Nazis extolled the cult of virility, and they hated homosexual artists. When they attacked a film, a novel, or a play, pro-Nazi critics would often use this expression: "a work that is Jew-ified and effeminate." This was how Alain Laubreaux, a critic from *Je suis partout*,[1] succeeded in having Cocteau's *La Machine infernale* banned. Laubreaux also tried to have himself made director of the Comédie-Française, but, in the face of an indignant reaction by its members, the Germans gave up the attempt to impose their protégé. The scene in which Depardieu punches the face of an anti-Semitic critic in the film really took place during the war. Jean Marais actually fought with Laubreaux.

How did you get the idea of making this film?

The idea came to Suzanne Schiffman and me after having read the autobiography of Jean Marais, and then memoirs by other actors, such as those by Corinne Luchaire, Ginette Leclerc, Van Parys, René Lefèvre, and many others as well. I concluded that, in each case, the most fascinating chapter was the one that dealt with the Occupation. I had been wanting to make a film about theater for a long time. I was also interested in doing a film about the period during the Occupation. *The Last Metro* allowed me to mingle these two wishes. I asked Nestor Almendros to be my cinematographer for the ninth time, given that the photography for this film required a lot of care and inventiveness in order to avoid a feeling of anachronism, which is all the more dangerous when one is dealing with a relatively recent period.

How did you develop the screenplay, which, like Day for Night, *involves many characters and plot times simultaneously?*

Suzanne Schiffman and I drafted a script by drawing upon our own memories. Suzanne's parents were in hiding during the war, her mother did not come back after being deported. One of my uncles who was a member of the Resistance got caught at the Gare de l'Est, but he was able to signal to a friend who came to meet him and prevented him from being arrested. And so on ... We wrote the script in two months last year, but for more than a year we were searching through our memories, interviewing friends, and reading all the books we could find about theatrical life during the War, and about the collaborationist press. I also read memoirs by women who had directed theaters during that time. I thought about Jewish artists who had worked secretly. While thinking about Louis Jouvet who had left for South America, I asked myself: what would have happened if Jouvet had remained hidden in his Athénée theater, and if he had continued to direct the house?[2] That is how the story came about.

And the Jewish issue? Or rather that of anti-Semitism in your film?

We were not thinking about that very much when we began the screenplay, but in the course of all the preliminary reading and perusal of documents, the importance of this issue during that period gradually impressed itself on us. The emphasis on the Jewish theme was probably owing to the fact that two years ago, in France, there was a radio broadcast of *La Vie des Français sous l'Occupation*, which I was talking about earlier, in which we heard many documents from the period read out. They were stupefying. I included some of them in *The Last Metro*. That is the origin of the retort: "It would not be necessary to make them wear a yellow star if Jews had blue skin." And "It's important to recognize those people because they are dangerous." These are documents that had been forgotten, and I find that it is worth the effort to ensure that they are heard again because we are now seeing, it has to be said, a renewed intolerance.

I am not saying that one has to hunt down anti-Semites during peace time. Everyone should be able to express their opinions, however displeasing they may be—that's necessary for there to be a play of ideas. But to be anti-Semitic in 1942 was despicable. To be responsible for the life and death of someone else, with the emphasis on death rather than life, is intolerable. I like the saying of an Italian dandy at the end of the War: "Finally, we can return to being anti-Semitic of our own free will!" That is an insolent and cynical statement, but I prefer it to pathological, hysterical attitudes of this sort: "They are taking our most beautiful women from us!" You get that a lot in the writing of Rebatet, for example.[3]

> *You have written before this that cinema is a woman's art and that, for you, the great moments of cinema involve "the convergence of the gifts of a director and those of an actress who is being directed by him." Could that be applied to* The Last Metro? *Does that account for the choice of Catherine Deneuve as the female star of your film, ten years after* Mississippi Mermaid?

To a degree. I think she is really good in this film. The role was written for her. I was thinking of her natural authority, and also of her age: she is now thirty-five, and it is time she give up playing young women with hair down to their shoulders. On the other hand, it was during the War that women began to manage theaters. And so, I invested her with this responsibility.

From Simone Berriau to Marguerite Jamois, from Yvonne Printemps to Alice Cocéa, from Parysis to Mary Morgan, there were many female theater directors in Paris during the Occupation who had to confront the same problems. Catherine Deneuve is both feminine and energetic, in a plausible way. I like the way that she always seems to project on the screen a double life: an apparent life, and a secret life. One gets the impression that she is keeping her thoughts to herself, and that her inner life is at least as important as her outer life.

> *You also cast Sabine Haudepin once again.*

Yes, I cast her in her debut role as the young girl in *Jules and Jim*. After that, we lost touch with one another. Sabine has returned to theater and, against my usual practice, I wasn't able to resist the pleasure of going to embrace her in the wings after her performance in *Three Sisters* in the Théâtre de la Ville, last winter.

> *You don't like people talking about "directing an actor." Why?*

People overuse this expression. It conveys the idea of authority. I was very unhappy in the army: I don't want people to direct me, and I don't want to direct others.

One cannot help noticing that Catherine Deneuve acts differently with you than with Claude Lelouch, for example. Does this arise from a different style of directing?

Yes, because Lelouch is seeking to capture spontaneous reality, and I am not at all interested in this reality. I prefer to have very scripted dialogue, I ask an actor to project, I want people to understand everything—I am rather obsessive in that regard. In effect, it is another way of working. I don't like improvisation. I have never seen an actor come up with a text that was better than the one that had been written for him. However much I like actors, I prefer them to utter the text that I have prepared for them. I find that they are not very inventive.

If you are not directing them, what are you doing?

Perhaps I am in fact directing them, and it's the word itself that displeases me. I prefer to speak of signaling, as when you direct trains . . .

When you signal to Catherine Deneuve, are you hoping to make people forget about Chanel No. 5?[4]

Chanel No. 5 was almost part of the character. At the beginning of the film, she is talking about how her husband came to know her, and says, "When he came to find me at Mademoiselle Chanel's . . ." We even suspect that she has been a model for Chanel. Actors have a kind of social reality that you can't get around very easily. All the roles that an actor has performed accumulate to give him or her an image that it is impossible to overcome entirely. It is better to go with it.

Insofar as The Last Metro *is a film about actors, one can understand why you cast a Deneuve and a Depardieu who, at the present time, are almost archetypes of their profession. Nevertheless, it was a great surprise to discover the name of Gérard Depardieu in the credit sequence, at the time of shooting, given that he, when all is said and done, is not at all similar to Jean-Pierre Léaud or Charles Denner!*

I had wanted to work with Depardieu from the time I saw him in a small role in *Stavisky* in 1973.[5] There is a scene in which he encounters Jean-Paul Belmondo, who plays Stavisky, in a stairway and exchanges several words with him. For me, that symbolized a meeting of two generations of actors—not that Belmondo's career is over, but it was the beginning of Depardieu's. The events of May 1968 mark the dividing line for me. Before that, actors would never have thought of appearing without being at least partially dressed. After that, they were capable of accepting that they could be required to appear naked, like Depardieu in *Going Places*.[6]

After your adoption of Jean-Pierre Léaud, is it Depardieu's turn?

I have no possessive feelings where actors are concerned. It is Depardieu himself who has provoked the phenomenon whereby we want to do everything with him. At the very moment he is shooting one scene, he inspires you with another. One can imagine him as an escaped convict. You say to yourself that he could do *The Count of Monte-Cristo*. In addition, he is not content with merely acting. He is endowed with a fabulous presence that relaxes the atmosphere. He has the gift of being able to soothe the slightest bit of tension.

In fact, it was he himself who discovered the key to the interpretation of his character, shortly before shooting began; he said to me, "I think the main attribute of this character is a certain kindness." We talked about that for a little while, and then I didn't need to give him any further direction for the rest of the shoot!

The Last Metro is a rather nocturnal film.

It was important to bear in mind the fact that the impression of this period is often conveyed by memories that are presented in black and white, as in photos and films from the time. So I had to take account of that as a given, and I think I resolved the problem by talking a lot about the period with Nestor Almendros, and then taking a number of decisions.

Among these decisions, there is one very simple one, which is that we never see a daytime scene until after forty-five minutes of the film have elapsed. The first forty-five minutes take place at night, in the dark, which is not really historically accurate, given that the film has a precise date, and the date is one month before the invasion of the free zone, around April–May 1942, at a time when evenings were under German time—like the daylight saving time we now have in summer—so as to economize on petrol, which means that it was actually still daylight until ten o'clock at night. In spite of that, I preferred to sacrifice historical accuracy and to have an aesthetic accuracy, as it were, so that my story would seem more plausible. People would feel more as if they were experiencing the War period if I filmed the whole of the first part at night. In my opinion, it is during daytime scenes that anachronisms creep in, so that people say, "Hold on, that street doesn't look as if it's from that period," and then they start to look to see whether there are TV aerials on the roofs. They are going to start seeing all kinds of anachronistic modern elements—they will seek out everything modern in the image that works against what the director was wanting to do—while with night scenes, one can light only parts of the image, one can maintain a much more mysterious atmosphere, and, strangely, doing so more powerfully evokes this period of the War.

Were you surprised by the film's success?

When I decided to make the film, I suspected that the subject was going to interest people in their forties, but I didn't imagine that young people would feel involved. Moreover, throughout the shoot I was rather worried. It was the first time that I was presenting characters with so little depth, characters that I didn't think were very strong, and which marked a change for me compared with a character like that of *Adele H.* In *The Last Metro*, no one is fully developed. Deneuve and Depardieu embody antiheroes, compromising characters because, during the Occupation, people lived with compromises, for good reasons. I was also astonished by the capacity for sympathy that spectators felt toward these characters.

The Last Metro *was not only successful in France, where it won ten Césars, but was also nominated for a Hollywood Oscar.*

I am happy that *The Last Metro* was successful beyond France, but I know that it is full of details that are hard for anyone who did not live through the German Occupation in France to understand. I can give you one example. In *The Last Metro* we have a young boy who lives next to the theater, and is growing tobacco plants. That is significant, because in France tobacco is a monopoly, meaning that it is forbidden for anyone to grow tobacco in their garden, and it was an even more serious offense during the War. During the War, there were no cigarettes, nor tobacco. Many people did that—sometimes on the balconies of their windows. And when I went to introduce *The Last Metro* in Israel—it was the first country in which the film was released—they subtitled that scene with the tobacco as if it were a drug, because they were incapable of thinking that it was tobacco. Those were the things that struck me as a child. It is strange, because in *The Last Metro*, one does not see that the child does indeed have a small role to play. I am convinced, however, that it is a vision of the Occupation that is my child's vision. I was eight years old at the beginning of the War, and twelve at the end. But someone who was an adult during the War would not create the same screenplay. He would perhaps deal with the same story, but he would not keep the same details. I filled it with details that had impressed themselves on the child that I was.

NOTES

1. *Je suis partout* was a right-wing French newspaper founded in 1930 that embraced fascism and anti-Semitism, aligning itself with the Nazis during the Occupation, until it ceased publication after the Liberation of Paris.

2. Louis Jouvet (1887–1951) was a French actor and theater director who controlled major national theaters between June 1940 and June 1941, when he left with his troupe for a tour of Latin America, not returning to France until 1945. His secretary, Charlotte Delbo, had returned to France in November 1941 to join the Resistance, but was arrested in 1942 and died in Auschwitz.

3. Lucien Rebatet (1903–1972), a French novelist, journalist, and intellectual, who, like Alain Laubreaux, wrote for the anti-Semitic right-wing newspaper *Je suis partout*.

4. Catherine Deneuve made a series of print ads and TV executions for Chanel No. 5 from 1968 through the end of the 1970s that "cemented [her] international stardom and underlined the perfume's iconic status." See Mark Tungate, *Branded Beauty: How Marketing Changed the Way We Look* (London and Philadelphia: Kogan Page, 2011), 122.

5. *Stavisky* (Alain Resnais, 1974).

6. *Les Valseuses* (Going Places, Bertrant Blier, 1974).

CHAPTER 28

1981: *THE WOMAN NEXT DOOR*

> Perhaps I am not modern because in modern art the entertainment value of the representation is destroyed. In this sense, if I were to make a comparison in terms of literature, it is rather as if I were making nineteenth century novels. Cinema did not exist in the nineteenth century, but I love films that have a link to the nineteenth century—in other words, ones that pursue the same ends as Stendhal, for instance.
>
> *Interview with Joël Saucin, Hebdo-Belge, November 1981*

When did the idea for The Woman Next Door *arise?*

It depends upon which aspect of the film you are talking about, the story or the theme. Let us talk about the theme. Let's say that bringing a man and a woman who had loved each other in the past face to face had been a theme that I had had in my head for several years, and on which I had been taking notes. At the time, my sketch was called "On Track"—which was not really a very good title! The essential thing was to find an ideal couple . . . I thought of Fanny Ardant when I saw *Les Dames de la côte* on television.[1] I instantly wanted to work with her. That took place just before the shooting of *The Last Metro*, in which I felt I had not made the most of Gérard Depardieu, given that he was only one of seven characters in the film, and not the most important one at that. I was all the more keen to work with Gérard because I had got on with him marvelously. So, on the night of the Césars, I introduced Gérard to Fanny Ardant. From there, I took up my story, which, at the time, was above all a story of nervous breakdown following a breakup.

How do you construct a screenplay of this sort?

You have to exploit your memory, the things you recollect. For example, the character of Madame Jouve comes from a woman I had known fifteen years earlier. I was in the south of France with Jean-Louis Richard—we must have been in the process of writing the screenplay for *Mata Hari*[2]—and, while looking for evening wear to attend a gala performance by Charles Trenet, we met this lady in Old Nice who was renting out dinner jackets . . . When I remembered this person, I suddenly thought of her for the confidante in *The Woman Next Door*.

This is a screenplay that was written very quickly, if I'm not mistaken?

In two or three weeks. I had some deadlines to meet because Gérard was leaving to film in Mexico, while Fanny was meeting Nina Companeez for a further series. So we left for Grenoble with a script of only thirty-five or forty pages, which simply told the story and no more. And given that I had my actors at hand, I could write the dialogue as I went along, on Sundays, which I like doing.

Do you often work in this way?

When I can, and when my films are not too complicated; when the number of characters is not too great. When the actors are anxious, it is better to reassure them by giving them all their lines before the shoot.

I imagine that with The Last Metro *that had not been possible . . .*

In that instance I had had to write everything in advance. When the actors are performing on stage—in the theater sequences—there were two separate columns in the script: the text of the play they were performing, and the text with the sentences to be said in the wings . . . The screenplay for *The Last Metro* was very detailed . . .

There has been a lot of talk about the ten Césars you won for that film . . .

That didn't affect me owing to the fact that I had enjoyed success in the past: *The 400 Blows*, *Jules and Jim*, and *Day for Night* . . . And also *Stolen Kisses* . . . After a success like that of *The Last Metro*, you simply end up with more obligations because you are invited everywhere. Now, I didn't want to spend my year traveling—which meant that I seized the chance to make *The Woman Next Door*! While it is a pleasure to go to London or to a festival in New York to present a film, I nevertheless feel I am living a more normal life when I am involved in a shoot. That is what I like best, along with writing the script and the editing.

How do you respond to your status as a "star director"?

Very normally! I have a feeling that the opposite would be abnormal! I have had disappointments, as you will have observed! When I begin to get concerned is when I have two flops in a row. In this regard, I have to admit that *The Green Room* was manifestly a flop, just like *Love on the Run*. I was therefore relieved by the success of *The Last Metro*. That has given me oxygen and four or five years in which I have carte blanche—but that is not entirely true. After the failure of *Two English Girls* and *A Gorgeous Girl Like Me*, fortunately I had *Day for Night* to help me climb back up the slope! Up until now, I have been lucky . . .

You really believe that it is a matter of luck . . .

In any case, the result of a film—and furthermore, it's a good thing—is not proportional to the amount of work it involves, nor the money spent, nor the intelligence deployed. It is not proportional to anything at all. It depends upon a kind of chemistry that happens or not. Very often, I have gone to huge efforts on films that have been a failure . . .

In France, most actors want to work with you. This is not necessarily by accident . . . How would you explain it?

I would like to say that it is logical, quite simply because I give precedence to the characters. They are more important than the decor, the story, or the atmosphere. My films are films with characters, and actors are people who have chosen this profession in order to play characters. In recent years, especially after 1968, people have often made the mistake of believing that, for an actor, it is enough simply to appear before a camera. Moreover, in many films, one doesn't even bother to give the character a name! Now, actors do not want to play themselves, or to play the same character each time. That's how it is with Depardieu, for example. After *The Woman Next Door*, we left hoping to get together again soon on another film. I get a feeling that we will be able to make quite a few films together . . .

This is, in addition, the first time that you have made two films in a row with the same actor.

That's right, because he is someone who is destined, in the religious sense of the word, for film. The first time you work with someone, you get to know him, but it is on the editing table, as a result of looking at and rewatching scenes, that you really discover him. In Gérard's case, he is someone for whom acting has to be a game. In addition, what I like a lot about him is that he doesn't do anything to assert his virility, being perfectly happy with the idea that there is a very strong feminine element in men in general, and all the more so in actors. He acts with the feminine part of him, he enjoys that . . . Sometimes in the past I have had problems with men who were scared of being overshadowed by the feminine roles. Let's say that often, in my films, feminine characters are more dynamic, more enterprising. With Gérard, that doesn't annoy him at all!

That is, in fact, what happens to some degree in The Woman Next Door, *between him and Fanny Ardant . . .*

The film is constructed in two parts. At the beginning, he is the one who is anguished by meeting her again, and then, from the middle onwards, the film turns upside down, and it becomes the opposite as soon as he goes too far—I mean the scene in which he hits her.

In The Woman Next Door, *as in most of your films, women are not filmed like the men. You get closer to their faces, for example . . .*

I am not consciously aware of that. What I saw fairly quickly is that Depardieu is better in the first takes, when he has just received his lines and doesn't know them completely as yet, whereas Fanny becomes more and more moving as the takes are repeated. When you have an actress like Jeanne Moreau or Fanny Ardant in front of the camera, you feel that the screenplay is in the process of being elevated, and the film that has been shot becomes precious.

I would like you to talk about your relationship with the actors. Just now you said, "I saw Fanny Ardant in Les Dames de la côte *and I wanted to make a film with her." Just as you said to me, "I saw Isabelle Adjani in* L'École des femmes *and I wanted to make* Adele H*." In the case of Fanny Ardant, what happened?*

She made me think at once of the Brontë sisters, in whom I had been very interested at the time of *Two English Girls*. I said to myself, "That girl is like the three Brontë sisters all by herself!" And then I met her, and we got to chatting... I went to see her in the theater... That's what happened.

Finally, television has sometimes led you to discover actors?

Yes. Before the advent of television, when one had a story with ten characters, one could have ten stars—it was good. The better known the actors were, the better the film. Television has changed that. We must not forget that when films are released, the actors come to be interviewed on television, with various extracts being played from the film concerned, which means that even people who don't go to the cinema know about all the year's productions... So, these days, all that brings about new requirements for credibility.

Generally, what is it that determines your choice of actors?

From the outset, I try to think of roles that would be best played by famous actors and those that would be better played by new faces. I could have put one of four or five great French actresses alongside Depardieu in *The Woman Next Door*: I would have come up with a film, but not the same one! A mythological dimension was less important to me here than the impression of reality that I wanted to create—I found it more interesting to have the impact of an encounter between an actor one sees four or five times a year on the screen and a new actress.

In your films, you get rid of as much scenery as you can...

In that respect, too, it's a way of resisting television! I do many things with the idea of reacting against television. Each night television presents us with an incredible array of images, both in reporting and fiction, it saturates us with images... Because of that I think that if people have made the effort to come to see a film, rather than remaining at home, a film should be as unified as possible, so as to capture their interest. Before television, one would have thought otherwise. Today, it is necessary to give them the essential elements of the story at once, and then to try and hold the audience, because people are much less receptive now than twenty years ago.

Why did you take the narrative approach you did in The Woman Next Door?

I had the subject of *The Woman Next Door* in my head for several years, but I couldn't make up my mind to go ahead with it. There was something too symmetrical about it. Everything became resolved when I introduced the character of Madame Jouve, the confidante, the narrator. When one is living through a love story, one experiences it very intensely, feeling as if the rest of the world has stopped. Twenty years later, one smiles at realizing how excessive one had been. Madame Jouve represents this indispensable hindsight. When you reread love letters, one is amazed at the intensity of the blows people deal to each other. You say that all of that should have been much gentler.

You will probably not agree with me, but I have found that The Woman Next Door *is a kind of extension of* Mississippi Mermaid. *There is passion, loneliness . . . and then with Depardieu-Belmondo, two "strong men" who become weak . . .*

There is certainly a relationship between the two films. It is true that since *Two English Girls* my love films have become more intense . . . In Europe, we are very sensitive to the metaphysical dimension of life. In contrast to the United States, we know that social ambition is empty. So it is easier for us to make stories about love, passion, obsessions—what I call films that push things to extremes, which quickly end up in death.

Is this what you like, love stories that go to an extreme?

They are more exhilarating. In addition, you know, when one is writing, when one is filming, it is satisfying to make characters suffer in your place. I see people at the moment who tell me that they were devastated by *The Woman Next Door*, whereas it makes me feel euphoric. It's exactly like the old Jewish story. A guy is in bed and cannot go to sleep. "It is because I am unable to pay the money I owe to the tailor across the street!" he explains to his wife. She gets up, opens the window, and calls to the neighbor, "My husband won't be able to pay you the money he owes!" She gets back into bed and says to her husband, "There, now it's he who will not be able to sleep!" Also, I often heard it said around me that this woman is in hospital, she has broken down, and that that man is being treated for insomnia . . . Strangely enough, one finds echoes of all these breakdowns and rifts in books and newspapers, but not often in films.

I find that The Woman Next Door *is a fairly difficult film for men.*

Really? There is one scene with which I am not happy, and which is one of the things I regret when I see the finished film. I didn't sufficiently reveal Depardieu's state of mind in the second part. I find that when Madame Jouve says to Depardieu, "I have seen this girl, she's in a bad state, you ought to go see her," at that point I made the scene too short. I should have shown that he was sincere in saying that he doesn't think it would be a good thing for him to go there. Because I get the impression that people really think that at that moment he is being egotistical, and shallow. For me, on the other hand, there was this idea, which I didn't really know how to convey, that the very excess of his violence, in the scene in which he practically knocks her to the ground, has left him feeling healed.

With The Woman Next Door, *we encounter yet again the need you have, above all else, to tell stories . . .*

That definitely comes from my love of books. I dream of making a film in which the only action would comprise events that have already occurred, and which are being retold. One of my favorite moments in *The Woman Next Door* is when Depardieu recalls to Fanny Ardant how they met. It is very disturbing, because it involves making the audience believe that what one hears is in the process of taking place! To do this, you have to make the audience listen to a dialogue that cannot be at all abstract. It is not enough to say, "I loved you, you loved me . . ." One has to say, "You were cutting bread at the bottom of the garden . . ." Things that conjure up images . . . When that happens, I think one has something interesting. When Madame Jouve recounts her attempted suicide, it is visual.

So writing occupies an important place. How did you collaborate with Jean Aurel . . . ?

This was perhaps the first time that he attached his name to a collaboration with me, but in actual fact, I have often asked his advice. Usually he collaborates in the editing. It is very rare for me to bring out a film in which Aurel has not participated in one way or another. When I have higgledy-piggledy material that is giving me vertigo, he helps me to clarify my ideas.

One gets the feeling that you carefully premeditated the surprises that the film reveals as it unfolds . . .

That's true. I never launch into a film without having the final quarter hour of it firmly in my head. I am always scared of disappointing people. I find that it is so easy to create brilliant beginnings that are often followed by a boring continuation. I often have laborious beginnings—and that is too bad—but at least I want to be very happy with what happens near the end of the film.

A film like this one depends upon arousing sympathy. One can't look at my characters as if they were insects. I sincerely believe in that—telling a story, generating something emotional between those in the hall and what is happening on the screen. It is necessary at the outset to know whether one wants to be an essayist, a philosopher, or a storyteller. If one has chosen to be a storyteller, one must accept the naïve aspect inherent in any story. Without naïveté, there is no story! Moreover, fiction needs melodrama. Songs bring that with them. I love songs, I don't need pretentious references, such as "as Althusser has said . . . ," et cetera.

That prompts me to talk about the importance of songs for you.

There are no songs in the film.

There was "Mon amant de Saint-Jean" in The Last Metro, *a song by Trenet in* Stolen Kisses *earlier and, in* The Woman Next Door, *there is talk about songs, their truths, their lies . . . What importance do they have for you?*

When I was working with Suzanne and Aurel, I said to them that this film ought to be in relation to *Stolen Kisses* what Édith Piaf is to Charles Trenet—in other words, for me, *The Woman Next Door* is an Édith Piaf film. It was also a bit like "*L'Hymne à l'amour*" and "*Ne me quitte pas*" by Jacques Brel, that is, great songs on fundamental things.

About cries of anguish, at the same time . . .

That's right, there is often something fundamental—that's what makes them beautiful; I am very envious of song lyricists because I know that I wouldn't be able to do it. It requires an ability to achieve simplification and ellipsis to write a song, whereas I find it very easy to write dialogue. And I feel that I would have loved to be able to write songs. Although it is not expressed in a polemical manner in the film, in my head it was a bit polemical, and a sign of my mistrust of what these days is called a "cultural discourse." Let us say that I, for one, find that very suspect; I listen to talk shows on the radio from time to time, in which people say that Juliette Gréco is "cultural," whereas Mireille Mathieu is not. I don't like that, and I mistrust it—because I think that people ought to know themselves, and, moreover, that the issue is not even to know what is cultural and what is not. I think that what is cultural is what helps us to live. And even though a song may be considered boring by intellectuals, because one hears it the whole year long, if it has helped a whole lot of people, this song is important. So it is with this in mind that I wrote this very pointed dialogue: "Songs tell the truth—even if they are stupid, they tell the truth," then she resumes, saying, "Furthermore, they are never stupid because they are never silly." Because, of course, "Your absence has wrecked my life" is a great expression, and "Let me become the shadow of your shadow" is a great expression also. So, yes, I have felt that for a long time. I could almost stretch it at a pinch to include the feminine press—romance magazines, which are often attacked by intellectuals and the intelligentsia. I have very clear memories of romance magazines, because when I was with the army in Germany, in an artillery regiment, at one time I managed to get myself assigned to work in the lobby, where all the newspapers were delivered. Once a week, there were almost three or four hundred copies of *Nous deux*, which disappeared in the first two hours.³ All those young soldiers, what did they throw themselves on? On *Nous deux*. It was fantastic—I was very impressed by that. Of course, *Nous deux* also had a "miss lonelyhearts" column, which is to say that in the army one has a great need to write and receive letters, but the soldiers also read the stories that were in it. So it was from that time that I concluded one should not be contemptuous of things just because they are popular or mass-produced. We still have that sort of thing today when people are ironic on television . . . I am not a fan of Guy Lux,⁴ because he does that without any grace, but I always defend singers.

Apart from Fahrenheit 451, *you have never made a film abroad. Why?*

I don't feel French in the patriotic sense of the word, but I am so all the same. I have never had a sense of nationalism. Cinema is my country, my family. I have a feeling of belonging to cinema, but when I go overseas, I don't feel as if I am representing France. I represent my work, that's all. In contrast, I feel very French in the dialogue I write. If one is a filmmaker of images, one can certainly make a film in any country in the world, but when you are writing dialogue, there are oblique ways of saying things that you can only find in your own language. When Depardieu says to Madame Jouve that Fanny Ardant belongs to the kind of women who "go to find midday at two in the afternoon,"⁵ that is a barbed expression that pretends not to be saying much while actually saying a lot. So, I could never find the equivalent of this phrase in English! I don't want to find myself at the mercy of scriptwriters. Many filmmakers who emigrated to Hollywood could master the lighting, the image, the work with actors, but I think that fundamentally they could not control what they were doing because of the language.

The Woman Next Door is your twentieth film. Do you feel you are in mid-career?

More than halfway through—two-thirds. I am not thinking of making more than ten films now. There is the problem of adapting to new techniques. There are things that are starting to rattle me. I am, for example, attached to the manual aspect of editing, to have the film in my hand. With electronic editing, this contact is lost. It's a bit like the difference between wood and plastic! I sometimes think that to tell a story, to make a normal film, is becoming anachronistic. You see, I remain attached to this notion of a "normal" film. I cannot do otherwise. It would be very artificial on my part. As long as the form of narration I like continues to work, I ought to take advantage of it! In a few years, people will be used to new video recorders, you are going to have accelerated speed with control on the screen. What this means is that young people who invite each other to see films will switch from important scenes to important scenes, jumping over the rest. Already, the American audience is incapable of following a story for two hours. Even a story that moves quickly like *The Woman Next Door* will perhaps prove boring for people one day. That will be the end of our conception of cinema; that will be the moment for us to leave it . . .

Notes

1. *Les Dames de la côte* was a TV series written and directed by Nina Companeez in 1979, set on the coast of Normandy in 1913, involving a young woman, Fanny Villatte, who renews her acquaintance with Marcel and Raoul Deccourt until the War intervenes.

2. *Mata Hari, agent H21* (Jean-Louis Richard, 1964), starring Jeanne Moreau and Jean-Louis Trintignant, with cameo appearances by Jean-Pierre Léaud and Charles Denner.

3. *Nous deux* is a popular French weekly magazine established in 1947 that specializes in the publication of love stories in the form of photo-novels.

4. Guy Lux (alias Maurice Guy, 1919–2003) was a French game show host.

5. A French expression meaning "to complicate matters unduly."

CHAPTER 29

1983: *CONFIDENTIALLY YOURS*

> I want my audience to be constantly captivated, spellbound ... that they come out of the theater dazed, amazed to be on the sidewalk. I would like them to forget the time, the place in which they find themselves, like Proust plunged in his reading at Combray. Above all, I want to create emotion—tears, and laughter when humor is the order of the day. When I listened to a recording taken during a private screening of *Confidentially Yours*, and I heard spectators laughing at the things that had so amused us during the making of the film, I was happy.
>
> *Interview with Corinne Blanche,* Jacinthe, *October 1983*

After the melodramas, after the stories about childhood, after the cycle of your autobiographical films, you have returned to the classical themes of the thriller ...

Let us say that with this last film I explore the themes of a conjugal thriller, a thriller without gangsters, in which the detectives only appear in the background, and in which the plot is governed, from one end to the other, by the imagination of a woman. It has nothing to do, or almost nothing, with the genre of *Day for Night* in which I was taking a risk in handling around ten characters of equal importance: here, following a crime story by Charles Williams, *The Long Saturday Night*, I was conjuring up a *Série noire* atmosphere, and that is what pleased me. After my "summing up" films (from *Stolen Kisses* to *The Last Metro*), I needed a story that was more simple, more linear, in which, from the beginning of the film, I could shadow a single heroine.

The number of characters in a film, then, for you, is a decisive factor . . .

That's obvious. On this point, I have always followed the advice of Henry James, who recommended that writers choose an odd number of characters to tell their story. With an even number—two couples, for example—one seldom escapes from the burdens of symmetry, and hence a certain conformity in the narrative. On the other hand, the unforeseeable, the unusual always sneaks in thanks to uneven numbers. And, for a *Série noire* film, that was indispensable.

As was, apparently, the fact that the film is shot in black and white . . .

The black and white is another matter: in one sense, I wanted to achieve a self-critique with respect to one of my older films, *The Bride Wore Black*, in which I had made the mistake of having too much sun, too much light, and in which, because of this, the mysterious aspect of William Irish's novels had been lost. That is why this film is not only in black and white, but also has three quarters of the action taking place at night, in rain.

But why this mistrust regarding light?

Because, with light, you see everything in the image, and mysteriousness instantly disappears. Generally, a night scene is always preferable to its daytime version because the former is more enigmatic: the nighttime atmosphere carries the fiction. It is as if you are photographing a face: by itself, it is only itself, but if you include, in the frame, the beginning of a shoulder or someone's neck, you already have the beginning of a story. In my work, I am always guided by a hatred of documentaries, and a documentary is designed to show us things or people without a trace of fiction. Now, an excess of light destroys fiction, constricts it, and impoverishes it. I don't like it if the sky is too blue in Westerns, so blue, almost white, that one sees the grain of the screen. In this case, one should imitate painters, and film in such a way that the canvas becomes invisible. In Westerns, as soon as heroes enter into some undergrowth, so that their silhouettes stand out against a dark background, I believe in it, but as soon as I see the sky, I no longer believe in it. To be filled, and filled well, the screen has to mistrust light. I should add that, for *Confidentially Yours*, I wanted to film Fanny Ardant as a mysterious, nocturnal heroine: what purpose would color serve in that regard?

From the beginning, then, your films tend to be inspired by the face of a woman?

Not by the face of an actress, but by the face of the heroine, the face required by the role. The actress only comes afterwards. I have always thought that stories, tales, can only be built around a woman, because women—and it is equally true in literature—convey the plot more naturally than men. It is, if you like, the opposite of Ford's Westerns, in which, as soon as something happens—the Indians attack—the women are made to hide in the coach while the men fight; if I were making a Western, I would certainly find a way of making sure that the women did not take shelter under the coach. Otherwise, I would get the feeling that nothing was happening on the screen.

Furthermore, that is what you did in The Last Metro, *in which the man stays in the coach, in other words, in a cellar, while Catherine Deneuve moves the story along. And, in* Confidentially Yours, *Trintignant is hidden the whole time while Fanny Ardant leads the investigation . . .*

Yes, as soon as I write a screenplay that is how things come about: the action belongs to the women—which is perhaps unrealistic in an absolute sense, but this is how I see things.

What triggered Confidentially Yours?

The idea came to me during a session in which we were viewing the rushes of *The Woman Next Door*. We were screening a nighttime scene in which Fanny Ardant was roaming around the house in a raincoat. Someone remarked, "That's a *Série noire* atmosphere." In effect, Fanny Ardant looked like a *Série noire* heroine.

Why Charles Williams?

Charles Williams, whose *The Diamond Bikini* makes you laugh at every page, committed suicide six or seven years ago, on the boat where he was spending the greater part of the year, without the American newspapers devoting a single paragraph to his death . . . It is difficult for French people to understand the solitude in which writers who have chosen popular literature live in the United States. French fans of *Série noire* fiction, without necessarily reading everything that is translated into our language, are quickly able to recognize the talent of this or that novelist and to make him known. The bush telegraph does the rest, and this is how the names of David Goodis, Dolores Hitchens, William Irish, Dorothy B. Hughes, Henry Farrell, Jim Thompson, Joseph Harrington, Harry Whittington, and that, more recently, of the English writer Patrick Alexander, have come to circulate by word of mouth and acquire a reputation among specialists. There is nothing similar in the United States. In 1962, while I was in New York to promote *Jules and Jim*, when I announced that I was hoping to make *Fahrenheit 451*, I discovered that not one out of ten American journalists even knew the name of Ray Bradbury.

There is only one explanation for this obscurity, which, in the case of Charles Williams, Goodis, and Irish has continued after their death: overproduction, the incredible number of books published each year, the incredible number of publishers, not only clustered in New York, but distributed across the whole of America.

What has drawn you to these novelists?

Each time I have approached a writer in the *Série noire*, I have been struck by his modesty, his professionalism, and also his sadness. There is often something despairing and fatalistic in the fate of a novelist who makes his living by telling crime stories.

Because the critics never mention them, because they never feel as if they have "their" audience, popular novelists who seem to write hastily, and only for money, reveal themselves more intimately through their fiction than one might think, and probably because they don't think they are doing so. Imagining themselves to be well concealed behind several corpses and some revolvers, they unveil themselves, confess, and achieve, through this constraint, a work of great freedom. Similarly, in the old oppressive Hollywood system, B series filmmakers believed themselves to be mere employees of the studio, whereas they were artists who were sincere and inspired. Being underground writers—I am employing the word in an almost literal sense, very different from "underground" as a term suggesting a flirtation with what is fashionable—the writers of *Série noire* novels are to Hemingway, Norman Mailer, and Truman Capote what dubbed actors are to stars on the screen. One can compare them, as Max Ophüls did with respect to dubbing artists, to wildflowers that grow in cellars.

For someone like me, for whom the story is very important, I find that *Série noire* novels bring with them an "excessive" dimension that usually we don't dare to invent. In general, an original screenplay tends to be too close to reality. It needs to be violated through the invention of powerful scenes. For example, in *The Piano Player*, adapted from a noir novel by David Goodis, I remember that I was happy when I filmed the scene in which Nicole Berger makes her confession in the presence of Charles Aznavour and throws herself out the window. I thought, "Here is a scene that I would never have dared to invent." Similarly, with regard to *Stolen Kisses*, an original screenplay I wrote with Bernard Revon and Claude de Givray, I thought, "We need a death. Even though the film is lighthearted in tone, we need a death." So we made an old man die, an old detective—an accidental death, which occurred while he was making a phone call. That was a victory: I had been capable of inventing a death.

Do you think the real heroine is the secretary?

Yes, that's the reason I selected this particular book. Charles Williams is a magnificent writer, but *Confidentially Yours* was very difficult to adapt. However, I liked the idea that an enquiry could be conducted by an ordinary person! Besides, the *Série noire* books I had adapted didn't normally involve gangsters or detectives; they dealt with people from ordinary life. I consider that to be more entertaining. Nevertheless, there is a mystery: one has to guess who the guilty person is, which the spectators probably do before the characters in the film . . . There is not a great deal to say about a film of that sort . . . Let us say that it is a "film for Saturday evenings" designed simply to give pleasure. There is no hidden intention. The action is not given a particular location. I have always had a theory that films adapted from American books should avoid a transposition that is too detailed. We shot in Hyères,[1] but there is nothing to indicate where we are! And given that the film takes place almost entirely at night, the "un-located," timeless aspect of it is intensified.

Given this situation, how did you approach the film?

This film has no ambition to be journalistic or to debunk anything. It is not one of those films that are considered to be "disturbing" . . . It doesn't disturb anyone! There is no aim other than to intrigue: in other words, basically to show simple things presented in an indirect way . . . All films have an experimental aspect to them. In this case, it was to see if, at the end, our mixture of scenes treated as a joke and those treated with a certain degree of real tension was harmonious.

In what respect was the adaptation of Charles Williams's book particularly difficult?

Because it largely consisted of things that took place by telex, telegrams, and telephone . . . and because the action was rather static. I didn't realize that immediately. So we (Suzanne Schiffman, Jean Aurel, and myself) kept the beginning and the end of the book, but we had to invent everything that took place in between, in order to create a visual impact on the screen. As a result of that experience, I realized how difficult it was to create a *Série noire* story: it involves specialized material. To write a *Série noire* story, you have to have undergone some training (in reality, there are only a limited number of original scenarios in *Série noire* fiction). The one in *Confidentially Yours*, even though it was childish and very simple, took much longer, and was more difficult to get off the ground, to construct, and write than, for example, *The Woman Next Door*. This was because *The Woman Next Door* was written in four days, elaborated in about ten days, with the dialogue being composed as we went along during the shooting. In this case, no . . . It involved a lot of work for a result that ought to create an impression of lightheartedness, of ease.

Should one regard this film, then, as a respite in the context of your other work?

It's a respite for the spectator because it is not demanding to watch, but strangely, it was demanding to make. That is bizarre! It is a respite, perhaps, because this film does not deal with any general issues, whereas *The Woman Next Door* and *The Last Metro* were informed by general issues. At the same time, I notice that, in these terms, a "light film" is more demanding than a film that is emotionally violent like *The Woman Next Door*. That was a film with a lot of tension, but it was incredibly easy to make, easy to write, easy to shoot. With this one, it involved things that you only know after they have happened. While you are watching, you have a suspicion that you want to see proved right.

Is this the first time you have made a film with Trintignant?

Although he is an actor whom I like a lot, and with whom I could certainly have made films during the past twenty years, until then I had only worked with him very indirectly. I chose him particularly for the sake of balancing the couple, because even in a fantasy film, you need a certain degree of realism with regard to a couple. The fact that Trintignant was fifteen years older than Fanny Ardant made the relationship between the secretary and the boss work.

> *You have the reputation of being a filmmaker who pays a lot of attention to his screenplays. And yet in your film there are improbabilities. Why?*

Strangely, this kind of film is often made with a lot of complicity on the part of the audience. Each time that you have situations that are too unrealistic, you have to add realistic details to accredit a feeling of realism. They might be boring, but one is obliged to give pointless explanations so as to justify certain things.

I assume that people want things to work. Spectators will accept anything so long as you give them the impression you know what you're doing. For example, *Confidentially Yours* is performed at great speed. People don't have time to analyze it. There is a kind of intoxication. During the filming, you have to sense the moments when you need to apply some realism, and those when you need to deflect attention. Stories are always unrealistic, but that is not important if the pleasure they elicit is strong enough. Pleasure has to overcome analysis. Lubitsch, for example, greatly enjoyed making the audience believe it knew what was going to happen, and then, at the end of the scene, there is a complete surprise. Something else happens. It's a game.

One doesn't create a screenplay in the same way one writes a poem. You write a screenplay by constantly saying to yourself, "What are people thinking at this particular moment?" They think such and such. So, we're going to switch to that aspect. One's sense of the audience constantly comes into play in one's work. Sometimes you seek to stun them, at other moments, you take them with you—or, to the contrary, you seek to surprise them. For instance, I was apprehensive about the two scenes in the police station. How to avoid clichés? I had already filmed in an immense kitchen with white tiles, from several levels, which didn't look like a police station. One thinks that it is a police station that has been set up where it was convenient because, basically, there is no characteristic type of police station. From then on, in each scene I needed to have something that broke with convention. For the first scene, I remembered something I had experienced two years earlier. I couldn't find my car one morning on the Fourteenth of July; it had been impounded because it was in the way of a procession. Having gone to the police station, I saw a Yugoslav there who was asking for political asylum. The police commissioner said, "Oh dear! Political asylum on the Fourteenth of July? You are not making things easy. All right, then, I will go and see what I can do."

In the second scene, I asked the property man to tamper with the tap of the kitchen in which we were filming. I imagined that in the middle of his interrogation, the commissioner would go to pour himself a glass of water. The tap would explode, there would be water everywhere, but that would not stop the vehemence of his questioning. He would wipe his face and continue with the questioning. Here, again, we breached convention. Such things help me a lot. They provoke laughter and a kind of relief. But above all, they help the audience to believe in what is said immediately before and immediately after.

> *Over time, you have created the impression that you are steadily going down your own road, remaining unresponsive to changing fashions.*

That's true. I do not believe in the idea of forms that self-destruct one after the other. I am persuaded that if *The Magnificent Ambersons* came out today, it would be the best film of the year.

I regard cinema as a classical art. Above all, it was magical. And that has ceased to be so, to some degree, because of television. My job is to try and rediscover some of that magic.

When I made *The Last Metro*, this was my chief concern. I thought: "I have to ensure that people enter into this atmosphere and don't leave it." That is why for the first forty minutes I do not depict a single scene shot during daytime. I thought: "They have to feel as if they are living under the Occupation."

For *Confidentially Yours*, I asked Nestor Almendros to film very quickly. At first, he was shocked: "I don't understand why you are in such a hurry, you earned so much money with *The Last Metro*." It was not because I wanted to reduce costs. But to make a film that resembles a B-series film, you can only devote very little time to each shot—otherwise the actors are going to lose interest. It is necessary that they remain committed. So we made the film in seven and a half weeks. I could have made it in ten weeks, but I preferred to sustain a breathless tone, a rather feverish one. For me, that is an intrinsic part of the genre.

The idea of sincerity is an important idea when you start out. It might be enough to assert oneself by proclaiming "I am here," especially in a first film. Afterwards, there is the notion of a career. Sincerity is no longer enough. A certain authority is needed. One forges laws. One obeys them. One becomes rather obsessive over everything. And that produces the risk of a cinema that is cold. As a result, there remains a need to do things with a kind of feverishness.

Television presents us with great variety. Ah well, I am going to give something concentrated! I am going to enclose you in a world in which you are going to believe! The idea is to fight against everything that resembles a documentary, everything that resembles an interview, everything that seems like improvisation—everything that we are shown on the television news each evening. You need classical rigor: if possible, the three unities—a small village, an action that takes place over four days. I try to take people on board. In earlier days, it was relatively easy—up until 1950–1955. Now it is much more difficult. In cinema, they want to speak with their neighbors, because, sitting in front of their television sets, they're used to talking. As far as I am concerned, I would like people to watch a film with their mouths wide open.

Note

1. Hyères is a town in Provence, in the Var department of the Provence-Alpes-Côte d'Azur region.

CHAPTER 30
1975–1984: OVERVIEW 3

Would it be accurate to say that your feelings regarding the New Wave, or what remains of it, are pessimistic?

Not really. As you know, pessimists and optimists don't exist, as a moralist has said, but only sad fools and happy fools. But there has been a lot of talk about the New Wave recently because it is the twentieth anniversary of the series of films that began to come out in 1959. And in a movement of this kind, apart from any artistic considerations, friendships, individual and group relationships, and their inevitable deterioration have to be taken into account. In France, the situation is particularly complicated, and not only in the domain of cinema, because of the fallout from May 1968. If one thinks of those among us who met at each other's places at a time when the future seemed promising for everyone, well, those relationships have somewhat deteriorated since then. Certain of them are in poorer health than they were twenty years ago. Others had hopes that have been disappointed. Friendships have been betrayed. People whose good looks improve with age are pretty rare, but there are exceptions. My thoughts concerning the New Wave are therefore not particularly optimistic. Exaggerating a little, you could say that we were young at the time, handsome, and likeable. And each individual will need to make up his or her own mind as to whether the last part of this sentence is still applicable.

In France, for a young person without money or connections, is it easier to make a film nowadays than it was twenty years ago?

No, insofar as in 1959 there was a sudden opening up of opportunities, and anyone at all could make a film. Now the situation has become stabilized, but there are still around thirty first films made in France each year by unknowns, thanks to the system of financial support provided by the *avance sur recettes*.¹

The situation for films is increasingly coming to resemble that of books. It is not very difficult to get a book published. The hard part is to get the book displayed in the shop windows of bookstores and succeed in getting it bought and read. It's the same thing with cinema. People are making more and more good films, but they don't get the distribution that they deserve. It even seems as if the most intelligent and cultured spectators prefer a simple yet appealing film to an intelligent but ham-handed film. Intellectuals often reject intellectual films made by intellectuals for intellectuals. A case in point, in France, is that of Pierre Kast, a highly cultured and well-read director who writes dialogue that is well constructed and marvelously convincing, but only makes films about intellectuals.² But his films are rejected by his intellectual peers who prefer to see, shall we say, a naïve and poorly made Western rather than an intelligent Western—unless, of course, it has been judged a masterpiece.

The problem for many new films, and not just in France, is that their ambition is often greater than the technical knowledge with which they are made. To put it another way, there are a number of films around that are uneven because of the gap between their philosophical and moral intentions, which are too lofty, and their realization, which is often really weak. It is true to say that this is the crisis confronting cinema today.

If you take Hollywood's cinematic production from before the 1940s or even the 1950s, you find films that give an impression of naïveté on the screen, but which are actually made in a very intelligent way. I think that this is true of *The Big Sky*, *Red River*, and *Air Force* by Hawks, for example, films that intellectuals might find naïve, catering to the tastes of the popular audience, and not very concerned with psychological verisimilitude, but which in reality were made with a great deal of intelligence behind the camera.³

For me, the first film that marks the period of cinema's decadence was the original James Bond film—*Dr. No*.⁴ Until then, the role of cinema had been largely to tell a story in the hope that the audience would believe it. There had been several minor films that were parodies of this narrative tradition; but, for the main part, a film told a story, and the audience wanted to believe this story. And it is in that regard that one could reopen the old polemic concerning Hitchcock. For years, English critics were reluctant to recognize that the films Hitchcock made in America were superior to those he had made in England. For me, the difference resides in the fact that Hitchcock's desire to have you believe in the story is stronger in his American films than in his English films.

But the reason why I talk of a period of decadence inaugurated by the James Bond films is that up until then this kind of parody had pleased only a minority and a number of snobs, whereas with the James Bond films it became a popular genre. For the first time, throughout the whole world, the audience at large was exposed to what amounted to a degradation of the art of cinema, to a cinematic genre that had no relation either to real life, or to any romantic tradition, but only to other films, and always in a way that diminished them. What is more, Hitchcock's career began to suffer from the moment the first James Bond films appeared because they were a kind of plagiarism of *North by Northwest*, his best thriller. He could not compete with the James Bond films, and after that, he was increasingly obliged to make low-budget films. Perhaps, too, he was simply becoming too old. For example, if he had been ten years younger, he would have been able to make disaster films. It should not be forgotten that he went to America to film *The Titanic*, but that ended up being replaced by *Rebecca*.

Don't you think that disaster films and super-productions are also, in one sense, a degradation of cinema—at least cinema as you conceive it?

No, they mark a return to the origins of cinema, to the first ten or fifteen years. That does not concern me at all. Cinema is condemned to make remakes because too many films are being made, and there are too many dramatic situations available. The whole of cinema history, therefore, is dotted with remakes, and this is not annoying so long as the remakes are better than the originals. Films with six reels are better than films with three reels. There was a loss of quality with the first talkies, but the introduction of sound did not prevent a film such as *King Kong* from being very fine in its conception and very ambitious visually.[5] And there are different blends. For example, for a long time it was the custom to make period films that were too reverent and lacked the physical freedom that we find in modern love films. So a remake of, say, *The Scarlet Pimpernel*, the subject of which is very daring, could be a very positive thing if it had been filmed from a more erotic angle and was more believable from a sexual point of view.[6]

The problem now, however, is how to combat color. How wrong we were to think that color would be an improvement and not a handicap!

This is surely only a manifestation of a general nostalgia you have?

No. Perfection in cinema consists of knowing that, come what may, there is a barrier between a film and "reality." Color has eliminated this last barrier.

If there is nothing false in a film, it is not a film—one is competing with the documentary and the result is very boring, just like most of the films made for American television, which I find lacking in every dimension that pertains to fiction—they are anti-dramatic, too much like documentaries, and very boring. And a large proportion of modern cinema is like that as well.

Color is an enemy. For me, it is now much more interesting to construct an apartment in a studio than to film a real apartment, because in a studio one at least has a chance of winning the battle against the ugliness of color, for example, by using many takes filmed at night, or by concentrating on specially contrived aspects.

Was color important in The Green Room?

That was not a problem. I didn't film either *The Green Room* or *Adele H.* in the same way I would have done had I used black and white. I avoided showing streets, period reconstructions, and extras in costumes. Dangers reside in all these areas. Also, in these two films the largest part of the action takes place at night, and night almost becomes part of the decor.

You have to come back to artifice if you want films to stop resembling documentaries. I think that is probably what drew me in the first instance to Hitchcock. If there is one thought that has remained constant in my life, it is a conviction that the enemy of the kind of cinema I personally like is the documentary. I have never filmed a documentary in my life, and I hope never to do so. This doesn't mean that I can't admire certain filmmakers who have made documentaries, such as Marcel Ophüls with *The Sorrow and the Pity*.[7] But what first drew me to cinema was my love of fiction, and what led me to want to make films was a desire to structure a fictional story.

Are there any cinematographers who share your ideas about color?

There are some who at least are asking the same questions. For example, it's not by chance that Nestor Almendros received an Oscar this year for his work in Terry Malick's *Days of Heaven*.[8] And there are five or six excellent cinematographers in France whose aesthetic matches mine. They fight against natural light, they try to invent an artificial kind of lighting, to rediscover the secrets of the cameramen who shot in black and white, and to apply them to color—that's what it's all about.

And new French directors? Which ones, in your opinion, are at the same level as you and capable of replacing you one day?

The one I prefer is Éric Rohmer, but of course he is of my generation, in fact older than me. But among the new ones, I think that one of the best is Claude Miller.

Who acted in one of your films?
I don't think so.

Yes he did, he acted in The Wild Child.
Oh yes, that's right, with his wife and baby. He has worked a lot for me since, not so much as an assistant, but as a production manager. I like his films very much. And then there is Jean-François Stévenin, who acted a part in *Day for Night*, and also in *Small Change*. He is a very good actor and director, but I think I prefer him as an actor, and, in any case, he has only directed one film. Someone else who has worked with me (and it is not simply because people have worked with me that I think they are good!) is Pierre Zucca, who took stills of the filming of *Day for Night*, and who has made a sophisticated, erotic-literary film called *Roberte*, which is a very fine movie.[9]

Can we speak, then, of the emergence of a Truffauldian school?
No, not at all, because those filmmakers have all been influenced by other directors apart from me. Stévenin was influenced by Bob Rafelson and John Cassavetes, and not at all by me. Claude Miller has certainly been influenced by Bergman, but, even though he has some points in common with me, it is more a question of affinities. For example, I share his taste for Bergman, but there is certainly no question of a school, not the slightest.

And what about you? Have you been influenced personally by the work of the young directors?
I think that one is influenced, above all else, by what one has seen and experienced prior to when you begin to make films. It is difficult to be influenced once you have started. That can happen from time to time, but the most profound influences occur much earlier, say, between eight and eleven years old in terms of emotions, and between fifteen and twenty-five as far as style is concerned. After that, you refine, you constantly polish your personal code, you even fight against it, but it seems to me that one is no longer subject to many other influences.

But isn't there a danger, in this case, of sticking too closely to a formula that is too rigid, knowing that if you have resolved a problem in a particular way in one film, you are going to tend to adopt the same solution in the films that follow?

Not entirely, in my opinion. It's true, my films often go in pairs. There is often one film that resembles another I made three or four years earlier, but I often seek to complicate the issue or resolve a new difficulty. Sometimes I want to improve something and the result is worse than the original, and what happens then is that a third film eventuates which is a synthesis of the two preceding ones. I think that this is the way I work.

You are talking about technical problems?

I would say aesthetic ones rather than technical ones. For example, how can I make a film that follows a single line without deviating from it? For me, issues present themselves in that way. How can I film a novella that seems to last only an hour when in reality it lasts an hour and a half? Or, on the other hand, how can I make a film in which all the characters are equally important? These are developmental exercises—partly technical, partly literary, given that they are linked to the development of the screenplay.

Could you give us some examples?

Not really. It's simply this alternation between films that depend on one character and those that are seeking to create a balance between the characters. For example, the last film with Antoine Doinel, *Love on the Run*, borrows certain things from the preceding films in this cycle, but it is close in its construction to *The Man Who Loved Women* because of its use of a voiceover, its commentary, and its attempt to meld very disparate material into a unity.

Is the commentary important because it gives a literary tone?

No, more of a first-person, confiding tone. And the influence here goes back to my childhood and the War years. It is the influence of Sacha Guitry and the charm of stories narrated in the first person.

In this regard, haven't you also been influenced by Henri-Pierre Roché, given that you have adapted two of his novels for the cinema? Doesn't The Man Who Loved Women *also owe a lot to Roché?*

Not much. I tried to avoid being poetic in this film. I gave the hero a scientific occupation and I wanted him to talk to women from a scientific angle. I was thinking of Howard Hughes, who sent a very famous memo about the way Jane Russell's bra ought to be made for *Outlaw*—an extraordinary, very moving memo of thirty or forty lines, in which he talks about this bra with incredible precision as if an aircraft engine were involved. So I think that it was this scientific aspect that I was looking for in *The Man Who Loved Women*, when Denner says that women's legs are compasses... This is not the atmosphere of Roché, who is a sentimentalist. The sexual element in Roché doesn't cause any suffering: everything is delicious; everything is fine; it's too easygoing. In my film, there is more suffering.

But I have certainly been very influenced by Roché. In certain respects, I was tempted to describe him as better than Cocteau because he achieves the same "poetic" effects of style with a greater economy of means. When Cocteau was describing *Antigone* and *Œdipe roi*,[10] he would say that they presented a view of Greece from the air. In my opinion, Roché achieves the same effect more simply. What I like about Roché is his phenomenal refinement, which allows him to use very few words. One always has the feeling that he has the vocabulary of a peasant, or of someone who has never read a book, or has just learnt to read and write—that's the height of refinement. If you examine his manuscripts, you see that he achieved this intentionally dry style through merciless cutting. I don't have a great admiration for my own film version of *Jules and Jim* (I am happy that it has a good reputation, but it is not as good as its reputation), but it is true that if I listen to the words, I still admire the same sentences. You remember when they are leaving for Greece? "*Il s'étaient fait faire de clairs costumes pareils.*"[11] Only Roché could have written that.

And he had a love for all women in general—a refusal to be interested in one kind of woman rather than another, and the idea that if a woman has a strong personality, one has to admire her, but above all, a refusal to prefer one kind of woman to another.

I wanted to ask you about your fascination with language. You are a "literary" director who has talked a lot about language in your films and elsewhere. Could you try to evaluate the importance of language in your work and its function as an aid, or obstacle, to communication? I am thinking, in particular, of Fahrenheit 451, Bed and Board, *and* The Wild Child.

This is not something I have been particularly conscious of before reading articles and critics. I have been attracted by certain themes, and I have sometimes wanted to show books in my films, and at least the importance of the written word, but I don't have a theory about it. Incidentally, it is true that in real life I always prefer to write a letter rather than use the telephone. Telephones are aggressive. I hate the sound of one ringing. With a letter, you can read it when it arrives, or later. You can reply when you want, or not at all. That seems more democratic to me, less authoritarian. So, in my films, people often communicate by letter. And books are also important.

As far as communication is concerned, I am a great optimist. I am very skeptical about the idea that genuine communication is impossible. I think people have grossly overexaggerated this notion, which has become something fashionable to believe. For my part, I believe in communication and comprehension. Things can be communicated. One can describe what one is feeling. One can talk about it.

To switch to a more personal level, how would you explain your difficulty in learning English?

I have difficulty reproducing sounds, but that is paradoxical because, after having seen a film twice, I know the music by heart—so there is something strange about it. I simply cannot manage to reproduce the sounds of English—perhaps because I started late and didn't have much education. I therefore had a tendency to learn only what seemed essential to me and useful for making a living. I have never had the kind of discipline that people usually develop during their secondary school studies. Perhaps at an unconscious level I also reject it. I don't know why, but it is very frustrating.

I was very happy when I first learned to read English. The first thing I read was David Selznick's collection of memos, which is fantastic. I was very happy, because the year before, I had been unable to read it. I have still not attempted novels, only biographies and books about cinema. But that represents considerable progress. To speak and understand, however, will always be difficult for me, and I will never completely achieve it.

You often depict a lonely man, living on the edge of society. Does this portrait of the loneliness of man reflect your own philosophy?

Not my philosophy of life, but in cinema there is a kind of film that particularly moves me, and these are films with a commentary—for example, *Les Enfants terribles*, *The Story of a Cheat*, and *Diary of a Country Priest*. It's as if the director is directly addressing himself to me, and confiding in me while I am sitting there in the dark. In contrast, I have been disappointed, even with films made by directors I admire, when the main character is given a friend or a confidant. My pleasure is ruined because, even if I want to be interested in the hero, as soon as I know he has a friend, I am less interested in what he has to say. One example of this is Bresson's *Pickpocket*. I like the film, but the pickpocket has a friend who guesses his secret, and, because of this, I cannot completely sympathize with him, since I am not that friend. The same thing is true of *This Sweet Sickness* by my friend Claude Miller.[12]

Thus, when I make a film, I pay a lot of attention to this aspect. In *The Man Who Loved Women* there is a direct allusion to this in the dialogue when someone says, "You will never see this guy with a man after six o'clock in the evening." At all events, he has no friends, but after six o'clock in the evening, he cannot bear the presence of a man. I believe this is the reason why the audience can feel sympathy for, and intimacy with, Charles Denner. In *Adele H.*, if I had given Adele a confidante, there would not have been any film. The audience is alone with her. That's the feeling I particularly try to arouse. It probably comes from my feelings of identification with a hero in my childhood. I have no time for modern theories of anti-identification. If theoreticians, and even directors, want to take pleasure in such things, so be it, but for me a film in which the audience identifies with the hero is not an inferior one. To the contrary, it is what moves me most.

I reached the age of nineteen without having seen a single film with Errol Flynn because he was only making period films, and I never went to see period films. It took time before I would choose films on account of the director. My primary criterion at that time was the subject, and I needed to guess it from the title. Hollywood films always dealt with love more than anything else at that time—love plus an adventure, and love plus a Western, and love plus a thriller (my favorite was love plus a thriller because there were always characters dressed in modern-style raincoats, and because it was easy to identify with them). I therefore preferred Alan Ladd to Errol Flynn; but, of course, the one I liked the best was Bogart and Hollywood psychological films—not that the psychology in them was particularly subtle—and films based around characters who had a secret, and films with a certain intensity, and, above all, they had to be modern. The company of these rather lonely characters gave me a lot of pleasure.

There are, of course, also autobiographical reasons. The fact that I was an only child, as you know, is an important factor. I think that I get on better with people who were an only child than with those who had many brothers and sisters. I understand the psychology of an only child much better. With an only child, there is far less of a feeling of competition. Personally, I don't think that I am very competitive in life. I belong to French cinema, but the thought of being superior to all other directors never enters my mind.

One criticism leveled at you is that you have not really made much progress in your films. I know that you accept Renoir's principle that a director only makes one film in his life, and that the following ones are only a reformulation of the ideas in this first film, but do you think you have relied too heavily on autobiography, or do you consider that to be inevitable? Do you have any desire to set off in a completely different direction?

I am not bothered by the fact that people say I haven't progressed. I accept the view than any progress one makes is always really very small. One invests the richest part of oneself in what you do at the outset. One could even probably say that it isn't worth the effort to make an entire career in cinema. One could just make, say, three or four films which, like three or four songs by a singer or a composer, will be the richest ones. But, because it is the thing you like doing the most, you continue. In spite of everything, I sometimes make films on difficult subjects . . .

Like The Green Room?

Yes, films like that in which I "muddle through," an expression I prefer to use rather than saying "succeed"—films which I have rather muddled through, and I can say that ten years earlier I could never have achieved, I wouldn't have "won the bet." Take the case of *Adele H*. It was a gamble, and I didn't lose it, but it required a certain degree of experience in the "business" before being able to make a film with so few elements. I also don't think that anyone could have made *Day for Night* as a first film. It needed experience and a certain mastery of cinema, and naturally one has a lesser degree of mastery at the beginning of one's career.

You are still talking of a need to "take a gamble," as you have been doing for a number of years now. Nineteen years ago, with Shoot the Piano Player, *you took many risks. Many people in England consider it to be your most exciting film even though it was a commercial flop. With a few very rare exceptions, you don't seem to have taken a risk since. You now have a solid financial foundation. Couldn't you risk taking a new departure, instead of returning, for example, to the themes and characters in the Doinel cycle, as you have done in* Love on the Run?

I think that the charm of *The Piano Player* comes from an element of chance, and this same element is present in *Stolen Kisses*. What these two films have in common is that, in each case, it is impossible to know what is going to happen. And it is true that apart from the Doinel films, I always know what is going to happen before filming begins—at least generally, although it is obviously possible to improvise certain details, given that I have confidence in the actors. But during the filming of *The Piano Player*, I suffered from not knowing what was going to happen to the main character, or what it was really about. It was a genuine experiment, and it is true that I no longer have the courage to try anything as experimental as that.

If I were making *The Piano Player* now, I would say to myself, "Who is this man? What does he want?" I would understand the story, whereas at the time, if I wanted to shoot a particular scene, I was happy to just go ahead and do it, and to follow it with another scene that was completely different. Moreover, I think that it was more acceptable in the climate that prevailed at the beginning of the 1960s. I think that if the film came out now, it would be greeted with even greater indifference than it was at the time. Nevertheless, if there were a crime film I wanted to film, I would still do it, but not with the same degree of naïveté, simply because I no longer want to be so naïve. In *The Piano Player*, there was an element of luck and the charm of Marie Dubois and Nicole Berger, and then the strangeness of the character played by Aznavour. It could have been better and it could have been worse, but I am not sure that it could have been remade. When I made *The Bride Wore Black*, I was convinced it would be like *The Piano Player*, but better. But it was worse, although I think the use of color in it might have been partly responsible for that. It was a film that should have been mysterious, and yet wasn't. Then I thought that I had another chance with *Mississippi Mermaid*, which turned out to be a huge flop. I like the love story, but the thriller side of it is completely botched. In effect, it is always rather artificial and absurd to take these American stories and import them into France.

Will you continue to revisit the same issues?

I don't know. There are certain films I have not yet made, that I will definitely make. For example, I would love to make a love story against a background of classical music. I would also like to make a film about France under the Occupation. That would require me to reopen my files, and that I meet certain Jews who were working clandestinely in Paris during the War, and who will tell me about their experiences. I am also meeting some young musicians from the Conservatoire and, depending upon what riches emerge from these conversations, I will decide what I am going to film. I will probably choose the subject that requires the least research.

So you still need this foundation of "truth" and real life? In this respect, you have not changed over twenty years. And, similarly, you have remained disengaged socially and politically?

Yes, partly for autobiographical reasons. I don't feel one hundred percent French, and I don't know the whole truth about my origins. I have never tried to obtain a voter registration card, and so I am not entitled to vote. I would feel I was doing something very artificial if I were to vote, as if I were acting a part. So I don't feel an attachment to France and could live out the rest of my life in another country. Just as the notion of patriotism hasn't taken hold of me, so too, when people try to explain their religion to me, I remain skeptical, and I feel that they cannot be sincere—which is stupid, because they are sincere. I don't manage to achieve their belief. My religion is cinema. I believe in Charlie Chaplin, et cetera. As far as politics are concerned, I think that their importance has been greatly exaggerated and overvalued for these past ten years. Politics for me consists simply of doing the housework; if one needs to vacuum up the dust in the morning, one does it—without talking about it. If the ashtrays need emptying, one empties them, but this is not the most important work of the day. It is necessary, but if it becomes the sum total of our conversation and our day, then it is folly. It is the same with politics. Politicians don't deserve their status as stars. They should simply be cleaning ladies who are humble and efficient.

So politics don't change people's lives or the structure of society?

Only very slowly—and the more slowly that happens, the more effective it is. Changes are not spectacular. Furthermore, to think that, in twenty years, a film with political content will offer a clearer picture of the society in which it was made than a nonpolitical film is to deceive oneself completely. Certain sophisticated comedies from Hollywood say as much about things in America in years gone by as films that aim to denounce some particular social abuse. The idea that one has to reflect the society in which one lives is false—because one does that anyway, whether intentionally or not. Salvador Dalí gave this advice to painters: "Above all, don't worry about being modern, because, unfortunately, whatever you might do, you will end up being so."

There is a lot of pressure on filmmakers from the media to make them introduce a political dimension, however artificial, into their work. It is important to resist such pressures. To make a film ought to be a pleasure, not a duty. One has to be free to follow one's instinct in the choice of subjects. You don't make a film to please one particular segment of public opinion. You make a film for your own pleasure, and in the hope that the audience will share it. If making films were to become a duty, I would do something else. The important issue for me is to know how best to spend one's time. One ought to give oneself a schedule that one likes, which is the reason I chose cinema. Apart from that, I could perhaps write. But the most important thing for me is to be free from all constraints.

The political blackmail of the past few years is a negative and disagreeable aspect of our times. Fortunately, it is coming to its end—in a cruel manner. Thanks to the paradox of history; thanks to the fact that Ayatollah Khomeini is worse than the former Shah of Iran; thanks to the fact that the Vietnamese have invaded Cambodia, and that the Chinese have supported the Cambodians; thanks to all these bloody paradoxes, it is clear that people cannot be pushed in a single direction. Life is full of paradoxes, and cinema has to reflect these paradoxes. In so-called political films, there is no life because there are no paradoxes. The director goes to work knowing in advance who is the corrupt police inspector, who is the dishonest real-estate promoter, who is the brave young reporter, et cetera. For a long time, in France, André Cayatte was the only director making this kind of film.[13] Since 1968, there has been a vogue for what I call "neo-Cayattism" which, as a spectator, I absolutely refuse to see, and, as a director, I absolutely refuse to practice.

Notes

1. The "*Avance sur recettes*," established in 1959 by André Malraux, is a form of financial aid awarded by the Centre national du cinéma et de l'image animée (CNC) for the making of feature films.

2. Pierre Kast (1920–1984) was a French film director who made many well-regarded short films and feature films, including *Amour de poche* (*Girl in His Pocket*, 1957), about a professor who accidentally shrinks his dog and his female lab assistant.

3. *The Big Sky* (Howard Hawks, 1952); *Red River* (Howard Hawks, 1948); and *Air Force* (Howard Hawks, 1943).

4. *Dr. No* (Terence Young, 1962).

5. *King Kong* (Merian C. Cooper and Ernest B. Schoedsack, 1933).

6. *The Scarlet Pimpernel* (Harold Young, 1934).

7. *Le Chagrin et la Pitié* (*The Sorrow and the Pity*, Marcel Ophüls, 1969), a film about the collaboration between the Vichy government and Nazi Germany.

8. *Days of Heaven* (*Les Moissons du Ciel*, Terence Malick, 1978).

9. *Roberte ce soir* (*Roberte*, Pierre Zucca, 1979), based on the eponymous novel by Pierre Klossowski (1905–2001), which provoked controversy because of its graphic depiction of sexuality.

10. *Antigone* is a version of Sophocles' myth, written in 1922; *Oedipe roi* refers to his play *The Infernal Machine*, based on the myth of Oedipus, which premiered in 1934.

11. "They had identical light-colored suits made."

12. *Dites-lui que je l'aime* (*This Sweet Sickness*, Claude Miller, 1977), starring Gérard Depardieu and Miou-Miou.

13. André Cayatte (1909–1989) was a lawyer-filmmaker who made films focusing on themes of crime, justice, and ethical responsibility, such as *Justice est faite* (*Justice Is Done*, 1950), *Nous sommes tous des assassins* (*We Are All Murderers*, 1952), and *La Raison d'état* (*State Reasons*, 1978).

LIST OF FILMS DISCUSSED BY TRUFFAUT

7 Women (*Frontière chinoise*, John Ford, 1966)
8½ (*Huit et demi*, Federico Fellini, 1963)
À bout de souffle (*Breathless*, Jean-Luc Godard, 1960)
Adam's Rib (*Madame porte la culotte*, George Cukor, 1949)
Adieu Philippine (Jacques Rozier, 1962)
Adolphe, ou l'âge tendre (Bernard Toublanc-Michel, 1968)
Air Force (Howard Hawks, 1943)
Alphaville (Jean-Luc Godard, 158)
Au Hasard Balthazar (Robert Bresson, 1966)
Baisers volées (*Stolen Kisses*, François Truffaut, 1968)
Ben Hur (William Wyler, 1959)
Bonne chance Charlie (*Good Luck Charlie*, Jean-Louis Richard, 1962)
Bonnie and Clyde (Arthur Penn, 1967)
Boudu sauvé des eaux (*Boudu Saved from Drowning*, Jean Renoir, 1932)
Boulevard (Jean Duvivier, 1960)
Brief Encounter (*Brève rencontre*, David Lean, 1945)
Brigitte et Brigitte (Luc Moullet, 1966)
Brumes d'automne (Dimitri Dirsanoff, 1929)
Casque d'or (Jacques Becker, 1952)
Ce soir ou jamais (*Tonight or Never*, Michel Deville, 1961)
Chiens perdus sans collier (*The Little Rebels*, Jean Delannoy, 1955)
Chronique d'un été (*Chronicle of a Summer*, Edgar Morin and Jean Rouch, 1961)
Cinéastes de notre temps (TV series, 1964–1972)

Citizen Kane (Orson Welles, 1941)
City Lights (*Les Lumières de la ville*, Charles Chaplin, 1931)
Days of Heaven (*Les Moissons du Ciel*, Terence Malick, 1978)
De Man die zijn haar kort liet knippen (*The Man Who Had His Hair Cut Short*, André Delvaux, 1966)
Death in Venice (*Mort à Venise*, Luchino Visconti, 1971)
Der blaue Engel (*The Blue Angel*, *L'Ange bleu*, Josef von Sternberg, 1930)
Détruire dit-elle (Marguerite Duras, 1969)
Dites-lui que je l'aime (*This Sweet Sickness*, Claude Miller, 1977)
Domicile conjugal (*Bed and Board*, François Truffaut, 1970)
Dr. No (Terence Young, 1962)
El Dorado (Howard Hawks, 1966)
Ensayo de un crimen (*The Criminal Life of Archibald de la Cruz*, Luis Buñuel, 1955)
Et Dieu . . . créa la femme (*. . . And God Created Woman*, Roger Vadim, 1956)
Europa '51 (*Europe '51*, Roberto Rossellini, 1952)
F for Fake (Orson Welles, 1973)
Fahrenheit 451 (François Truffaut, 1966)
Family Life (Ken Loach, 1971)
Germania anno zero (*Germany Year Zero*, *Allemagne année zéro*, Roberto Rossellini, 1948)
Gone with the Wind (*Autant en emporte le vent*, Victor Fleming, George Cukor, Sam Wood, 1939)
Goupi mains rouges (*It Happened at the Inn*, Jacques Becker, 1943)
Hiroshima mon amour (*Hiroshima Mon Amour*, Alain Resnais, 1959)
I Confess (*La Loi du silence*, Alfred Hitchcock, 1953)
Il Casanova di Federico Fellini (*Le Casanova de Fellini*, Federico Fellini, 1976)
Il grido (*Le Cri*, Michelangelo Antonioni, 1957)
Il vangelo secondo Matteo (*The Gospel According to St. Matthew*, Pier Paolo Pasolini, 1964)
It Should Happen to You (*Une femme qui s'affiche*, George Cukor, 1954)
Ivan Grozniy (*Ivan the Terrible*, Sergei Eisenstein, 1944, 1958)
Jeux interdits (*Forbidden Games*, René Clément, 1952)
Johnny Guitar (Nicholas Ray, 1954)
Journal d'un curé de campagne (*Diary of a Country Priest*, Robert Bresson, 1951)
Jules et Jim (*Jules and Jim*, François Truffaut, 1962)
King Kong (Merian C. Cooper and Ernest B. Schoedsack, 1933)
King of Kings (*Le Roi des rois*, Nicholas Ray, 1961)

Kiss Me, Stupid (*Embrasse-moi, idiot*, Billy Wilder, 1964)
L'Amour à la chaîne (*Tight Skirts, Loose Pleasures*, Claude de Givray, 1965)
L'Amour à vingt ans (*Love at Twenty*, Shintarô Ishihara, Marcel Ophüls, François Truffaut, and others, 1962)
L'Amour en fuite (*Love on the Run*, François Truffaut, 1979)
L'Année dernière à Marienbad (*Last Year in Marienbad*, Alain Resnais, 1961)
L'Argent de poche (*Small Change*, François Truffaut, 1976)
L'Arroseur arrosé (*Tables Turned on the Gardener*, Louis Lumière, 1895)
L'Atalante (Jean Vigo, 1934)
L'Eau à la bouche (Jacques Doniol-Valcroze, 1960)
L'École des femmes (Raymond Rouleau, 1973)
L'Enclos (*The Enclosure*, Armand Gatti, 1961)
L'Enfance nue (*Naked Childhood*, Maurice Pialat, 1968)
L'Enfant sauvage (*The Wild Child*, François Truffaut, 1970)
L'Histoire d'Adèle H. (*The Story of Adele H.*, François Truffaut, 1975)
L'Homme de Rio (*That Man from Rio*, Philippe de Broca, 1964)
L'Homme qui aimait les femmes (*The Man Who Loved Women*, François Truffaut, 1977)
L'Immortelle (Alain Robbe-Grillet, 1963)
L'Œil du Malin (*The Third Lover*, Claude Chabrol, 1962)
La Baie des Anges (*Bay of Angels*, Jacques Demy, 1963)
La Belle et la Bête (*Beauty and the Beast*, Jean Cocteau, 1946)
La Bête humaine (*La Bête Humaine*, Jean Renoir, 1938)
La Cage de verre (*The Glass Cage*, Philippe Arthuys, Jean-Lous Levi-Alvarès, 1965)
La Chambre verte (*The Green Room*, François Truffaut, 1978)
La Chienne (Jean Renoir, 1931)
La Chinoise (Jean-Luc Godard, 1967)
La Collectionneuse (*The Collector*, Eric Rohmer, 1967)
La Dénonciation (Jacques Doniol-Valcroze, 1962)
La Duchesse de Langeais (*Wicked Duchess*, Jacques de Baroncelli, 1942)
La Femme d'à côté (*The Woman Next Door*, François Truffaut, 1981)
La Femme et le Pantin (*The Woman and the Puppet*, Jacques de Baroncelli, 1929)
La Fiancée des ténèbres (Serge de Poligny, 1945)
La Fille aux yeux d'or (*The Girl with the Golden Eyes*, Jean-Gabriel Albicocco, 1961)
La Gifle (*The Slap*, Claude Pinoteau, 1974)
La Grande illusion (*La Grande Illusion*, Jean Renoir, 1937)

La Guerre est finie (*The War Is Over*, Alain Resnais, 1966)
La Loi du survivant (*Law of Survival*, José Giovanni, 1967)
La Longue Marche (Alexandre Astruc, 1966)
La Mariée était en noir (*The Bride Wore Black*, François Truffaut, 1968)
La Morte-Saison des amours (Pierre Kast, 1961)
La Musica (Marguerite Duras, Paul Seban, 1967)
La Nuit américaine (*Day for Night*, François Truffaut, 1973)
La Passion de Jeanne d'Arc (*The Passion of Joan of Arc*, Carl Theodor Dreyer, 1928)
La Peau douce (*The Soft Skin*, François Truffaut, 1964)
La Pointe courte (Agnès Varda, 1956)
La Proie pour l'ombre (*Shadows of Adultery*, Alexandre Astruc, 1961)
La Pyramide humaine (*The Human Pyramid*, Jean Rouch, 1961)
La Récréation (Fabien Colin and François Moreuil, 1961)
La Règle du jeu (*The Rules of the Game*, Jean Renoir, 1939)
La Sirène du Mississipi (*Mississippi Mermaid*, François Truffaut, 1969)
La Tête contre les murs (*The Keepers*, Georges Franju, 1959)
La Tour, prends garde! (*King on Horseback*, Georges Lampin, 1958)
La Vie de château (*A Matter of Resistance*, Jean-Paul Rappeneau, 1966)
Lady in the Lake (*La Dame du lac*, Robert Montgomery, 1947)
Le Baron fantôme (*The Phantom Baron*, Serge de Poligny, 1943)
Le beau Serge (*Le Beau Serge*, Claude Chabrol, 1958)
Le Chagrin et la Pitié (*The Sorrow and the Pity*, Marcel Ophüls, 1969)
Le Chemin des écoliers (Michel Boisrond, 1959)
Le Corbeau (*Le Corbeau: The Raven*, Henri-Georges Clouzot, 1943)
Le Coup de grâce, (Jean Cayrol, Claude Durand, 1965)
Le Coup du berger (Jacques Rivette, 1956)
Le Crime de M. Lange (*The Crime of Monsieur Lange*, Jean Renoir, 1936)
Le Départ (*The Departure*, Jerzy Klolimowski, 1967)
Le Dernier Métro (*The Last Metro*, François Truffaut, 1980)
Le Diable au corps (*Devil in the Flesh*, Claude Autant-Lara, 1947)
Le Genou de Claire (*Claire's Knee*, Éric Rohmer, 1970)
Le Joli Mai (Chris Marker, 1963)
Le Lys dans la vallée (Marcel Cravenne, 1970)
Le Mépris (*Contempt*, Jean-Luc Godard, 1963)
Le Panier à crabes (Joseph Lisbona, 1960)
Le Passage du Rhin (*Tomorrow Is My Turn*, André Cayatte, 1960)
Le Petit Soldat (*The Little Soldier*, Jean-Luc Godard, 1963)

Le Président (*The President*, Henri Verneuil, 1961)
Le Puits et le Pendule (Alexandre Astruc, 1964)
Le Rideau cramoisi (*The Crimson Curtain*, Alexandre Astruc, 1953)
Le Roman d'un tricheur (*The Story of a Cheat*, Sacha Guitry, 1936)
Le Signe du lion (*Sign of the Lion*, Éric Rohmer, 1962)
Le Temps du ghetto (Frédéric Rossif, 1961)
Le Testament d'Orphée, ou ne me demandez pas pourquoi (*Testament of Orpheus*, Jean Cocteau, 1960)
Le Vieil Homme et l'enfant (*The Two of Us*, Claude Berri, 1967)
Les Amants (*The Lovers*, Louis Malle, 1958)
Les Anges du péché (*Angels of Sin*, Robert Bresson, 1943)
Les Bonnes Femmes (*The Good Time Girls*, Claude Chabrol, 1960)
Les Carabiniers (*The Soldiers*, Jean-Luc Godard, 1963)
*Les Cœurs vert*s (Édouard Luntz, 1966)
Les Cousins (Claude Chabrol, 1959)
Les Dames de la côte (TV series, 1979)
Les Dames du Bois de Boulogne (*Ladies of the Park*, Robert Bresson, 1945)
Les Deux Anglaises et le continent (*Two English Girls*, François Truffaut, 1971)
Les Enfants du paradis (*Children of Paradise*, Marcel Carné, 1945)
Les Enfants terribles (Jean-Pierre Melville, 1950)
Les Grandes Personnes (*Time Out for Love*, Jean Valère, 1961)
Les Honneurs de la guerre (*The Honors of War*, Jean Dewever, 1961)
Les Lions sont lâchés (*The Lions Are Loose*, Henri Verneuil, 1961)
Les Mauvais Coups (François Leterrier, 1961)
Les Mauvaises Rencontres (*Bad Liaisons*, Alexandre Astruc, 1955)
Les Mistons (François Truffaut, 1957)
Les quatre cents coups (*The 400 Blows*, François Truffaut, 1959)
Les Valseuses (*Going Places*, Bertrant Blier, 1974)
Les Visiteurs du soir (*Les Visiteurs du Soir*, Marcel Carné, 1942)
Lettre de Sibérie (*Letter from Siberia*, Chris Marker, 1957)
Lola (Jacques Demy, 1961)
Lola Montès (Max Ophüls, 1955)
Lolita (Stanley Kubrick, 1962)
Los Olvidados (*Los olvidados*, Luis Buñuel, 1950)
Macbeth (Orson Welles, 1948)
Masculin Féminin (Jean-Luc Godard, 1966)
Mata Hari, agent H21 (Jean-Louis Richard, 1964)

Metropolis (Fritz Lang, 1927)
Moby Dick (John Huston, 1956)
Moderato cantabile (*Seven Days . . . Seven Nights*, Peter Brook, 1960)
Modesty Blaise (Joseph Losey, 1966)
Monsieur Verdoux (Charles Chaplin, 1947)
More (Barbet Schroeder, 1969)
Mouchette (Robert Bresson, 1967)
Mr. Arkadin (*Monsieur Arkidin*, Orson Welles, 1955)
Muriel ou Le temps d'un retour (*Muriel, or The Time of Return*, Alain Resnais, 1963)
Naked Dawn (*Le Bandit*, Edgar G. Ulmer, 1955)
Nana (Jean Renoir, 1926)
Nattvardsgästerna (*Winter Light*, Ingmar Bergman, 1963)
North by Northwest (*La Mort aux trousses*, Alfred Hitchcock, 1959)
Nuit et Brouillard (*Night and Fog*, Alain Resnais, 1955)
Orfeu Negro (*Black Orpheus*, Marcel Camus, 1959)
Paisà (*Paisan*, Roberto Rossellini, 1946)
Paradis perdu (*Four Flights to Love*, Abel Gance, 1940)
Paris brûle-t-il? (*Is Paris Burning?*, René Clément, 1966)
Paris nous appartient (*Paris Belongs to Us*, Jacques Rivette, 1961)
Pickpocket (Robert Bresson, 1959)
Picratt, roi du rail (*Fuzzy, King of the Railway*, Mack Sennett, 1919)
Pierrot le Fou (Jean-Luc Godard, 1965)
Pontcarral, colonel d'empire (Jean Delannoy, 1942)
Portrait-robot (*Portrait-Robot*, Paul Paviot, 1962)
Psycho (*Psychose*, Alfred Hitchcock, 1960)
Rear Window (*Fenêtre sur cour*, Alfred Hitchcock, 1954)
Rebecca (Hitchcock, 1940)
Red Line 7000 (*La Ligne rouge 7000*, Howard Hawks, 1965)
Red River (*La Rivière rouge*, Howard Hawks, 1948)
Roberte (*Roberte ce soir*, Pierre Zucca, 1979)
Romeo and Juliet (Franco Zeffirelli, 1968)
Rue des Prairies (*Rue de Paris*, Denys de La Patellière 1959)
Sait-on jamais (*No Sun in Venice*, Roger Vadim, 1957)
Shadow of a Doubt (*L'Ombre d'un doute*, Alfred Hitchcock, 1943)
Si c'était vous (TV series)

Snow White and the Seven Dwarfs (*Blanche-Neige et les sept nains*, William Cottrell, David Hand, 1937)
Sommaren med Monika (*Summer with Monika*, Ingmar Bergman, 1953)
Sommarlek (*Summer Interlude*, Ingmar Bergman, 1951)
Spartacus (Stanley Kubrick, 1960)
Sunrise: A Song of Two Humans (*L'Aurore*, F. W. Murnau, 1927)
The African Queen (John Huston, 1951)
The Awful Truth (*Cette sacrée vérité*, Leo McCarey, 1937)
The Barefoot Contessa (*La Comtesse aux pieds nus*, Joseph L. Mankiewicz, 1954)
The Bible: In the Beginning . . . (*La Bible*, John Huston, 1966)
The Big Sky (*La Captive aux yeux clairs*, Howard Hawks, 1952)
The Big Sleep (*Le Grand Sommeil*, Howard Hawks, 1946)
The Bridge on the River Kwai (*Le pont de la rivière Kwai*, David Lean, 1957)
The Burglar (Paul Wendkos, 1957)
The Devil Is a Woman (*La Femme et le Pantin*, Josef von Sternberg, 1935)
The Diary of a Chambermaid (Jean Renoir, 1946)
The Golden Coach (*Le Carrosse d'or*, Jean Renoir, 1952)
The Kid (*Le Kid*, Charles Chaplin, 1921)
The Lady from Shanghai (*La Dame de Shanghai*, Orson Welles, 1947)
The Last Laugh (*Le Dernier des hommes*, F. W. Murnau, 1924)
The Magnificent Ambersons (*La Splendeur des Amberson*, Orson Welles, 1942)
The Misfits (*Les Misfits*, John Huston, 1961)
The Naked Jungle (*Quand la marabunta gronde*, Byron Haskin, 1954)
The Quiet Man (*L'Homme tranquille*, John Ford, 1952)
The Outlaw (*Le Banni*, Howard Hughes, Howard Hawks, 1943)
The Red Badge of Courage (*La Charge victorieuse*, John Huston, 1951)
The Roots of Heaven (*Les Racines du ciel*, John Huston, 1958)
The Scarlet Pimpernel (Harold Young, 1934)
The Stranger (*Le Criminel*, Orson Welles, 1946)
The Thing from Another World (*La Chose d'un autre monde*, Christian Nyby and Howard Hawks, 1951)
The Young Lions (*Le Bal des maudits*, Edward Dymytryk, 1958)
Thomas l'Imposteur (*Thomas the Imposter*, Georges Franju, 1965)
Tirez sur le pianiste (*Shoot the Piano Player*, François Truffaut, 1960)
Toni (Jean Renoir, 1935)
Touch of Evil (*La Soif du mal*, Orson Welles, 1958)

Trans-Europ-Express (Alain Robbe-Grillet, 1966)
Tystnaden (*The Silence*, Ingmar Bergman, 1963)
Un condamné à mort s'est échappé ou Le vent souffle où il veut (*A Man Escaped*, Robert Bresson, 1956)
Un couple (*A Couple*, Jean-Pierre Mocky, 1960)
Un homme et une femme (*A Man and a Woman*, Claude Lelouch, 1966)
Une aussi longue absence (*The Long Absence*, Henri Colpi, 1960)
Une belle fille comme moi (*A Gorgeous Girl Like Me*, François Truffaut, 1972)
Une femme est une femme (*A Woman Is a Woman*, Jean-Luc Godard, 1961)
Une grosse tête (*A Swelled Head*, Claude de Givray, 1962)
Une histoire d'eau (*A Story of Water*, Jean-Luc Godard and François Truffaut, 1961)
Une visite (François Truffaut, 1955)
Unfaithfully Yours (*Infidèlement vôtre*, Preston Sturges, 1948)
Viaggio in Italia (*Journey to Italy*, *Voyage en Italie*, Roberto Rossellini, 1954)
Vivement dimanche! (*Confidentially Yours*, François Truffaut, 1983)
Viskningar och rop (*Cries and Whispers*, Ingmar Bergman, 1972)
Vivre sa vie (*My Life to Live*, Jean-Luc Godard, 1962)
Zazie dans le métro (Louis Malle, 1960)
Zéro de conduit (*Zero for Conduct*, Jean Vigo, 1933)

SOURCES

1. Childhood

Pierre Ajame, *Les Nouvelles littéraires*, no. 1837, 15 November 1962
Janick Arbois, *Télérama*, no. 865, 14–29 August 1966
Guy Artiban, *Playboy* [France], January 1975
Pierre Bénichou, *Le Nouvel Observateur*, no. 277, 2–8 March 1970
Anne de Gaspari, *Les Nouvelles littéraires* 54, no. 2524, 18 March 1976
Paul Henrickson, *Washington Post*, 22 February 1979
Charles Highan, *Action 9*, February 1974
Philippe Labro, *Lui*, no. 9, September 1964
Dominique Maillet, *Cinématographe*, no. 105, December 1984 [text from 1974]
Michèle Manceaux, *L'Express*, 23 April 1959
Franck Maubert, *Lire*, no. 80, April 1982
Marcel Mithois, *Réalités*, no. 220, May 1964
Colette Portefaix, *Télé 7 jours*, 6–12 August 1983
Georges Sadoul, *Les Lettres françaises*, no. 775, 28 May–3 June 1959

2. The New Wave

Pierre Billard, *France-Observateur*, no. 501, 3 December 1959
Jean Collet, Michel Delahaye, Jean-André Fieschi, André S. Labarthe, Bertrand Tavernier, *Cahiers du cinéma* 23, no. 138, December 1962
Jean-Louis Comolli, Jean Narboni, *Cahiers du cinéma*, no. 190, May 1967
Guy Léger, *Signes du temps*, no. 12, December 1959
Dominique Maillet, *Cinématographe*, no. 105, December 1984 [text from 1974]
Louis Marcorelles, *France-Observateur*, no. 598, 19 October 1961
André Parinaud, *Arts*, no. 720, 29 April–5 May 1959
Luce Sand, *Jeune Cinéma*, no. 31, May 1968

3. The Auteur Theory
Pierre Billard, *Cinéma* 62, no. 62, January 1962
Dan A. Cukier, Jo Gryn, *Script*, no. 5, April 1962
R. M. Franchi, Lewis Marshall, *New York Film Bulletin* 3, no. 3, Summer 1962

4. 1954: *Une visite*; 1957: *Les Mistons*; 1958: *Histoire d'eau*
Dominique Maillet, *Cinématographe*, no. 105, December 1984 [text from 1974]

5. 1959: *The 400 Blows*
Yvonne Baby, *Le Monde*, 21 April 1959
Pierre Billard, *Cinéma* 59, no. 37, June 1959
Michel Capdenac, *Les Lettres françaises*, no. 1179, April 1967
Dan A. Cukier, Jo Gryn, *Script*, no. 5, April 1962
Claude Dupont, *Ciné-Jeunes*, no. 78, 1974
[Interview] *Cinéma* 67, no. 112, January 1967
Dominique Maillet, *Cinématographe*, no. 105, December 1984 [text from 1974]
Michel Mardore, *Les Lettres françaises*, no. 911, 25–31 January 1962
André Parinaud, *Arts*, no. 720, 29 April–5 May 1959
Georges Sadoul, *Les Lettres françaises*, no. 775, 28 May–3 June 1959
Paul-Louis Thirard, *Les Lettres nouvelles*, 1959
Pierre Wildenstein, *Télé-Ciné*, no. 83, June–July 1959

6. 1960: *Shoot the Piano Player*
Yvonne Baby, *Le Monde*, 24 November 1960
Jean Collet, Michel Delahaye, Jean-André Fieschi, André S. Labarthe, Bertrand Tavernier, *Cahiers du cinéma* 23, no. 138, December 1962
Dan A. Cukier, Jo Gryn, *Script*, no. 5, April 1962
[Interview] *Cinéma* 61, no. 52, January 1961
[Interview] *France-Film—Cinéma nouveau*, no. 9, February 1961
[Interview] *Télé-Ciné*, no. 94, March 1961
[Interview] *Art et Essai*, no. 8, March 1966
[Interview] *Cinéma* 67, no. 112, January 1967
Dominique Maillet, *Cinématographe*, no. 105, December 1984 [text from 1974]
Michèle Manceaux, *L'Express*, 24 January 1963
Michel Mardore, *Les Lettres françaises*, no. 911, 25–31 January 1962
Henri Rode, *Cinémonde*, no. 1421, 31 October 1961

7. 1962: *Jules and Jim*
Guy Artiban, *Playboy* [France], January 1975
Yvonne Baby, *Le Monde*, no. 5294, 24 January 1962
Pierre Billard, *Cinéma* 62, no. 62, January 1962
Dan A. Cukier, Jo Gryn, *Script*, no. 5, April 1962
Pierre Delot, *Clarté*, no. 42, March 1962
[Interview] *Art et Essai*, no. 7, February 1966
[Interview] *Art et Essai*, no. 8, March 1966
Claude de Givray, *Cinéma et Télé-Cinéma*, no. 341, October 1966
Michel Mardore, *Les Lettres françaises*, no. 911, 25–31 January 1962
David Sterritt, *Christian Science Monitor*, 27 November 1978

8. 1962: *Antoine and Colette*
[Interview] *Art et Essai*, no. 8, March 1966
[Interview] *Cinéma 67*, no. 112, January 1967
Dominique Maillet, *Cinématographe*, no. 105, December 1984 [text from 1974]

9. 1964: *The Soft Skin*
Pierre Ajame, *Le Nouvel Adam*, no. 19, February 1968
Yvonne Baby, *Le Monde*, no. 6018, 22 May 1964
Raymond Bellour, Jean Michaud, *Les Lettres françaises*, no. 1000, 24–30 October 1983
Pierre Billard, *Cinéma 64*, no. 87, June 1964
Pierre Billard, Christiane Collange, Claude Veillot, *L'Express*, no. 883, 20–26 May 1968
Martine Cadieu, *Les Nouvelles littéraires*, no. 1916, 21 May 1964
Jean Collet, *Télérama*, no. 733, 2–8 February 1964
Jean-Louis Comolli, Jean Narboni, *Cahiers du cinéma*, no. 190, May 1967
[Interview] *Art et Essai*, no. 8, March 1966
[Interview] *Télé-Ciné*, no. 128, May-June 1966
[Interview] *Cinéma 67*, no. 112, January 1967
Michèle Manceaux, *L'Express*, 14 May 1964

10. 1966: *Fahrenheit 451*
Yvonne Baby, *Le Monde*, no. 6744, 18–19 September 1966
Pierre Bénichou, *Le Nouvel Observateur*, no. 277, 2–8 March 1970
Anne Capelle, *Arts-Loisirs*, no. 51, 14–20 September 1966
Jean-Louis Comolli, Jean Narboni, *Cahiers du cinéma*, no. 190, May 1967
[Interview] *Lectures pour nous*, December 1966
René Gilson, *Paris-Match*, no. 912, 1 October 1966
Claude de Givray, *Cinéma et Télé-Cinéma*, no. 341, October 1966
Marcel Martin, *Les Letters françaises*, no. 1148, 15–21 September 1966
Claude-Jean Philippe, *Télérama*, no. 872, 2–8 October 1966
Stacy Waddy, *Midi-Minuit fantastique*, no. 15–16, December-January 1967

11. 1967: *The Bride Wore Black*
Yvonne Baby, *Le Monde*, no. 7236, 18 April 1968
Jean Collet, *Télérama*, no. 954, 28 April–4 May 1968
Gilles Jacob, *Cinéma 67*, no. 121, December 1967
Gérard Langlois, *Les Letters françaises*, no. 1229, 10–16 April 1968
Claude-Jean Philippe, *Télérama*, no. 872, 2–8 October 1966
Luce Sand, *Jeune Cinéma*, no. 31, May 1968

12. 1968: *Stolen Kisses*
M. Aranias, Robert Malengreau, *Pourquoi* [Belgium], 1970
Étienne Ballerini, Alain Thery, Roger Caracache, Bernard Oheix, *Jeune Cinéma*, no. 77, March 1974 [unpublished extract]
Jean Collet, *Télérama*, no. 954, 28 April–4 May 1968
[Interview] *Cinéma et Télé-Cinéma*, no. 422, October 1968
[Interview] *Photo*, no. 33, 1970
Gérard Langlois, *Les Letters françaises*, no. 1229, 10–16 April 1968
Pierre Loubière, Gilbert Salachas, *Télé-Ciné 23*, no. 160, March 1970

Dominique Maillet, *Cinématographe*, no. 15, October–November 1975
Sébastien Roulet, *Cahiers du cinéma*, no. 200–201, April–May 1969
Luce Sand, *Jeune Cinéma*, no. 31, May 1968
Noël Simsolo, *Image et son, revue du cinéma*, no. 245, December 1970

13. May 1968
Philippe Labro, "*Mai 68: Ce n'est qu'un début*," Special Edition, *Éditions et Publications premières*, no. 2, Paris, Denoël

14. 1959–1968: Overview 1
Cinéma 64, no. 86, May 1964. Interview by Pierre Billard
Cahiers du cinéma, no. 190, May 1967. Interview by Jean-Louis Comolli and Jean Narboni

15. 1969: *Mississippi Mermaid*
Guy Artiban, *Playboy* [France], January 1975
Yvonne Baby, *Le Monde*, no. 7600, 21 May 1969
[Cinéastes de notre temps] *Télé-Ciné* 23, no. 160, March 1970
Jacques Fieschi, *Cinématographe*, no. 27, May 1977
Sanche de Gramont, *New York Times*, 15 June 1969
Monique Sobieski, *Journal du show-business*, no. 36, 27 June 1969
Claude-Marie Trémois, *Télérama*, no. 1013, 14–21 June 1969

16. 1970: *The Wild Child*
M. Aranias, Robert Malengreau, *Pourquoi* [Belgium], 1970
Pierre Bénichou, *Le Nouvel Observateur*, no. 277, 2–8 March 1970
Guy Braucourt, *Les Nouvelles Littéraires* 48, no. 2242, 10 September 1970
[Filmmakers of our time: François Truffaut] *Télé-Ciné* 23, no. 160, March 1970
[Interview] *The National Observer*, 12 October 1970
Anne Gillain, *Wide Angle* 4, no. 4, 1981
Guylaine Guidez, *Cinémonde*, no. 1844, September 1970
Pierre Loubière, Gibert Salachas, *Télé-Ciné* 23, no. 160, March 1970

17. 1970: *Bed and Board*
Étienne Ballerini, Alain Thery, Roger Caracache, Bernard Oheix, *Jeune Cinéma*, no. 77, March 1974 [unpublished extract]
Pierre Bénichou, *Le Nouvel Observateur*, no. 277, 2–8 March 1970
Guy Braucourt, *Cinéma 70*, no. 150, November 1970
Guy Braucourt, *Les Nouvelles Littéraires* 48, no. 2242, 10 September 1970
Gérard Langlois, *Les Letters françaises*, no. 1350, 9–15 September 1970
Pierre Loubière, Gilbert Salachas, *Télé-Ciné* 23, no. 160, March 1970
Michel Pérez, *Le Matin de Paris*, 24 January 1979
Noël Simsolo, *Image et son, revue du cinéma*, no. 245, December 1970

18. 1971: *Two English Girls*
Yvonne Baby, *Le Monde*, no. 8356, 25 November 1971
Claude Beylie, *Écran* 72, no. 1, January 1972

Guy Braucourt, *Les Nouvelles Littéraires*, no. 2306, 3–9 September 1971
[Interview] *Télérama*, no. 1126, 14–21 August 1971
Anne Gillain, *Wide Angle* 4, no. 4, 1981

19. 1972: A GORGEOUS GIRL LIKE ME
Étienne Ballerini, Alain Thery, Roger Caracache, Bernard Oheix, *Jeune Cinéma*, no. 77, March 1974 [unpublished extract]
Fred Barron, Paul Michaud, *Real Paper*, 2 January 1974
Claude Beylie, *Écran 73*, no. 17, July–August 1973
[Interview] *Technicien du film*, no. 191, 15 March 1972
Agathe Godard, *Vingt Ans*, 3 January 1973
Dominique Maillet, *Cinématographe*, no. 15, October–November 1975
René Quinson, *Le Soir* [Marseilles], 29 March 1972
Claude-Marie Trémois, *Télérama*, no. 1161, 15–22 April 1972

20. 1973: DAY FOR NIGHT
Yvonne Baby, *Le Monde*, no. 8815, 18 May 1973
Claude Beylie, *Écran 73*, no. 17, July–August 1973
Dominique Maillet, *Cinématographe*, no. 15, October–November 1975
Joanne Ney, *Village Voice*, no. 19, 24 January 1974
Chris Petit, Verina Glaessner, *Time Out*, no. 197, 30 November–6 December 1973

21. 1969–1974: OVERVIEW 2
Cinéma/Québec 3, no. 4, December–January 1974. Interview by André Leroux and Laurent Galiardi

22. 1975: THE STORY OF ADELE H.
Anne Gillain, *Wide Angle* 4, no. 4, 1981
Dominique Maillet, *Cinématographe*, no. 15, October–November 1975
Joël Saucin, *Hebdo-Belge*, November 1981
Claude-Marie Trémois, *Télérama*, no. 1319, 27 April–2 May 1975

23. 1976: SMALL CHANGE
Claude Beylie, *Écran 76*, no. 45, 15 March 1976
Jean Delmas, *Jeune Cinéma*, no. 95, May–June 1976
Anne Gillain, *Wide Angle* 4, no. 4, 1981
Dominique Maillet, *Cinématographe*, no. 15, October–November 1975
Larry Van Dyne, *The Chronicle Review* [Washington], 19 March 1979

24. 1977: THE MAN WHO LOVED WOMEN
Jacques Fieschi, *Cinématographe*, no. 27, May 1977
Anne de Gasperi, *Le Quotidien de Paris*, 26 April 1977
Anne Gillain, *Wide Angle* 4, no. 4, 1981
Dominique Maillet, *Lumière du cinéma*, no. 4, May 1977

25. 1978: THE GREEN ROOM
Samuel Lachize, *Humanité-Dimanche*, 7 April 1978

Catherine Laporte, Danièle Heymann, *L'Express*, no. 1392, 13–19 March 1978
Michel Pérez, *Le Matin de Paris*, 29 March 1978
Claude-Marie Trémois, *Télérama*, no. 1473, 8–15 April–2 1978

26. 1979: *Love on the Run*
Anne de Gasperi, *Les Nouvelles littéraires*, 22 February 1979
Anne Gillain, *Wide Angle* 4, no. 4, 1981
Simon Mizrahi, press kit for *L'Amour en fuite*, 1978
Michel Pérez, *Le Matin de Paris*, 24 January 1979
Yoïchi Umemoto, Takehito Deguchi, *Eureka* [Tokyo], 15 April 1980

27. 1980: *The Last Metro*
Michel Boujut, *Les Nouvelles littéraires*, no. 2754, 18 September 1980
Tom Buckley, *New York Times*, 14 October 1980
Serge Dussault, *La Presse* [Montreal], 21 February 1981
Anne de Gasperi, *Le Quotidien de Paris*, 11 June 1980
Julien Mazurelle, *Film-Bruxelles*, October 1980
Franco Nuovo, *Journal de Montréal*, 17 February 1981
Nathalie Petrowski, *Le Devoir* [Montreal], 21 February 1981
Joël Saucin, *Hebdo-Belge*, November 1981

28. 1981: *The Woman Next Door*
Michel Boujut, *Les Nouvelles littéraires*, 1 October 1981
Dominique Maillet, *Première*, no. 4, October 1981
Pierre Murat, *Télérama*, no. 1655, 30 September 1981
Luce Vigo, *Révolution*, 2 October 1981

29. 1983: *Confidentially Yours*
Paul Ceuzin and Gilles Costaz, *Le Matin de Paris*, 8 August 1983
François Guérif, Pilote, *August* 1983
Jean-François Josselin and Jean-Paul Enthoven, *Le Nouvel Observateur*, 5 August 1983
Dominique Maillet, *Première*, February 1981
Michèle Régnier, *Révolution*, 12 August 1983

30. 1975–1984: *Overview 3*
Sight and Sound 48, no. 4, 1979. Interview by Don Allen

INDEX

7 Women (*Frontière chinoise*, John Ford), 182
8½ (*Huit et demi*, Federico Fellini), 180, 236, 243, 291
400 Blows, The. See *Les quatre cents coups*

À bout de souffle (*Breathless*, Jean-Luc Godard), 17, 41, 89, 109, 283
Adam's Rib (*Madame porte la culotte*, George Cukor), 58
Adieu Philippine (Jacques Rozier), 32, 43
Adjani, Isabelle, 256, 259, 273, 313
Adolphe, ou l'âge tendre (Bernard Toublanc-Michel), 119
African Queen, The (John Huston), 184
L'Aigle à deux têtes (Jean Cocteau), 92
Air Force (Howard Hawks), 329
Aldrich, Robert, 54
Alexander, Patrick, 322
Allen, Lewis, 116
Allio, René, 42
Almendros, Nestor: *La Chambre verte* and, 286, 291; *Le Dernier Métro* and, 306; *L'Enfant sauvage* and, 245; *L'Histoire d'Adèle H.* and, 261; *L'Homme qui aimait les femmes* and, 280; mentioned, 225, 303, 331; praised by Truffaut, 258; *Vivement dimanche!* and, 326
Alphaville (Jean-Luc Godard), 92
Althusser, Louis, 316
Les Amants (*The Lovers*, Louis Malle), 29, 82
L'Amour à la chaîne (*Tight Skirts, Loose Pleasures*, Claude de Givray), 151

L'Amour à vingt ans (*Love at Twenty*, Shintarô Ishihara and others), 12, 113, 151, 216, 294, 295, 296
L'Amour en fuite (*Love on the Run*, François Truffaut): Antoine Doinel, characterization of, 296; earlier films, relations to, 294; editing of, 297; flop, as, 311; genesis of, 295; mentioned, 298, 333
Amouroux, Henri, 302
Amphitryon (Jean Giraudoux), 207
Andersson, Bibi, 240
Andress, Ursula, 148
Les Anges du péché (*Angels of Sin*, Robert Bresson), 282
L'Année dernière à Marienbad (*Last Year in Marienbad*, Alain Resnais), 33, 34, 39, 89, 157
Anouilh, Jean, 301
Antoine et Colette (*Antoine and Colette*, François Truffaut), 113
Antonioni, Michelangelo, 31, 186
Apollinaire, Guillaume, 221
Archibald de la Cruz (Luis Buñuel), 287
Ardant, Fanny: acting style of, 312; *La Femme d'à côté* and, 309–310; reminds Truffaut of Brontë sisters, 313; *Vivement dimanche!* and, 321, 325
L'Argent de poche (*Small Change*, François Truffaut), 262, 263, 266, 270, 277, 332
L'Arroseur arrosé (*Tables Turned on the Gardener*, Louis Lumière), 31
L'Art d'être grand-père (Victor Hugo), 271

Astruc, Alexandre, 10, 14, 31, 38
L'Atalante (Jean Vigo), 11
Aubry, Cécile, 68
Audiard, Michel, 28, 42, 103, 228
Audiberti, Jacques, 84, 91, 120, 186, 204, 229
Audin, Maurice, 35
Au Hasard Balthazar (Robert Bresson), 177
Aumont, Jean-Pierre, 235, 239
Aurel, Jean: collaboration with Truffaut, 47, 294, 296, 315; film critic, as, 60; mentioned, 178, 316, 324
Aurenche, Jean, 79, 108
Une aussi longue absence (The Long Absence, Henri Colpi), 33
Autant-Lara, Claude, 36, 238
author theory, the, 51, 52, 53, 54
L'Avare (Molière), 267
Awful Truth, The (Cette sacrée vérité, Leo McCarey), 212
Aznavour, Charles, 83, 84, 85, 90

La Baie des Anges (Bay of Angels, Jacques Demy), 234
Baisers volés (Stolen Kisses, François Truffaut): casting of, 153, 157, 203; characters in, 155, 156, 158–159, 234, 277; Le Dernier Métro and, 300; improvisation in, 114, 151; mentioned, 93, 190, 194, 208–209, 216, 295–296; La Nuit Américaine, compared with, 236, 238, 240, 263; privileged scenes in, 154; shooting of, 150; style of, 151, 156; theme of, 158; Tirez sur le pianiste and, 338; writing of, 323
Balzac, Honoré de, 7, 117, 124, 158, 196; influence on Truffaut of, 7, 15
Barbin, Pierre, 150
Bardot, Brigitte, 16, 190
Barefoot Contessa, The (La Comtesse aux pieds nus, Joseph L. Mankiewicz), 90
Le Baron fantôme (The Phantom Baron, Serge de Poligny), 4
Bataille, Georges, 298
Baud, Linda, 119, 120
Baudelaire, Charles, 137
Bazin, André: death of, 69; eulogized by Truffaut, 231; filmmaker, as, 24; mentioned, 11, 15; mentors Truffaut, 11–13
Bazin, Janine, 199, 245
Le beau Serge (Le Beau Serge, Claude Chabrol), 46
Becker, Jacques, 36, 52, 54, 120, 181, 287
Bed & Board (Truffaut). See Domicile conjugale
La Belle et la Bête (Beauty and the Beast, Jean Cocteau), 142, 284

Une belle fille comme moi (A Gorgeous Girl Like Me, François Truffaut): audience response to, 271; autobiographical elements in, 231; characters in, 229; confusion of genres in, 232; L'Enfant sauvage, relation to, 230; failure of, 311; genesis of, 227; mentioned, 79; reaction against Les Deux Anglaises, as, 80, 228, 259; shooting of, 248
Belmondo, Jean-Paul, 102, 130, 189, 190, 193, 197, 305
Benedetti, Nelly, 76
Ben Hur (William Wyler), 31
Bérard, Henri, 38
Berger, Nicole, 338
Bergman, Ingmar: eroticism of, 275; filmmaker, as, 181; influence of, 62, 332; mentioned, 29, 45, 54, 105, 240; praised by Truffaut, 247–248; Truffaut's admiration for, 183, 186
Berri, Claude, 42, 44, 163, 164, 176, 215
Berriau, Simone, 304
La Bête humaine (La Bête Humaine, Jean Renoir), 55, 75, 193
Bible: In the Beginning . . ., The (John Huston), 184
Big Sky, The (Howard Hawks), 329
Big Sleep, The (Le Grand Sommeil, Howard Hawks), 284
Bisset, Jacqueline, 235, 239, 298
Bitsch, Charles L., 38
Björnstrand, Gunnar, 240
Blain, Gérard, 17, 61
Bleu d'outre-tombe (Jean-René Clot), 132
Blondin, Antoine, 60
Bluwal, Marcel, 65
Bogart, Humphey, 9, 11, 251
Bonne chance Charlie (Good Luck Charlie, Jean-Louis Richard), 40
Les Bonnes Femmes (The Good Time Girls, Claude Chabrol), 32
Bonnie and Clyde (Arthur Penn), 249
Borgeaud, Nelly, 273
Bost, Pierre, 79, 108
Boudu sauvé des eaux (Boudu Saved from Drowning, Jean Renoir), 176
Boulevard (Jean Duvivier), 113
Bouquet, Michel, 126, 141, 146, 147, 190, 191
Bradbury, Ray, 116, 129–130, 133–134, 190, 322
Brando, Marlon, 269
Braque, Georges, 221
Brassens, Georges, 102
Braucourt, Guy, 183
Braunberger, Pierre, 63

Brel, Jacques, 316
Bresson, Robert, 44, 52, 54, 177, 258, 336
Brialy, Jean-Claude, 24, 63, 96
Bride Wore Black, The (François Truffaut). See *La Mariée était en noir*
Bride Wore Black, The (William Irish), 140
Bridge on the River Kwai, The (*Le Pont de la rivière Kwai*, David Lean), 83, 143
Brief Encounter (*Brève rencontre*, David Lean), 143
Brigitte et Brigitte (Luc Moullet), 42
Bronson, Charles, 240
Brontë sisters, 220, 313
Brooks, Peter, 116
Brooks, Richard, 60
Browning, Tod, 287
Brumes d'automne (Dimitri Dirsanoff), 16
Buñuel, Luis, 56, 156, 183, 186, 282, 287
Burglar, The (Paul Wendkos), 83

La Cage de verre (*The Glass Cage*, Philippe Arthuys, Jean-Lous Levi-Alvarès), 43
Cahiers du cinéma, 23, 24, 34, 44
Caillois, Roger, 132
Camus, Marcel, 22
Capote, Truman, 322
Capra, Frank, 42
Les Carabiniers (*The Soldiers*, Jean-Luc Godard), 43
Cargol, Jean-Pierre, 200, 234
Carlsen, Henning, 294
Carné, Marcel, 25
Carol, Martine, 243
Casanova (Fellini), 284
Casque d'or (Jacques Becker), 287
Cassavetes, John, 332
Cayatte, André, 340
Ceccaldi, Daniel, 153
"Une certaine tendance au cinéma français," 52
Ce soir ou jamais (*Tonight or Never*, Michel Deville), 32
Chabrol, Claude, 22, 24, 32, 38, 46, 181
Le Chagrin et la Pitié (*The Sorrow and the Pity*, Marcel Ophüls), 331
La Chambre verte (*The Green Room*, François Truffaut): celebration, as, 288; cinematic references in, 287; color in, 331; conception of, 286; deaf-mute child in, 288–289; emotions expressed in, 290; fairy tale, as, 289; mentioned, 337, 311; music in, 291; theme of, 287
Le Chanois, Jean-Paul, 36
Chaplin, Charlie, 10, 31, 56, 77, 181, 224, 300, 339

Chaplin, Geraldine, 163
Chase, James Hadley, 142
Le Chemin des écoliers (Michel Boisrond), 22
La Chienne (Jean Renoir), 192
Chiens perdus sans collier (*The Little Rebels*, Jean Delannoy), 67, 68
La Chinoise (Jean-Luc Godard), 45
Christie, Julie, 134, 235, 273
Chronique d'un été (*Chronicle of a Summer*, Edgar Morin and Jean Rouch), 33
Cinéastes de notre temps (TV series, 1964–1972), 199
Citizen Kane (Orson Welles), 9, 133, 178, 237
City Lights (*Les Lumières de la ville*, Charlie Chaplin), 11
Clair, René, 52, 83, 154, 190
Claudel, Paul, 8, 301
Clément, René, 52, 68
Clerval, Denys, 194
Clift, Montgomery, 178, 251
Clot, Jean-René, 132
Clouzot, Henri-Georges, 208, 282, 340
Cocéa, Alice, 304
Cocteau, Jean: compared with Roché, 109, 222, 334; influence of, 61, 69, 92, 142; mentioned, 44, 140, 149, 286, 288, 302, 334; *La Nuit Américaine*, referenced in, 239; Truffaut's admiration for, 54, 186
Les Coeurs verts (Édouard Luntz), 42
Cognani, François, 59
Cohen, Albert, 298
Cohn-Bendit, Daniel, 161
La Collectionneuse (*The Collector*, Eric Rohmer), 176
Companeez, Nina, 310
Un condamné à mort s'est échappé ou Le vent souffle où il veut (*A Man Escaped*, Robert Bresson), 16, 177
Confidentially Yours (François Truffaut). See *Vivement dimanche!*
Constantine, Jean, 39, 174
Contempt (Alberto Moravia), 91
Les Contes du lundi (Alphonse Daudet), 14
Cooper, Gary, 11
Le Corbeau (*Le Corbeau: The Raven*, Henri-Georges Clouzot), 4, 6, 14, 44, 282, 340
Le Coup de grâce (Jean Cayrol, Claude Durand), 43
Le Coup du berger (Jacques Rivette), 24, 60
Un couple (*A Couple*, Jean-Pierre Mocky), 32
Les Cousins (Claude Chabrol), 29, 32, 82
Coutard, Raoul, 37, 145

Crane, Stephen, 184
Cries & Whispers (Ingmar Bergman). See Viskningar och rop
Le Crime de M. Lange (The Crime of Monsieur Lange, Jean Renoir), 181
Cukor, George, 58

Dabadie, Jean-Loup, 256
Dali, Salvador, 132, 339
Les Dames de la côte (TV series), 309
Les Dames du Bois de Boulogne (Robert Bresson), 282
Daquin, Louis, 36
Darbon, François, 113, 153
Dark Passage (David Goodis), 83
Daudet, Alphonse, 14
Daves, Delmer, 83
Day for Night (François Truffaut). See La Nuit Américaine
Days of Heaven (Les Moissons du Ciel, Terence Malick), 331
Death in Venice (Mort à Venise, Luchino Visconti), 284
De Bosi, Gianfranco, 122
de Broca, Philippe, 70
Decaë, Henri, 37, 67, 69, 70
Decaë, Jacqueline, 78
De Gaulle, Charles, 148, 160
Deglane, Henri, 25, 47
Delannoy, Clément, 52
Delannoy, Jean, 53, 283, 340
Delerue, Georges, 100, 174, 175
Delluc, Louis, 31, 32
Delon, Alain, 190
De Man die zijn haar kort liet knippen (The Man Who Had His Hair Cut Short, André Delvaux), 179
De Mille, Cecil B., 25
de Monferrand, Jean, 1
Demy, Jacques, 92, 147, 225, 234
Deneuve, Catherine, 190, 193, 197, 273, 304, 305
Denner, Charles: La Chambre verte, and, 288; L'Homme qui aimait les femmes, and, 273–275, 285; mentioned, 126, 277, 279; Truffaut's view of, 278
La Dénonciation (Jacques Doniol-Valcroze), 41
Depardieu, Gérard, 302, 305, 306, 307, 309, 310, 312, 313, 314, 315, 317
Departure, The (Le Départ, Jerzy Klolimowski), 153
Der blaue Engel (L'Ange bleu, Josef von Sternberg), 192

Le Dernier Métro (The Last Metro, François Truffaut): autobiographical memories in, 303; Catherine Deneuve in, 304; Depardieu in, 305–306, 309–310; earlier works, relation to, 300; mentioned, 316, 320, 321, 324, 326; Occupation, depiction of, 301–302; success of, 307, 311
Desailly, Jean, 121, 122, 170, 174
Design for Living (Sérénade à trois, Ernst Lubitsch), 210
Détruire dit-elle (Marguerite Duras), 214
Les Deux Anglaises et le continent (Two English Girls, François Truffaut): conception of, 245–246; failure of, 227, 311; L'Histoire d'Adèle H., relation to, 258; mentioned, 80, 228, 233, 260, 314; method of directing in, 259; mise-en-scène in, 242–243; reaction against Jules and Jim, as, 226; relation to source novel of, 219, 220, 221; Roché and, 222; style of, 224–225; visual Truffaut's criticism of, 257
Les Deux Anglaises et le continent (Henri-Pierre Roché), 96, 218
Devil Is a Woman, The (La Femme et le Pantin, Josef von Sternberg), 192
Dhermit, Édouard, 239
Le Diable au corps (Devil in the Flesh, Claude Autant-Lara), 119
Le Diable au corps (Raymond Radiquet), 108
Diamond Bikini, The (Charles Williams), 321
Diary of a Chambermaid, The (Jean Renoir), 55
Diary of a Country Priest, The (Georges Bernanos), 266
Dickens, Charles, 77, 153
Dites-lui que je l'aime (This Sweet Sickness, Claude Miller), 336
Domicile conjugal (Bed & Board, Truffaut): characters in, 203; influence of Renoir on, 212; mentioned, 209, 223, 280, 294; sadness of, 208; shooting style of, 210; Truffaut's dissatisfaction with, 216
Doniol-Valcroze, Jacques, 24, 32, 58, 59, 61
Dorfmann, Robert, 38
Douchet, Jean, 181
Dreyer, Carl, 160, 292, 294, 340
Dreyfus, Alfred, 35
Dr. No (Terence Young), 329
Dubois, Marie, 338
Duhamel, Antoine, 194
Duhamel, Claire, 153
Duras, Marguerite, 37

L'Eau à la bouche (Jacques Doniol-Valcroze), 32
L'École des femmes (Raymond Rouleau), 256

L'Éducation sentimentale (Gustave Flaubert), 158
Eichmann, Adolf, 34
Eisenstein, Sergei, 29, 178
El Dorado (Howard Hawks), 182
L'Enclos (*The Enclosure*, Armand Gatti), 43
L'Enfant sauvage (*The Wild Child*, François Truffaut): autobiographical element in, 226; *Une Belle Fille comme moi*, relation to, 230; casting of, 200; childhood, vision of, 271; ending of, 260; genesis of, 201; *L'Histoire d'Adèle H.*, relation to, 255; Janine Bazin, influence of, 244–245; mentioned, 78, 93, 234, 243, 263, 288; pre-adolescence, depiction of, 265; screenplay, shaping of, 254; style of, 205, 224, 258; themes in, 197, 202, 204, 208–209; Truffaut as actor in, 236–237; Truffaut's satisfaction with, 249
Les Enfants du paradis (*Children of Paradise*, Marcel Carné), 6, 44
Les Enfants sauvages (Lucien Malson), 198
Les Enfants terribles (Jean Cocteau), 92
Les Enfants terribles (Jean-Pierre Melville), 108, 278
Ensayo de un crimen (*The Criminal Life of Archibald de la Cruz*, Luis Buñuel), 285
Epstein, Jean, 31
Et Dieu créa . . . la femme (*. . . And God Created Woman*, Roger Vadim), 16, 106
Eugénie Grandet (Honoré de Balzac), 14, 274
Europa '51 (*Europe '51*, Roberto Rossellini), 68, 104, 137

Fahrenheit 451 (François Truffaut): books in, 132, 233, 242, 256, 279; censorship theme in, 131; characters in, 125, 134, 203; communication in, 334; construction of, 167; editing of, 297; English language and, 191; English location of, 136; genesis of, 116, 130, 170; Julie Christie and, 235, 273; mentioned, 93, 146, 152, 154, 166, 209; *La Peau douce*, relation to, 134; *Les quatre cents coups*, relation to, 134; science fiction and, 129, 132; screenplay of, 133; themes of, 135–138, 197, 201, 204, 224, 291
Falcon, André, 153
Family Life (Ken Loach), 79
Farrell, Henry, 227, 229, 322
Favre-Le Bret, Robert, 163
Fellini, Federico, 183, 215, 236, 282, 284, 291
La Femme d'à côté (*The Woman Next Door*, François Truffaut): absence of songs in, 316; casting of, 313; genesis of, 309; mentioned, 311, 315, 318; *La Sirène du Mississipi*, relation to, 314; screenplay for, 310, 324; structure of, 312
Une Femme est une femme (*A Woman Is a Woman*, Jean-Luc Godard), 32, 89
La Femme et le Pantin (*The Woman and the Puppet*, Jacques de Baroncelli), 192
Fernandel, 28
Ferrière, Martine, 153
Feuillère, Edwige, 116
Feyder, Jacques, 25, 31
F for Fake (Orson Welles), 294
La Fiancée des ténèbres (Serge de Poligny), 4
La Fille aux yeux d'or (*The Girl with the Golden Eyes*, Jean-Gabriel Albicocco), 32
Finch, Peter, 137
Flaherty, Robert, 31
Flynn, Errol, 117, 336
Fonda, Henry, 251
Ford, John, 42, 182, 321
Fossey, Brigitte, 68, 276
Frankenheimer, John, 9
French quality tradition, 52
Fresnay, Pierre, 9, 11, 28
La Fugue d'Antoine (François Truffaut), 64
Fuller, Samuel, 84

Gabin, Jean, 28
Gance, Abel, 25, 31
Garfield, John, 11
Garrel, Philippe, 92, 235
Genet, Jean, 136, 186; influence on Truffaut of, 13
Le Genou de Claire (*Claire's Knee*, Éric Rohmer), 46
Germany Year Zero (*Allemagne année zéro*, Roberto Rossellini), 67
Gide, André, 13, 107, 193, 281
La Gifle (*The Slap*, Claude Pinoteau), 256
Gilles, Guy, 43
Giovanni, José, 42
Gish, Dorothy, 233
Gish, Lillian, 233
Givray, Claude de, 39, 151, 211, 323
Godard, Jean-Luc: Cocteau, influence of, 92; color, use of, 225; contemporary preoccupations of, 185; *Une histoire d'eau*, making of, 62–63; ideological filmmaker, as, 136; May 1968 and, 162; mentioned, 31, 89, 122, 153, 155, 186; New Wave and, 42, 43, 45, 46; Truffaut's relationship with, 10–11, 14, 15, 17, 209. See also *À bout de souffle*, *Alphaville*, *La Chinoise*, *Le Mépris*, *Le Petit Soldat*, *Les Carabiniers*,

Godard, Jean-Luc (*continued*)
   Masculin Féminin, Pierrot le fou, Une Femme est une femme, Une histoire d'eau, Vivre sa vie
Golden Coach, The (*Le Carrosse d'or*, Jean Renoir), 186, 238
Gone with the Wind (Victor Fleming, George Cukor, Sam Wood), 98
Goodis, David, 82–84, 92, 141–142, 190, 322–323
Gorgeous Girl Like Me, A (François Truffaut). See *Une belle fille comme moi*
Gospel According to St. Matthew, The (*L'Évangile selon saint Matthieu*, Pier Paolo Pasolini), 224
Goupi mains rouges (*It Happened at the Inn*, Jacques Becker), 288
La Grande Illusion (*La Grande Illusion*, Jean Renoir), 11, 196
Les Grandes Personnes (*Time Out for Love*, Jean Valère), 32
Grant, Cary, 9, 11, 117, 137, 189
Greco, Juliette, 102, 316
Green Room, The (François Truffaut). See *La Chambre verte*
Grémillon, Jean, 31
Il grido (*Le Cri*, Michelangelo Antonioni), 29
Griffith, D. W., 11, 25, 31, 42, 224
Grimm's Fairy Tales, 186
Une grosse tête (*A Swelled Head*, Claude de Givray), 40
Gruault, Jean: *Jules et Jim* and, 96, 97, 106, 219–221; mentioned, 198, 224, 255, 257, 287; New Wave, and, 11; storyteller, as, 254
La guerre de Troie n'aura pas lieu (Jean Giraudoux), 207
La guerre est finie (*The War Is Over*, Alain Resnais), 180
Guillemin, Henri, 124
Guillemot, Agnès, 213
Guillie, Frances Vernor, 253
Guimard, Paul, 60
Guitry, Sacha, 8, 15, 212, 297, 333, 340

Hanoun, Marcel, 37
Harrington, Joseph, 322
Haudepin, Sabine, 304
Hawkins, Jack, 137
Hawks, Howard, 129, 182, 292, 329
Hemingway, Ernest, 322
Herrmann, Bernard, 259
Hiroshima mon amour (*Hiroshima Mon Amour*, Alain Resnais), 29, 33, 37, 41, 82
L'Histoire d'Adèle H. (*The Story of Adele H.*, François Truffaut): Adèle, characterization of, 336; *L'Argent de poche*, relation to, 262; color, use of, 331; conception of, 254; double take (French and English) of, 261; experimental aspect of, 258; genesis of, 253; Isabelle Adjani in, 256; mentioned, 278, 282, 286, 289, 307, 337; music in, 255, 258–259, 260; Nestor Almendros, and, 280; screenplay of, 257; style of, 283
Une histoire d'eau (*A Story of Water*, Jean-Luc Godard and François Truffaut), 62
Hitchcock, Alfred: American films of, 329–330; box office success of, 56; emotions, and, 148, 181, 186; influence on Truffaut of, 73, 74, 134, 181–183, 331; Lubitsch's influence on, 210–211; *La Mariée était en noir* and, 141; mentioned, 42, 167, 178, 180, 185, 203, 300; music, use of, 259; *North by Northwest*, and, 101; *Rear Window*, and, 85; *Shadow of a Doubt*, and, 213, 292; *La Sirène du Mississipi*, and, 250; time, treatment of, 113; Truffaut's interviews with, 184; VistaVision, use of, 177
Hitchens, Dolores, 322
Hitler, Adolf, 34
L'Homme de Rio (*That Man from Rio*, Philippe de Broca), 42
Un homme et une femme (*A Man and a Woman*, Claude Lelouch), 42
L'Homme qui aimait les femmes (*The Man Who Loved Women*, François Truffaut): Casanova, relation to, 284; characterization of hero in, 336; Charles Denner, and, 273, 285, 288; cinematic influences on, 285; cinematography of, 280; ending of, 290; flashbacks in, 275; genre of, 278; Roché, extent of debt to, 333–334
Les Honneurs de la guerre (*The Honors of War*, Jean Dewever), 40
Hughes, Dorothy B., 322
Hugo, Adele, 253, 255
Hugo, Léopoldine, 254
Huston, John, 31, 183, 184, 202, 203
Huxley, Aldous, 130

I Confess (*La Loi du silence*, Alfred Hitchcock), 178
Les Illusions perdues (Honoré de Balzac), 14
L'Immortelle (Alain Robbe-Grillet), 42
Irish, William, 141, 142
Isabelle (André Gide), 13
It Should Happen to You (*Une femme qui s'affiche*, George Cukor), 58
Ivan Grozniy (*Ivan the Terrible*, Sergei Eisenstein), 29

Jaccoud, Pierre, 115, 118, 119
Jack (Daudet), 14
Jade, Claude, 153
James, Henry, 286, 320
Jamois, Marguerite, 304
Jaubert, Maurice, 255, 258, 259, 260, 290, 291
Jeanson, Henri, 25, 26, 28
Jessua, Alain, 42
Jeux interdits (*Forbidden Games*, René Clément), 68
Joan of Arc, 2, 177
Johnny Guitar, 91, 138, 194, 229
Le Joli Mai (Chris Marker), 43
Journal d'un curé de campagne (*Diary of a Country Priest*, Robert Bresson), 278
Le Journal du voleur (*The Thief's Journal*, Jean Genet), 13
Jouvet, Louis, 303
Jules et Jim (*Jules and Jim*, François Truffaut): autobiographical roots of, 109, 110; casting of, 99, 171; characters in, 102, 106; *Les Deux Anglaises* (Roché) and, 218, 219; earlier films, relation to, 98; *Fahrenheit 451* and, 256; fairy story, as, 146; freeze frames in, 108; Gruault's input into, 220; Jeanne Moreau and, 239; love theme of, 257; *La Mariée était en noir*, compared to, 144, 145; mentioned, 107, 113, 127, 140, 168, 226, 300; music in, 175; Oscar Werner in, 135; pace of, 225; *La Peau douce*, relation to, 79, 120, 215, 259; photography of, 246; Roché's novel and, 96; screenplay of, 173–174; shooting of, 95, 134; style of, 178; Suzanne Schiffman and, 281; theme of, 97, 104, 105; Truffaut's personal investment in, 100
Jules et Jim (Roché), 95–96, 97, 109, 221, 334

Kast, Pierre, 41, 44, 329
Kid, The (*Le Kid*, Charlie Chaplin), 77
King Kong (Merian C. Cooper and Ernest B. Schoedsack), 330
King of Kings (*Le Roi des rois*, Nicholas Ray), 31
Kiss Me, Stupid (*Embrasse-moi, idiot*, Billy Wilder), 182
Kubrick, Stanley, 9
Kurosawa, Akira, 45

Lachenay, Robert, 3, 7, 9, 13
Ladd, Alan, 336
Lady from Shanghai, The (*La Dame de Shanghai*, Orson Welles), 185
Lady in the Lake (Robert Montgomery), 73
Lafont, Bernadette, 61, 229

La Fontaine, Jean de, 106, 186
Lancaster, Burt, 240
Lang, Fritz, 181, 227, 340
Langlois, Henri: *Baisers volés* and, 194; *Domicile conjugale* and, 209; mentioned, 11, 156, 214; sacking of, 150, 154, 160; Truffaut's support for, 151, 161
Last Laugh, The (*Le Dernier des hommes*, F. W. Murnau), 172
Last Metro, The (François Truffaut). See *Le Dernier Métro*
Latouche, Michel, 63
Laubreaux, Alain, 302
Laurent, Jacques, 60
Law of Survival (*La Loi du survivant*, José Giovanni), 177
Léaud, Jean-Pierre: *Antoine et Colette*, and, 113; casting of, 77; closeness to Truffaut, 271; *Domicile conjugale*, reaction to, 208; mentioned, 73, 112, 114, 190, 209, 234, 305; *Les quatre cents coups*, in, 66; Truffaut's direction of, 98, 178, 222; Truffaut's view of, 153, 193, 240, 241, 252
Léautaud, Paul, 221, 275
Leclerc, Ginette, 302
Lefèvre, René, 302
Lelouch, Claude, 43, 163, 251, 305
Lemaire, Philippe, 17
Lester, Richard, 163
Lettre de Sibérie (*Letter from Siberia*, Chris Marker), 33
Lévy, Raoul, 130
Les Lions sont lâchés (*The Lions Are Loose*, Henri Verneuil), 103
Lisbona, Joseph, 51
Lola (Jacques Demy), 32, 39, 43
Lola Montès (Max Ophüls), 16, 90, 99
Lolita (Stanley Kubrick), 119
London, Jack, 153
Long Saturday Night, The (Charles Williams), 320
La Longue Marche (Alexandre Astruc), 43, 178
Lonsdale, Michael, 153, 157
Lorre, Peter, 11
Los Olvidados (Luis Buñuel), 156
Love on the Run (François Truffaut). See *L'Amour en fuite*
Lubitsch, Ernst, 154, 210, 211, 212, 230, 251, 267, 325
Luchaire, Corinne, 302
Lugosi, Bela, 287
Lumet, Sidney, 9
Lumière, Auguste and Louis, 31, 32

Lux, Guy, 317
Le Lys dans la vallée (Honoré de Balzac), 14
Le Lys dans la vallée (Marcel Cravenne), 119

Macbeth (Orson Welles), 185
La Machine infernale (Jean Cocteau), 302
Madame Bovary (Gustave Flaubert), 5, 118, 119, 120
Mademoiselle (Tony Richardson), 180
Magnificent Ambersons, The (*La Splendeur des Amberson*, Orson Welles), 9, 133, 186, 224, 326
Mailer, Norman, 322
Malle, Louis, 22, 24, 42, 162
Malraux, André, 148
Malson, Lucien, 198
Mann, Claude, 234
Man Who Had His Hair Cut Short, The. See *De Man die zijn haar kort liet knippen*
Man Who Loved Women, The (François Truffaut). See *L'Homme qui aimait les femmes*
Marais, Jean, 302
Marat-Sade (Peter Weiss), 136
La Mariée était en noir (*The Bride Wore Black*, François Truffaut): American cinema, relation to, 142, 196; character of Julie in, 144, 145; color, use of, 320, 338; fairy story, as, 146; improvisation, absence of, 248; long takes in, 145, 152; mentioned, 46, 177, 179, 190, 249, 273; source of, 140; style of, 145–146; theme of love in, 143; Truffaut's critique of, 148
Marker, Chris, 10, 12
Marx, Harpo, 200
Masculin Féminin (Jean-Luc Godard), 152, 153
Mata Hari, agent H21 (Jean-Louis Richard), 166, 310
Mathieu, Mireille, 317
Matisse, Henri, 34
Mauriac, Claude, 41
Maurier, Claire, 76, 78
Les Mauvais Coups (François Leterrier), 32
Les Mauvais Coups (Roger Vailland), 38
Les Mauvaises Rencontres (*Bad Liaisons*, Alexandre Astruc), 14, 90
Max, Harry, 153
Mayer, Louis B., 183
McCarey, Leo, 210, 212
Melville, Jean-Pierre, 41, 108
Menegoz, Robert, 36
Le Mépris (*Contempt*, Jean-Luc Godard), 178
Mérimée, Prosper, 16
Metropolis (Fritz Lang), 9
Miller, Claude, 332, 336
Minnelli, Vincente, 5, 298

Miser, The (Molière), 267
Misfits, The (John Huston), 106
Mississippi Mermaid (François Truffaut). See *La Sirène du Mississipi*
Mississippi Mermaid (William Irish), 190
Les Mistons (François Truffaut): Bernadette Lafont and, 229; child actors in, 268; editing of, 172; Les Films du Carrosse and, 62; genesis of, 61; *Jules et Jim*, relation to, 98; *La Mariée était en noir*, relation to, 143; mentioned, 24, 60, 64, 200; Philippe de Broca, assistance of, 70; Roché, shown to, 96; shooting of, 58; Truffaut's lessons from, 59
Mizoguchi, Kenji, 45
Moby Dick (John Huston), 184
Moderato cantabile (*Seven Days... Seven Nights*, Peter Brook), 33, 102
Modesty Blaise (Joseph Losey), 176
Monroe, Marilyn, 189
Monsieur Verdoux (Charlie Chaplin), 11, 285
Montessori, Maria, 198
Montherlant, Henri de, 301
Moravia, Alberto, 86, 91
More (Barbet Schroeder), 275
Moreau, Jeanne: actress, as, 29, 146, 148, 241, 312; *Jules et Jim*, and, 98, 99, 239; *La Mariée était en noir*, and, 140, 144–145; mentioned, 91, 179, 234; Roché's response to, 96
Morgan, Mary, 304
Morgan, Michèle, 28
La Morte-Saison des amours (Pierre Kast), 32
Les Mots (Jean-Paul Sartre), 79, 148
Mouchette, Robert Bresson), 177
Moullet, Luc, 42
Moussy, Marcel, 28, 41, 65, 166
Mr. Arkadin (*Monsieur Arkidin*, Orson Welles), 185
Muriel ou Le temps d'un retour (*Muriel, or The Time of Return*, Alain Resnais), 43, 120, 280
Murnau, F. W., 11
La Musica (Marguerite Duras, Paul Seban), 42

Le Nabab (Alphonse Daudet), 14
Naked Childhood (*L'Enfance nue*, Maurice Pialat), 203
Naked Dawn (*Le Bandit*, Edward G. Ulmer), 95, 96
Naked Jungle, The (*Quand la marabunta gronde*, Byron Haskin), 196
Nana (Jean Renoir), 119, 192
Nattvardsgästerna (*Winter Light*, Ingmar Bergman), 181

New Wave, The: aims of, 45; beginnings of, 24; characteristics of, 22, 30, 31, 32, 277, 283; concept of, 21; criticism of, 87; definition of, 21, 29, 43; diversity of, 22, 42; evolution of, 41–42; genesis of, 23; mentioned, 36, 39, 47, 82, 242; shooting style of, 27; tendencies in, 32; Truffaut's role in, 44–45; waning of, 30, 42, 44, 328

North by Northwest (*La Mort aux trousses*, Alfred Hitchcock), 101, 330

Nouvelle Vague, La. *See* New Wave, The

La Nuit américaine (*Day for Night*, François Truffaut): aim of, 243–244; *Le Dernier Métro*, relation to, 300–303; documentary quality of, 234; genesis of, 233; mentioned, 242, 248, 276, 288, 294, 332, 337; mise-en-scène in, 298; multi-character film, as, 263, 277, 319; recapitulation film, as, 235–236; screenplay of, 246; success of, 311; Suzanne Schiffmann and, 245; Truffaut as actor in, 236–237

Nuit et Brouillard (*Night and Fog*, Alain Resnais), 104

Nureyev, Rudolf, 200

Œdipe roi. See *La Machine infernale*

L'Œil du Malin (*The Third Lover*, Claude Chabrol), 41

Ophüls, Max, 52, 54, 55, 56, 107, 227, 322, 331

Orfeu Negro (*Black Orpheus*, Marcel Camus), 29

Pagnol, Marcel, 298

Paisà (*Paisan*, Roberto Rossellini), 68

Le Panier à crabes (Joseph Lisbona), 51

Paradis perdu (*Four Flights to Love*, Abel Gance), 2

Les Paravents (Jean Genet), 136

Paris brûle-t-il? (*Is Paris Burning?*, René Clément), 176

Paris nous appartient (*Paris Belongs to Us*, Jacques Rivette), 46

Le Passage du Rhin (*Tomorrow Is My Turn*, André Cayatte), 85

La Passion de Jeanne d'Arc (*The Passion of Joan of Arc*, Carl Theodor Dreyer), 2

Paviot, Paul, 41

La Peau de chagrin (Honoré de Balzac), 14

La Peau douce (*The Soft Skin*, François Truffaut): casting of, 170, 171, 274; characters in, 120, 124, 174; ending of, 125; failure of, 116, 127, 203; freeze frames in, 108; genesis of, 116, 118; mentioned, 126, 134, 172, 176, 208, 235, 243; montage in, 123; music in, 175; response to *Jules and Jim*, as, 79, 120, 215, 259; style of, 122, 123, 178; title of, 240; Truffaut's critique of, 115, 124, 212

Perier, François, 170

Perrault, Charles, 84, 106, 186

Pétain, Philippe, 8, 203

Le Petit Soldat (*The Little Soldier*, Jean-Luc Godard), 89

Peyrefitte, Roger, 298

Philipe, Gérard, 28

Piaf, Édith, 316

Picasso, Pablo, 35, 221

Piccoli, Michel, 178

Pickpocket (Robert Bresson), 336

Picratt, roi du rail [*Fuzzy, King of the Railway*] (Mack Sennett), 107

Picture (Lillian Ross), 183

Pierrot le fou (*Pierrot le Fou*, Jean-Luc Godard), 45, 196

Pisier, Marie-France, 112, 113, 294, 295

La Pointe courte (Agnès Varda), 33

Polanski, Roman, 162, 215

Politique des auteurs, la, 52, 53, 54, 57

Pons, Maurice, 61, 172

Pontcarral, colonel d'empire (Jean Delannoy), 4, 340

Porcile, François, 255

Portrait-Robot (Paul Paviot), 41

Preminger, Otto, 60, 168

Le Président (*The President*, Henri Verneuil), 103

Prévert, Jacques, 16, 25, 102, 235, 277

Printemps, Yvonne, 304

La Proie pour l'ombre (*Shadows of Adultery*, Alexandre Astruc), 32

Psycho (*Psychose*, Alfred Hitchcock), 34

Le Puits et le Pendule (Alexandre Astruc), 137

La Pyramide humaine (*The Human Pyramid*, Jean Rouch), 33

Les quatre cents coups (*The 400 Blows*, François Truffaut): autobiographical elements in, 1, 8, 10, 13–14, 65, 99–100, 271; *Baisers volés* as sequel to, 151; casting of, 66–67; characters in, 76, 102, 105, 178, 270; children in, 265; compared with *Jules et Jim*, 98, 104; compared with *La Peau douce*, 120; compared with *Tirez sur le pianiste*, 93, 104; documentary quality of, 168, 243; Doinel series, and, 297–298; editing of, 173; fairy tale elements in, 147; genesis of, 64; Hitchcock's influence on, 73–75; improvisation in, 171; influences on, 62, 67–69, 75, 78; Jean-Pierre Léaud and, 77; Marcel Moussy, contribution of, 28, 65; mentioned,

Les quatre cents coups (*The 400 Blows*, François Truffaut) (*continued*) 37, 79, 88, 91, 96, 113, 216; music in, 174–175; parents' resentment of, 17, 110; reception of, 80, 169; Renoir's influence on, 75, 78; Rossellini's influence on, 78; shooting of, 69–71; social critique, as, 204; success of, 82–83, 89, 112, 127
Queneau, Raymond, 32, 186, 227, 281
Quiet Man, The (*L'Homme tranquille*, John Ford), 182

Radiguet, Raymond, 61
Rafelson, Bob, 332
Raimu (alias, Jules Auguste Muraire), 9
Ray, Nicholas, 60, 84, 91, 138
Raynaud, Fernand, 267
Rear Window (*Fenêtre sur cour*, Alfred Hitchcock), 85
Rebatet, Lucien, 304
Rebecca (Hitchcock), 330
La Récréation (Fabien Colin and François Moreuil), 32
Red Badge of Courage, The (*La Charge victorieuse*, John Huston), 183
Red Line 7000 (*La Ligne rouge 7000*, Howard Hawks), 182
Red River (*La Rivière rouge*, Howard Hawks), 186, 329
La Règle du jeu (*The Rules of the Game*, Jean Renoir), 11, 14, 55
Reinhardt, Gottfried, 183, 184
La Religieuse (Denis Diderot), 136
Renoir, Jean: approach of, 186; author theory and, 53, 54–55; death of, 300; influence of, 62, 75, 78, 117, 141, 181–182, 194; mentioned, 25, 31, 90, 194, 212, 237, 249; personal filmmaker, as, 52; *Les quatre cents coups*, view of, 204; *La Sirène du Mississipi* and, 250; themes of, 105, 224
Resnais, Alain: approach to filmmaking of, 180–181, 280; mentioned, 10, 12, 31, 37, 61, 63; New Wave and, 22, 38, 42; *Nuit et Brouillard*, and, 88; protest at Cannes, and, 162; Truffaut's view of, 32–33, 256; *Une visite* and, 59
Revon, Bernard, 151, 211, 323
Rich, Claude, 163
Richard, Jean-Louis, 39, 116, 125, 130, 166, 310
Richardson, Tony, 180
Richer, Jean-José, 59
Le Rideau cramoisi (*The Crimson Curtain*, Alexandre Astruc), 14
Rispal, Jacques, 153

Rivette, Jacques: cinephile, as, 10, 14, 44, 60; *Les Deux Anglaises*, view of, 225; friendship with Truffaut, 15, 178; influence on Truffaut, 6, 44, 46, 58, 59, 61, 138; May 1968 and, 162; mentioned, 92, 175, 212, 248, 282; New Wave and, 24, 38, 45
Robbe-Grillet, Alain, 178
Roberte ce soir (*Roberte*, Pierre Zucca), 332
Roche, France, 66
Roché, Henri-Pierre: *Les Deux Anglaises* and, 219–221; influence on Truffaut of, 92, 178, 224, 333–334; *Jules et Jim* of, 96, 100, 109; mentioned, 223, 227; Truffaut's identification with, 222
Rohmer, Éric: cinephile, as, 60; filmmaker, as, 43, 46, 282; influence of, 44; mentioned, 14, 45, 180; New Wave and, 38; storyteller, as, 176–177; Truffaut's respect for, 186, 332
Le Roman d'un tricheur (*The Story of a Cheat*, Sacha Guitry), 14, 15, 335
Romeo and Juliet (Franco Zeffirelli), 119
Rooney, Mickey, 11
Roots of Heaven, The (*Les Racines du ciel*, John Huston), 184
Ross, Lillian, 184
Rossellini, Roberto: English actors, view of, 137; influence of, 16, 67, 78, 104; mentioned, 31; Truffaut works as assistant of, 17
Rouch, Jean, 228, 269
Le Rouge et le Noir (Stendhal), 108
Le Roux, Maurice, 174
Rue des Prairies (*Rue de Paris*, Denys de La Patellière), 42

saganisme, 30
Saint-Laurent, Yves, 194
Sait-on jamais (*No Sun in Venice*, Roger Vadim), 175
Sarris, Andrew, 301
Sartre, Jean-Paul, 9, 79, 148, 231, 301
Saura, Carlos, 163
Scarlet Pimpernel, The (Harold Young), 330
Schary, Dore, 184
Schiffman, Suzanne, 245, 263, 281, 294, 296, 302, 303, 324
Schroeder, Barbet, 275
La Séquestrée de Poitiers (André Gide), 107
Serre, Henri, 99, 102
Seyrig, Delphine, 153, 154, 157
Shadow of a Doubt (*L'Ombre d'un doute*, Alfred Hitchcock), 213, 285

Shoot the Piano Player (François Truffaut). See *Tirez sur le pianiste*
Si c'était vous (TV series), 28
Le Signe du lion (Éric Rohmer), 43
Simenon, Georges, 91, 120, 275, 298
La Sirène du Mississipi (*Mississippi Mermaid*, François Truffaut): adaptation, as, 190, 192; casting of, 193; Catherine Deneuve and, 304; earlier films, relation to, 209; failure of, 338; *La Femme d'à côté*, relation to, 314; improvisation in, 191; influence of Renoir on, 195; mentioned, 189, 203, 224; personal projection in, 226; representation of women in, 273; themes in, 193–194, 196, 247; tonal rupture in, 249
Situations (Jean-Paul Sartre), 231
Skolimowski, Jerzy, 153, 248
Small Change (François Truffaut). See *L'Argent de poche*
Snow White and the Seven Dwarfs (*Blanche-Neige et les sept nains*, William Cottrell, David Hand), 196
Soft Skin, The (François Truffaut). See *La Peau douce*
Sommaren med Monika (*Summer with Monika*, Ingmar Bergman), 62
Sommarlek (*Summer Interlude*, Ingmar Bergman), 62
Le Soulier de satin (Paul Claudel), 207
Spaak, Charles, 25, 87
Spartacus (Stanley Kubrick), 31
Stavisky (Alain Resnais), 305
Steinbeck, John, 155
Stendhal, 309
Stévenin, Jean-François, 269, 270, 332
Stevens, George, 184
Stewart, James, 9, 11, 117
Stolen Kisses (François Truffaut). See *Baisers volés*
Story of Adele H., The (François Truffaut). See *L'Histoire d'Adèle H.*
Stranger, The (*Le Criminel*, Orson Welles), 185
Stroheim, Erich von, 11, 31
Subor, Michel, 100
Sunrise (*L'Aurore*, F. W. Murnau), 172, 205

Tati, Jacques, 44, 52, 54, 212
Le Temps du ghetto (Frédéric Rossif), 33
Tendeter, Stacey, 259
Le Testament d'Orphée (*Testament of Orpheus*, Jean Cocteau), 46, 113

La Tête contre les murs (*Head Against the Wall*, Georges Franju), 83, 84
Thomas l'Imposteur (*Thomas the Imposter*, Georges Franju), 176
Thompson, Jim, 322
Tirez sur le pianiste (*Shoot the Piano Player*, François Truffaut): adaptation, as, 83, 88, 190, 323; American cinema and, 91, 93, 181, 195; approach to, 168; audience, and, 41; Aznavour in, 84–85; casting of, 84; charm of, 338; editing of, 173; failure of, 203; fairy tale, as, 84; genesis of, 82; improvisation in, 171; influences on, 92, 138; mentioned, 100, 126, 147, 209, 212, 297, 337; music in, 175; *Les quatre cents coups*, relation to, 79, 89, 146; setting of, 229; Suzanne Schiffmann and, 245; theme of, 83; tone in, 178, 249; Truffaut's critique of, 86, 90, 101; Truffaut's other films, relation to, 104
Toni (Jean Renoir), 55
Touch of Evil (*La Soif du mal*, Orson Welles), 103
La Tour, prends garde! (*King on Horseback*, Georges Lampin), 66
Tracy, Spencer, 9
Trans-Europ-Express (Alain Robbe-Grillet), 176
Trenet, Charles, 151, 152, 233, 310, 316
Trintignant, Jean-Louis, 324
Truffaut, François: adaptation, views on, 246–247; American cinema, view of, 9, 90–91; audience, awareness of, 168, 326; autobiographical elements in films of, 64–65, 118, 225–226, 231, 264, 276, 337; characters of, 34, 36, 105, 117, 120, 167, 255; children, working with, 269; cinemascope, use of, 70; Cocteau, influence on, 92; color, views on, 225, 246, 258, 280, 283, 331; commentary, use of, 278, 335–336; dialogue, views on, 137; documentary, view of, 78, 243, 331; editing, view of, 172, 173; film critic, as, 15; film distribution, view of, 39, 40; freeze frames, use of, 108; genre-mixing, and, 248, 279; improvisation, use of, 171; interviews, attitude toward, 215; iris shots, use of, 223; Léaud, relationship with, 240; mise-en-scène, view of, 183; music, importance of, 174, 175, 259; parents, relations with, 17; privileged scenes, theory of, 154; storytelling, view of, 176; subjective cinema, view of, 73; voice-over commentary, use of, 96. See also *Antoine et Colette*, *Baisers volés*, *Domicile conjugale*, *Fahrenheit 451*, *Jules et Jim*, *L'Amour en fuite*, *L'Argent de poche*, *L'Enfant sauvage*, *L'Histoire d'Adèle H.*, *L'Homme que aimait les femmes*, *La Chambre verte*, *La Femme d'à*

Truffaut, François (*continued*)
    côté, La Mariée était en noir, La Nuit Américaine, La Peau douce, La Sirène du Mississipi, Le Dernier Métro, Les Deux Anglaises et le continent, Les Mistons, Tirez sur le pianiste, Une Belle Fille comme moi, Une Histoire d'eau, Une visite, Vivement dimanche!
Tystnaden (*The Silence*, Ingmar Bergman), 275

Unfaithfully Yours (*Infidèlement vôtre*, Preston Sturges), 285

Vadim, Roger, 106
Valéry, Paul, 235
Les Valseuses (*Going Places*, Bertrant Blier), 306
Van Parys, Georges, 302
Varda, Agnès, 32
Varte, Rosy, 113
Ventura, Lino, 252
Verne, Jules, 118
Viaggio in Italia (*Voyage en Italie*, Roberto Rossellini), 16
Vian, Boris, 60
Vidor, King, 42
La Vie de château (*A Matter of Resistance*, Jean-Paul Rappeneau), 42
La Vie des Français sous l'Occupation (Henri Amouroux), 302, 303
Le Vieil Homme et l'enfant (*The Two of Us*, Claude Berri), 42, 176
Vigan, Robert le, 85
Vigo, Jean, 24, 25, 31
Visconti, Luchino, 284
Une visite (François Truffaut), 58, 59, 60
Les Visiteurs du soir (*Les Visiteurs du Soir*, Marcel Carné), 4, 340
Viskningar och rop (*Cries & Whispers*, Ingmar Bergman), 247

Vitti, Monica, 162
Vivement dimanche! (*Confidentially Yours*, François Truffaut): adaptation, as, 323–324; filming of, 326; genesis of, 321; style of, 325
Vivre sa vie (*My Life to Live*, Jean-Luc Godard), 89

Wademant, Annette, 67
Walsh, Raoul, 42, 250
Waltz into Darkness (William Irish), 192
Welles, Orson: ethical stance of, 103; idiosyncratic filmmaker, as, 185; mentioned, 248; mise-en-scène, purpose of, 183; *La Nuit américaine* and, 237; style of, 186; Truffaut's esteem for, 56, 284
Werner, Oscar, 99, 102, 107, 135, 239
Whittington, Harry, 322
Wicked Duchess (*La Duchesse de Langeais*, Jacques de Baroncelli), 119
Wild Child, The (François Truffaut). See *L'Enfant sauvage*
Wilder, Billy, 182, 211, 228, 292, 298
Williams, Charles, 320, 321, 323
Woman Next Door, The (François Truffaut). See *La Femme d'à côté*
Woolrich, Cornell. *See* Irish, William
Wyler, William, 184

Young, Terence, 162
Young Lions, The (*Le Bal des maudits*, Edward Dymytryk), 87

Zazie dans le métro (Louis Malle), 32
Zéro de conduit (*Zero for Conduct*, Jean Vigo), 11, 67
Zinnemann, Fred, 184
Zola, Émile, 17
Zucca, Pierre, 332

ANNE GILLAIN is Professor Emerita at Wellesley College. She is author of *François Truffaut: The Lost Secret* (IUP, 2013) and is co-editor with Dudley Andrew of *A Companion to François Truffaut*.

ALISTAIR FOX is Professor Emeritus of English at the University of Otago. He is author of *Speaking Pictures: Neuropsychoanalysis and Authorship in Film and Literature* (IUP, 2016), *Jane Campion: Authorship and Personal Cinema* (IUP, 2011), and is translator of *François Truffaut: The Lost Secret* (IUP, 2013).

www.ingramcontent.com/pod-product-compliance
Lightning Source LLC
Chambersburg PA
CBHW031411230426
43668CB00007B/277